PRAISE FOR *USING OL

This is a much needed and most rewarding volume. For some time now, a number of volumes on political biblical criticism have appeared. These have examined the ways in which biblical texts can be invoked and deployed regarding key issues in contemporary society and culture. In so doing, these works bring the past and the present together in highly creative and sophisticated ways. This volume by Greg Carey on public biblical criticism continues in this vein. Its unique contribution to this ongoing discussion is an analysis of the dynamics and mechanics at work in any such criticism. Carey's volume is an excellent mixture of personal voice, critical expertise, and gentle disposition. I find it a most welcome addition to this important strand of contemporary criticism.

–Fernando F. Segovia, Oberlin Graduate Professor of New Testament and Early Christianity, The Divinity School, Vanderbilt University

Carey does in one book what would normally take three: he epitomizes salient information on the history of interpretation of the Bible, he surveys the landscape of contemporary methods, and he calls readers to engage in the public square regarding biblical interpretation for the sake of our common life together as global citizens. Real people's lives depend upon it.

–Jaime Clark-Soles, Professor of New Testament, Altshuler Distinguished Teaching Professor Director, Baptist House of Studies, Perkins School of Theology, Southern Methodist University

The Bible is a public document and should not be left only to mystical interpreters, ecclesial enthusiasts, or political partisans. Greg Carey provides an effective and exhaustive guide to those who wish to practice biblical interpretation conscientiously for the publics they engage. We do well to heed Carey's reliable advice.

–Emerson Powery, professor of Biblical Studies, Messiah College

This is a splendid, accessible survey of how scholarship illuminates the Bible. It's also an impassioned appeal, urging anyone who reads and interprets Scripture to expand their perspectives, examine their presuppositions, and learn from others. No matter who you are, whether you've never consulted a footnote in a study Bible or you've earned a degree in biblical studies, you're going to learn something new and useful here.

–**Matthew L. Skinner**, professor of New Testament, Luther Seminary

In a period of history when U.S. readers of the Bible are divided both politically and theologically on a myriad of social and cultural issues, *Using Our Outside Voice: Public Biblical Interpretation* is an indispensable guide for anyone intending to participate in employing biblical interpretation in the public arena. Carey provides a clear and lively discussion in understanding people's commitments and arguments on sexuality, race, politics, geo-politics, and a host of other issues in relationship to the Bible

–**Francisco Lozada, Jr**, Charles Fischer Catholic Associate Professor of New Testament and Latina/o Church Studies, Brite Divinity School

Using Our Outside Voice responds to the ongoing claim by many evangelicals that progressives have a low view of Scripture. Here one will find an introduction to biblical hermeneutics that is pointed without being polemical, alert about how we move the Bible into the public without being pedantic, and most of all, Carey offers us all a wonderful example of how a first-rate teacher works out interpretation with students. What we say about the Bible works ripple-like into our culture and *Using Our Outside Voice* reminds us that what we professors and preachers say, what we write, and what we claim matters more than we may ever know.

–**Scot McKnight**, Julius R. Mantey Chair of New Testament, Northern Seminary

Using Our Outside Voice

USING OUR OUTSIDE VOICE

Public Biblical Interpretation

GREG CAREY

Fortress Press

Minneapolis

USING OUR OUTSIDE VOICE

Public Biblical Interpretation

Copyright © 2020 Fortress Press, an imprint of 1517 Media. All rights reserved. Except for brief quotations in critical articles or reviews, no part of this book may be reproduced in any manner without prior written permission from the publisher. Email copyright@1517.media or write to Permissions, Fortress Press, PO Box 1209, Minneapolis, MN 55440-1209.

Cover illustration: Jing Jing Tsong c/o Theispot

Cover design: Laurie Ingram

Print ISBN: 978-1-4514-9633-8

eBook ISBN: 978-1-5064-6378-0

To Jennifer

CONTENTS

	Abbreviations	xi
	Preface	xiii
1.	Public Biblical Interpretation	1
2.	Bridging the Gap: History, Language, Culture	44
3.	Tell Me a Story: Literary Modes of Interpretation	106
4.	The Virtuous Reader	142
5.	Flesh and Blood	173
6.	Bringing It Home, Taking It Outside	220
	Bibliography	235
	Index of Modern Authors	262
	Index of Key Terms	270
	Index of Scriptural and Ancient Texts	276

ABBREVIATIONS

ATR	*Anglican Theological Review*
AYBRL	Anchor Yale Bible Reference Library
BibInt	*Biblical Interpretation*
BMW	The Bible in the Modern World
CRINT	Compendia rerum iudaicarum ad Novum Testamentum
Doctr. chr.	Augustine, *De doctrina christiana*
ExpTim	*Expository Times*
HUT	Hermeneutlische Untersuchungen zur Theologie
IDB	*Interpreter's Dictionary of the Bible*
Int	*Interpretation*
JAJ	*Journal of Ancient Judaism*
JBL	*Journal of Biblical Literature*
JBQ	*Jewish Biblical Quarterly*
JSNT	*Journal for the Study of the New Testament*
JSOT	*Journal for the Study of the Old Testament*
JSOTSup	Journal for the Study of the Old Testament Supplement Series
LNTS	Library of New Testament Studies
NCBC	New Cambridge Bible Commentary
NIB	*New Interpreter's Bible*
NIDB	*New Interpreter's Dictionary of the Bible*
NovT	*Novum Testamentum*
OTL	Old Testament Library
Princ.	Origen, *de Principiis*

RBS	Resources for Biblical Studies
RSN	*Religious Studies News*
SBLSymS	Society of Biblical Literature Symposium Series
SemeiaSt	Society of Biblical Literature Semeia Studies
SRR	Studies in Rhetoric and Religion
USQR	*Union Seminary Quarterly Review*
VCSup	*Vigilae christianae*: Supplement Series
WBC	Word Biblical Commentary
WUNT	Wissenschaftliche Untersuchen zum Neuen Testament

PREFACE

Twenty-five years of academic teaching have led me to frame my vocation in terms of *public biblical interpretation*. I practice public interpretation, and I educate divinity students in equipping themselves for their work as public interpreters in religious communities and beyond. When I taught undergraduates, I was guiding them to interact with public biblical interpretation as part of their formation as critically informed and reflective citizens. I hope this book will prove useful to both secular and religious readers.

I certainly did not set out to write a book like this, but now I see it as a key moment in my vocational trajectory. It integrates the things I value most in my work. The project began with a conversation with Neil Elliott, a splendid New Testament scholar and then an academic editor for Fortress Press. I am grateful to Neil for the invitation to pursue this project and for his encouragement. Over time, the project has taken several turns. Originally conceived as the first volume in a series, it now stands on its own. Without the gracious and (again) encouraging guidance of Scott Tunseth at Fortress, it would never have seen publication.

I have consulted with several colleagues regarding specific issues that surface here: special thanks to Dirk Lange, Bryce Rich, Emma Wasserman, and Rob Seesengood. My understanding of "public biblical interpretation" has benefited enormously from participation in a two-year consultation, "Teaching Exegesis in Theological Schools," sponsored by the Wabash Center for Teaching and Learning in Theology and Religion. I am grateful to our conveners, Matthew L. Skinner and Christine Roy Yoder, and to the nine other colleagues with whom these conversations continue. Above all, I am grateful to my students and colleagues at Lancaster Theological Seminary, where we pursue wisdom and understanding in community. Without sabbatical research leaves granted by our administration and trustees, I could not imagine taking on a project like this. For twenty years I've been blessed to work alongside Julia M. O'Brien, without whose example and insight I would be a different person and this, a very different book.

Many of the issues addressed in this book are inflected by my identity as a Christian scholar who teaches in an ecumenical Protestant theological seminary in the United States. When I speak of the Bible, I am generally referring to the Protestant canon. I frequently refer to the Jewish Scriptures, sometimes the Hebrew Bible, to refer to the Scriptures Christianity shares with Judaism. I rarely refer to those Scriptures as the "Old Testament," a usage that obscures their integrity as the Scriptures of Israel. Nor do Christian Old Testaments correspond exactly to the Hebrew Bible. The biblical canons of Catholic and Eastern Christian communions differ from Protestant Bibles. Unless otherwise noted, all translations from the Bible are taken from the New Revised Standard Version.

Although I have sought to minimize footnotes, I find that students and readers often benefit by entering into conversation with other scholars. Therefore, I often identify the scholars who advance important insights as a way of personalizing the discussion. I have made no attempt to engage the full range of opinion or to cite every important voice, even voices that have shaped my understanding of particular issues. All citations and references to other scholars are here for the benefit of the reader.

My wife Jennifer Craighead Carey and I began dating around the time I began work on this book. We'll have been married just over three years when this book is published. From the beginning we've relished lively and critical conversations about the things that matter to us both, including the role of religion and biblical interpretation in our society. I cannot separate this book from my hope that she will find it meaningful and useful, enough so that we'll have lots to disagree about as she works her way through it. Those conversations form part of the foundation of our relationship, and I thank God for Jennifer's love, for the family life we're building, and for her passion for justice. I dedicate this book to her.

CHAPTER 1.

PUBLIC BIBLICAL INTERPRETATION

Not many people worked tougher jobs than I did while paying my way through school. I held a summer job performing chemical analyses of chicken litter—in Alabama, outdoors, wearing a hardhat, breathing mask, goggles, rubber gloves, long sleeves, and boots. Did you know chicken manure is a powder? In another job I held patients down during their electroshock therapy, then wheeled them back to their units. And I served as an instructor in a course for convicted domestic violence offenders: in exchange for avoiding jail time, the offenders were required to take a lengthy course. They resented being there, and it wasn't exactly a piece of cake for us instructors. I'm told that, compared to other options, the course works. But teaching it? Hardly pleasant.

Here's what I didn't know about domestic violence. At some point in the curriculum, many offenders would appeal to the Bible, making the point that women are obliged to have sexual intercourse with their husbands.

The men were correct—sort of. The apostle Paul does in fact command husbands and wives to have sex together. Literally, Paul writes, "The husband should give to his wife her conjugal rights, and likewise the wife to her husband" (1 Cor 7:3). He goes on to argue that the woman does not govern her own body, but the man does, as likewise the woman governs the body of the man (7:4). The larger context of Paul's argument presupposes that he is talking about married couples. As one can see, this passage opens itself to all sorts of wicked applications, for in abusive relationships men seek to control ("govern") the bodies and lives of women who associate with them. This includes coercing women by means spiritual, psychological, and physical to provide sex.

I was taken aback to learn that so many abusers know that the Bible contains such teaching. That is not to say that many of these men knew *where* such a passage occurs in the Bible. Few of them indicated that they were particularly religious, though some did. But somehow word gets around among abusers that the Bible commands women to offer their bodies to men. One shudders to imagine the effect.

People appeal to the Bible for all sorts of reasons. The work of public biblical interpretation involves a level of accountability both scholarly and moral. Public interpreters should develop some proficiency in historical, cultural, and literary modes of interpretation: interpretive strategies that translate to almost all fields of cultural study. They also cultivate familiarity with a broad range of interpretive options, including those from diverse cultural locations and historical points of view. Many interpreters adhere to particular faith traditions and are accountable for engaging those traditions in meaningful, constructive ways. Public interpreters also are accountable for the ethical implications of our work. Faced with Paul's advice in 1 Corinthians 7, and knowing the horrific ways in which it has been applied, what are we to do?

An interpreter *might* appeal to Paul's social and historical contexts. The *New Oxford Annotated Bible*, the most commonly used study Bible in classrooms, includes notes pointing out, "That the partnership of marriage includes the bodies of the husband and wife was also affirmed by the Stoic philosopher Musonius."[1] So Paul's outlook is not unique for his time and place. Also citing Musonius, other scholars treat Paul as a relative progressive in his day, as he "applies Stoic friendship themes to marriage, emphasizing mutuality" in a culture that was brutally patriarchal.[2] More optimistically, one historian of ancient Greco-Roman literature defends Paul, who "rebels against the unmitigated chauvinistic attitudes [he] would have found in Greco-Roman households" wher-

---

1. Laurence L. Welborn, "1 Corinthians" (study notes), in *The New Oxford Annotated Bible*, ed. Michael Coogan et al., 4th ed. (New York: Oxford University Press, 2010), 2008.
2. Carolyn Osiek and David L. Balch, *Families in the New Testament World: Households and House Churches*, Family, Religion, and Culture (Louisville: Westminster John Knox, 1997), 116.

ever he may have traveled.[3] In this passage, and in the larger context of 1 Corinthians 7, Paul assumes that women exercise the same freedom over their sexual lives as do men.[4] Our interpreter might say that Paul promoted mutuality rather than domination, and that to use Paul to coerce sex is to misunderstand, and misuse, his writings.

I suspect few domestic violence offenders would care. Nor would they be impressed by other contemporary lines of interpretation. For example, with respect to the Pauline letters, many interpreters have shifted their focus from the apostle himself and his point of view toward what we can learn about the Pauline communities through these letters. Feminist interpreters have largely shaped this change in focus. For centuries readers have debated Paul's outlook on matters, gender prominent among them. "Would Paul endorse women for leadership in churches?" we might ask. But his letters also reveal, sometimes accidentally, the activities and interests of women, who apparently provided key leadership to the movement (consider the names and activities reflected in Rom 16:1–16) and held vocal roles in their assemblies (as reflected in passages like 1 Cor 11:2–16). We might ask: "What activities and beliefs lie behind Paul's instructions on marriage and sexuality in 1 Corinthians 7?" Paul indicates that he is responding to questions *from* the Corinthians rather than simply imposing his own opinion (7:1). Paul's discussion reflects the likelihood that some (many?) among the Corinthians, men and women alike, are promoting sexual abstinence.[5] Perhaps people believed sexual abstinence freed the spirit for profound, even ecstatic, spiritual experiences. This belief might have been especially attractive among women, for whom patriarchal marriage posed a forbidding prospect.[6]

It may be tempting to say that domestic abusers "abuse" the Bible for their own purposes. But they hardly stand alone in insisting upon women's submission. Many Christians maintain that the Bible enjoins

---

3. Sarah Ruden, *Paul among the People: The Apostle Reinterpreted and Reimagined in His Own Time* (New York: Pantheon, 2010), 97.
4. Sandra Hack Polaski, *A Feminist Introduction to Paul* (St. Louis: Chalice, 2005), 49.
5. William Loader, *The New Testament on Sexuality* (Grand Rapids: Eerdmans, 2012), 198.
6. Judith M. Gundry-Volf, "Celibate Pneumatics and Social Power: On the Motivations for Sexual Asceticism in Corinth," *USQR* 48/3–4 (1994): 105–26; see Kate Cooper, *Band of Angels: The Forgotten World of Early Christian Women* (New York: The Overlook Press, 2013), 80–81.

male leadership and female submission. Their number includes Leah Kelley, an advocate of "Christian domestic discipline." The Christian domestic discipline movement teaches not only that wives should submit to their husbands but also that husbands should punish disobedient wives by means of corporal punishment—spanking. The boundaries between submission, punishment, and abuse are vanishingly small. (For my part, I don't believe such boundaries exist: religiously sanctioned submission is inherently abusive.) In any case, Kelley counsels wives *never* to decline their husbands' advances.[7]

The larger movement that promotes male leadership and female subordination calls itself "complementarianism," the idea that women and men are equal in dignity and status, at the same time that God has ordained that men provide leadership in the home and in the church. This general view hardly belongs to one group, but many students of American religion identify complementarianism as the defining characteristic of evangelical and fundamentalist Christianity. Only men serve as ordained priests in Roman Catholic and Eastern Orthodox churches, but gender doctrines track fairly closely with liberal/conservative divisions in Protestant Christianity. For example, women serve as ordained ministers among mainline Presbyterians, Lutherans, and Episcopalians, but their more conservative counterparts regard women's ordination as unbiblical.[8] (We should also note that many evangelicals reject complementarianism.) Although they may disagree on the historical particulars, many historians regard male supremacy as the primary defining characteristic of evangelical and fundamentalist Protestantism.[9]

---

7. *Christian Domestic Discipline Bible Study for Wives* (n.p.: Christian Domestic Discipline, 2006), 46. Cited, with quotation in a footnote, in Linda S. Schearing and Valarie H. Ziegler, *Enticed by Eden: How Western Culture Uses, Confuses (and Sometimes Abuses) Adam and Eve* (Waco, TX: Baylor University Press, 2013), 76.

8. Those more conservative bodies include the Presbyterian Church in America, the Evangelical Presbyterian Church, the Associate Reformed Presbyterian Church, the Reformed Presbyterian Church, the Lutheran Church—Missouri Synod, the Wisconsin Evangelical Lutheran Synod, and the Anglican Church in North America, among others.

9. Betty A. DeBerg, *Ungodly Women: Gender and the First Wave of American Fundamentalism* (Macon, GA: Mercer University Press, 2000 [1990]); Sally Gallagher, *Evangelical Identity and Gendered Family Life* (New Brunswick, NJ: Rutgers University Press, 2003); Brenda Brasher, *Godly Women: Fundamentalism and Female Power* (New Brunswick, NJ: Rutgers University Press, 1998).

If some invoke the Bible to promote women's submission, others obviously will provide feminist interpretations of the very same passages. Elisabeth Schüssler Fiorenza's classic reconstruction (her word) of Christian origins introduced feminist biblical scholarship to a broad audience. She emphasizes that 1 Corinthians reflects Paul's vision that the gospel overcomes all barriers that divide people from one another, including barriers related to gender. Paul attributes to women (most of) the same prerogatives he ascribes to men, and his promotion of celibacy actually encourages women to defy Roman laws that promoted marriage. Although Paul's vision is limited, Schüssler Fiorenza argues, he did broaden the choices open to "ordinary" Christian women.[10]

This reflection on Paul's instruction in 1 Corinthians 7 began with people who rarely read the Bible and generally have little formal education in biblical studies. We also considered popular Bible teachers and cultural movements, especially "complementarians" who teach women's subordination. And we have surveyed some of the ways in which academic biblical scholars, including feminist interpreters, have approached this text.

Public biblical interpretation inhabits such contested spaces. Religious communities search the Scriptures in the process of discerning sacred truth. Political leaders and ordinary citizens alike consult the Bible to authorize their public policy positions. Professional biblical scholars may or may not participate in all these activities, while they also explore the literary, historical, and cultural dimensions of biblical and related literature, along with the origins of Judaism and Christianity. Biblical scholars and other researchers seek to understand how the Bible has functioned and has been understood in diverse historical contexts. As we have seen from our discussion of 1 Corinthians 7, no one person or group determines how others understand the Bible. No one controls the Bible or its meaning.

---

10. Elisabeth Schüssler Fiorenza, *In Memory of Her: A Feminist Theological Reconstruction of Christian Origins* (New York: Crossroad, 1983), 220–26.

USING OUR OUTSIDE VOICE: PUBLIC BIBLICAL INTERPRETATION

"Use your inside voice," our elementary school teachers used to say. As children, we shouted inside and outside. The things we wanted to say were important to us. We felt enthusiasm, anger, or fear. What's more, it was hard to get attention. Everybody was shouting, so we did too. How else could we be heard? "Of course," we shouted! "Use your inside voice!"

Relying on those worn-out words we inherited from our teachers, many of us who have worked with children as parents, teachers, or volunteers find ourselves repeating them: "Use your inside voice." As we catch ourselves in the act, we feel a mix of embarrassment and nostalgia. For my part, I'd like to go back to my childhood teachers and apologize: "You were right. Now I know." I bet they hear that all the time.

This book, scheduled for publication during a US presidential election year, has confronted me with a challenge. The culture I live in is more polarized than it's been since my childhood. I was born in 1965 at the height of the Civil Rights struggle and just as the United States was doubling down on its military intervention in Vietnam. When I was three or four years old, someone gave me an oversized T-shirt bearing an American flag and the caption "America: Love It or Leave It." How could I know I was sleeping in a political statement? That period, of course, saw the assassinations of Robert F. Kennedy and Martin Luther King Jr., along with a spate of race riots across the country. Protests against the Vietnam War intensified. The United States wasn't the only Western democracy in distress. Many people felt as if society was tearing itself apart.

It feels that way now too. Having grown up white in the American South, I remember when white adults would voice openly racist sentiments in public. By the time I was in school, we children "knew better." Not only did we refrain from speaking in that way; we were offended when other people did. As I write in 2019, I find it profoundly distressing that openly racist, misogynist, and homophobic language is back in the public square. People don't even apologize for it anymore.

As I was discussing this with a circle of friends, I looked to my friend Rob Seesengood. Rob is a New Testament scholar himself, almost my age, who also grew up in the South. "How would we say that in the South, Rob? Would we say, 'They're saying these things out loud'?"

Rob put it just right, in a tone of mocking surprise: "They're using their outside voice."

Public biblical interpretation calls us to practice—and use—our outside voices. This isn't to say we should be shouting—by no means! To speak in our outside voice means to take accountability for how we interpret the Bible. Public biblical interpretation, in the sense I intend here, involves the process of informed, dialogical interpretation of the Bible and related topics. Faced with such diverse readers and readings of the Bible, and with no reasonable hope of managing the Bible's meaning, people continue to practice public interpretation in academic, religious, and other settings. But what qualifies someone to function as a responsible interpreter of the Bible? No institution is giving out badges to Deputy Interpreters, and frankly, few would be impressed if they did. I would contend that responsible public biblical interpretation implies the ability to enter a conversation about the Bible, to understand the various arguments in play, to weigh the ethical and theological implications of our views, and to offer informed opinions that others can understand. This role requires not only basic knowledge but also identifiable skills, habits, and dispositions. No one is suggesting that public interpreters of the Bible are smarter, more insightful, or more correct than are other people. However, public biblical interpretation involves participating in reasoned conversations about the Bible and its significance.

WE ALREADY KNOW

We perform critical interpretation all the time, but rarely self-consciously.

In 1998 the American Film Institute produced a list of the "100 Greatest American Films." Back in the day when you would drive to the nearest video store, I began renting as many of these films as I could find. My favorite really old movie was *The Maltese Falcon*, a 1941 *film noir* starring Humphrey Bogart as a cynical detective. Based on a 1930 novel of the same name, it features the great character actor Peter Lorre as Joel Cairo, an international criminal who tends to dress formally and relies on deception to get what he wants. The novel makes it clear that Cairo is gay. Just prior to his first appearance, the detective's secretary announces, "This guy is queer." The filmmaking conventions of 1941 would not allow such direct characterization of homosexuality, leaving viewers to draw their own conclusions.[11]

Back to 1998. According to the polling company Gallup, in 1998 about 37 percent of Americans would affirm that they had friends or relatives who had told them, personally, that they were gay or lesbian. By 2013 that percentage had more than doubled to 75 percent. To make this personal, by 1998 I knew quite a few people who identified themselves to me as gay or lesbian. But that was relatively new to my experience. Having grown up in a small Southern city, I'd literally known no one who was out to the general public until I became an adult. Joel Cairo was an interesting character, but in 1998 his sexuality didn't cross my mind.

Around 2013 I watched *The Maltese Falcon* again. Fifteen years had passed, but this time it was absolutely clear to me that Joel Cairo was gay. So I developed an experiment. When the seminary in which I teach developed a new course, "Interpreting in Context," I decided to begin the course with a two-minute clip from the film, the first scene in which Joel Cairo appears. I've now done this several times, and the results are predictable.

First, I briefly introduce the film and ask students to pay particular attention to Joel Cairo, as we'll discuss him after watching the clip. When the clip is over, I simply ask the class to offer one-word descriptions of Cairo. I make a list of their terms on the board: criminal, sneaky, formal, exotic, international, stylish, suspicious. Among the terms come some words that approach conversations about gender and sexuality: students may judge Cairo as weak or effeminate. In some classes a student will suggest that he's gay.

For each of these characteristics, I ask what leads students to their conclusions. Ultimately, I want to discuss Cairo's sexuality, but we talk about all the descriptors. For example, Cairo could be judged as sneaky or exotic because he carries three passports, not all of which bear the same name. He's formal because he enters the room in a tuxedo with white gloves and a hat. If a student observes that Cairo is gay, some students immediately agree. It's our first class session, and they don't know what's safe to discuss and what isn't, so they've kept their opin-

---

11. Dashiell Hammett, *The Maltese Falcon* (New York: Alfred A. Knopf, 1930). By the way, in 1998 the Modern Library ranked the novel number 56 among its 100 best English-language novels of the twentieth century ("100 Best Novels," http://www.modernlibrary.com/top-100/100-best-novels/).

ions to themselves. Other students express surprise; Cairo's sexuality had never crossed their minds. And several remain unconvinced. We watch the video a second time, and we develop a list of "factors": What kinds of evidence would make the case for Cairo as a gay character?

What students do at this point is remarkable. Without prompting on my part, they appeal to various kinds of evidence. Consider figure 1.1.

Factors in the Scene	How the Scene Is Filmed	Historical and Cultural Considerations
Cairo's business card smells like gardenia.	When the secretary announces Cairo, a little musical riff accompanies him.	Assumptions about gay men have changed significantly since 1941. Back then gay men were assumed to be weak and dishonest. Gay men were assumed to be effeminate, and effeminate men were considered likely to be gay.
Cairo's dress is excessively formal, including his gloves, ring, and decorated umbrella.		
	When Cairo and the detective struggle, the camera angle accentuates the detective's larger stature.	
While speaking with the detective, Cairo rubs his umbrella handle against his lips in a suggestive way.[12]		
		Films in 1941 were precluded from explicit presentations of sexuality or sexual orientation.
Cairo's manner of speaking includes an exotic accent and a hint of femininity.		
The detective easily overcomes Cairo in a physical struggle.		

Fig. 1.1

I record students' comments on the whiteboard as they articulate their thoughts, organizing them according to the categories in this table. Without thinking about it, students have covered some of the primary factors in critical interpretation, whether of the Bible or of any cultural artifact: the data itself, the artistry by which it is developed, and historical and cultural factors many contemporary people may not know.

But there's something most students haven't done: until it's named, they haven't recognized the interpretive rules by which they've been

---

12. See the discussion of this point in Virginia Wright Wexman, "Kinesics and Film Acting: Humphrey Bogart in *The Maltese Falcon* and *The Big Sleep*," in *Star Texts: Image and Performance in Text and Television*, ed. Jeremy G. Butler (Detroit: Wayne State University Press, 1991), 209.

playing. Clarifying these categories reveals that we perform the basic moves of biblical scholarship all the time: with music, novels, movies—you name it. It's when we name these interpretive moves, weigh them, and reflect on them critically that interpretation becomes *disciplined*. Public interpretation requires that we pay disciplined attention.

The *Maltese Falcon* exercise includes one more dimension. I tell the students the story you've just read: how the passage of fifteen years changed my perception of Joel Cairo. I also share that I immediately consulted Google: Do film critics discuss Cairo's sexual orientation? This marks another dimension of public interpretation: conversation with experts. Sure enough: there's lots of discussion about Cairo's sexual orientation, some going back decades.[13] When we're doing public interpretation, it's important that we consult the opinions of others, especially highly skilled or academic interpreters.

I press this extra step further. Some critics, I suggest to the class, have even speculated that Sam Spade, the hard-boiled detective who encounters and defeats Cairo, is either gay-curious or bisexual. "No way!" is the general response, as Spade is the epitome of the tough guy, and his affairs with women attest to his straightness. But we replay the scene. When Spade's secretary, Effie, introduces Cairo's business card, scented with gardenia, Spade exclaims, "Quick! In with him, darling!" And when Cairo suggestively rubs the tip of his walking stick against his lips, Spade places his cigarette to his lips and takes a long drag. When Cairo frisks Spade, noticeably on his buttocks, Spade overcomes his new adversary. The camera slows down to emphasize Spade's joy in overcoming Cairo. I point out that when Spade strikes Cairo again later in the movie, he says, "And when you're slapped, you'll take it and like it!" All these observations I encountered in an online search years ago, but hours of searching now have not led me to the source. Nevertheless,

---

13. Markus Spöhrer, "Homophobia and Violence in Film Noir: Homosexuality as a Threat to Masculinity in John Huston's *The Maltese Falcon*," *Journal of Literature and Culture* 6 (2016): 56–71; Dion Kagan, "Representing Queer Sexualities," in *The Routledge Companion to the Media, Sex and Sexuality*, ed. Clarissa Smith and Fiona Attwood with Brian McNair (New York: Routledge, 2018), 95; Richard Barrios, *Screened Out: Playing Gay in Hollywood from Edison to Stonewall* (New York: Routledge, 2003), 187–88; and classically, Vito Russo, *The Celluloid Closet: Homosexuality in the Movies*, rev. ed. (New York: Harper & Row, 1987), 94.

none of us would have complicated Spade's "obvious" heterosexuality had I not derived those insights from film critics.

We all perform critical interpretation in one context or another, making judgments about movies, songs, and other works of art. We apply the same criteria professionals do: some literary, some cultural. And from time to time we consult what others, particularly experts, have to teach us. Biblical interpretation draws upon the same skill sets.

THE BIBLE IN THE PUBLIC SQUARE

In July 2015 I attended a wedding in a large Southern Baptist church. The young couple were both members of this church. During the service the pastor frequently emphasized that in marriage the husband should lead the household, sacrificing his own preferences for the welfare of his wife. The wife in turn should follow her husband's leadership. Having grown up Southern Baptist myself, I was struck by the intensity of this emphasis. Biblical complementarianism is hardly a new idea, but its importance has grown enormously in Southern Baptist denominational life. Reflecting this emphasis, in 1998 the denomination added a statement affirming complementarianism to its doctrinal confession. That statement also defines marriage "as the uniting of one man and one woman." Throughout the service the pastor referred to a key passage, Ephesians 5:21–33, as the model for male leadership in the household.

Meanwhile, several of my gay and lesbian friends were planning their own weddings. Just weeks before that wedding, the Supreme Court of the United States had issued the *Obergefell v. Hodges* ruling. A mere 5–4 majority ruled that the US Constitution requires states to allow marriages between same-sex couples. Public support for same-sex marriage rights had been growing rapidly over just a few years, but not uniformly. The idea was far more popular in some states than others. Churches were sharply divided on the issue. A few major denominations have opened the possibility that ministers may perform weddings for same-sex couples, others suffer bitter conflict, and still others—the majority as I am writing—will not allow such practices. Again, the Bible plays a critical role in these debates. Opponents of same-sex marriage cite several passages they view as condemning same-sex sex. Advocates try to explain away those passages or develop alternative arguments for inclusion. Some insist wrangling over biblical passages is simply wrongheaded due to the enormous cultural gulf that separates our world from biblical societies. In every case biblical interpretation stands at the heart of such debates.

Biblical interpretation has long played this troubled role in US history. One side piles up verses to support its opinion, while the other side finds their own verses. Advocates describe the biblical cultures in contradictory ways. We played out such conflicts with respect to slavery, which split the Presbyterian, Methodist, Baptist, and German Reformed churches between North and South. Baptists never reunited; Presbyterians and Methodists took more than a century. Less divisive were conflicts concerning divorce: Could the church acknowledge the marriages of divorced people? Could divorced persons, remarried or not, serve as local church officers or as clergy? Divisive again was the question of women's ordination, which still splinters various denominational traditions. So, the sexual orientation and gender identity question looks quite familiar.

Yet, public biblical interpretation requires us to enter these conversations in disciplined and effective ways. We may reject the practice of biblical proof-texting, but we cannot avoid the fact that many people turn to Scripture for guidance, while some rely on it to bolster their preexisting convictions.

ASSUMPTIONS AND ENDS IN BIBLICAL INTERPRETATION

The gender and sexuality debates highlight the Bible's role as a resource for rhetoric, or public argumentation. People use the Bible in this way not only to address ethical questions but also to resolve theological debates. The religious culture in which I grew up, like those shared by many of my students and other people I encounter, often featured such debates. One of the most illuminating controversies involved how believers experience the Holy Spirit. Most Christians believe the Holy Spirit enters the lives of people upon their baptism or upon their conversion. We may experience occasional periods of spiritual transcendence. Some special people seem spiritually tuned in more often and to a greater degree than the rest of us. But the Spirit's presence does not change in any fundamental way. Other Christians, however, believe in a "second blessing," the possibility that a person may—and should—be "filled" with the Holy Spirit at some point after her conversion. Remarkably, these debates center on the book of Acts, which offers case studies for both positions. For example, when Peter first shares the gospel with Gentiles, the Holy Spirit comes upon them immediately, even before their baptism (Acts 10:44–47). On the other hand, Paul encounters a group of believers who have not even heard of the Holy Spirit (19:1–7). Not surprisingly, such debates could continue endlessly.

Beyond argumentative uses, the Bible performs a wide variety of functions in our society and in others. Many people turn to the Bible for personal inspiration and devotional use. The forms of devotional Bible reading vary. Some people simply read several chapters of the Bible daily, reading the Bible all the way through over a period of time or reading through individual books. Readers may highlight especially meaningful passages, take notes, or consult available reference materials such as Bible dictionaries or atlases. Other readers rely on guides that point them to select passages for each day, often accompanied by inspirational meditations and guided prayer. A growing number of readers are turning to an ancient practice, *lectio divina* or divine reading. Some religious orders and countless individuals practice *lectio divina* daily, reading a text, meditating upon its details, and then moving into prayer.

All devotional approaches to Bible reading hold two things in common: they expect the Bible to "speak" to the reader in a direct way. More accurately, devotional readers seek communication from God through their Bible reading through the work of the Holy Spirit. Devotional reading also is personal and individual. A reader may or may not consult the opinions of others or seek out scholarly resources. Moreover, a devotional reader feels no obligation to explain his understanding of the text to other people. Meaning occurs in the interaction between the Bible and an individual reader.

Far removed from devotional readers are those who study the Bible out of historical, cultural, or literary interest. Their interests may vary greatly. Some students seek to understand religion as a cultural phenomenon. Reading the Bible differs little from reading other foundational religious texts from around the world. Some people expect to find wisdom or inspiration in sacred texts like the Bible; others are simply curious about how religions emerge and adapt. For example, what does it mean to call Judaism a religion—and does such terminology make sense of the movement to which Paul refers in Galatians 1:14? For that matter, at what point in history is it meaningful to call Christianity a religion among other religions? What literary and cultural influences contributed to the emergence of apocalyptic literature in Judaism and Christianity? How did material conditions such as agriculture, travel, housing, health, and government shape family life in biblical cultures? Questions like these pose fascinating intellectual challenges.

Some colleges and universities include parts of the Bible in "Great Books" or Western Civilization courses. Such curricula aim to equip students as well-informed global citizens. Just as often, however, these classes create opportunities for students to engage fundamental human questions. While reading Plato's *Republic*, we may discuss the value and privilege attached to education. The *Bhagavad Gita* provides an opportunity to reflect on the tension between individualism and duty. Might we read the Genesis creation stories in conversations about climate change, or could Paul's letters nurture discussions concerning the meaning of suffering? Perhaps we might read Paul alongside the *Gita* and the Roman Stoics.

Over the past few decades biblical scholars have devoted increasing attention to the Bible's influence or use in diverse cultural contexts. Opportunities for research in this area are literally endless. How have missionaries used the Bible and Bible translation in colonial contexts? How do artistic depictions of Moses adapt from one cultural context to another? How did Southern defenders of slavery use the Bible to defend their position, and did apologists for segregation employ the same arguments or different ones?

Unlike devotional interpretation, historical and cultural investigations need not lead to religious insight or experience. But another factor distinguishes historical and cultural readers from those who read the Bible devotionally. When people read devotionally, they often do not consult scholarly opinion. Nor do they generally feel accountable to reason through or explain the reasons for their interpretations. Of course, some people do consult Bible dictionaries and other resources in their devotional study, and some people share their devotional experiences with people they know. Generally, however, a devotional reader's interpretations are her own, and rarely does one person criticize another on the basis of their devotional understanding. Devotional Bible reading is a form of personal religious experience. In contrast, those who study the Bible for historical or cultural reasons often do so in public settings: classrooms, museums, academic societies, and faith communities. They share their understandings with others, they read or participate in academic biblical scholarship, and they know they may need to explain their perceptions to other people. When people participate in broader conversations concerning the Bible—including biblical scholarship and the give-and-take of reasoned arguments—they are participating in public biblical interpretation.

Devotional users naturally read the Bible for religious ends, but so do many other kinds of readers. In countless settings, including homes, prisons, synagogues, and churches, Bible study groups explore the Bible in community. Religious leaders study the Bible as they prepare to preach and teach. The range of biblical-studies resources available to preachers is staggering, including academic biblical commentaries, commentaries just for preachers, magazine columns, and countless online resources. Religious leaders also study the Bible for guidance in their counseling and administrative ministries. Rabbis, ministers, and theologians take the Bible into consideration as they respond to pressing ethical issues and theological questions. These readers are all interpreting the Bible theologically. That is, they are seeking guidance, inspiration, or insight from the process. Some of them interact with biblical scholarship more than others. Some expect to articulate their understandings for other people, while for others that possibility is somewhat remote.

All of these readers come to the Bible with different assumptions, interests, and aims. Some expect religious or spiritual benefits, while others bring different kinds of curiosity. Some interpret the Bible in public settings, with a give-and-take of opinions and reasons, while for others the process is an individual pursuit. Some seek out the opinion of academic "experts"; others wouldn't notice if a spaceship gathered those experts together with a tractor beam and whisked them to another galaxy. Yet despite the differences among these approaches, people routinely cross the lines that would divide them. Lots of people read the Bible in devotional, academic, *and* religious contexts, and with different goals from moment to moment and context to context.

This little book, however, addresses people who will participate in the work of public biblical interpretation. What does a person need to know, what does a person need to do, and what kind of person should one be, in order to be an effective public interpreter of the Bible?

WHERE PUBLIC BIBLICAL INTERPRETATION HAPPENS

Public biblical interpretation occurs in many settings. Some, like classrooms, involve face-to-face interaction. Others occur online or in print. In all settings only a few marks distinguish public biblical interpretation.

- We seek to arrive at reasoned understandings.
- We draw upon widely shared criteria in articulating our points of view.
- We take seriously the work of other interpreters.
- And we prepare to articulate our conclusions with reasons other people can understand.

Public biblical interpretation calls for a certain kind of awareness. The work of interpretation may seem theoretical, abstract, removed from pressing concerns such as war and peace, economic opportunity, or even love. Then again, a reflective look at current events reveals the degree to which biblical interpretation bears precisely on these issues. The nation of Israel figures mightily in the American political consciousness: Is Israel the beacon of democracy in a chaotic region, or is Israel the occupying force that oppresses Palestinians? If we scratch the surface just a little bit, we find religion, particularly biblical interpretation, lying at the heart of our debates. According to a Pew Research Center poll, white evangelicals in the US are by far Israel's strongest supporters. Forty-six percent of white evangelicals expressed the view that the United States does not support Israel enough, a percentage significantly higher than that of Jews and overwhelmingly higher than those for white mainline Protestants (26 percent), black Protestants (19 percent), and Catholics (20 percent). Such wide differences in opinion reflect many complicated factors, but surely biblical interpretation counts as one of them. As opposed to about half of other Protestants, white evangelicals (82 percent) and Orthodox Jews (84 percent) overwhelmingly affirmed the proposition that "God gave Israel to the Jews."[14] The shaping of white evangelical opinion regarding Israel does not come down to disputes over individual Bible passages, though peo-

---

14. Michael Lipka, "More White Evangelicals Than American Jews Say God Gave Israel to the Jewish People," Pew Research Center, October 3, 2013, https://tinyurl.com/u9xbjmr.

ple will cite them from time to time. Instead, it reflects broader assumptions regarding the shape of the biblical story and its contemporary relevance. Many Christians, not only white evangelicals, apply biblical teachings about ancient Israel to contemporary geopolitics. As the theologian David Tracy once wrote, "At times, interpretations matter."[15]

We could multiply examples. Many Christians believe in clearly distinguished gender roles: To what degree do their understandings of the Bible influence their behavior as employers, colleagues, and voters? Many believe the Bible proclaims faith in Jesus as the only path to salvation, with everyone else misguided and lost: To what degree do attitudes about world religions shape public debates concerning the status of Muslim immigrants and visitors? Some prominent preachers and churches teach that faith leads to material prosperity: one journalist has suggested that this message contributed to the housing crash of 2008.[16] I am skeptical, but come to think of it, the value of my own home took more than five years to recover.

Without belaboring the point, we might move from public debates to matters of personal piety. Many people of faith wonder about God's role in suffering and adversity, and they tend to turn to the Bible for guidance. Not all expect the Bible to answer their questions in some direct way, but in their search for meaning they might ponder books such as Proverbs and Job. According to Proverbs, a person who lives well will typically prosper. Job imagines a man who is exceedingly righteous yet endures enormous suffering. Others ponder a passage like Romans 8:28, which poses all sorts of interpretive problems. Does the passage essentially say, "Everything happens for a reason," or does it simply affirm that God is present in all circumstances, working for good? Even our earliest manuscripts of Romans reflect ancient debates over the passage's meaning, as copyists attempted to clarify the wording with subtle changes. Few questions occupy our minds like suffering and adversity. Using the Bible as a resource for sorting through such things, religious leaders influence how their audiences respond to hard times.

Sometimes interpretation does matter, and public biblical interpretation involves the process of bringing interpretation to a level of articu-

---

15. David Tracy, *Plurality and Ambiguity: Hermeneutics, Religion, Hope* (San Francisco: Harper & Row, 1987), 7.
16. Hannah Rosen, "Did Christianity Cause the Crash?" *The Atlantic*, December 2009, https://tinyurl.com/scu85w3.

lation and accountability. That is, it requires us to spell out the rationale for our own interpretations, assess the views of others, and engage the diverse range of options. Our goals may vary. Some of us seek to understand biblical books, or passages of them, with greater insight; others may be interested in the historical process by which the Bible came to be as it is; and still others want to explore how people use the Bible as they do.

At a series of conferences about twenty years ago, I heard two presentations concerning the book of Revelation. One, by a white North American feminist, critiqued the book's misogyny. The feminine imagery in Revelation, she argued, fixates on women's sexual status: whore, mother, and virgin are the only options. Women have literally no constructive place in the book (see 14:1–5). Indeed, even contemporary apocalyptic movies tend to reduce women to such roles. Moreover, Revelation fantasizes about sexualized violence against women who do not conform to its vision (see 2:20–23; 17:15–18). A second presenter, a male Latin American theologian who identified with the struggles of poor peasants, praised Revelation's call for economic justice. Revelation condemns economic exploitation (see 18:11–19) and envisions the overthrow of oppressive powers. Responding to questions from North American feminists, this interpreter argued that (a) Revelation's feminine symbolism simply drew upon stock imagery from the Hebrew prophets and (b) that its emphasis on justice should not be sacrificed due to other concerns.[17]

The two presentations and the conversation that ensued revealed to me what is at stake in biblical interpretation. Technically, both scholars were "correct." Both appealed to Revelation's literary patterns and attempted to make sense of the book in its social, historical, and religious contexts. For the most part, both interpreters agreed on the same "rules" of interpretation. Both interpreters also sought to address Revelation in ways that were relevant to contemporary people and their struggles. If anything, their greatest difference resided in their loyalties: What readers and what concerns most drove their thinking? They

---

17. The papers have been published, but the discussion has not. Tina Pippin, "'And I Will Strike Her Children Dead': Death and the Deconstruction of Social Location," in *Reading from This Place*, ed. Fernando F. Segovia and Mary Ann Tolbert (Minneapolis: Fortress, 1995), 1:191–98; and Néstor Míguez, "Apocalyptic and the Economy: A Reading of Revelation 18 from the Experience of Economic Exclusion," in Segovia and Tolbert, *Reading from This Place*, 2:250–62.

never came to an agreement. I have to admit that I left the session unsettled myself. But their presentations modeled for me why biblical interpretation can be important. Both interpreters are actively involved in real-world struggles for justice, and their interpretations reflected those real-world relationships and commitments. Public interpretation provides a space for the full expression of these commitments and arguments.

Interpretation is an ongoing process. This is true in part because interpreters and our circumstances change according to time and place. That's often a good thing. Many people are wired to prefer closure and certainty, but one moment's confidence gives way to another's embarrassment.

Prior to World War II, biblical interpreters frequently described ancient Judaism in extremely prejudicial ways. Dominated by Christian—mostly Protestant—scholars, the field reflected the influence of the Protestant Reformation. According to Martin Luther and other reformers, the apostle Paul had found himself trapped by Judaism and its legal requirements: in their eyes Judaism represented an oppressive system of ritual and performance, not a dynamic, living spirituality. This characterization of Judaism resonated with the portrait of the Pharisees and other Jewish leaders we encounter especially in the Gospels. It was also quite common for interpreters to privilege some forms of supposedly more authentic expressions of faith—such as the Hebrew prophets—over against priestly and legalistic interpretations. Jesus's parables, for example, were treated as more creative or poetic than were the parables and allegories of the rabbis.[18] The trouble was, few Christian interpreters were deeply investigating the primary sources of ancient Judaism for its own sake.

Not all interpreters treated Judaism in this way, of course. However, for quite some time Christian biblical scholars routinely compared the faith of Jesus, Paul, and the early Christians to the purported formalism and hypocrisy of Judaism. That Jesus, Paul, and others were in fact Jews and probably derived their fundamental religious categories from their native culture seems to have passed interpreters by.

The Holocaust fundamentally transformed the context for biblical

---

18. Shawn Kelley, "Race, Aesthetics, and Gospel Scholarship: Embracing and Subverting the Aesthetic Ideology," in *Prejudice and Christian Beginnings: Investigating Race, Gender, and Ethnicity in Early Christian Studies*, ed. Laura Nasrallah and Elisabeth Schüssler Fiorenza (Minneapolis: Fortress, 2009), 191–209.

scholarship. Academic biblical studies had flourished especially in Germany, where many Christians were all too complicit in the annihilation of Jews. Without question, Christian biblical scholarship contributed to anti-Semitic attitudes. After the war a gradual reassessment began to emerge, most notably in E. P. Sanders's classic *Paul and Palestinian Judaism*, which spelled out the fundamental critique I have just described.[19] Today biblical scholars recognize that previous interpretations were not only harmful; they were inaccurate due to their dependence on theological categories of the sixteenth and seventeenth centuries. With an enormous assist from the discovery of the Dead Sea Scrolls, archaeological research, and enhanced attention to the primary sources, research on ancient Judaism has undergone revolutionary transformation.

Interpreters disagree with one another, and interpretations change over time. These realities often provoke frustration among students: "If the experts can't agree, then what am I supposed to write?" Biblical interpretation rarely leads to certainty, and why should we expect it to? In the United States the Supreme Court resolves our most vexing constitutional questions, but rarely does the Court achieve total consensus. More commonly the votes are split 7–2, 6–3, or 5–4. Moreover, a court must choose between two sides of an argument; biblical interpreters face endless options. We are rarely in a position to say we have "proven" a conclusion or "won" an argument. Instead, we aim to develop the most compelling understanding we can achieve with the resources available to us. In David Tracy's words, we seek "relative adequacy."

> Relative adequacy is just that—relative, not absolute adequacy. If one demands certainty, one is assured of failure. We can never possess absolute certainty. But we can achieve a good—that is, a relatively adequate—interpretation: relative to the power of disclosure and concealment of the text, relative to the skills and attentiveness of the interpreter, relative to the kind of conversation possible for the interpreter in a particular culture at a particular time. Somehow relatively adequate interpretation and conversations suffice.[20]

---

19. E. P. Sanders, *Paul and Palestinian Judaism: A Comparison of Patterns of Religion* (Minneapolis: Fortress, 1977), esp. 33–59. For a full-length study of racialized and anti-Semitic discourse in the field, see Shawn Kelley, *Racializing Jesus: Race, Ideology and the Formation of Modern Biblical Scholarship* (London: Routledge, 2002).

20. Tracy, *Plurality and Ambiguity*, 22–23.

According to Tracy, many factors shape, limit, and influence the work of interpretation. The texts we are interpreting don't always answer the questions we bring to them. If they did, interpretation would be a lot simpler. We might derive mixed messages from the texts themselves or their historical contexts. And as interpreters we bring our own personal and cultural biases to the process. We choose to ask some questions but not others, while some aspects of the text grab our attention while others do not. Biases can be helpful: if we don't have questions, we won't have curiosity. But we cannot pretend that texts are obvious or that our interests are purely objective. We seek relative clarity, not absolute certainty.

Let's consider an example, one with significant implications for understanding Paul's basic theology. On several occasions Paul's letters include the phrase *pistis Christou* or *pistis Jēsou Christou*. Most English translations have rendered this phrase "faith in (Jesus) Christ," but more recently many interpreters have recommended the translation, "faith of (Jesus) Christ" (see especially Rom 3:22, 26; Gal 2:16, 20; 3:22; Phil 3:9).[21] From a purely grammatical standpoint both translations can be correct. (Technically, we're talking about the difference between an objective and a subjective genitive in Greek grammar.) The difference may seem insignificant at first glance, but it is not. In Paul's view, do people experience salvation (or justification, in Paul's language) because of their own faith or because of Jesus's faithfulness on behalf of humanity?

Interpreters who address this problem appeal to many kinds of evidence. The word *pistis*, often translated "faith," has a range of meanings and can just as easily point to faithful*ness* rather than belief. There's the matter of Greek syntax, how words relate to one another in meaningful ways. We can be more specific and look into how Paul uses genitive constructions with other phrases: Does he usually use genitives in objective or subjective ways? Interpreters look into the context of the passages in question: What seems to be Paul's larger line of argument in each case? And we can look at the problem from the perspective of Paul's larger theology: Apart from this particular question, how does Paul seem to understand the relationships among justification, Jesus, and faith (or faithfulness)? How did other Jews and Christians under-

---

21. Jouette M. Bassler provides an especially lucid and concise explanation of the problem in *Navigating Paul: An Introduction to Key Theological Concepts* (Louisville: Westminster John Knox, 2007), 27–32.

stand justification? All of these factors and others contribute to our problem-solving. In the end, however, no one knows the absolute truth. For all we know, Paul may have *intended* his language to remain ambiguous. He may have had both possible meanings in mind at once. A final resolution may elude us, but the process of working through all these questions can only deepen our understanding of the problem and of Paul's letters in general.

YOU DO IT ALL THE TIME

Many people express apprehension about interpreting the Bible. We might not know it from the confidently nutty ways people sometimes use it, but most people approach interpretation as a daunting task. For one thing, the Bible's been around for nearly two thousand years. What can one say that hasn't already been said?

People have other good reasons to hesitate. A vast distance separates us from the times and cultures in which the biblical books were composed. The Bible mentions people who were famous in their day but—apart from their biblical appearances—would be unrecognizable to most college history majors. Consider Sennacherib, Cyrus, Herod, and Bernice. We could say the same for biblical place names and even ethnicities: How many English speakers know who the Elamites were? There are reasons people publish Bible atlases and dictionaries. Readers know, however, that the cultural divide extends far wider than the names of people and places. We may not express our grief in the ways the ancients did, but we understand what's going on when people rend their garments, beat their chests, or refuse to eat. Yet other cultural logics baffle us. What's going on when Abraham sacrifices several animals, cuts them into two pieces, and leaves the body parts aligned over against one another overnight (Gen 15:9–21)? Why does one Hebrew man place his hand under another's genitals when they make an important pact (Gen 24:2, 9; 47:29)? What on earth does Paul have in mind when he commands women who pray or prophesy in public to cover their heads (literally, "have authority over their heads") "because of the angels" (1 Cor 11:10)? Commentators still argue over that one.

Culture and history pose a problem, but many readers—I can say this for my students, at least—feel more intimidated by the process of interpretation. In the popular imagination Bible reading has a mystical quality, as if one needs a magic decoder ring to make sense of its stories and poems. There's a widely shared sense that every passage in the Bible must convey a deep personal or spiritual message or that interpretation requires readers to possess expert knowledge in order to achieve understanding. "I read the same passage," students say, "but I didn't see the things you pointed out."

Not only do we possess the tools necessary for insightful interpretation; we use them all the time. In 2014 the insurance company GEICO launched a commercial based on this very premise. Often called the "Horror Movie Commercial," it features four young adults, two women and two men, running through the moonlit woods. One stumbles and falls. When they come upon a cabin in the woods, one suggests, "Let's hide in the attic." Another replies, "No, in the basement." A third offers a wiser alternative, "Why can't we just get in the running car?" But the fourth is having none of that: "Are you crazy? Let's hide behind the chainsaws." There awaits the masked murderer, rolling his eyes at his victims' stupidity. Then we hear the voiceover: "If you're in a horror movie, you make poor decisions. It's what you do. If you wanna save 15 percent or more on car insurance . . ."

The Horror Movie Commercial entirely relies on the literary competence of TV watchers. Before a word is spoken, the eerie setting, the panicked running, and the youthfulness of the actors give away the horror movie premise. We've all seen enough horror movies to know where and how people meet bad ends. The ad's humor resides in our ability to perform a fairly sophisticated literary analysis intuitively and quickly. We do it all the time.

When my daughters were little, they enjoyed the Newberry Medal-winning novel *Bridge to Terabithia*.[22] The story pairs a preteen boy and girl as best friends who explore a fantasy life in their forest hideaway. It's a bit of a coming-of-age story: through the friendship and adventures he shares with Leslie, Jesse gains self-confidence and strength. Tragically, Leslie dies in an accident, leaving the young man to come to terms with his grief.

Decades later the novel was adapted into a major feature film, which I watched with my daughters. As we all know, it's all but impossible for a movie to follow a novel detail for detail, but one moment particularly caught our attention. After Leslie's death, Jesse visits her home. In an instant, just vaguely, it seems as if he sees her roaming through

---

22. Katherine Paterson, *Bridge to Terabithia* (New York: HarperCollins, 1977).

the house—a detail that does not occur in the novel. The moment is so subtle, and it happens so quickly, that I wasn't even sure what had happened. I definitely did not know what it meant. After we left the theater, my daughters and I discussed why those who created the movie chose to add this detail. We finally landed on an answer that satisfied us: the novel goes to great lengths to show how Jesse's friendship with Leslie continues to influence him even after her death. These things play out in ways that might be too slow-paced for film. Leslie's almost ghostly appearance, we decided, was the film's way of suggesting her continuing presence in Jesse's life. My daughters were both young at the time. I don't know the degree to which my own education influenced our conversation, but I remember they were making the same observations and asking many of the same questions I was. Works of art invite the work of interpretation.

This interpretive work goes on all the time. Pay television and the rise of internet services like Netflix have led to an era of great television series. Many series deal in symbolic gestures, cultural allusions, and inside references from one episode to another. We also enjoy the opportunity to watch missed episodes at our convenience or even binge-watch an entire series in a weekend. If something grabs our attention or leaves us confused, we know we can ask our friends the next morning. If we can't wait even that long, we can go online as soon as an episode ends to find Twitter debates and real-time blogs addressing our questions.

We perform these tasks with all sorts of media: visual art, music, cartoons—you name it. Most often we do so for our own amusement. Did Bessie Smith *really* mean what I thought she meant in her 1928 song "Empty Bed Blues"? We also notice that our cultural competence increases over time, even as cultural artifacts acquire new significance with the passing of time: the 1972 hit "Too Late to Turn Back Now" has always been a lovely love song. But in the film *BlackKkKlansman*, the producer transforms that song into a luxurious celebration of African American culture. Having seen the movie, I resonate with the song at a very different level. As time passes, we gain experiences and cultural knowledge that enhance our skills in critical appreciation.

Applying our interpretive skills to movies and songs is usually fun, but our public debates sometimes concern weightier matters. In 1994 controversy erupted over a planned exhibit by the Smithsonian Institution's National Air and Space Museum. Anticipating the fiftieth anniversary of the Hiroshima and Nagasaki bombings, the Smithsonian planned to look into the suffering of Japanese victims and the logic behind the American decision to deploy the bombs. New historical research suggested that the traditional rationale given for the decision, that using the bombs saved countless lives, was incorrect—and that the United States knew this to be the case before using the bombs. When news of the planned exhibit broke out in 1994, many citizens, especially veterans organizations representing persons who had fought in the Pacific War, rose up in protest. The exhibit, they said, would dishonor those who had fought against Japan, and it would shift attention away from the atrocities committed by the Japanese themselves. The final exhibit was much more modest than what had been projected. During the controversy Tom Crouch, the Smithsonian's curator, pointedly asked:

> Do you want to do an exhibit to make veterans feel good, or do you want an exhibit that will lead our visitors to think about the consequences of the atomic bombing of Japan? Frankly, I don't think we can do both.[23]

The Enola Gay exhibit controversy reflects how diverse factors can complicate the work of public interpretation—and how those factors indicate what lies at stake in that work. With the generation that had fought the Pacific War rapidly dying off, veterans organizations wanted to ensure that their courage, service, and sacrifice would receive the attention they deserve. Others sought to dramatize the consequences of nuclear war, including the perils attending national policy that relies upon nuclear weapons as a deterrent. Some sought to protect the ideal of the United States as a heroic and virtuous actor on the world scene, particularly during World War II, while others were more deeply committed to the humanity of all persons who suffer, including the Japanese. The Enola Gay exhibit wasn't simply about the past; it involved the relationship between how we describe our past and what we value in the present.[24]

---

23. Quoted in Edward T. Linenthal, "Anatomy of a Controversy," in *History Wars: The Enola Gay and Other Battles for the American Past*, ed. Edward T. Linenthal and Tom Engelhardt (New York: Henry Holt, 1996), 35.
24. See Michael J. Hogan, "The Enola Gay Controversy: History, Memory, and the Politics of Presentation," in *Hiroshima in History and Memory*, ed. Michael J. Hogan (New York: Cambridge University Press, 1996), 200–32.

BIBLICAL INTERPRETATION IN HISTORICAL PERSPECTIVE

The Dead Sea Scrolls amount to a diverse collection of ancient Jewish texts discovered in eleven caves at a site called Khirbet Qumran in what was then Jordan, now the West Bank. Among the first seven scrolls to appear in 1947 was the *Habakkuk Pesher* (1QpHab), a running commentary on chapters 1–2 of the biblical book of Habakkuk. The document has grown immensely important for at least four reasons: (1) As one of the first scrolls discovered, translated, and published, it exercises perhaps outsized influence. (2) It may record some of the history and self-understanding of the community that produced or maintained the scrolls. (3) The Hebrew text of Habakkuk included in the commentary corresponds closely to the Masoretic Text, the medieval text of the Jewish Scriptures that serves as the primary basis for most modern translations. (4) It reflects how some ancient Jews interpreted the Bible in the century or two between the Maccabean Revolt (167–164 BCE) and the time of Jesus.

Text from Habakkuk (included in the *Pesher*)	Commentary
[*Oracle of Habakkuk the prophet. How long, O Lord, shall I cry*] *for help and Thou wilt not* [*hear*]? (1:1–2)	[Interpreted, this concerns the beginning] of the [final] generation....
So the law is weak [*and justice never goes forth*] (1:4a–b)	[Interpreted] this concerns those who have despised the Law of God....
[*For the wicked encompasses*] *the righteous.* (1:4c)	[*The wicked* is the Wicked Priest, and *the righteous*] is the Teacher of Righteousness....
[*Behold the nations and see, marvel and be astonished; for I accomplish a deed in your days, but you will not believe it when*] *told.* (1:5)	[Interpreted, this concerns] those who were unfaithful together with the Liar, in that they [did] not [listen to the word received by] the Teacher of Righteousness from the mouth of God....

Fig. 1.2

Interpretation of Habakkuk in the *Habakkuk Pesher*

The *Habakkuk Pesher* interprets biblical Habakkuk as an oracular prophecy that outlines the history and context of the Qumran community. A few excerpts from the commentary, paired with the relevant text from biblical Habakkuk, reveal the commentary's basic logic: see figure 1.2.[25]

The commentary goes on, of course, but even this small sample invites curiosity. It introduces a set of characters: Who are those who have despised the law and those who were unfaithful, the Wicked Priest, the Teacher of Righteousness, and the Liar? The commentary alludes to other characters and events, to such a degree that many interpreters believe it sketches a partial history of the Qumran community. Perhaps the group experienced internal strife, in which the Liar opposed the leader called the Teacher of Righteousness. Perhaps there was external conflict, in which the Teacher of Righteousness opposed the high priest in Jerusalem. According to commentary on Habakkuk 2:15, the Wicked Priest "pursued the Teacher of Righteousness to the house of his exile" on the Day of Atonement. This detail suggests conflict regarding the correct calendar, a major topic of debate among Jews of the period. The *Pesher* includes disparaging comments on the Romans, whom it calls the Kittim.[26]

For our purposes, the *Habakkuk Pesher* provides one example of ancient Jewish biblical interpretation. The biblical text is taken to speak directly to the context of the hearer. It has a certain oracular quality: the text conveys supernatural wisdom, but a highly skilled reader is required for proper interpretation. As James L. Kugel points out, ancient interpreters assumed the Bible's divine authorship. That belief implied the sense that every aspect of the Bible provides relevant teaching for all readers, even when the biblical text itself doesn't make obvious sense. As we see in the *Habakkuk Pesher* and other sources, the task of interpretation requires creativity and wisdom: since the Bible is assumed to speak authoritatively to every situation, and since the text itself doesn't make that outcome easy, interpreters must somehow decode the Bible in order to find insight.[27]

According to one common narrative, premodern people would allow their imaginations to run wild, twisting texts to mean whatever they wanted. The cultural revolution embodied in the Renaissance revived

---

25. Translation of 1QpHab from Geza Vermes, *The Dead Sea Scrolls in English*, 3rd ed. (New York: Penguin Books, 1987).
26. See James C. VanderKam, *The Dead Sea Scrolls Today* (Grand Rapids: Eerdmans, 1998), 47–48, 100–04.
27. James L. Kugel, *The Bible as It Was* (Cambridge, MA: Belknap/Harvard, 1997), 17–23.

an interest in historical and naturalistic investigation. The Protestant Reformation can partly be explained as a transitional period between the Middle Ages and Renaissance thinking, with key figures like Martin Luther and John Calvin reading the Bible in its original languages and taking seriously its historical contexts. According to this model they favored straightforward "common-sense" readings over allegorical and other fanciful modes of interpretation, clearing the path for modern biblical interpretation. This common model is helpful in some ways: the return to history does mark a sea change in interpretive sensibility. But ancient Jews and Christians thought a lot about biblical interpretation, developing fairly sophisticated approaches of their own. Several of the things they considered should also occupy our attention.

Many ancient readers employed *allegorical*, or *spiritual*, methods of interpretation, a model that looks silly to moderns. Allegorical interpretations take discrete elements of a text and link them to realities that lie beyond the text in question. For example, the apostle Paul develops an extended interpretation of the stories concerning Sarah and Hagar (Gal 4:21–31). In Genesis Sarah and her husband Abraham cannot produce offspring. Sarah delivers her enslaved woman Hagar for Abraham's sexual use, and she bears Abraham's first son, Ishmael. Later Sarah conceives a son of her own, Isaac. Genesis features two versions of the story, but in both Sarah eventually drives Hagar out of the household (Gen 16:1–16; 21:9–21). In taking up this story Paul explicitly calls his interpretation allegorical (Gal 4:24). Sarah corresponds to the heavenly Jerusalem, which implies the gospel, promise, freedom, and Spirit. Hagar aligns with the earthly Jerusalem, accompanied by slavery and the flesh. "So then, friends," Paul writes, "we are children, not of the slave but of the free woman."

We can only guess how effectively Paul persuaded his audience, but we easily imagine his opponents mocking his line of thought. Allegorical interpretation can make almost any sort of meaning out of a text. On the other hand, one can only refute an allegorical interpretation by offering an even more compelling counter-interpretation or by showing a logical flaw within the interpretation itself. Perhaps Paul's opponents pointed out that it is Sarah's descendants, after all, who receive the Torah on Mount Sinai, not Hagar's: How can Paul say that "Hagar is Mount Sinai in Arabia" (Gal 4:25), using her story to discourage adherence to the law?

Ancient interpreters, of course, understood the dangers of allegorical interpretation, but they also thought things through at multiple levels. In Alexandria, perhaps the ancient Mediterranean world's most learned city, a Jewish thinker and community leader named Philo applied allegorical interpretation in many settings. Even in the garden of Eden, Philo said, God assigned meanings to the Tree of Life and the Tree of Knowledge (*Plant.* 36).[28] Philo understood the persuasive power of more straightforward, literal readings. Unfortunately, sometimes literal readings of the text create unflattering portraits of God or seem to promote unethical behavior. Following similar logic, Augustine speculates that the vast majority of deeds reported in the Old Testament are to be understood figuratively as well as literally (*Doctr. chr.* 3.32). Origen explicitly names Philo's influence on his own approach to interpretation,[29] an influence that extended to figures as notable as Clement of Alexandria, Jerome, and Augustine.

Premodern Christian interpretation appealed to two primary criteria in judging faithful interpretation: the rule of faith and the rule of love. The rule of faith implies adherence to a fixed set of beliefs, something very similar to the great creeds such as the Nicene Creed. This criterion rules illegitimate interpretations that promote beliefs that contradict the rule of faith, or that portray the Bible as doing so. The rule of love involves both devotion and ethics. Proper interpretation should enhance love of God and love of neighbor. Augustine argued:

> Whoever ... thinks that he understands the divine Scriptures or any part of them so that it does not build the double love of God and of our neighbor does not understand it at all. (*Doctr. chr.* 1.40)[30]

Premodern Christian interpretation, then, fell within the boundaries of what was already regarded as true doctrine and proper conduct. Where the biblical texts seemed reluctant to fit into those boundaries, allegorical interpretation was called for. Augustine maintains, "Whatever

---

28. Cited in Robert M. Grant and David Tracy, *A Short History of the Interpretation of the Bible*, 2nd ed. (Minneapolis: Fortress, 1984), 53.
29. David T. Runia, "Philo and Origen: A Preliminary Survey," in *Philo and the Church Fathers: A Collection of Papers* (VCSup 32; Leiden: E. J. Brill, 1995), 117–25; Peder Borgen, "Philo of Alexandria as Exegete," in *A History of Biblical Interpretation*, ed. Alan J. Hauser and Duane F. Watson (Grand Rapids: Eerdmans, 2003), 1:114–43.
30. Augustine of Hippo, *On Christian Doctrine*, trans. D. W. Robertson Jr., Library of Liberal Arts (New York: Macmillan, 1958).

appears in the divine Word that does not literally pertain to virtuous behavior or to the truth of faith you must take to be figurative" (3.14).

Early Christian interpreters such as Origen and Augustine sought not only to provide guidelines for appropriate interpretation; they also cared about interpreters as persons. They did not regard biblical interpreters as blank slates, idealized readers who would read and understand unaided. Augustine insisted that interpreters needed grounding in the fear and love of God, including a humble sense of Scripture's authority. He also believed readers should have a general familiarity with the whole Bible before engaging in public interpretation (*Doctr. chr.* 2.9–14). In short, in premodern Christian interpretation one's spiritual formation and moral character constituted fundamental elements in the process of interpretation.

Often overlooked in surveys of ancient Christian interpretation is the ongoing interaction between Christian and Jewish interpreters, including the also overlooked contributions of Jewish Christians. Many noncanonical Jewish writings survive precisely because Christians transmitted and cared for them, and many of those writings reflect how some ancient Jews, and probably Christians, interpreted the Bible.[31] For example, Jewish interpreters frequently filled in the gaps of biblical narratives or expanded those stories to address issues that were important to them. From important texts such as 1 Enoch and Jubilees we encounter an explanation for the flood. According to Genesis 6:1–4, the "sons of God" impregnated mortal women, producing a race of giants. Immediately following this account comes the story of Noah and the great flood: human wickedness had reached a critical state (6:5). First Enoch and Jubilees understand the interspecies reproduction between angels and women as the cause for the flood. Likewise, ancient Jewish noncanonical literature includes final blessings ("testaments") from great figures of the past to their heirs, in which the patriarchs outline important beliefs and other expansions of the biblical accounts, along with biographies ("lives") of the prophets. The rabbinic tradition of *midrash* similarly involves the elaboration of biblical narratives, usually revising old material and adding new content, as a means of interpretation.

Ancient Jewish interpretation often records dialogue or debate rather

---

31. Torleif Elgvin, "Jewish Christian Editing of the Old Testament Pseudepigrapha," in *Jewish Believers in Jesus: The Early Centuries*, ed. Oskar Skarsaune and Reidar Hvalvik (Peabody, MA: Hendrickson, 2007), 278–304.

than the articulation of a single interpretive conclusion. We observe this pattern in both exegetical works (often called *midrashim*) and the classical rabbinic literature, where passages of Scripture are quoted, dissected, and debated at length. The purpose often involves knowing how to live when the Torah is unclear or when circumstances are complicated. Sometimes the discussion can be more speculative. For example, the Genesis Rabbah includes a discussion of why creation begins not with *aleph*, the first letter of the alphabet, but with *bet*. (In Hebrew, the phrase often translated "In the beginning" begins with the letter *bet*.) One rabbi answers that this factor reveals that there is not one world but two, the present world and the world to come. Also, it indicates that creation is an act of blessing, since the Hebrew word for blessing also begins with *bet*. And on goes the conversation (*Gen. Rab.* 1.10).[32] A distinguishing mark of rabbinic interpretation involves presenting multiple points of view, even when the conversation leads to a preferred resolution. We might further note that some medieval Jewish scholars, such as Rashi (Rabbi Solomon ben Isaac, d. 1105), preferred "contextual" over allegorical and midrashic interpretation, while others advanced grammatical understanding of biblical Hebrew, anticipating by centuries views held by the Protestant Reformers.[33]

The Protestant Reformation provides a handy way to assess the transition from premodern to modern modes of interpretation. Martin Luther and John Calvin, the most prominent of the reformers, straddled the intellectual world of the Middle Ages and that of the Renaissance. In general, they both preferred "plain," "common-sense," or even "literal" interpretation over figurative and allegorical modes. Yet they also valued and consulted the works of medieval commentators. In contrast to most medieval interpreters, both studied the biblical languages, reflecting the humanist tendency to consult original sources. In resolving exegetical disputes, both Luther and Calvin sought to understand the intentions of the biblical authors and took account of the historical contexts addressed by the biblical texts. None of these points represents an absolute break from earlier interpreters; however, the overall picture reflects changing sensitivities and commitments in

---

32. Cited in Gary G. Porton, "Rabbinic Midrash," in Hauser and Watson, *A History of Biblical Interpretation*, 1:215–16.

33. Robert A. Harris, "Medieval Jewish Biblical Exegesis," in Hauser and Watson, *A History of Biblical Interpretation*, 2:141–71.

interpretation. Finally, it would never have crossed the mind of either Luther or Calvin that proper interpretation could occur apart from the life of faith and prayer. For both Luther and Calvin, a skilled interpreter learns languages and history, consults previous interpreters, practices carefully reasoned and easily understood methods of interpretation, and integrates interpretation with the life of faith.

Reformation biblical interpretation promoted simplicity, but it also led to confusion. It foregrounded biblical interpretation as a means of engaging controversy. Although Luther and Calvin respected earlier interpreters, they also treated interpretation as a means of determining theological truth. Once that cat had escaped the bag, interpreters frequently defied church authority. The Enlightenment's commitment to "pure" reason, as if reason divorced from emotion, desire, or history were possible, led the way to new questions and answers. The tradition of critical biblical interpretation—interpretation that subjects the Bible to the judgment of scholarly, even "scientific," inquiry—emerged in European universities. Believers and unbelievers alike began to question not only the Bible's meaning but also the processes by which the biblical books were composed. Traditional views, such as Moses's authorship of the Torah and the authorship of the Gospels by Jesus's disciples and their friends, were abandoned. Scholars exposed historical problems in the biblical histories. Even the historical reliability of the Gospels came into question, with "lives of Jesus" investigating the historical nature of Jesus's teaching and activities. Historical-Jesus research remains the most common way in which popular audiences encounter biblical scholarship.

The turn toward history marks the primary distinction between modern and premodern scholarship.[34] For premodern interpreters, theological criteria governed public interpretation. Interpretations that did not promote faithful belief and behavior were regarded as deficient. Although the vast majority of public interpreters adhere to religious communities and seeks theological insight, modern academic interpretation has elevated historical criteria to the forefront. Historians do not appeal to divine intention or activity in accounting for past events. Likewise, modern biblical interpreters have sought ordinary human explanations for matters such as how the biblical books were com-

---

34. Stephen Fowl, "Theological and Ideological Strategies of Biblical Interpretation," in *Scripture: An Ecumenical Introduction to the Bible and Its Interpretation*, ed. Michael J. Gorman (Peabody, MA: Hendrickson, 2005), 164.

posed; the social settings and developments of ancient Israel, Judaism, and Christianity; and the events narrated in biblical accounts. All of those issues can and do bear religious significance, but modern scholarship does not apply theological criteria to such questions. Indeed, modern interpretation welcomes contributions from believers and nonbelievers alike.

Christian fundamentalism has rejected historical criticism since the dawn of the twentieth century, regarding it as antithetical to proper faith. If Moses didn't compose the Torah, if books like Isaiah were composed over centuries rather than by a single author, and if Jesus didn't do and say all the things recorded in the Gospels, what remains for faithful interpretation? But another reaction against the historical-critical paradigm emerged in the late twentieth century. From a literary perspective, historical criticism seemed to chop the Bible into little pieces of source material, traditional development, and redactional editing. A biology student can learn lots by dissecting a frog, but all the dissected frogs in the lab are dead. Likewise, many argued, historical criticism stripped away the literary and poetic power of the Bible. From a theological perspective, historical criticism tended to shy away from the main reasons people read the Bible: for religious and moral wisdom and inspiration. Historical criticism remains basic to most public interpretation, while efforts to reclaim the Bible's literary and theological value also occupy important public space.[35] Most contemporary interpreters blend historical and literary approaches, and many integrate all these perspectives with theological interest.

One theological tradition, Eastern Orthodoxy, has largely exempted itself from the historical-critical ethos of contemporary scholarship. Historical criticism tends to assume the inferiority of earlier, especially

---

35. The literature pertinent to these conversations is immense. On historical criticism's relevance for religious interpretation among Jews, Protestants, and Catholics, see Marc Zvi Brettler, Peter Enns, and Daniel J. Harrington, S.J., *The Bible and the Believer: How to Read the Bible Critically and Religiously* (New York: Oxford University Press, 2012). A classic exposition of literary approaches to the Bible may be found in the work of Robert Alter, *The Art of Biblical Narrative* (New York: Basic Books, 1981); and *The Art of Biblical Poetry* (New York: Basic Books, 1985). For contemporary attempts to emphasize theological interpretation, see Ellen F. Davis and Richard B. Hays, eds., *The Art of Reading Scripture* (Grand Rapids: Eerdmans, 2003); Steven E. Fowl, *Theological Interpretation of Scripture*, Cascade Companions (Eugene, OR: Cascade, 2009); and Michael J. Gorman, ed., *Scripture: An Ecumenical Introduction to the Bible and Its Interpretation* (Peabody, MA: Hendrickson, 2005).

premodern, interpretations in favor of newer, "critical" interpretations. Orthodoxy, however, seeks wisdom especially in the ancient "church fathers," whose commentaries, sermons, and devotional writings still survive.[36] In Orthodox traditions all interpretation primarily serves the work of spiritual edification. One practical way in which Orthodox interpretation often differs from historical-critical interpretation lies in the relationship between the "Old Testament" (the Jewish Scriptures, including the Apocrypha or not, as treasured by Christians) and the New. Orthodox readers see Jesus as the center of the biblical story, with the Old Testament pointing toward the new in a figural (not necessarily predictive) way. In contrast, historical critics interpret Old Testament passages as speaking to places and times far removed from the early Christian communities that appropriated them.[37]

Religious and theological research stands apart from other areas of academic inquiry in important ways. In most cities one does not expect to find bookstores dedicated to historical, sociological, or legal research. However, religious and theological bookstores appear in most significant cities and many smaller ones. Religiously affiliated publishers provide important resources that are consulted by academic and general audiences alike. Although many colleges and universities provide secular courses related to biblical studies, many others approach the subject from a theological or confessional perspective—not to mention the hundreds of theological seminaries in which biblical scholars work. For these reasons the role of faith in academic biblical scholarship sometimes emerges as a contentious issue: To what degree do religious commitments determine the categories that receive scholarly attention? Does study that serves the church count as "real" scholarship, or should academic research guard itself from sectarian influence? My own view is that theologically informed research does contribute to scholarship; however, it is entirely fair to question its influence on what counts as important or unimportant. It is also reasonable to point out and critique how theological (and other) commitments influence the work of scholars.

From the Enlightenment on, modern biblical interpretation has

---

36. John Anthony McGuckin, "Recent Biblical Hermeneutics in Patristic Perspective: The Tradition of Orthodoxy," *Greek Orthodox Theological Review* 47 (2002): 308.

37. Ronald D. Witherup, "The Interpretation of the Bible in Roman Catholic and Orthodox Churches," in Gorman, *Scripture: An Ecumenical Introduction*, 211.

tended to minimize the person of the interpreter, the real flesh-and-blood reader who reads and makes sense of the Bible. I teach in a theological seminary, where a plaque commemorates "William C. Schaeffer, Professor of New Testament Science." The idea was that interpretation is an intellectual discipline. If interpreters could agree upon the basic rules of interpretation, in theory they could achieve consensus regarding the history and meaning of texts. Many textbooks devoted to biblical interpretation reflect this assumption by featuring chapter after chapter on "methods" of interpretation without discussing the person of the interpreter at all—or as part of particular chapters. Although this traditional model has undergone criticism and revision, such textbooks encouraged readers to set aside their personal histories and commitments in the search for "objectivity." They labeled proper biblical interpretation "exegesis," which involved bringing meaning out from (*ex*) the text. A great sin, *eisegesis*, was considered to have occurred when interpreters read into (*eis*) the text from their own interests and biases.

Twentieth-century developments in philosophical hermeneutics, the study of meaning-making, called for renewed attention to the personal and cultural formation of interpreters. We all encounter texts through the mediation of culture. Put another way, we read the Bible within the flow of our larger culture's encounter with it and with a host of other values. We cannot escape that reality, nor should we try. But we can cultivate self-awareness regarding how our reading occurs within a broader cultural perspective—and what is at stake in that process. For example, perhaps the most important work of New Testament scholarship is Albert Schweitzer's *The Quest of the Historical Jesus*. For all its brilliance, the book begins with a paean to German intellectual life: no other culture, Schweitzer writes, possesses the unique genius that empowered German theology.

> When, at some future day, our period of civilisation shall lie, closed and completed, before the eyes of later generations, German theology will stand out as a great, a unique phenomenon in the mental and spiritual life of our time. For nowhere save in the German temperament can there be found in the same perfection the living complex of conditions and factors—of philosophic thought, critical acumen, historical insight, and religious feeling—without which no deep theology is possible.[38]

---

38. Albert Schweitzer, *The Quest of the Historical Jesus: A Critical Study of Its Progress from Reimarus to Wrede* (New York: Macmillan, 1968 [1906]), 1.

Schweitzer is known as a great humanitarian, a recipient of the Nobel Peace Prize. But his own nationalism—his *Quest* appeared less than a decade before the outbreak of World War I—profoundly shaped how he interpreted Jesus.

Cultural insight empowers interpretation in all sorts of ways. Many cultures apply the metaphor of light and dark to good and evil, respectively. Many biblical texts, most notably the Gospel of John, rely upon this metaphor (see John 3:19–21). But that comparison has also served evil ends, as when, on biblical grounds, defenders of slavery and segregation regarded dark skin as a curse from God.[39] The Botswanan interpreter Musa W. Dube counters such interpretations by recalling the positive presence of darkness in her own cultural context, where children play outside at night. If European colonizers stigmatized Africa as "the Dark Continent," Dube suggests that interpreters can transcend that metaphor by learning "to play in the dark, seek in the dark, and to see the breath-taking million stars shining in the dark."[40]

Philosophers also demonstrated that our biases and commitments can foster insight. Indeed, they are necessary for our learning. Necessity often proves itself the mother of invention. The challenges posed by space travel led to dozens of inventions, from joysticks to memory foam. As for matters of interpretation, the questions we bring to the Bible often shape what we find in it. Enslaved Africans in the United States told and retold the exodus story, where God liberates Israel from bondage in Egypt.[41] The narrative goes on to grant the Israelites land that had once belonged to their neighbors. God promises, "I will hand over to you the inhabitants of the land, and you shall drive them out before you" (Exod 23:31). That same story has proven problematic for Native Americans, Palestinians, and others, who have lost their ancestral lands to people who claimed them in the name of the exodus

---

39. Several examples occur in Stephen R. Haynes, *Noah's Curse: The Biblical Justification of American Slavery*, Religion in America (New York: Oxford University Press, 2007).
40. Musa W. Dube, "Decolonizing the Darkness: Bible Readers and the Colonial Cultural Archive," in *Soundings in Cultural Criticism: Perspectives and Methods in Culture, Power, and Identity in the New Testament*, ed. Francisco Lozada Jr. and Greg Carey (Minneapolis: Fortress, 2013), 42.
41. Demetrius K. Williams, "The Bible and Models of Liberation in the African American Experience," in *Yet with a Steady Beat: Contemporary U.S. Afrocentric Biblical Interpretation*, ed. Randall C. Bailey, SemeiaSt 42 (Atlanta: Society of Biblical Literature, 2003), 34.

promise. For example, under the banner of "Manifest Destiny" white Americans appropriated Israel's acquisition of a promised land as God's will. The decimation of Native American populations echoes the biblical narrative in which Israelites drive out and exterminate the inhabitants of Canaan. By identifying themselves with this biblical motif, people minimize the guilt of genocide and displacement. Our social embeddedness markedly informs how we understand the Bible.[42]

Moreover, the increasing number of women and other previously marginalized voices in academic conversations has led to renewed attention to "flesh-and-blood" readers.[43] In addition to religious faith or non-faith dispositions, countless factors both individual and cultural shape how we make meaning. Well into the twentieth century, academic biblical scholarship was conducted mostly by ordained white men. Conversations regarding gender, race, ethnicity, colonialism, social class, and sexual orientation have exerted dramatic influence upon the field. Imagine a study of Mary the mother of Jesus, as she is presented in the Gospels of Matthew and Luke, conducted by a woman from India such as Sharon Jacob. Jacob takes seriously the experiences of real women—specifically, poor Indian women who accept payment to serve as surrogate mothers for wealthy Westerners. Seeking to better their own lives and those of their families, these women carry other people's babies in economic relationships that recapitulate centuries-old colonialist relations. How might the stories of such women illuminate the story of Mary, who carries God's baby in her own body for benefits unnamed? What of her husband Joseph, who, like Indian husbands, acquiesces in the arrangement?[44] In a sense we return to premodern interpretation when interpreters draw meaning from their own identities and the cultural histories of other flesh-and-blood peo-

---

42. See Robert Allen Warrior, "A Native American Perspective: Canaanites, Cowboys, and Indians," in *Voices from the Margin: Interpreting the Bible in the Third World*, ed. R. S. Sugirtharajah, 2nd ed. (Maryknoll, NY: Orbis, 1995), 277–85; and Naim S. Ateek, "A Palestinian Perspective: Biblical Perspectives on the Land," in Sugirtharajah, *Voices from the Margin*, 267–76.

43. For the phrase "flesh-and-blood reader," see Fernando F. Segovia, "Toward a Hermeneutics of the Diaspora: A Hermeneutics of Otherness and Engagement," in Segovia and Tolbert, *Reading from This Place*, 1:57–59.

44. Sharon Jacob, *Reading Mary alongside Indian Surrogate Mothers: Violent Love, Oppressive Liberation, and Infancy Narratives*, The Bible and Cultural Studies (New York: Palgrave Macmillan, 2015).

ple. Objectivist, historicist analysis takes a back seat to the project of meaning-making.

People may choose to interpret the Bible in a purely cultural and historical framework, restricting its meaning to points in the past. But when readers seek contemporary meaning from the Bible, they necessarily invoke the sort of analogical and figural reasoning that marked premodern interpretation. The construction of contemporary meaning requires that readers draw some sort of analogies between the biblical text and its environment and the readers' own cultural moment. Interpretation necessarily entails the work of the imagination. What kinds of correspondences does the interpreter draw between the ancient text and our own cultural moments?[45] In a fundamental sense, the Bible says nothing to us today—at least, not until we invite it to speak.

INTERPRETATION IN THE UNITED STATES

The United States bears its own history and legacies with respect to biblical interpretation. The culture is and always has been religiously diverse, more so now than ever, but the influence of Protestantism and revivalism shapes the context in which we read. European Christianity eventually settled into Protestant (usually Reformed or Lutheran) areas and Roman Catholic areas, with scattered Anabaptists and other minorities present from place to place. When sects conflicted with one another or rulers shifted their loyalties, violence often resulted. Indeed after the Reformation, European Christians died at one another's hands in greater numbers than had been the case under Roman persecution. Until the modern age of missionary expansion, Christians in most other areas of the globe identified with national churches: Ethiopic, Coptic, Syriac, Armenian, Russian, and so forth.

But distinctive forces shaped religion in the United States. Spanish Mexico and South America, like French Canada and other regions, expressed loyalty to Roman Catholicism. Some of the US colonies began with express commitment to one blend of Christianity or another, while a few did not, but rapidly religion became an elective matter within the emerging United States. The Constitution declares that "no religious test" may be applied to potential employees or rep-

---

45. Ellen F. Davis, "Teaching the Bible Confessionally in the Church," in *The Art of Reading Scripture*, ed. Ellen F. Davis and Richard B. Hays (Grand Rapids: Eerdmans, 2003), 11–12; Fowl, *Theological Interpretation of Scripture*, 56–63.

resentatives of the federal government. In the eighteenth and nineteenth centuries church attendance waxed and waned, with periods of intense religious excitement (revivals) popping up from time to time. As a result, the new country played host to endless religious innovation and competition among sects, each deploying the Bible in an effort to demonstrate its superior faithfulness. Amid such competition Protestants became especially adept at hanging arguments upon frameworks of carefully chosen Bible verses. To be sure, their European predecessors had already developed similar strategies: for example, the influential Westminster Confession of Faith (1646) included footnotes with Scripture "proofs." This mode of interpretation flourished especially in the United States.

The debates over slavery, which escalated in the decades leading up to the Civil War, provided the classic arena for argumentation via Bible verse. The rupture went deep, as the largest Protestant denominations—Methodist, Baptist, and Presbyterian—all split over the issue prior to the Civil War. Baptists have yet to reconcile due to a host of other issues, but Northern and Southern Methodists (1939) and Presbyterians (1983) took their own time in reuniting. Abolitionists and slavery apologists alike produced detailed arguments for their positions, including not only individual verses but often analyses of the historical contexts of the relevant biblical passages. Pro-slavery advocates advanced biblical passages that promote slavery, along with those passages that tell enslaved people to obey their masters. Robert L. Dabney voiced their confidence: "Here is our policy, then, to push the Bible continually, drive abolitionism to the wall, to compel it to assume an anti-Christian position. By so doing, we compel the whole of Christianity of the North to array itself on our side."[46] Opponents of slavery also appealed to the Bible, but they typically pointed to general principles such as the exodus or the equality of all peoples before God rather than to passages that specifically address slavery and enslaved people. Church historian Mark A. Noll observes, "The power of the proslavery scriptural position—especially in a Protestant world of widespread intuitive belief in the plenary inspiration of the whole Bible—lay in its

---

46. Quoted in Clarice J. Martin, "'Somebody Done Hoodoo'd the Hoodoo Man': Language, Power, Resistance, and the Effective History of Pauline Texts in American Slavery," *Semeia* 83/84 (1998): 215–16, citing Thomas Cary Johnson, *The Life and Letters of Robert Lewis Dabney* (Richmond, VA: Presbyterian Committee of Publication, 1903), 129.

simplicity," and "those who defended . . . the legitimacy of slavery had the easiest task."[47]

The slavery arguments may seem outdated to contemporary readers, but they set the tone for a series of other debates, all conducted on similar lines: May divorced persons, or divorced persons who remarry, receive the church's blessing or serve in positions of ordained ministry? Does the Bible condemn mixing of the races, whether through desegregation or interracial marriage? Does the Bible prohibit or authorize the ministerial leadership of women, especially the authority to preach? And the most divisive issue among Christian churches today—does the Bible condemn same-sex eroticism or same-sex marriage? All of these topics have proven divisive in the twentieth and twenty-first centuries. Apart from the question of race, contemporary churches still differ from one another with respect to divorce, the role of women, and same-sex love.

As inheritors of the European Reformation heritage, the Protestants (including Quakers and Mennonites) who argued over slavery shared many common assumptions. So do their descendants who deploy the Bible to debate other topics. They agree on the value of learning the historical and cultural contexts in which the Bible emerged. They share respect for the biblical languages. They value common-sense interpretation over allegorical and figural reading.

But they also share a didactic and propositional understanding of the Bible. That is, they treat the Bible as containing discrete lessons for life, morality, and doctrine. When a biblical author speaks directly to a subject such as work, money, gender, sexuality, or slavery, the reader is obligated to clarify the Bible's teaching and to follow it. A defender of slavery might observe that several of Jesus's parables include enslaved people as characters. One parable begins, "Which of you, owning a slave . . ." (Luke 17:7, my translation). Might one not conclude that Jesus imagines his disciples as slaveholders? Even when the Bible does not provide explicit teaching on a given subject, such readers assume it contains moral and theological lessons. For example, I once heard a sermon on Noah and the great flood in which the preacher identified eight learning points concerning the topic of endurance. The story never mentions endurance, of course, but a preacher who approaches the

---

47. Mark A. Noll, *The Civil War as a Theological Crisis* (Chapel Hill: University of North Carolina Press, 2006), 33, 50. See James Albert Harrill, *Slaves in the New Testament: Literary, Social, and Moral Dimensions* (Minneapolis: Fortress, 2006), 165–92.

Bible as a trove of moral lessons will extract them from the story one way or another.

Nave's Topical Bible provides a particularly fine example of this propositional approach. One still finds it in bookstores; because it has exhausted its copyright, an online version also exists. First published in 1896 by military chaplain Orville James Nave, this topical Bible quotes 10,000 passages under 20,000 topics. (This, according to *Wikipedia*.) For example, for the word *obduracy* (or stubbornness) we find nineteen passages and cross-references to other subjects like Pharaoh, the Bible's prime example of stubbornness. Sex and intercourse lack entries, but the one for marriage is quite extensive. This entry includes consanguineous marriage, or marriage between relatives; parents contracting marriages for their children; bridal ornaments; wives obtained by kidnapping and wives obtained through heroic feats; and many more subtopics. *Nave's Topical Bible* reflects the assumption that the Bible is a compendium of teachings regarding discrete subjects.

Those who adopt the propositional approach usually assume the Bible's unity and consistency; that is, they believe the Bible speaks with a single clear voice on all topics. This assumption requires interpreters to explain away apparent contradictions. For example, the book of Proverbs generally teaches that wise and righteous conduct leads to positive outcomes. What to do, then, with the book of Job, in which the protagonist is exposed to enormous suffering precisely because of his own righteousness? (Job was probably composed in part to respond to the kind of outlook we encounter in Proverbs.) Did Jesus encourage his followers to disregard the Torah in some instances? This question would have been extremely important in Christianity's first generations. Mark 7:19 reports that Jesus declared all foods clean. Not only does Matthew's account of the same story (15:1–20) omit that saying, but Matthew's Jesus explicitly instructs his disciples that every detail of the law still stands (5:17–20). The difference between the two accounts is almost surely intentional rather than accidental. We could multiply examples of diverse points of view within the Bible, all of which problematize a propositional approach.

Common-sense, propositional approaches limit the kinds of meaning we might find in the Bible. They tend to reduce literary forms like myth, legend, poetry, and parable into single-point "lessons," stifling the potential of story and poem to shape emotion and attitude. These approaches cut off the possibility of finding conversations and debates within the Bible rather than unified teaching. These approaches are hardly limited to US Protestantism, but they have been especially prominent here—and they have gone global through missions and evangelism efforts.

Propositional approaches to the Bible also restrict its interest to the communities of religious adherents. Many readers find the Bible interesting beyond its devotional and theological value. They may study it as an example of meaning-making in specific cultural contexts, for case studies in social adaptation, as a contributing witness for ancient Mediterranean history, and for a host of other reasons.

CONCLUSION

Public biblical interpretation happens when readers enter into conversation with one another, both hearing a diversity of opinions and prepared to share and assess one another's reasons for understanding things as we do. It requires acts of disciplined imagination, in which widely shared criteria shape our deliberations. We might appeal to linguistics, ancient political and cultural history, models from the social sciences, and the conventions of literary interpretation, among other considerations. We may also take account of who is doing the reading and what is at stake for all of us, opening our attention to questions of cultural power and difference.

Some of us read for religious and theological reasons. Others do not. Religious readers may value theological considerations as valid criteria in the work of interpretation, privileging other religiously inclined conversation partners. In doing so, they should not be surprised that some will appreciate their interpretations more than others. In public interpretation, however, we often learn from readers very different from ourselves.

As we move ahead in this study, we will explore the role of historical and cultural factors in interpretation, followed by literary approaches to reading. We will then turn our attention to ourselves—to ideal and actual readers. What makes for a virtuous reader? Does interpretation reward, or even cultivate certain values, sensitivities, and skills? And how do we factor in the contributions and liabilities that come with being real people, with our own personal and cultural histories? Finally, we will explore how ordinary interpreters may interact with the work of professional scholars. How much authority do we grant to the professionals, and how may we access their work most efficiently?

CHAPTER 2.

BRIDGING THE GAP: HISTORY, LANGUAGE, CULTURE

A friend thought he had learned Danish. Having taken a table in a restaurant, he confidently placed his order. The waiter politely asked if he *really* wanted what he'd ordered. My friend reasserted his confidence. The waiter walked to a nearby table, where a customer had brought his dog, then took the dog to meet my friend. "*This* is what you ordered. Are you sure?"

We all expect some cultural adjustment when we travel. I hadn't learned this when I first traveled back in the eighties, but people are more sophisticated now. It's far more common for college and even high school students to experience overseas trips. Just the same, even sophisticated travelers would find ourselves overwhelmed if we were to visit the biblical world. If Westerners struggle to cope with the poverty today in, for example, an Indian city, imagine what would happen if we were confronted by the crowded and unsanitary conditions of an ancient city, with its conventional gender roles, treatment of children, and widespread presence of enslaved people. Imagine our sitting down to share even a common meal: Would we recognize the food, know how to eat it, or follow appropriate etiquette? In some social contexts it's a deadly mistake to say the wrong thing: imagine our fear walking the streets of one of those cities.

Such historical awareness arrived fairly recently on the cultural scene. Walk through an art gallery, and one quickly notices how paintings of biblical scenes reflect the people and cultures that produced the artwork rather than the dress or topography of the biblical world. As late as the eighteenth century, painters tended to dress historical characters in the costumes with which they were familiar. Murillo's *Flight into Egypt*, completed in 1650, depicts Joseph in a hat that must have been stylish in the Seville of his own day. Giotto's early-fourteenth-century rendering of the same scene leaves Joseph hatless. One might guess that men typically didn't wear hats in Giotto's Italy, as his work shows no awareness of historical context. Giotto's *The Kiss of Judas* features soldiers in late medieval Italian uniforms. When a contemporary artist such as the Chinese He Qi dresses the Holy Family as Chinese peasants, we understand his work as making a deliberate choice. He knows Jesus was not Chinese, but his work provides a Chinese interpretation of biblical stories. Not long ago that wasn't the case.

Modern readers intuitively know we must interpret ancient texts in their historical contexts. The question of context provokes frequent debate among readers, but almost everyone accepts the value of historical knowledge. (In this chapter we explore how historical context sometimes proves problematic; in the next chapter we discuss persons who regard historical context as unimportant or unnecessary.) If we accept the significance of historical *context* for biblical texts, more controversial are questions associated with their historical *production*. A forensic art historian might scrape through layers of a painting in order to assess a work's authenticity. A textual historian attends to the diverse styles of handwriting and ink that appear on a manuscript and draws conclusions regarding the history of that manuscript. Can modern readers look into and "through" biblical texts to discern the history of their composition? Can we identify diverse sources that lie beneath the biblical text as it now stands? Is it possible to discriminate earlier from later material? And should we even try to address such questions? These and other issues provide the subject matter for this chapter.

HISTORICAL CONTEXT

Genesis 18:1–33 includes two fascinating stories. In the first, "three men" appear to Abraham, who rushes to prepare a feast for them. The men inquire regarding Abraham's wife Sarah, and one of the men promises that "in due season" Sarah will bear a son. This is remarkable, as Sarah and Abraham have grown old without producing children. Overhearing the preposterous conversation, Sarah laughs. Then in verse 13 something remarkable happens: "The Lord" (Yahweh) chides Sarah for laughing, identifying himself as one of the three "men" who has spoken with Abraham.

In summarizing the story, I have skipped over one little detail. The story begins by explaining that "the Lord" (Yahweh) has appeared to Abraham. It then goes on to introduce "three men" (and not Yahweh) standing before him. Are we to assume the three men in verse 2 represent the form in which "the Lord" appeared to Abraham in verse 1? When the story returns to mention Yahweh in verse 13, it brings things full circle. "The Lord" has appeared as "three men." Yahweh has been present in the story all along. From this point in the story forward, we no longer read of the "three men"; instead, Yahweh shares with Abraham his plan to destroy the wicked cities of Sodom and Gomorrah. Abraham bargains back and forth with Yahweh, securing the promise that if only ten righteous men reside in Sodom, Yahweh will withhold the devastation. Apparently, Yahweh is open to reason.

A second disclosure occurs when the narrative shifts away from Abraham and Sarah to Sodom and Gomorrah. Genesis 19:1 begins with "two angels" sent to survey Sodom that evening. Are we now to conclude that the "three men" who visited Abraham and Sarah earlier in the day (18:2) included Yahweh, attended by two angels?

The story of Abraham, Sarah, Yahweh, the "three men," and the "two angels" raises several historical questions. We might divide them into two basic categories: cultural context and the history of the story's composition. In terms of the story's composition, historians will note several remarkable features:

- Genesis includes not one but two stories in which God promises that Abraham and Sarah will produce an heir. The key point here is Sarah: on multiple occasions God has promised Abraham many offspring (12:1–3; 13:14–17; 15:1–6). But here God promises that Sarah will give birth to this heir. The first such story occurs in Genesis 17:15–22, immediately before the one we're now discussing. Whenever Genesis includes multiple accounts of very similar events, historians often wonder whether the book has incorporated multiple independent literary traditions. For example, Genesis includes two accounts of creation, two stories of the great flood that are intertwined with one another, two stories of Hagar and her son Ishmael, and two stories in which Abraham passes off Sarah as his sister. One key sign of multiple traditions has to do with the deity's name: in 17:15–22 it is "God" (*Elohim*) or "God Almighty" (*El Shaddai*) who makes the promise, but in 18:1–15 it is Yahweh. This is part of a larger pattern in Genesis, and it accompanies other factors that indicate that Genesis, along with the rest of the Pentateuch, has a long and complicated prehistory.[1]

- The question of just who visits Abraham and Sarah, and later Sodom, poses a fascinating problem. Could the apparent confusion (we use the term "apparent" advisedly) be the result of shrewd literary craftwork, or might it result from a lengthy process involving the editing, or redaction, of earlier literary sources? (These two possibilities are not mutually exclusive.) It is entirely possible that a skilled ancient writer might shape the story's entertainment value by withholding important information early in the account, only to supply that information later. So we learn that Yahweh visited Abraham, then wonder who the three men might be, only to find that the "three men" are Yahweh and two angels. It's just as likely, however, that the story's current form also reflects redaction. One can easily imagine a story about Abraham and Sarah encountering *three mysterious men*, later redacted to offer a more theologically acceptable picture in which Yahweh directs the proceedings.

Both sets of observations involve the historical process by which Genesis attained its present form. They suggest a lengthy process by which earlier literary sources were incorporated into later works, and those works once again woven to form Genesis as we know it today. This view would prove highly controversial in some theological circles, but the basic set of assumptions and conclusions is widely held. We might also pursue another set of historical questions, however, based on the historical context of the stories. Here we examine especially 18:1–15, the scene that focuses upon Abraham and Sarah and their visitors. Human behaviors make sense in some historical contexts but not others. In this story we observe several dynamics.

First, Abraham is committed to providing hospitality to his visitors. Interpreting this passage, commentators routinely observe the high level of hospitality expected in ancient Near Eastern cultures. It appears that some of Abraham's hospitality creates a sense of literary exaggeration. Abraham does not simply bring out a snack. Indeed, his level of hospitality exceeds reason in some respects. It takes time to bake bread and to slaughter and cook a calf, but this is what Abraham does. The bread cakes come from the finest flour—and an enormous amount at that. And how are his guests supposed to eat a whole calf? So Abraham's extravagance exceeds ordinary courtesy. Nevertheless, the story

---

1. Although he does not agree on every point presented here, Joel Baden presents a contemporary appraisal of this approach in *The Composition of the Pentateuch: Renewing the Documentary Hypothesis*, AYBRL (New Haven: Yale University Press, 2012), esp. 13–33.

does reflect ancient sensibilities concerning hospitality, reflected today in many cultures.

The story also reflects ancient views of status, placing Abraham at a level below his guests and above the members of his household. He identifies his guests as "my lord" (18:3), perhaps hinting to the reader of the three men's identity. According to the story, he runs here and there, and he and his household repeatedly hurry to prepare the feast. When Abraham meets the men, he bows down to the ground. While they eat, he stands beside them like a table waiter. Just "a little water," Abraham offers, and just "a little bread," but he brings curds and milk instead of water, Sarah prepares rich cakes, and he serves his guests a specially prepared calf. In every respect, Abraham demonstrates his inferiority to his guests—beyond the ordinary expectations of hospitality.

Abraham may be inferior to his guests, but not to his wife Sarah or his enslaved person. The story's cultural context includes both gender and slavery. Abraham commands his wife and his enslaved person alike to prepare the meal. In relation to Abraham, Sarah and the anonymous enslaved person share inferior status. Earlier in Genesis, and again later, when Sarah wants the enslaved person Hagar expelled from the household, she does not cast Hagar out herself but brings her complaint to Abraham (16:5–6; 21:9–14). Abraham has taken Hagar as his wife, and she has produced a son. Sarah can no longer exercise authority over Hagar without Abraham's permission. Sarah also remains inside during the visit of the "three men," avoiding public view until she is called for. (Yet in other stories powerful men see her beauty in public spaces.) As for the enslaved person, we note that biblical translations often gloss over the vocabulary of slavery, rendering words that ordinarily mean "slave" as "servant." The term here in Genesis, *šipḥah*, means "slave-girl."

A reader attuned to cultural history will want to know more about ancient households, slavery, marriages, and the like. Such a reader might wonder if the relational patterns reflected in Genesis indicate a particular moment in history. After all, social arrangements in Israel, like other societies, did change over the course of history. Slavery and patriarchy never went away, but the structure of household life did evolve. The rule of kings and emperors produced an emphasis upon the nuclear family as the basic economic unit, as opposed to the larger kinship networks that sustained people in periods marked by less centralized government. The Bible includes material that reflects both realities.[2]

Almost all interpreters agree on the value of this sort of cultural history. Consider the diverse questions one might pose. After introductions, a preview of the syllabus, and a discussion of routine business matters, I have often begun my classes with demographics. What difference would it make to pursue religion when the average life expectancy for women lies between the ages twenty-five and thirty (for men, forty or so), when women on average must deliver five living babies in order for the population to hold steady, and in a world without germ theory or antibiotics? (These realities hold true for the New Testament period.) Societies marked by a relative shortage of women, prevalent slavery, and vast wealth inequality generate an abundance of men who cannot expect to marry: Might that reality prove relevant for thinking through celibacy in the New Testament?

DATING THE BIBLE

Social and historical contexts come in many forms. We might consider the question of when biblical books were written and how the time of composition relates to the events to which those books refer. Examples abound, but one classic case involves the book of Daniel. Daniel's story refers to the Babylonians, Medes, and Persians, locating Daniel and his activities in the sixth century BCE. The story itself is full of historical problems, not least explaining how Daniel has managed to enter a series of royal courts in three empires, along with the simple fact that no Darius the Mede, the emperor who dominates chapter 6 of Daniel, is known to history. (Several Persian Dariuses did make their mark.) As a result, one might conclude that the specific historical contexts to which Daniel refers may not be particularly helpful for understanding the book. For example, Daniel 6:12 relies upon the notion that Persian edicts are irrevocable—not only an impractical practice, but one we have no evidence ever existed.[3] Nevertheless, some researchers have

---

2. Ronald A. Simkins, "Family in the Political Economy of Monarchic Judah," *The Bible and Critical Theory* 1 (2004): 1–17. See Julia M. O'Brien, "The Economics of Family: Changing Biblical Norms," *Biblical Archaeology Review* 36/5 (September–October 2010): 30, 76.

3. Ben Zion Katz, "Irrevocability of Persian Law in the Scroll of Esther," *JBQ* 31 (2003): 94–96.

uncovered Babylonian and Persian practices and sensibilities reflected in Daniel.[4] Some awareness of Babylonian and Persian history will illuminate aspects of Daniel.

Other signs, however, indicate that Daniel reached its final form much later in history, almost surely in the period surrounding the Maccabean Revolt of 167–164 BCE. The book does not say so directly, but several factors suggest this conclusion. For one thing, the book includes some Greek technical vocabulary, a clear indication of material that took shape much later than the sixth century. Second, Daniel 11 includes what interpreters of apocalyptic literature call a "review of history," a series of predictions after the fact that tracks the career of Antiochus IV, the ruler of the Seleucid Empire whom the Maccabees drove out from Judea. Antiochus's death in 164 BCE turned Seleucid attention from Judea and cleared the path for a political settlement. Daniel 11 accurately tracks Antiochus's career until it turns to "the time of the end" at verse 40. Because the book reflects no knowledge of how Antiochus's life turned out, we have a clear sense of when it reached its final form.

Perhaps most interesting, we identify a third factor in identifying the context in which Daniel reached its final form. Daniel 1–6 provides a series of legends about faithful Judean boys and men in the courts of dangerous kings. Time and again the misguided, often comical, rulers threaten the lives of the young men, but God delivers these young men from peril. When we turn to chapter 7, the book takes a different tack. No longer are we reading entertaining stories; we are in a literary apocalypse, a book of dramatic revelations. And no longer are foreign rulers depicted as good-willed if dangerously unstable; now they are wicked and malevolent. The apocalyptic section sets forth the ultimate victory of Israel's God and of that God's faithful followers. Reading between the lines of Daniel provides a plausible historical context for the book's final form. Jewish sources portray Antiochus as a tyrant who compelled Judeans to violate their ancestral laws under threat of execution. In order to encourage nonviolent resistance to Antiochus's program, Daniel's final form combines legends of divine rescue with an apocalyptic message of divine deliverance in another mode. When we read Daniel in this historical context, the entire book begins to make sense.

4. Shalom M. Paul, "The Mesopotamian Background of Daniel 1–6," in *The Book of Daniel*, vol. 1: *Composition and Reception*, ed. John J. Collins and Peter W. Flint (Boston: Brill Academic, 2002), 55–68.

NAMING THE MOMENT

The example of Daniel demonstrates that identifying the historical context of a biblical book or passage brings multiple factors to bear. Information *external* to the text provides part of the context: What political forces were in play, how did ordinary people lead their lives, and what cultural influences were prevalent? But we also read between the lines: What *internal* clues shed light on the moment at which a book emerged? With Daniel we turn to major moments in history, the stuff of kings and armies. Other biblical texts invite us to a lower level of historical prominence. For example, Paul's letters challenge readers to identify (guess?) the interpersonal and communal circumstances of his audiences. Beyond simply identifying the time in which a biblical writing or section emerged, attention to these internal clues helps us understand the specific situations and motivations for writing.

One example at first gives the impression of being simple but then demonstrates its complexity. The epistle to Philemon is the shortest of Paul's letters, coming in at only twenty-five verses. (For ease of reference verse numbers were added to the biblical text centuries after their composition.) The letter mentions three primary characters: Paul is writing to a believer named Philemon concerning someone he calls Onesimus. Reading between the lines, however, we glean additional information—but we are also left with new questions.

- We see that Philemon is not the letter's only recipient. Paul addresses the letter to Philemon, as well as "to Apphia our sister, to Archippus our fellow soldier, and to the church in your house" (2). The letter sounds as if Paul is leaving things up to Philemon, when, in fact, he presents the question before the entire church. This sly strategy on Paul's part places Philemon in a bind. He must respond before the entire community that gathers in his own house. As patron of the church, and likely its most prominent member, Philemon is on the spot.

- Many readers assume, I suspect correctly, that Onesimus is or has been Philemon's enslaved person. Paul asks Philemon to regard Onesimus no longer as an enslaved person but as a brother. Most interpreters take "slave" to indicate Onesimus's literal status and "brother" his metaphorical relationship to Philemon within the church (16). Moreover, Paul employs a wordplay when he refers to Onesimus, whose name means "useful," by claiming that Onesimus had been useless to Philemon but is now useful to Paul. But it is not obvious that Onesimus is or has been an enslaved person.

- Indeed, some interpreters have suggested that Onesimus was really Philemon's brother, whom Philemon metaphorically treated like an enslaved person.

- Even if we grant that Onesimus is or was Philemon's enslaved person, we struggle to imagine the story behind Paul's letter. Has Onesimus run away, perhaps hoping Paul will protect him? Paul alludes to the possibility that Onesimus may have wronged Philemon or may owe Philemon a debt (18–19). Paul calls himself a prisoner: Did Philemon send Onesimus to help Paul during his stay in prison?

- For what, exactly, is Paul asking? If Onesimus is a runaway enslaved person, Paul may be asking Philemon to receive him back with kindness. Perhaps Paul is asking Philemon to set Onesimus free from his slavery. Some interpreters propose that Paul wants Onesimus for himself, perhaps as an apprentice in ministry while still enslaved.[5] We later hear of an Onesimus who conducted missions on Paul's behalf (Col 4:9). These proposals all assume that somehow Onesimus is or has been enslaved to Philemon.

Reading between the lines of a text for hints regarding its audience or the intentions of its author is all but unavoidable. Revelation 2–3 addresses individual letters to seven churches in the Roman province of Asia (western Turkey to modern readers). Because each letter alludes to the circumstances of a single church, interpreters look into these letters for hints as to Revelation's context and purpose. For example, Revelation 2:13 mentions "Antipas my witness, my faithful one, who was killed among you." Many take this as an indication that Revelation was written to address ongoing or anticipated persecution.

Someone might object that Philemon and Revelation make sense on their own, without needing to posit particular historical contexts. For one thing, such historical reconstructions necessarily involve guesswork. We don't *really* know from reading these books what was actually going on in those moments. Our discussion of Philemon shows that, despite mounds of research, historians still haven't reached consensus. The same holds for Revelation on important points. Moreover, many readers experience the literary and religious value of texts without dependence on historical research. Apart from academic and professional study, countless people have found value in reading the Bible without elaborate historical investigation. Premodern readers certainly did so. We will return to these debates later.

---

5. J. Albert Harrill, *Slaves in the New Testament*, 6–16.

SOCIAL FACTORS

Throughout the development of modern biblical interpretation, however, readers tend to ask historical questions, seeking a larger context that might inform interpretation. Over the past several decades the Bible's political contexts have enjoyed increasing levels of attention. Although politics have always played an important role in biblical interpretation, the focus of these questions has changed in recent years. This follows larger trends in historical studies generally, which zoom out from particular rulers, battles, and great cultural accomplishments to the ordinary conditions of people's lives.[6] For example, readers of Jeremiah will benefit from knowledge about the Babylonians, King Josiah's reform, and the exile, of course. However, a closer look into the social dynamics of the exile—who was taken away, and who was left behind—informs our understanding of the book and its purposes. If indeed, the poorest of the population, who constituted the great majority, remained in and around Jerusalem, Jeremiah's concern with the exile voices the interests of those cultural elites who traveled to Babylon. The book's very composition and survival, decades later in the Persian province of Yehud (Judah/Judea), also reflects the perspectives of a later generation of cultural elites.

More detailed attention to the lives of ordinary people and pervasive realities such as gender, poverty, status, and empire shape contemporary historical research. A massive resource such as *The Oxford Encyclopedia of the Bible and Gender Studies* suggests the depth and breadth of this work.[7] In partnership with historians of the ancient Near East and Mediterranean, biblical scholars delve into popular medicine, family and household structures, diet and dining, and a host of other matters that once received scarce attention.

Human sexuality has proven the most controversial topic in churches over the past twenty years or more. As a result, I receive invitations to speak to church groups on topics like "The Bible and Sexuality," "The Bible and Marriage," or "The Bible and Homosexuality." One of the most important points I try to convey is that it is nearly impossible to map biblical passages onto modern discussions of marriage, family,

---

6. Anne Thayer, "What's New in the History of Christianity?" *Religion Compass* 1 (2007): 4–9.

7. Julia M. O'Brien et al., eds., *The Oxford Encyclopedia of the Bible and Gender Studies*, 2 vols. (New York: Oxford University Press, 2014).

and sexuality. Ancient Mediterranean marriages often featured quite young women—thirteen or fourteen years of age—with older men in an arrangement designed to sustain the population, provide labor, and ensure lines of inheritance. Thus, biblical marriage laws regulate the sexuality of women in ways that do not apply to men: for example, adultery is defined as sexual relations between a married woman and a man other than her husband, but there is no law against married men having sex with unattached women.[8]

In showing how big a difference culture can make even for "universal" human concerns like sexuality, I often use thought experiments. One experiment asks participants to name the reasons people get married. The list ranges from things like falling in love, experiencing companionship, passion, and building a life together to the pragmatics of tax returns, personal finances, and legitimating children. Then I ask the group, "Can you think of any biblical marriages that occur for any of those reasons?" Occasionally someone will note that Jacob loved Rachel, spending fourteen years working for her father in order to take her as wife. But of course, the story says nothing about Rachel's feelings for Jacob, reflecting the difference between ancient love and modern romance.

In a second experiment, directing the group to close their eyes and say nothing out loud, I ask, "How many of you would feel comfortable having sex while knowing children were present in the room?" The point, of course, is that in our cultural context no one would. In one church a man in the back row apparently couldn't help himself. He blurted out, "I don't know if I *could*." But the part of Pennsylvania where I live has many eighteenth-century farmhouses: most consist of two rooms, and one is the kitchen. In other words, not long ago in this very part of the country where I work, people experienced the relationship between childhood and sexuality very differently than we do now. All the more so with biblical sexuality: as Carolyn Osiek and David L. Balch put it, "Virtually all modern persons would experience intense culture shock over sexual relationships in the Corinthian church."[9] What's more, family structures and sexual conventions shifted

---

8. See Jennifer Wright Knust, *Unprotected Texts: The Bible's Surprising Contradictions about Sex and Desire* (San Francisco: HarperOne, 2011), 49–64; Annalisa Azzoni, "Marriage and Divorce: Hebrew Bible," in O'Brien, ed., *Oxford Encyclopedia*, 1:483–88.
9. Osiek and Balch, *Families in the New Testament World*, 116.

markedly among the various cultures of the biblical world, so that the Bible reflects no single set of values and expectations. Indeed, debates concerning matters of gender, family, and sexuality occur within the Bible itself.

One emerging interest has involved the matter of empire.[10] Every part of the Bible reflects the interaction of multiple ancient empires. For most of their history Israel and Judah stood under the direct control of a greater power or found themselves negotiating for survival among the powers of their day. Empire-oriented approaches to the Bible have at least as much to do with contemporary realities as with the ancient world. The twentieth century witnessed the independence of most former European colonies, but relationships of economic, cultural, and military domination persist.[11] Not coincidentally, the same period has generated the growing influence of global voices in biblical scholarship, particularly interpreters from societies that once lived under European colonialism. This demographic transformation roughly accompanied the emergence of Global South liberation theologies, which interpreted the gospel as a call for social justice on local and global levels. In other words, interpreting empire in the Bible bears directly upon contemporary political and theological concerns.

Within that liberationist framework many interpreters mine the Bible for good news from an anti-imperial perspective.[12] Interpreters generally realize that the Bible does not speak with a single voice with respect to empire, but the liberationist impulse implies a tendency among many to find straightforward good news from a liberationist perspective, along with a tendency to pass over dehumanizing aspects of the Bible.[13] With respect to the Hebrew Bible, Norman Gottwald

---

10. Greg Carey, "Early Christianity and the Roman Empire," in *The State of New Testament Studies* (ed. Scot McKnight and Nijay K. Gupta; Grand Rapids: Baker Academic, 2019), 9–34.

11. Antonio Negri and Michael Hardt, *Empire* (Cambridge, MA: Harvard University Press, 2001).

12. For example, Richard A. Horsley, ed., *In the Shadow of Empire: Reclaiming the Bible as a History of Faithful Resistance* (Louisville: Westminster John Knox, 2008), to which I contributed a chapter on Revelation. Horsley acknowledges that "biblical books are not unanimously or unambiguously anti-imperial or pro-imperial" ("Introduction: The Bible and Empires," 7).

13. Here I am drawing heavily upon the language of R. S. Sugirtharajah, *The Bible and the*

called attention to an anti-monarchical ethos of early Israel that informed both postexilic Judah and the emergence of rabbinic Judaism. John Dominic Crossan portrayed Jesus as a countercultural and anti-imperial sage who built grassroots-level networks of reciprocity, while Richard A. Horsley and Ched Myers presented Jesus as more directly involved in anti-imperial politics, albeit nonviolently.[14] Neil Elliott proposed that Paul could easily be read as fostering small communities that countered the ethos of domination that defined Roman imperialism,[15] a movement Horsley described as "an international counter-imperial (alternative) society."[16] Meanwhile, Warren Carter modeled anti-imperial readings of the New Testament with studies of Matthew and John.[17]

These selections, chosen for their wide influence, illustrate empire-critical approaches to the Bible. The approach is thoroughly historiographical. One analyzes the historical contexts of biblical figures or books, then interprets the biblical material over against ancient imperial realities. The Roman Empire, for example, posited only one "lord" (*kyrios* in Greek), who reigned as son of God, was regarded as savior of the world, and received credit for inaugurating a new age of salvation. (For a classic example, see Virgil's *Aeneid* 6.1.791.) Many interpreters have noted the similar language early Christians applied to Jesus, including *Lord, Son of God, savior,* and *the kingdom of God.* This line of comparison often leads to identifying early Christianity as a counter-imperial movement.

A theoretical twist on empire-critical studies came on the scene with

Third World: Precolonial, Colonial, and Postcolonial Encounters (New York: Cambridge University Press, 2001), 240–41.

14. John Dominic Crossan, *The Historical Jesus: The Life of a Mediterranean Jewish Peasant* (San Francisco: HarperCollins, 1993); Richard A. Horsley, *Jesus and Empire: The Kingdom of God and the New World Disorder* (Minneapolis: Fortress, 2003); Ched Myers, *Binding the Strong Man: A Political Reading of Mark's Story of Jesus* (Maryknoll, NY: Orbis, 1988).

15. Neil Elliott, *Liberating Paul: The Justice of God and the Politics of the Apostle* (Minneapolis: Fortress, 2006 [1994]).

16. Richard A. Horsley, "Paul and Slavery: A Critical Alternative to Recent Readings," *Semeia* 83/84 (1998): 176.

17. Warren Carter, *The Roman Empire and the New Testament: An Essential Guide*, Essential Guides (Nashville: Abingdon, 2006); *Matthew and Empire: Initial Explorations* (Harrisburg, PA: Trinity Press International, 2001); *John and Empire: Initial Explorations* (New York: T&T Clark, 2008).

postcolonial interpretation. Far beyond biblical and religious studies, literary and cultural critics emerging from previously colonized contexts exhibited a different set of sensibilities—still historical, but with a very different inflection. Postcolonial hermeneutics is not a method or procedure but a recognizable conversation about the effects of empire and resistance to empire within cultures.[18] For one thing, postcolonial critics reject the idea that cultural products ever resist imperial patterns "purely," without bearing the traces or symptoms of the discourses they resist. This concept, *hybridity*, implies that anti-empire and postcolonial texts are necessarily complicated—and never purely liberatory. This concept distinguishes postcolonial approaches from empire-critical ones.[19] As a case in point, Tat-siong Benny Liew argues that Mark does not so much reject Roman imperial language as reinscribe it by applying it to Jesus, whose rule very much resembles Roman domination.[20] Postcolonial interpretation takes seriously the Bible's historical contexts, particularly the realities of empire and resistance. What distinguishes postcolonial reading is that it interprets those historical realities through the lenses of modern cultural theory.[21]

---

18. Following Stephen D. Moore, "Postcolonialism," in Adam, *Handbook of Postmodern Biblical Interpretation*, 182–83, I suggest the following landmark works of postcolonial criticism: Bill Ashcroft, Gareth Griffiths, and Helen Tiffin, eds., *The Empire Writes Back: Theory and Practice in Post-Colonial Literatures* (London: Routledge, 1989); Homi Bhabha, *The Location of Culture* (New York: Routledge, 1994); Edward Said, *Orientalism: Western Conceptions of the Orient* (London: Penguin, 1978); and Gayatri Chakravorty Spivak, "Can the Subaltern Speak? Speculations on Widow-Sacrifice," in *The Post-Colonial Studies Reader*, ed. Bill Ashcroft, Gareth Griffiths, and Helen Tiffin (New York: Routledge, 1995 [1985]), 24–28.
19. Sugirtharajah, *The Bible and the Third World*, 240–43; Moore, "Postcolonialism," 186–88.
20. Tat-siong Benny Liew, "Tyranny, Boundary and Might: Colonial Mimicry in Mark's Gospel," *JSNT* 73 (1999): 7–31; cited in Moore, "Postcolonialism," 187–88.
21. The literature on postcolonial biblical interpretation is vast. In addition to other works cited here, see Tat-siong Benny Liew and Fernando F. Segovia, eds., *Colonialism and the Bible: Contemporary Reflections from the Global South* (Lanham, MD: Lexington Books, 2018); Stephen D. Moore and Fernando F. Segovia, eds., *Postcolonial Biblical Criticism: Interdisciplinary Intersections*, The Bible and Postcolonialism (New York: T&T Clark, 2005); R. S. Sugirtharajah, *Postcolonial Criticism and Biblical Interpretation* (New York: Oxford University Press, 2002); R. S. Sugirtharajah, ed., *The Postcolonial Bible*, The Bible and Postcolonialism (Sheffield: Sheffield Academic, 1998); R. S. Sugirtharajah, *The Bible and the Third World*; and Fernando F. Segovia and

Postcolonial interpretation expands historical interpretation in a second way. In addition to the Bible's ancient contexts, postcolonial interpreters demonstrate interest in how the Bible has been deployed in more recent colonial history. As mentioned in chapter 1, Musa W. Dube, a Botswanan feminist, looks into the biblical language of light and darkness. The contrast between light and dark is tremendously important, for example, in John's Gospel. Dube investigates how European missionaries designated Africa as the "Dark Continent," primarily because they perceived Africans as culturally and religiously ignorant, but also with an implicit commentary on dark skin. Dube turns the light/dark metaphor on its head by recalling her childhood, when children enjoyed playing in the dark, by the light of the moon. Darkness need not be fearful or negative, she points out. Her interpretation of the light/dark motif bears upon both Africa's colonial history and biblical discourses of light and darkness.[22]

SOCIAL SCIENCES AND HISTORICAL ANALYSIS

Biblical scholarship has always interacted with other academic disciplines, including the social sciences. When the University of Chicago opened the nation's first department of sociology in the 1890s, biblical scholars Shailer Mathews (1863–1941) and Shirley Jackson Case (1872–1947), colleagues at Chicago, turned to sociology to interpret early Christian history.[23] From the outset Mathews labeled his interpretation of Jesus a "Christian sociology"—that is, an attempt to discern the "social philosophy and teachings" of Jesus.[24] Indeed, Mathews's *The Social Teaching of Jesus* first appeared as a series of essays in the *American Journal of Sociology*. And in 1927 Case argued, "no return to Jesus will be adequate that is not at the same time a return to the living conditions of his own time," and "each gospel revealed the distinctive social experience of its particular writer and his immediate associates within one

---

R. S. Sugirtharajah, eds., *A Postcolonial Commentary on the New Testament Writings*, The Bible and Postcolonialism (New York: T&T Clark, 2007).

22. Dube, "Decolonizing the Darkness."
23. James Albert Harrill, *The Manumission of Slaves in Early Christianity*, HUT 32 (Tübingen: Mohr Siebeck, 1995), 5.
24. Shailer Mathews, *The Social Teachings of Jesus: An Essay in Christian Sociology* (New York: Macmillan, 1897), 1–3.

or another area of growing Christianity."[25] The idea that the Gospels reflect their own social settings was hardly unique to Case, but his explicit interaction with sociological theory was distinctive at the time.

Perhaps theological considerations shaped both Mathews and Case as much as did sociological ones: both were influenced by the social gospel movement, a late-nineteenth-century interpretation of Christianity as a movement of progressive social change. Moreover, sociology had just emerged as an academic discipline. It had yet to develop a scientific research model, nor had it generated the sophisticated concepts and research models that would emerge in later decades.

Social-scientific criticism distinguishes itself not so much by attention to ancient social realities as by its reliance upon modern social-scientific models. We might characterize this distinction in terms of social history versus sociological interpretation. Social history might ask, "How densely populated were ancient cities?" The answers provide relevant information for understanding the ancient world. But sociological interpretation might ask, "How do models of honor-shame cultures help us understand the stories of David?" In biblical scholarship this movement to embrace sociological theory emerged most visibly in the 1970s and still marks social-scientific interpretation. To take one specific example, gift-giving and its relationship to reciprocity have long posed classic topics for anthropological investigation. People exchange gifts for many reasons, including the advancement in social status that can accrue to gift-givers. Both givers and recipients of gifts may gain status through an exchange and the mutual recognition it implies. One might even dishonor a person by giving a gift so large that the recipient cannot possibly reciprocate it. Having surveyed social-scientific research on gift-giving, Victor H. Matthews examines the story of Jacob and Esau. The story includes two accounts in which Jacob resorts to deceit and manipulation in order to acquire Esau's birthright. Jacob ventures to another land to build his household. Upon returning, and fearing possible revenge on Esau's part (Gen 27:42–45; 32:7), Jacob presents Esau with a series of fabulous gifts: two hundred female goats and twenty male goats; two hundred ewes and twenty rams, and so forth—a procession of gifts meeting Esau one at a time. For his part, Esau recognizes the obligation that attends the gifts he will receive and

---

25. Shirley Jackson Case, *Jesus: A New Biography* (Chicago: University of Chicago Press, 1927), 110, 106.

seeks to deflect them: "I have enough, my brother; keep what you have for yourself" (33:9). When Esau offers to leave some of his own retinue with Jacob, an attempt to exert his own status, Jacob likewise evades the gift (33:15–17). The two brothers go off on their separate ways, and the focus of the story resides with Jacob and his household. Both brothers have engaged in the ritual and power-brokering associated with gift-giving and the avoidance of gifts, an element brought into relief by social-scientific research.[26]

One of the most interesting applications of sociological models to early Christianity involves a full-time researcher in the sociology of contemporary religion, Rodney Stark. His book *The Rise of Christianity* has both exerted remarkable influence and gathered harsh criticism.[27] In explaining how a tiny movement grew to include the majority of the Roman Empire in about thirty decades, Stark opens himself to the criticism that he is writing a success story, one in which the outcome is guaranteed. Nevertheless, Stark's narrative provides an important case study and continues to influence interpreters, including me. In the modern world, Stark points out, new religious movements tend to flourish at relatively high strata of society. Following research by other historians of early Christianity,[28] Stark suggests that Christianity likewise built its appeal among relatively more privileged persons. As for the common narrative that martyrdom contributed positively to the movement's growth, Stark appeals to the sociological model of rational choice theory: People are more likely to embrace a religion that offers great value. That others might have been willing to die for their faith demonstrated how much they valued it. So long as there weren't *too* many martyrs, their example showed the value of Christian faith

---

26. Victor H. Matthews, "The Unwanted Gift: Implications of Obligatory Gift Giving in Ancient Israel," *Semeia* 87 (1999): 91–104.

27. Rodney Stark, *The Rise of Christianity* (Princeton: Princeton University Press, 1997). For an entirely different account of Christianity's progress, see Douglas Boin, *Coming Out Christian in the Roman World: How the Followers of Jesus Made a Place in Caesar's Empire* (New York: Bloomsbury, 2014). For one early critique of Stark, see Willi Braun, "Sociology, Christian Growth, and the Obscurum of Christianity's Imperial Formation in Rodney Stark's *The Rise of Christianity*," *RSN* 25/2 (April 1999): 128–32.

28. Wayne A. Meeks, *The First Urban Christians: The Social World of the Apostle Paul*, 2nd ed. (New Haven: Yale University Press, 2003 [1983]).

to believers and potential converts alike.[29] Stark also observes that early Christianity valued women more highly than did the Greek and Roman cultures in general, leading to a relative abundance of women in the church. (The Roman world suffered from a statistical shortage of women, largely due to the dangers of reproduction and to common infanticide of baby girls.) As a result, the movement produced more offspring than did the general population, while marriages between Christian women and "pagan" men led to the conversions of some men. Stark's models of status, rational choice, and demographic change energize his overall explanation for early Christian growth.

Stark's work represents the application of models derived from contemporary Western societies. More common are studies that build upon contemporary societies that may resemble those of biblical cultures in significant ways. Many interpreters have followed the lead of cultural anthropologists who have explicated how societies develop purity codes, cultures in which people vie for status in terms of public honor and shame, the role of magic and cursing in resolving conflict, and societies in which people openly acknowledge relationships of status and obligation among patrons, clients, and brokers. For example, Paul asks believers in Galatia who has bewitched them into following a teaching he opposes (Gal 3:1) and curses those who proclaim this "different gospel" (Gal 1:6–9; 5:12). Jerome H. Neyrey draws upon studies that define the characteristics of modern witchcraft societies and finds that those models usefully fit Paul's relationship with the Galatians—a context marked by close interaction among rivals who have no established means of resolving their differences.[30]

Social scientists test theoretical hypotheses by investigating relevant data, working back and forth between theory and data. Their ultimate aim is to establish useful theory rather than to collect data as an end in itself. In contrast, biblical scholars tend to apply widely accepted social-scientific theories to biblical texts and historical movements without questioning the theories themselves. One might say we apply modern sociological hypotheses to interpret ancient data. In the social sciences the data test the hypotheses, while in biblical studies the hypotheses

---

29. The idea that pervasive persecution defined early Christian experience has been largely discredited. See Candida Moss, *The Myth of Persecution: How Early Christians Invented a Story of Martyrdom* (San Francisco: HarperOne, 2013).

30. Jerome H. Neyrey, *Paul, in Other Words: A Cultural Reading of His Letters* (Louisville: Westminster John Knox, 1990), 181–206.

govern the interpretation of the data.[31] Social-scientific research has proven enormously helpful in the reconstruction of Israelite, Jewish, and early Christian history and in lending insight into our interpretations of ancient texts—so long as interpreters keep in mind the difference between social-scientific models and actual data.

INTELLECTUAL AND CULTURAL LIFE

College "Great Books" courses often begin with the ancient Near Eastern texts *Enuma Elish* and the *Epic of Gilgamesh*, perhaps even the *Aqhat Epic*, followed by the first three chapters of Genesis. This choice locates Genesis within the context of ancient Near Eastern "creation stories," which may not be the best category for describing them. Studies routinely inspect the law code of Hammurabi as a context in which to understand parts of the Torah. Commentaries on the Gospel of John routinely track the concept of the *logos* (or "word"; see John 1:1) from Plato through the Jewish intellectual Philo, along with the role of Lady Wisdom in the Hebrew wisdom traditions. Interpreters of Paul's letters likewise immerse themselves in Stoic ethical and moral teaching.

All these examples reflect the value interpreters place upon literary and cultural contexts for our understanding of the Bible. At the same time, this way of reading fosters a sort of tunnel vision, reducing such ancient texts to "contexts" for understanding the Bible and diminishing their independent worth. (We do similar things with noncanonical Jewish literature like the Dead Sea Scrolls and what we call the Pseudepigrapha.[32]) Especially problematically, this approach skews our understanding of the "contexts" themselves. In important ways *Enuma Elish* is a "creation story." Readers will note how its beginning tracks with Genesis 1.

> When above the heaven had not (yet) been named,
> (And) below the earth had not (yet) been called by name;
> (When) Apsû primeval, their begetter,

---

31. Mary Ann Tolbert, "Social, Sociological, and Anthropological Methods," in *Searching the Scriptures*, 2 vols., ed. Elisabeth Schüssler Fiorenza (New York: Crossroad, 1993), 266–67. See John H. Elliott, *What Is Social Scientific Criticism?* Guides to Biblical Scholarship (Minneapolis: Fortress, 1993), 48–49.

32. See Eva Mroczek, "The Hegemony of the Biblical in the Study of Second Temple Literature," *JAJ* 6 (2015): 2–35.

Mummu, (and) Ti'âmat, she who gave birth to them all,
(Still) mingled their waters together . . .

This translation, from a volume named *The Babylonian Genesis*,[33] resembles Genesis in several ways. It imagines a period "in the beginning" (Genesis), when the earth already existed but lacked form, its waters mingled together. In both Genesis and the *Enuma Elish* darkness shrouds the period before creation.[34] Other aspects of the *Enuma Elish* enlighten our understanding of the Hebrew texts—and not only Genesis. The concept that one god might emerge to reign in a heavenly council over all others occurs here, in the Psalms, and in other ancient Near Eastern literature. Psalm 82, for example, envisions God ruling amid other gods (*elohim*, in Hebrew), as do other passages such as 1 Kings 22:19–23 and Job 1:6; 2:1.[35] What we rarely encounter, at least in biblical scholarship, are straightforward interpretations of *Enuma Elish* in its own right. And since ancient Near Eastern scholarship remains dominated by an interest in biblical literature—a reality that seems to be changing—texts like *Enuma Elish* continue to be interpreted in terms of their background or in the context of comparative approaches to ancient religion. For example, *Enuma Elish* had a ritual function, being recited on the fourth day of Babylonian new-year festivals. I'd like to know more about those festivals and other Babylonian sacred observances.[36]

A MATERIAL CULTURE

The emergence of archaeology as a scientific discipline set off a predictable flurry of interest in the Bible, a precious text that clearly emerged from ancient societies and refers to historical persons, places,

---

33. Translation by Alexander Heidel, *The Babylonian Genesis*, 2nd ed. (Chicago: University of Chicago Press, 1951).
34. Peter Enns, *Inspiration and Incarnation: Evangelicals and Incarnation: Evangelicals and the Problem of the Old Testament*, 2nd ed. (Grand Rapids: Baker Academic, 2015), 15–16.
35. See Mark S. Smith, *The Origins of Biblical Monotheism: Israel's Polytheistic Background and the Ugaritic Texts* (New York: Oxford University Press, 2001), esp. 41–66.
36. Tammi J. Schneider, *An Introduction to Ancient Mesopotamian Religion* (Grand Rapids: Eerdmans, 2011), 43. For introductions to ancient Mesopotamian religion see Schneider, *Introduction*, and Daniel C. Snell, *Religions of the Ancient Near East* (New York: Cambridge University Press, 2011).

and events.[37] Dramatic discoveries such as the Dead Sea Scrolls (1946) and Qumran, the site at which they were found, provided fresh new texts from ancient Judaism, among other new sources of information. The Qumran finds have proven formative for our appreciation of Judaism's diversity and literature, with implications as well for the contexts that produced Jesus and the movement he inspired. At about the same time, the discovery of texts from Nag Hammadi in Egypt (1945) revealed an entirely new body of literature that contributes to new assessments of how early Christianity developed into the second and third centuries. Without question the Dead Sea Scrolls and the Nag Hammadi Library have forced a reassessment of ancient Judaism and Christian origins.

Unfortunately, biblical archaeology, as it has been called, has also generated a host of problems and controversies. In the nineteenth and twentieth centuries the movement tended to focus on confirming or disconfirming the historicity of biblical narratives, in the same way that archaeologists uncovered Troy, immortalized in Homer's *Iliad* and *Odyssey*. Research at Troy not only confirmed its destruction in the twelfth century BCE; it also uncovered thousands of years of human history. As for the Bible, excavations of sites related to ancient Jericho led to the conclusion that no great walled city existed on that site at any period that could possibly relate to the story of Jericho's destruction in Joshua 6. The biblical storyline of a massive exodus from Egypt, followed by a dramatic conquest of Canaan, simply does not comport with archaeological research in either Egypt or Israel/Palestine. In many cases the archaeological record refuses to confirm the biblical accounts.

Just as controversial, countless people have used archaeology to promote sensational new "revelations" about biblical persons or events, revelations often disconfirmed by later research. In 2012 Harvard professor Karen L. King, a highly regarded historian of early Christianity, announced the existence of a sensational "Gospel of Jesus's Wife." Although the "gospel" is only a small papyrus fragment, it includes a line in which Jesus speaks of his own wife. King's announcement intersects with popular theories that Jesus was not celibate, as the canoni-

---

37. On the historical development of archaeology's contribution to biblical studies, see Thomas W. Davis, *Shifting Sands: The Rise and Fall of Biblical Archaeology* (New York: Oxford University Press, 2004).

cal Gospels suggest, and may have been married to Mary Magdalene.[38] Unfortunately, other researchers claimed they had proven the Gospel of Jesus's Wife to be a forgery on several grounds. Much of the debate has occurred online,[39] with an issue of the journal *New Testament Studies* largely devoted to articles disproving the would-be gospel's authenticity.[40] Although the debate continues, by far most experts consider the fragment a modern forgery.[41] Similar dramatic announcements, often accompanied by flurries of news reports and even documentaries, pop up from time to time. Others use archaeology to promote one site or another as a tourist attraction. The intersection of archaeology, the Bible, and spiritual devotion attracts perhaps way too much money. Looting and fraud occur frequently. Moreover, contemporary political conflicts, many of which involve rights to land and conflicts over religious legacies, further complicate the role of archaeology in research, to the point that even terminology for the field is disputed. "Biblical archaeology" has largely yielded to "Near Eastern archaeology."

A key problem underlying archaeology's contribution to biblical studies has to do with what we expect from archaeological work. Beyond biblical studies and history, archaeology constitutes a fundamental element of anthropology, the study of human cultures. In proper research, archaeologists set out not to confirm whether or not an event occurred in the past but to understand how societies formed, organized themselves, and developed. Dramatic historical findings (and frauds) may make big news, but archaeology proves even more useful in helping us understand the material culture of biblical societies, an element that greatly enriches our grasp of biblical texts.

If I may share a personal example, I was once walking with the Israeli archaeologist Mordechai Aviam around the site usually identified with the Cana of John 2. We were filming a segment for a documentary on the life of Jesus, and the producers found it helpful to film segments on relevant archaeological sites. In that sense we were experiencing the

---

38. Harvard University, "Gospel of Jesus's Wife," http://gospelofjesuswife.hds.harvard.edu/.

39. The website of Mark Goodacre includes a guest post by Andrew Bernhard, "The End of the Gospel of Jesus' Wife Forgery Debate," *NT Blog*, September 8, 2015, https://tinyurl.com/rt5v26z.

40. *New Testament Studies* 61 (2015): 289–394.

41. Joel Baden and Candida Moss, "The Curious Case of Jesus's Wife," *The Atlantic*, December 2014, https://tinyurl.com/sddu79z.

intersection of money, media, piety, archaeology, and the Bible. With no training in and little knowledge of archaeology, I asked Professor Aviam if the villages of Galilee were observant of Jewish dietary practices. He immediately replied, "No pig bones." In other words, while other historians debated the level of observance among Galilean Jews around the time of Jesus, archaeologists had ascertained the diet of those local villages. "No pig bones" indicates a consistent level of Torah observance.

In her landmark study *Discovering Eve*, Carol Meyers explores the archaeological and literary evidence for life in the highlands of pre-monarchical Israel. Meyers suggests a subsistence-level economy marked by "the virtual absence of trade or the exchange of goods."[42] In a patriarchal society, with the household the "preeminent" locus of economic activity, women would have held strong roles in decision making. Indeed, Meyers now argues, it is more helpful to describe ancient Israelite society as heterarchical rather than patriarchal, in that status and agency would have been fluid depending upon the social contexts and the persons involved.[43] This relatively egalitarian structure, Meyers argues, provides the social context for the Song of Songs, the Bible's great erotic poem. In the Song the woman and the man both show agency, pursuing one another. The Song even mentions the "mother's house" of the woman (3:4; 8:2), reflecting a woman's authority over her own household in some circumstances. Meyers acknowledges that gender hierarchies likely existed in pre-monarchical Israel, as they certainly did in later periods, but she emphasizes women's agency in peasant households. This social context, informed by archaeological and literary evidence, complemented by contemporary anthropological models, shapes her reading of the Song of Songs.[44]

Attention to material culture can influence major questions in biblical interpretation. One very popular line of thinking portrays Jesus as building communities of solidarity in the face of Roman imperial exploitation. As the theory goes, the Galilee of Jesus's day would have suffered economic depletion as a result of heavy building projects and

---

42. Carol Meyers, *Discovering Eve: Ancient Israelite Women in Context* (New York: Oxford University Press, 1988), 174.

43. Carol Meyers, *Rediscovering Eve: Ancient Israelite Women in Context* (New York: Oxford University Press, 2013), 194–99.

44. Meyers, *Discovering Eve*, 174–81.

taxation. Under economic pressure, Galileans would have been forced to sell their property and seek labor opportunities, often resulting in the sort of absentee landowners featured in some of Jesus's parables and other literary sources. (See especially the parable of the tenants in Mark 12:1–12 par.) Some archaeologists, however, retort that the material evidence from Galilee during the period shows economic vitality rather than decline. Although these considerations may not prove or disprove the nature of Jesus's ministry, they do caution against characterizing Jesus's activities as a response to economic decline.[45]

"BEHIND" THE TEXT: HISTORICAL RECONSTRUCTION AND "HIGHER" CRITICISM

Almost all modern interpreters have embraced historical criticism in a general sense, including the historical contexts of the biblical writings as an essential factor in the process of interpretation. Especially (but not only) in religious contexts, controversy has intensified when interpreters peer "behind" the text into the history of its composition. In the late nineteenth and early twentieth centuries, fundamentalist Christians objected to such "higher criticism," which pressed beyond the immediate circumstances addressed by a text to identify the development of early, pre-literary tradition, the literary sources biblical authors blended together to create the texts as we now have them, and the processes of editing, or redaction, that led to the final form of the biblical text. The legacy of those early fundamentalists continues in many contexts, as attested by the regularity with which conservative Christian colleges and seminaries dismiss faculty members who embrace certain kinds of historical scholarship.[46] Antipathy against higher criticism manifests itself in textbooks on biblical interpretation that devote entire chapters to "historical and cultural backgrounds" but do not discuss the processes by which biblical books were composed.[47]

Three classic examples illustrate "behind"-the-text historical inter-

---

45. Eric M. Meyers and Mark A. Chancey, *Alexander to Constantine*, vol. 3: *Archaeology of the Land of the Bible*. AYBRL (New Haven: Yale University Press, 2012), 120–21.
46. Brandon G. Withrow and Menachem Wecker, *Consider No Evil: Two Faith Traditions and the Problem of Academic Freedom in Religious Higher Education* (Eugene, OR: Cascade, 2014).
47. As in Grant R. Osborne, *The Hermeneutical Spiral: A Comprehensive Introduction to Biblical Interpretation* (Downers Grove, IL: InterVarsity, 1991).

pretation. First, throughout the centuries, readers have noticed a problem with the Pentateuch, the Bible's first five books. In both Jewish and Christian traditions, these are the "books of Moses," attributed to Israel's great lawgiver. But the book of Deuteronomy narrates Moses's death. If Moses wrote the Pentateuch, how can he have described his own death, not to mention the mourning that followed (Deuteronomy 34)? Questions like these led many interpreters to question Moses's authorship.

In the eighteenth and nineteenth centuries, however, scholars began trying to explain other problems with the Pentateuch. Most notable were "doublets," dual and often contradictory retellings of the same account. Most famously, Genesis includes two creation stories. One (Gen 1:1–2:4a) describes an orderly process in which "God" (Hebrew: *Elohim*) creates the world through a series of utterances: "Let there be light," "Let there be a dome in the midst of the waters," and so forth. The other features a much more intimate, and less orderly, process through which "the Lord God" (*Yahweh Elohim*) forms humankind from dust and breathes life into the first human (2:4b–3:24). This second account includes the famous story of Adam and Eve. A reader who compares the two accounts will notice conflicting sequences in which creation occurs, different names and characteristics ascribed to the deity, and other stylistic differences. As one reads through the Pentateuch, one encounters other doublets, such as dual accounts of the Ten Commandments (Exod 20:1–17; Deut 5:6–21), Moses's striking the rock (Exod 17:1–7; Num 20:2–13), and Jacob's "acquisition" of Esau's birthright (Gen 25:29–34; 27:1–35). These are only a few of many examples in which interpreters began noticing predictable patterns with respect to the divine name and character, geography, and other variables.

In the 1870s and 1880s the German scholar Julius Wellhausen formulated a classic solution to the Pentateuch, the Documentary Hypothesis. According to Wellhausen these five books had been composed from four basic sources, each composed in a distinctive time and place with characteristic interests of its own. The book of Deuteronomy comprised one source (D), a Priestly source (P) is reflected in Leviticus and other specific passages, and the main narrative represented a blending of a Yahwistic (J) source from the southern kingdom, Judah, and the Elohistic source (E) from the northern kingdom, Israel. Countless scholars have revised and attacked Wellhausen's model, but his basic insight—that the Pentateuch represents a weaving together of at least three or four distinctive strands of literary tradition—remains the prevailing view.[48]

The second major controversy, one alive today in different forms, involves the Synoptic Problem, how to account for the remarkable similarities and differences among Matthew, Mark, and Luke. We call these three the Synoptic Gospels because they "see together" (*syn optic*) the career of Jesus and because we can see them together by placing their stories side by side. Not only do these three Gospels share a great deal of common material, they tend to relate their stories in a common order and with a common Greek vocabulary. When one Gospel includes material the others do not, that material rarely disrupts the Gospels' common sequence of stories.

Early Christians recognized the Synoptic Problem without naming it so. According to the common view, the author of Matthew wrote first, and Mark abbreviated Matthew's story. (We do not know who composed the Gospels. When referring to the Gospels, the names Matthew, Mark, Luke, and John provide a shorthand for the anonymous authors of these works.) Matthew and Mark together influenced the Gospel of Luke. We sometimes call this solution the Augustinian Hypothesis because it was held by the great bishop and theologian Augustine of Hippo (354–430 CE). Another view, once largely abandoned but now growing in popularity, posits that Mark was composed first, influencing first Matthew and then Luke. This is called the Farrer–Goulder Hypothesis.[49] A growing number of scholars, while not denying a process of literary influence from one Gospel to another, emphasize the process of oral storytelling or social memory, according to which differences among the accounts reflect the diverse ways in which early Christians recounted Jesus's story.[50]

Despite the presence of alternative explanations, not to mention a growing number of scholars who refrain from choosing among the options, the vast majority subscribes to a different model. The Two-Source Hypothesis, sometimes called the Four-Source Hypothesis,

---

48. Baden, *Composition of the Pentateuch*. For a popular explication, see Richard Elliott Friedman, *Who Wrote the Bible?* (Englewood Cliffs, NJ: Prentice Hall, 1987).

49. The Farrer–Goulder Hypothesis's most influential advocate is Mark Goodacre. See *The Case against Q: Studies in Markan Priority and the Synoptic Problem* (Harrisburg, PA: Trinity Press International, 2002).

50. See Rafael Rodriguez, *Structuring Early Christian Memory: Jesus in Tradition, Performance, and Text*, LNTS (New York: T&T Clark, 2010).

includes the following components: (1) Mark was the earliest of the Synoptic Gospels, providing the narrative structure for both Matthew and Luke. (2) Matthew and Luke indicate no dependence upon one another in any direction. (3) The substantial body of material shared by Matthew and Luke, but not by Mark, must derive from a literary source now lost to us. We call this source Q, short for the German *Quelle*, which means "source." By definition, Q is a hypothetical source. We possess no ancient copies of it. Yet the idea of Q carries great value for explaining why Matthew and Luke share some material and yet diverge from one another in important ways.

According to the Two-Source Hypothesis, Matthew and Luke wrote independently but shared two common sources, Mark and Q. The Four-Source Hypothesis simply recognizes that Matthew and Luke also drew upon their own independent material, M for material unique to Matthew and L for material unique to Luke.

TWO-SOURCE HYPOTHESIS

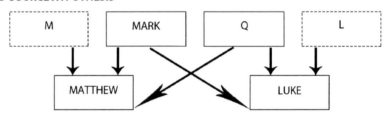

Fig. 2.1 The Two-Source Hypothesis

The Synoptic Problem and the Two-Source Hypothesis have proven controversial because they undermine the notion that the Gospels offer us direct and accurate recountings of Jesus's career and teachings. We derive the Gospels' titles from an ancient, and popular, tradition that attributed each Gospel to one of Jesus's followers or to a student of a first-generation believer. The Gospel of Luke represents a semi-exception in that it describes a process of research that led to its composition. If we take seriously that the Gospel authors drew upon earlier literary sources, we cannot expect eyewitness reporting from the Gospels. As we shall see, the Synoptic Problem opens the path to other important insights and implications.

A third controversial problem involves the authorship of the Pauline letters. The New Testament includes thirteen letters written in Paul's name. Seven of those letters are "undisputed"; that is, almost everyone agrees that Paul is their primary author. Three of the thirteen—1 and 2 Timothy and Titus—are called the Pastorals. Few scholars regard Paul as the primary voice behind the Pastoral Epistles, although 2 Timothy has more advocates than do the others. Three other epistles—Colossians, Ephesians, and 2 Thessalonians—remain disputed. Not many interpreters attribute Ephesians to Paul, while opinion is more evenly divided regarding Colossians and 2 Thessalonians. Let's remember that some biblical scholars are bound by their theological convictions to affirm that Paul wrote all thirteen letters attributed to him—at least, in some meaningful sense. My anecdotal impression is that, when we exclude people bound by theological presuppositions, a less than overwhelming majority attributes Colossians and 2 Thessalonians to someone writing in Paul's name. One technical term for writing under the name of someone else is *pseudepigraphy*; others prefer the word *forgery*.

Scholars offer multiple reasons for doubting Paul's authorship of particular letters. There's no question that early Jews and Christians sometimes practiced forgery: the extracanonical evidence lies beyond dispute. (Otherwise, how does one explain 3 Corinthians, the fictional correspondence between Paul and Seneca, and the Apocalypse of Paul?) The disputed letters often use vocabulary that does not occur in the undisputed letters—or they use the same words with significantly divergent nuances of meaning. Many believe the disputed letters reflect circumstances that make better sense after Paul's career than during it. Most importantly, the disputed letters advance ideas Paul seems not to have held, or they reflect a more highly articulated version of those ideas. All such considerations require judgment on the part of the interpreter, with some factors pulling more weight than others. The judgment depends on no single factor but on the accumulation of evidence.

To offer one particular example, Ephesians 2:8–10 either summarizes one high point of Paul's gospel or it represents a later interpretation of the apostle's thought.

> For by grace you have been saved through faith, and this is not your own doing; it is the gift of God—not the result of works, so that no one may boast. For we are what he has made us, created in Christ Jesus for good works, which God prepared beforehand to be our way of life.

In other letters Paul certainly affirms that salvation comes by grace through faith. However, it's the language of "works" that arrests our attention. This question bears upon all the points mentioned in the paragraph above: vocabulary, context, and content. In other letters, especially Galatians and Romans, Paul refers to "works of the law," specifically the defining practices of Jewish identity: diet, Sabbath, and (for men) circumcision. In Ephesians, however, "works" apparently refers to "good works," as "Paul" elaborates in 2:10. One might imagine feeding the hungry as an example of good works. This distinctive vocabulary usage implies both a new historical context and new teaching content: In the decades after Paul's career Christians debated the role of good works, not simply "works of the law," in salvation. No longer does the concern lie with the place of Gentiles, who lack "works of the law," in the church, as it does in the undisputed letters. Many interpreters see this passage as a development beyond what Paul himself taught, an appropriation of Paul's teaching for a later day.

The question of authorship can weigh heavily in debates concerning Paul's reputation. Paul has long been criticized as a patriarchal pig and a defender of slavery, while defenders of women's subordination and slavery have routinely appealed to the Pauline Epistles. Until fairly recently, most of the debate concerning the disputed epistles involved matters related to proper belief or church structure, things like eschatology, the role of bishops, and the like. Perhaps in an era in which women and people of color have a greater voice in public biblical interpretation, more attention has been devoted to the role of gender and slavery in Paul's letters. If we isolate the undisputed letters from the disputed ones, one factor jumps off the page: the clearest teachings concerning the subordination of women and enslaved persons all occur in the disputed letters. The undisputed letters certainly include controversial passages, but it is entirely possible to interpret those letters as relatively progressive regarding gender and slavery.[51]

The conversation regarding Paul's authorship underscores the value of public biblical interpretation. For one thing, the stands many people take on the issue often reflect their prior religious commitments. This is true of those who doubt Paul's authorship of certain books as much as it is of those who affirm it. Among theological readers, and those who find theology interesting, these debates also contribute to how we imagine what Paul "really" believed and taught. One major debate

51. Unfortunately, space prohibits a full discussion here. For the case for a progressive Paul, see Marcus J. Borg and John Dominic Crossan, *The First Paul: Reclaiming the Radical Visionary behind the Church's Conservative Icon* (San Francisco: HarperOne, 2009).

in Pauline interpretation involves whether the apostle taught against legalism in general or against the narrower question of how Gentiles might be incorporated into the churches. The position that Paul actually composed Colossians and Ephesians favors the more general anti-legalism interpretation, while the pseudepigraphal interpretation favors the latter. Modern Christians almost never defend slavery in any cultural context, but they do debate gender relations, including the roles women may fill in churches. Interpreters have appealed to Paul in such debates through the centuries, and cultural historians have devoted significant attention to the history of Paul's appropriation.

SOURCE CRITICISM

The Documentary Hypothesis and the Two-Source Hypothesis represent the two best-known cases of source criticism, the attempt to discern the discrete literary sources from which biblical books were built. The Documentary Hypothesis posits at least four literary sources that contribute to the Pentateuch, while the Two-Source Hypothesis maintains that Mark and Q provided the common sources upon which the authors of Matthew and Luke built their narratives. Source criticism works at multiple levels in biblical studies, from obvious but important divisions within biblical books to more controversial cases. Interpreters apply source criticism to noncanonical works like the Gospel of Thomas and even to the hypothetical Q document, for which we have no actual copies.

Let's begin with a fairly straightforward example, the book of Proverbs. The book begins, "The proverbs of Solomon son of David, king of Israel" (1:1). If we take this introduction at face value, we attribute the book to King Solomon. We might regard Solomon as the literary author, or we might consider the book a collection of sayings traced back to him. But when we arrive at chapter 10, we find another attribution: "The proverbs of Solomon" (10:1). Why do we need this additional inscription? A similar insertion appears still later: "These are other proverbs of Solomon that the officials of King Hezekiah of Judah copied" (25:1). At this point any reader would suspect that the book, composed of proverbs attributed to Solomon, includes two or more literary collections. Still later, "The words of Agur son of Jakeh. An oracle" (30:1). We know nothing of any Agur or Jakeh. Finally, "The words of King Lemuel. An oracle that his mother taught him" (31:1). We know no King Lemuel either.

It's fairly obvious that our book of Proverbs includes several sets of independent material. Naturally, scholars have spent quite some time trying to learn all they can about those sources, not only relying on the direct attributions we have just reviewed but also taking account of literary style and thematic content. Other biblical books practically invite source criticism. The books of 1 and 2 Chronicles clearly rely upon the books of Samuel and Kings for much of their content, but they allude to other books as well, "annals" of various kings (1 Chr 27:24; 2 Chr 20:34; 33:18). In turn, the books of Kings frequently refer to "the Annals of the Kings of Israel" and those of the kings of Judah. The book of Psalms divides itself into five "books," and many of the Psalms begin with headings that suggest earlier collections of psalms. Within the New Testament, we have already observed that the author of Luke's Gospel recognizes other narratives, presumably relying upon them from time to time.

More complicated questions emerge. Commentators commonly divide the book of Isaiah into three parts, chapters 1–39 (1 Isaiah), 40–55 (2 Isaiah), and 55–66 (3 Isaiah). Several factors justify this division. First Isaiah is generally (but not entirely) written in prose and holds close to stories involving the prophet Isaiah and his eighth-century BCE context. Second Isaiah transitions to poetry and mentions a Persian king, Cyrus, who reigned in the sixth century. It seems the material in 2 Isaiah aimed to encourage exiles to return to Judah from their captivity in Babylon. Third Isaiah seems to reflect a slightly later period, perhaps in the fifth century, in which the audience lives in and around Jerusalem, and the new (second) temple is fully operational. All commentators acknowledge that this neat division fails to explain particular parts of the book, such as the apocalyptic-sounding material in chapters 24–27, but most believe this general framework provides helpful context for understanding the book's disparate parts.

A classic New Testament case involves Paul's letters to the Corinthians, in which the apostle alludes to other correspondence, whether written or oral. A casual observer might think Paul wrote to the Corinthians twice, producing two letters, with perhaps some communication from the Corinthians in between. But the letters suggest a more complicated process.

- In 1 Corinthians Paul mentions having *already* written to the Corinthians (5:9–11).
- In 1 Corinthians Paul also mentions that he has received messages from Corinth, perhaps oral (1:11; 5:1) and certainly some written (7:1).
- In 2 Corinthians Paul refers to one or more letters he has sent on multiple occasions (2:3–9; 7:8–12; 10:11).

Complicating this picture, many readers have observed that 2 Corinthians easily divides into sections. For the most part, chapters 1–7 are conciliatory, as if Paul has already won the day in a conflict with opponents in Corinth and is seeking to heal the wounds. Meanwhile, chapters 10–13 take a more aggressive, even polemic tone, giving the sense that Paul is in the midst of a conflict he cannot count on winning. (What if 2 Corinthians 10–13 is the earlier letter to which Paul refers in chapters 1–7?) Interpreters also note that 2 Corinthians 8–9, in which Paul addresses a collection he is taking to support poor believers in Jerusalem, bears no obvious relationship to the rest of the book. Moreover, a reader could easily skip directly from 6:13 to 7:2 without missing anything (try it): Might 2 Corinthians 6:14–7:1 constitute a later insertion into the letter?

Interpreters have offered many proposals regarding the source history of 1 and 2 Corinthians, including theories that rely on letters we do not possess. Final certainty may always elude us. Is 2 Corinthians a composite of earlier letters and fragments? If so, how do they relate to one another? How does 2 Corinthians, or part of it, relate to 1 Corinthians? In my classroom, I suggest that students avoid making a detailed judgment on these source-critical questions, but I do recommend that they appreciate what part of the literature they are interpreting. Specifically, readers of 2 Corinthians should know the difference between its conciliatory and polemical sections.

Interpreters also look for sources within documents. For example, Luke includes a distinctive selection of parables that do not appear in the other Gospels. Some stand among the Bible's most popular passages: the Good Samaritan, the Prodigal Son, and the Rich Man and Lazarus. Several of these parables portray characters who begin with fairly stable lives and high status, then find their security directly threatened. These memorable stories also feature "interior monologue"—occasions when a character speaks to himself. (These characters are all male.) In other Gospels Jesus's parables do not have this feature.

> "I will say to my soul, Soul, you have ample goods laid up for many years; relax, eat, drink, and be merry." (12:19)

> "I will get up and go to my father . . ." (15:18)

> "What will I do, now that my master is taking the position away from me?" (16:3)

Because these parables have such distinctive characteristics, some interpreters have concluded that Luke possessed a special collection of Jesus's parables. Some have even speculated that the author of Luke is their true author or that the author embellished their literary style. We may never know, but we can observe that Luke sometimes inserts these parables into strategically significant contexts. For example, all three Synoptic Gospels include the man who asks Jesus how to inherit eternal life—but Luke uses the story to introduce the parable of the Good Samaritan (10:25–37).

Source criticism has been applied outside the canon. Almost all interpreters believe the Gospel of Thomas, as we now have it, adapts material from the Synoptic Gospels. But did a version of Thomas ever exist that was completely independent of the Synoptics' literary evidence? April DeConick posits a "Kernel Thomas" that predates the Synoptic Gospels, to which other material was added later, some of it related to the other Gospels.[52] Many interpreters understand Thomas along these lines, but others regard it as developing after the Synoptics and in relationship to them.[53] This source-critical debate has proven important for conversations regarding the nature of Jesus's teaching. If Thomas includes material that is independent of and predates the Synoptics, Jesus researchers must take those sayings into account.

Perhaps the most fascinating case study in source criticism involves Q, the hypothetical document from which Matthew and Luke commonly draw material. Q consists almost entirely of Jesus's sayings and lacks narrative structure. Although we have no copies of Q, some interpreters do believe the material Matthew and Luke share provides a

---

52. April DeConick, "The Gospel of Thomas," in *The Non-Canonical Gospels*, ed. Paul Foster (London: T&T Clark, 2008), 13–29.

53. Mark Goodacre, *Thomas and the Synoptics: The Case for Thomas's Familiarity with the Synoptics* (Grand Rapids: Eerdmans, 2012).

complete or almost complete text of Q. Others are less confident, to say the least. Nevertheless, John S. Kloppenborg developed a highly influential source-critical theory. According to Kloppenborg, Q's earliest layer (Q1) consisted of instructions from Jesus to a countercultural community of his followers; a second layer (Q2), composed after the community experienced conflict and rejection, carries a more defensive tone and prophesies judgment against outsiders; and a third layer (Q3) includes the temptation story we know from Matthew and Luke.[54] Naturally, some interpreters regard Q's development very differently. Dale C. Allison Jr., for example, sees instruction to a missionary community as the foundational layer, followed by more general instructions concerning daily living aimed at a broader audience, with the prophetic judgment sayings as Q's final layer.[55]

We have reviewed examples of source criticism that range from the fairly obvious to the more speculative. Source criticism examines two possibilities: first, that biblical authors drew upon previously available literary sources in composing their works; and second, that some biblical books may have developed over a long period of time. If Proverbs directly identifies earlier sources, Isaiah gives them away through its diverse literary styles and historical contexts. Sometimes interpreters reach near-consensus on source-critical matters: the Pentateuch reflects multiple independent traditions, Isaiah developed over a long period of time, and the Two-Source Hypothesis has persuaded most interpreters of the Synoptic Gospels. Other cases are more speculative, leading to more contentious debate.

FORM CRITICISM

Form criticism begins with a basic literary insight: every culture generates literary forms, or genres, in which its citizens develop general cultural competence. I'm from Alabama, where college football rules the cosmos. If someone tells me that Jesus was playing golf with revered football coaches Bear Bryant and Shug Jordan (of blessed memory), I prepare myself for a joke. If I sit down at the movie theater and a dateline scrolls across the screen accompanied by a vague electronic sound,

---

54. John S. Kloppenborg, *The Formation of Q: Trajectories in Ancient Wisdom Collections*, Studies in Antiquity and Christianity (Minneapolis: Fortress, 1987).
55. Dale C. Allison Jr., *The Jesus Tradition in Q* (Harrisburg, PA: Trinity Press International, 1997).

I know I'm in for a drama, possibly a James Bond sort of spy flick. The fun happens when people get inventive with these literary forms, confusing some of us but not others. Satirical news stories like those from *The Onion* have certainly embarrassed me a time or two, as I've confused fiction for news. I so enjoy it when it's someone else taking the bait. The Bible includes little literary forms, like oracles and parables, and complete literary genres such as Greek biography (the Gospels) and two apocalypses. Recognizing literary and cultural forms is essential for biblical interpretation, not to mention for general cultural competence.

Biblical form criticism moves beyond the recognition of genre in an effort to glean historical insight. The process is complex, often requiring multiple levels of guesswork, and it has received intense criticism. Indeed, one might say that form criticism has passed out of vogue. Nevertheless, form criticism has played such a constitutive role in the history of public biblical interpretation that it requires some discussion.

Form criticism combines attentiveness to literary conventions with social context. Many modes of communication primarily make sense in a limited range of social situations. Some of us are old enough to remember the breezy, casual style of school and community newsletters, which created the fiction that their readers belonged to a close-knit community of relatively hip people. For example, suppose friends are sharing a cup of coffee, and one unloads a story about his frustration at work. In a soothing voice, another friend replies, "And how do you feel about that?" The group might chuckle, acknowledging the mild humor. We associate a soothing voice drawing out someone's feelings with a therapist's office, not a coffee shop. Biblical scholars would identify the therapist's office as the primary life setting, or *Sitz im Leben*, for the soothing question, "How do you feel about that?"

We might well miss the joke. One classic contribution of form criticism involves the Psalms. People have long noted that this book includes different kinds of psalms: prayers for protection, angry protests, sad laments, and hymns of praise. Psalm 82 has drawn the attention of form critics: it begins by imagining a heavenly assembly in which the God of Israel judges the other gods. God delivers an indictment: "How long" will these lesser gods pervert justice (82:2)? And God pronounces a verdict and a sentence: "You shall die like mortals" (82:7). Historians might conclude that this psalm reflects developments in the history of Israel's religion. A heavenly court scene is a common motif in ancient Near Eastern literature, and Psalm 82 draws specifically upon this context. Modern readers may struggle to recognize this *Sitz im Leben* for a couple of reasons: we typically don't think of courtrooms filled with gods, and our notion of courts does not involve a royal throne room in which a king pronounces verdicts. Neither of these factors would discourage an ancient reader. Psalm 82 recalls the development of Israelite religion from its polytheistic origins through what we might call henotheism, the notion of one god ruling over the assembly of other gods. By the time we reach Psalm 82, we have an early expression of monotheism: the other gods have been sentenced to death.[56]

Along similar lines, form critics have found what they believe to be signs of early Christian worship in small passages from the New Testament. For example, Philippians 2:1–11 features Paul's call for the Philippians to share the mind of Christ, serving one another rather than looking out for themselves. The passage includes metrical lines, often called the "Christ Hymn," which apply the example of Jesus to these values. Many form critics believe Paul did not compose the hymn but drew upon a hymn already known to the Philippians to make his point. Likewise, Galatians 3:27–29 is a favorite passage in some quarters, for there Paul asserts that in Christ all social boundaries are overcome. Divisions between Jew and Greek, enslaved person and free, male and female—from Paul's male Jewish point of view, the fundamental dividing lines within humanity—are of no account. Form critics identify this passage as a baptismal formula. It begins, "As many of you as were baptized into Christ have clothed yourselves with Christ." Not only does this statement refer to baptism, but the imagery of putting on Christ recalls how early Christians apparently carried out baptisms: new believers removed their clothes, entered the water, then received white robes to wear after their baptisms. The language of putting on Christ or putting on the new self occurs several times in the Pauline epistles (Rom 13:14; Eph 4:24; Col 3:10), all in the context of moral exhortation. According to some interpreters, if Galatians 3:27–29 functioned as an early baptismal formula, an egalitarian ethos must have been formative in Pauline circles.

Perhaps the most fascinating example of New Testament form criticism involves Jesus's parables, the memorable stories and comparisons that appear in Jesus's teaching in the Synoptic Gospels. (The Gospel of

---

56. Walter Brueggemann and William H. Bellinger Jr., *Psalms*, NCBC (New York: Cambridge University Press, 2014), 354–59.

Thomas includes several parables, but John has none.) Many of Jesus's contemporaries, Jewish and non-Jewish alike, used parables, but Jesus's parables stand out for their quick surprises. Over the centuries, interpreters have come up with all sorts of interpretations for the parables, motivating modern scholars to try to pin them down in a more precise way. Are the parables simply nifty illustrations that convey Jesus's lessons? Do parables function as allegories, with each character, action, and key component corresponding to some reality beyond, or might each parable convey just one essential point? Perhaps the parables are more evocative, challenging readers (as they would have Jesus's audiences) to grapple with their ways of imagining God and the world on their own? Perhaps they empower audiences to take a critical look at the social and economic order in which they find themselves oppressed? More recently, interpreters have tended to shy away from one-size-fits-all approaches to the parables, but the basic discussion of what parables are and how they work remains an active conversation.[57]

For example, the parable of the Laborers in the Vineyard (Matt 20:1–16) has garnered many conflicting interpretations over the centuries, a process that is hardly slowing down today. Early in the morning, a landowner goes into the marketplace to hire workers, promising each a fair wage. He returns at noon, at three in the afternoon, and at five in the afternoon to hire more workers, also offering them a fair wage. At the end of the workday, he pays all of the workers the same amount, a typical daily wage, beginning with those who worked least and moving on to those who had worked all day. The daylong workers, expecting to receive more than those who had worked shorter hours, complain against the landowner, who defends himself: they had agreed on a fair wage from the beginning; should some workers complain about his generosity to others? Jesus concludes the parable with the saying, "So the last will be first, and the first will be last."

The basic meaning of the Greek word *parabolē* has to do with comparison. Our problem involves asking just what sort of comparison this parable would establish. Many, perhaps most, interpreters have

---

57. All of these options have been proposed and widely followed during certain periods. For a survey of scholarship on the parables, see David B. Gowler, *What Are They Saying about the Parables?* (Mahwah, NJ: Paulist, 2000). Although I disagree with the author on important points, for the most comprehensive (and excellent) recent study of the parables, see Klyne R. Snodgrass, *Stories with Intent: A Comprehensive Guide to the Parables of Jesus* (Grand Rapids: Eerdmans, 2008).

taken this parable somewhat allegorically: the landowner corresponds to God, the wages to salvation, and the workers to people. According to this view, the parable teaches that God grants salvation to people regardless of their relative merits. (This interpretation preaches very well in certain Protestant contexts, in which salvation does not depend upon the merit of a person's life.) A related interpretation emphasizes the element of time just as much as it does the wages: God grants people the same salvation, even to those who come to faith late in life. (Think of the so-called deathbed conversion.)

Other interpreters would respond by taking the world of the parable—a landowner, labor-market workers, and daily wages—very seriously. Nothing about the parable itself requires that we convert it into a lesson on salvation. Perhaps the landowner does communicate something about God, but labor and payment mean what they mean: not many employers show so much concern for their workers that they pay everyone a reasonable wage. According to this line of interpretation, the parable teaches something about the justice of God. In God's economy, everyone gets enough.

A third group might step away from finding correspondences between the parable and some external factor such as salvation or justice. The most surprising thing about this story isn't that everybody gets paid the same; it's that the daylong laborers are forced to watch while those who worked least receive their pay first. "The last will be first, and the first will be last." One might see the parable as undermining conventional assumptions about merit and status. Note that the passage immediately preceding this parable concludes with a very similar saying: "But many who are first will be last, and the last will be first" (19:30). Some interpreters have even seen the landowner's behavior as an attempt to undermine the solidarity among poor laborers, as seen when the first group of workers complains about the others.[58]

Form criticism has played a most significant role in historical Jesus research, with implications for other important questions. These applications combine form, source, and redaction criticism (discussed immediately below). Some historians isolate what they regard as the authentic kernel of the Jesus tradition within a passage. For example, with parables a form critic might begin by stripping away what she sees

---

58. William R. Herzog, *Parables as Subversive Speech: Jesus as Pedagogue of the Oppressed* (Louisville: Westminster John Knox, 1994), 79–97.

as later layers of tradition and interpretation. The key criterion for this source-critical assessment involves the critic's understanding of how Jesus's parables worked. The critic also seeks to isolate the parable from the ways in which an author has edited and packaged it (redaction).

The parable of the Persistent Widow and the Unjust Judge (Luke 18:1–8) offers a fairly complicated case study. A widow keeps seeking justice from a judge who neither fears God nor respects people until, worn out by her visits, the judge grants her justice. The passage begins with an introduction, almost surely provided by the author of Luke, telling us how to interpret the parable: disciples should persevere in prayer, just as the widow does with her case. But Luke 18:6–8 apparently provides two more explanations of the story, both placed on the lips of Jesus. According to the first, disciples can be confident that God, who is far superior to corrupt judges, will bring justice to the elect. The second is more obscure: "When the Son of Man comes, will he find faith on earth?"

A form critic rapidly disassembles the passage. The introduction, which interprets the parable as a lesson on prayer (18:1), is attributed to the Gospel author's redactional activity. The explanations at the end (18:6–8) likely reflect traditional interpretations that developed a generation or two after Jesus's career. The first one perhaps addresses a persecuted community that waits for Jesus's return: it encourages them that God will deliver justice for them before long. Here we see form criticism working not only to identify *Jesus's* authentic teaching but to specify the *Sitz im Leben* in which early Christians adapted his teaching. The original parable, found in the simple story of 18:2–5, is largely attributed to Jesus. It reminds ordinary, powerless people to be shameless in pursuing justice.[59]

This sample reading of Luke 18:1–8 demonstrates how scholars have applied form criticism to identify Jesus's authentic teaching and to trace the development of traditions about Jesus. This line of interpretation fits a historical Jesus who isn't much interested in the traditional trappings of religion, like prayer, instead passing along sage advice for communities of ordinary, vulnerable people. It further suggests that after Jesus's death—especially as they waited for his return—early Christians adapted his parables to address their own sense of powerlessness.

---

59. For a reading very much like the one provided here, with a summary of debates involving 18:6–8, see Bernard Brandon Scott, *Hear Then the Parable* (Minneapolis: Augsburg Fortress, 1988), 175–88.

As I mentioned above, such applications of form criticism have largely fallen into disfavor. Some recent interpreters are more optimistic about the power of oral tradition to pass along a fair representation of Jesus's teaching—not necessarily in detail, but with general accuracy concerning the impact Jesus's teaching had upon his hearers and those who followed them. More importantly, they are skeptical of our ability to separate authentic kernels from later developments.[60] Historically attuned readers will balance active investigation of our texts with critical humility.

REDACTION CRITICISM

Source and form criticism both attend to the *pre*history of a text. Form criticism analyzes the tiny bits of tradition from which a biblical book emerges, seeking to uncover how traditional materials developed over time, often in oral tradition, prior to their appearance in a larger unit. Source criticism has to do with written sources that biblical authors edited and incorporated into their larger works. That process of editing provides the focus for redaction criticism. *Redaction* is simply a technical word for the process of editing, one we often encounter in news reports involving government or legal affairs. Redaction criticism assumes not only that the biblical authors wove earlier literary sources into their writing; it also assumes these authors had motives for doing so—whether literary, theological, or cultural. Redaction criticism amounts to accounting for how biblical authors took these earlier sources and adapted them for their own uses, then assessing the thematic implications of the redaction process.

As we noted earlier, Hebrew Bible students quickly encounter the Documentary Hypothesis, a source-critical theory that posits four main literary sources that contribute to the Pentateuch's present form. Professors typically rely upon two case studies to illustrate the theory: the creation stories of Genesis 1–3 and the flood account of Genesis 6–8. We noted the creation story earlier: Genesis 1:1–2:4a presents a complete account of creation, as does 2:4b–3:24. The stories use different names for God, describe God's behavior in different ways, present different orders in which things were created, and so forth. Neither story refers to the other one.

---

60. See Chris Keith and Anthony Le Donne, eds., *Jesus, Criteria, and the Demise of Authenticity* (New York: T&T Clark, 2012).

The flood accounts create a more complicated problem. Genesis 1–3 presents first one story, then the other. At first glance, however, Genesis 6–8 reads as a continuous account, until one looks into the details. Upon closer inspection, we find the same kinds of problems that enabled scholars to identify two separate creation stories: two different names for God, matching different ways of imagining God's behavior, along with diverse sequences of events and conflicting accounts of the animals herded onto Noah's ark. For example, in one account Noah brings seven pairs of each clean (i.e., suitable for sacrifice) species onto the ark, while the other account provides for a single pair per species. Richard Elliott Friedman helpfully provides a translation of the story that identifies each account by placing one in a bold, small-cap font.[61]

Source critics identify the same two sources behind the creation and flood narratives: J and P. The P creation account (1:1–2:4a) characterizes God as creating through the force of the divine word, separating one set of realities from others. Classification is big in the P materials. The P account also culminates in the Sabbath, a significant concern for a (P)riestly author. The J story presents the Lord God creating not with a word but by "forming" and "breathing," and creating not in a linear fashion but through trial and error. J's deity can walk through the garden and wonder where the humans are. In contrast to J's "anthropomorphic" deity, whose behavior resembles that of mortals, P presents a more transcendent God.

The flood stories recapitulate some of these factors. In the J account, Yahweh ("the Lord") actually regrets creating humans (6:6) and later relishes the smell of Noah's sacrifice (8:21). Showing no such change of heart, P's God shows great concern for the classifications of animals, the sort of concern that pervades P material throughout the Pentateuch. In the P creation account, God speaks, and it is; in P's flood story, "Noah did this; he did all that God commanded him" (6:22).

All of these observations apply to source criticism, establishing J and P accounts behind the creation and flood stories with which Genesis begins. But what of redaction? Specifically, why would the final redactor of Genesis place the two creation stories side by side, then interweave two separate flood accounts into one story? Joel Baden offers two responses, one fairly straightforward and the other more complicated. The first has to do with literary style: the "compiler" (Baden's

---

61. Friedman, *Who Wrote the Bible?* 54–59.

word) allows stories to remain separate *unless* they describe an account that could happen only once. Most readers have had no trouble reading one creation story after the other, but two distinct accounts of Noah and the flood would not go over well.[62] The second combines style with theology. The compiler chose to begin the entire Pentateuch with the P creation account, which provides a normative framework for understanding God. The flood story, blending the two sources together, restores the sense of order that marks P's creation account: "The [P] priestly flood story portrays the flood as a reversal and renewal of creation, again with reference only to Genesis 1, not to Genesis 2."[63] Whereas God creates by setting boundaries between the water and the dry ground, the flood amounts to water overcoming those boundaries in a most violent fashion. Indeed, after the flood God recapitulates the order of creation: "birds and animals and every creeping thing that creeps on the earth" (8:17; see 1:20, 24–25). Indeed, these living beings receive the same command at creation and after the flood: "Be fruitful and multiply" (1:22; 8:17). So do humans (1:28; 9:1, 7). From a redaction-critical perspective, the choice to introduce Genesis (and the Pentateuch) with P's creation account shapes the significance of the flood stories.

Some interpreters have likened the combination of source, form, and redaction criticisms to an archaeological site. These approaches attempt to scrape back layers of a text's prehistory: from the final work of a redactor, through the strata of various literary sources, to the history and development of traditional materials. Each historical layer carries a significance of its own, sometimes rivaling the text itself in importance.

With the Hebrew Scriptures, redaction criticism has been applied to just about every book, from "historical" books (or Former Prophets) to literature like Job and the Psalms, to the entire collection of "Minor Prophets" (also known as the Book of the Twelve). Fewer of the New Testament books clearly represent composite documents, but redaction criticism has been applied to many, especially intensely to the Synoptic Gospels. If one accepts the basic Two-Source Hypothesis, it makes lots of sense to compare Matthew and Luke over against Mark. This process brings out not only editorial changes in specific passages but

---

62. Baden, *Composition of the Pentateuch*, 226.
63. Baden, *Composition of the Pentateuch*, 184.

also broader editorial tendencies on the part of Matthew and Luke. Those tendencies may be taken to reflect key points of emphasis for each author.[64]

The first example I use in my classes involves Peter's confession that Jesus is the Messiah (or Christ), which occurs in Matthew 16:13–23; Mark 8:27–33; and Luke 9:18–22. I create a chart, or "synopsis," with the three versions of the story in parallel columns. (Books of such comparisons, called *synopses*, are available for purchase in English and in Greek.) I then invite students to compare Matthew and Luke over against Mark, noting substantive differences. Students sometimes voice observations that seem unimportant; for example, Matthew calls Caesarea Philippi a "district," while Mark calls it "villages." Upon closer study, one might find that Matthew and Mark handle geography differently, but most commentators regard the difference as insignificant. (Mark is fonder of the term translated "village" than is Matthew.) But Luke redacts Mark's setting in a more significant way: Luke provides no location for the scene, but it occurs when Jesus is praying alone. We might regard Jesus's prayer as incidental, but Luke frequently depicts Jesus praying when the other Gospels do not, usually at key moments in his life: his baptism (3:21–22), at the beginning of his ministry (5:15–16), before he calls his twelve apostles (6:12–13), his transfiguration (9:29), the delivery of the Lord's Prayer (11:1), and just before his arrest (22:41–44). It may seem like a small detail within this story, but emphasizing Jesus's prayer life is one of Luke's distinctive tendencies, or themes.

The three accounts include a great deal of common material and common wording, but the most obvious difference among them is reflected in their relative length. Luke's is the shortest of the three; Matthew's the longest. Perhaps an overview of the structure of the three accounts will bring this out best.

---

64. Mark Allan Powell's textbook, *Introducing the New Testament: A Historical, Literary, and Theological Survey* (Minneapolis: Fortress, 2009), features remarkably helpful tables on "Matthew's Use of Mark" (110–11) and "Luke's Use of Mark" (152–53).

Matthew	Mark	Luke
Jesus asks his disciples who people say he is.	Jesus asks his disciples who people say he is.	Jesus asks his disciples who people say he is.
The disciples offer various answers.	The disciples offer various answers.	The disciples offer various answers.
Peter identifies Jesus as the Messiah and Son of God.	Peter identifies Jesus as the Messiah.	Peter identifies Jesus as God's Messiah.
Jesus blesses Peter and confers authority upon Peter and the church.		
Jesus asks his disciples who people say he is.	Jesus informs the disciples concerning the fate of the Son of Man.	
Peter takes Jesus aside to rebuke him.	Peter takes Jesus aside to rebuke him.	
Jesus rebukes Peter.	Jesus rebukes Peter.	

Fig. 2.2

Synoptic Gospel Presentations of Peter's Declaration about Jesus

The chart reveals the key differences: (a) only Matthew includes Jesus's blessing of Peter, accompanied by a pronouncement of authority upon Peter and the church, while (b) only Luke lacks the conflict between Peter and Jesus.

One might explain these differences by supposing that Matthew, Mark, and Luke possessed different traditions of this same account. Most interpreters, however, see redaction at work. All four Gospels, John included, offer a complicated portrayal of Jesus's inner circle of disciples: they initially do what Jesus commands, but they also demonstrate misunderstanding and in the end abandon Jesus. Peter, in particular, denies knowing Jesus during Jesus's trial. Mark's is the most negative portrayal of these disciples: their obedience and perception grow less secure until Jesus's arrest, when they all flee, never to be seen again within the story. Their only hope lies near the end of the Gospel: the women who visit Jesus's empty tomb are commanded to "go, tell his disciples *and Peter*" that the risen Jesus will meet them in Galilee (16:7).

This moment reveals Peter's crucial role in the emergence of early Christianity. Peter plays a prominent role in all four Gospels. At the beginning of Acts (written by the same author as Luke), Peter emerges as the first leader and spokesperson of the church in Jerusalem. On the whole, Matthew and Luke both treat Peter more kindly than Mark does, perhaps because of Peter's later importance among the churches. In redacting Mark 8:27–33, Matthew and Luke both soften Mark's portrayal of Peter. Luke simply omits the reference to Peter's conflict with Jesus. Matthew allows Peter to misunderstand and even to scold Jesus, but Matthew adds a particular blessing to Peter. In the end, Matthew and Luke both soften Mark's characterization of Peter, but they employ opposite means to do so. Matthew adds material, but Luke omits material. Careful attention to the Synoptic Gospels brings out countless similar examples.

Source and form criticism attempt to show *how* biblical books attained their present, or final, form. In addition to the *how* question, redaction criticism asks *why* the authors handled their materials as they did. Redaction criticism brings out the motives—the thematic, theological, literary, and social interests—behind the biblical books as we have them.

RECEPTION HISTORY

When referring to "historical criticism," we have usually pointed to a text's historical context (sometimes called "lower criticism") and the process of its composition ("higher criticism"). Recently more attention has drifted toward how biblical texts have functioned at various historical moments and cultures, something we might call "reception history," or *Wirkungsgeschichte*.

John F. A. Sawyer has provided a model study of how Christians have understood and appropriated the Hebrew Bible book of Isaiah. His title, *The Fifth Gospel*, emphasizes the ways in which early Christians turned to Isaiah to legitimate their claims about Jesus, particularly in debates with Jews.[65] The influential church leader Jerome, responsible for the Latin Vulgate translation of the Bible that functioned as the Roman Catholic Church's official Bible for centuries, referred to Isaiah as an "evangelist": he believed Isaiah proclaimed Jesus's birth ("a virgin will be with child and bear a son"; 7:14, NASB; see 9:6) and his suffering (see Isaiah 53). When Augustine asked his bishop, Ambrose, for vacation

---

65. John F. A. Sawyer, *The Fifth Gospel: Isaiah in the History of Christianity* (New York: Cambridge University Press, 1996).

reading suggestions, the bishop recommended Isaiah "because, I believe, he is more plainly a foreteller of the Gospel and of the calling of the Gentiles than are the others."[66]

Sawyer points out that all four Gospels, Acts, and Romans directly quote the same passage from Isaiah, in which the prophet learns that his people will reject his words. Early Christians turned to these passages to account for why the gospel did not receive widespread acceptance in Jewish circles. Likewise, the relatively obscure Ascension of Isaiah depicts the prophet as predicting Jesus's career, including his descent from the seventh level of heaven to take mortal form. The wicked king Manasseh martyrs the prophet, sawing him in two with a wood saw (see Heb 11:37!). The monastic movement found support in Isaiah, as did countless pieces of liturgy, song, and art. Isaiah's role in anti-Jewish polemic, with its catastrophic results, occupies an entire chapter of Sawyer's book.

Sawyer's study is extensive and impressive, covering scores of Christian figures and diverse forms of cultural expression. But Sawyer's focus remains largely with Western Christianity, at least after about the sixth century. The past forty years or so have witnessed an explosion of interest in global, or non-Western, readings of the Bible. This development coincides with two others: the global trend toward national independence on the part of formerly colonized peoples, and the rise of liberation theology. As discussed above, liberation theologies emphasize social, economic, cultural, and political liberation on the part of marginalized peoples.

One groundbreaking representative of liberationist biblical interpretation is Ernesto Cardenal's *The Gospel in Solentiname*, originally published in four volumes in 1975 (in English, 1976). Based on recordings of Bible study sessions among poor farmers on the Nicaraguan island of Solentiname, the collection offers interpretations of Gospel passages that surprised most European and North American readers. For example, the story of the wedding at Cana (John 2:1–12) is widely known: Jesus's mother Mary informs Jesus that the hosts have run out of wine, but Jesus seems reluctant to intervene—if not rude about it. In the end, Jesus transforms the water into wine: this first "sign" he performs in John leads his disciples to believe in him. The group in Solentiname focused on Mary's courage. Perhaps, they reasoned, Jesus's reluctance

---

66. Sawyer, *Fifth Gospel*, 1–2, citing Augustine's *Confessions*, 1.276.

resulted from his fear of bringing attention to himself, but Mary offers a model of courage. "That's the way every revolutionary mother ought to be with her revolutionary son," one farmer asserts.[67]

Sawyer's study of Isaiah's reception history, similar to others like it, tends to focus upon the producers of relatively high culture. The turn toward global interpretation, portended by *The Gospel in Solentiname*, often attends to people who will never write commentary that others will read. Gerald West, a white South African, has documented diverse interpretive strategies among liberationist black readers, what he calls "ordinary readers," in that context.[68] The Botswanan feminist Musa Dube has chronicled the interpretations of Botswanan women in African Independent Churches, contrasting their readings with those of white European and North American feminists. According to Dube, these Botswanan women engage the Bible deeply but with spiritual freedom, a commitment to liberation, and wisdom drawn from multiple religious traditions.[69]

The history of reception involves both historical and global dimensions. Sawyer's study of the reception of Isaiah peers into history, a largely Western Christian tradition of interpretation. Cardenal, West, and Dube invite us to expand our attention on a global scale, acknowledging relationships of colonial, economic, and cultural domination.

Readers who take reception history seriously must decide how we relate to the interpretations we encounter. We could investigate other interpretations as a matter of historical or cultural inquiry. Sometimes, for example, we encounter interpretations that strike us as clearly fanciful: we are interested in them as representatives of particular cultural moments, not because they will influence our own interpretive work. For example, an apocryphal Acts of John provides the first attestation that Revelation was composed in a cave. Contemporary tourists may still visit a cave supposed to be the dwelling of John of Patmos. The same Acts of John attributes the Gospel of John—but not Revela-

---

67. Ernesto Cardenal, *The Gospel in Solentiname* (Maryknoll, NY: Orbis, 2010 [1975, 1977]), 77.
68. Gerald West, *Biblical Hermeneutics of Liberation: Modes of Reading the Bible in the South African Context*, 2nd ed., Bible & Liberation (Maryknoll, NY: Orbis, 1995).
69. Musa W. Dube, *Postcolonial Feminist Interpretation of the Bible* (St. Louis: Chalice, 2000), esp. 39–43, 184–95.

tion!—to John's visionary experiences.[70] Those make interesting tidbits, but they're hardly likely to influence our basic understanding of the Apocalypse.

But what about the possibility that other interpreters might reveal layers of meaning to us? Often readers who operate with cultural assumptions and from historical contexts far different than our own become our teachers. To stay with Revelation for a moment, many readers grapple with the book's violence. Can we justify the suffering Revelation imagines for human beings? The South African activist Allan A. Boesak composed a study of Revelation from his experience fighting Apartheid, which includes his torture and imprisonment. Revelation depicts Jesus as a Lamb, wearing a robe dipped in blood. In his violent and repressive context, Boesak writes, "If [Christ's] cloak is spattered with blood, it is the blood of his enemies, the destroyers of the earth and of his children."[71] Having read Boesak, I could no longer evaluate Revelation's violence as a theoretical question divorced from the lived experience of violent suppression.

Some Christian traditions heavily value the history of interpretation, especially the ancient Christian writers often called the "church fathers." Roman Catholic and Eastern Orthodox communions explicitly value the tradition of interpretation. The 1993 Pontifical Biblical Commission document "The Interpretation of the Bible in the Church" insists upon the necessity for modern historical-critical scholarship of the sort we have discussed in this chapter, but the document also credits the church fathers with having "drawn out from the totality of Scripture the basic orientations which shaped the doctrinal tradition of the church." In other words, patristic interpretation set the basic categories for faithful interpretation through the centuries. Moreover, attention to the history of interpretation can "throw light upon" the meaning of individual passages.[72]

Although the great Protestant Reformers Martin Luther and John Calvin highly respected patristic interpretation, most Protestants have

---

70. Ian Boxall, *Patmos in the Reception History of the Apocalypse*, Oxford Theology and Religion Monographs (New York: Oxford University Press, 2013), 109–11.

71. Allan A. Boesak, *Comfort and Protest: The Apocalypse from a South African Perspective* (Philadelphia: Westminster, 1987), 124.

72. The Pontifical Biblical Commission, "The Interpretation of the Bible in the Church," in Dean P. Béchard, ed., *The Scripture Documents: An Anthology of Official Catholic Teachings* (Collegeville, MN: Liturgical Press, 2002), 244–316.

tended to favor more "direct" access to the Bible's meaning. Meanwhile, secular biblical scholarship largely models itself after the social and physical sciences, with the assumption that the passage of time brings progress to our understanding. Both Protestant and secular scholarship tend to relegate the church fathers to an antiquarian curiosity. More recent trends, often associated with the "Theological Interpretation of Scripture" movement, often seek to recapture ancient interpretation. Stephen Fowl calls for "contemporary believers to relearn the habits and practices that constituted a flourishing pattern of theological interpretation in the past."[73] Frances M. Young observes that the church fathers often interpreted the Bible in harmful ways, most notably anti-Jewish ways, yet she states that "we would know more about theological reading of Scripture if we could relearn from the fathers the notion that Scripture is a fountain."[74] "Theological interpretation of Scripture" advocates tend to value patristic interpretation above contemporary global interpretation.

One might argue that the question of real, flesh-and-blood readers marks one of the critical dividing lines among contemporary interpreters. The party of interpreters who attend to the actual working effects of biblical interpreters is growing, but many scholars proceed as if such concerns lie beyond the boundaries of biblical interpretation. Apart from one chapter on fundamentalism, the *Oxford Handbook of Biblical Studies*, a prestigious reference work that introduces readers to the field of biblical scholarship and is composed by a world-class team of scholars, devotes no attention to the history of interpretation or to real readers in a global context.[75] We will return to this question in chapter 5.

LANGUAGE, TEXT, AND TRANSLATION

Historical criticism has confronted significant challenges over the past several decades, particularly from theologically invested readers. Throughout the centuries, interpreters have assumed the value of his-

---

73. Fowl, *Theological Interpretation of Scripture*, 55.

74. Frances M. Young, "Patristic Biblical Interpretation," in *Dictionary for Theological Interpretation of the Bible*, ed. Kevin J. Vanhoozer et al. (Grand Rapids: Baker Academic, 2005), 570.

75. Judith M. Lieu and J. W. Rogerson, eds., *The Oxford Handbook of Biblical Studies* (New York: Oxford University Press, 2008).

torical information, even if historical context did not govern interpretation in every case. The simultaneous emergence of higher criticism and the theory of evolution in the nineteenth century created a rift among interpreters. Religious traditionalists held on to "lower criticism," the study of cultural and historical information about the biblical world, while rejecting "higher criticism" such as source, form, and redaction analysis. But in the 1960s and 1970s, many began to complain that historical criticism was stifling interpretation. Their concerns were many:

- Historical interests became ends in themselves, limiting interpretation to the knowledge of how or when a text was produced.
- Historical interpretation locates meaning in the past, cutting off the Bible's contemporary relevance.
- Biblical scholars' exclusive commitment to historical interpretation hindered readers from asking other kinds of questions and precluded other forms of interpretation. Interpretations that did not "count" as historical were rejected.
- Narrowly construed, historical criticism is simply analysis that chops the Bible into little lifeless bits. It treats the Bible like those frogs in high school biology labs to which we alluded earlier. If the frog isn't dead before we cut it open, it surely will be soon afterward.

Most interpreters can acknowledge the merit of such concerns, yet historical criticism remains the prevailing mode of contemporary biblical scholarship. Moreover, few scholars would deny its role, perhaps among other kinds of interpretation, in the interpretive process.

One area in which historical knowledge seems essential involves the actual text of biblical books and the translations we produce from those texts. Those of us who read the Bible in English depend upon committees of scholars who translate the Hebrew, Aramaic, and Greek texts on our behalf. And readers who know the biblical languages still depend upon teams of scholars who produce their Hebrew, Aramaic, and Greek editions of biblical books.

Philology, the study of language, is an inherently historical discipline. Languages interact with one another and evolve over time. Translators must attend to these dynamics. The Greek word *martys* ordinarily described witnesses in a courtroom or other public controversy, but the book of Revelation links witnesses and their testimony (*martyria*) with the risk of persecution, even death (e.g., 1:5; 2:13). While ancient people already knew about exemplary figures who suffered execution for their faithfulness, our modern concept of martyrdom may have taken a giant step with Revelation. Such historical context is necessary if we want to understand what Revelation means by calling Jesus a "faithful witness" (1:5; 3:14), or what it means for John to say he "was on the island called Patmos because of the word of God and the testimony (*martyria*) of Jesus" (1:9).

As a rule of thumb, almost all modern translations on the market are quite good. Committees of devoted experts, guided by specialists in translation and style, create these translations. The differences among them usually reflect predictable concerns. Some translations address readers with fairly advanced English reading skills, while others serve people with more limited vocabulary. The New Century Version, for example, reads at a fifth-grade reading level, in comparison with more widely used translations that read at something like an eighth-grade reading level. Naturally, differences in reading level result in variations in vocabulary and sentence structure. Translations sometimes differ due to conflicting commitments regarding gendered language: more recent translations tend to use gender-inclusive language for humans but not for God, a trend that was controversial a couple of decades ago. Translations also vary due to differences in philosophies concerning how language works. Some believe language makes sense primarily at the level of words, while others believe meaning happens in phrases and clauses. Verbal-equivalence translations like the English Standard Version and the New American Standard Bible adopt the first view, while dynamic-equivalence translations such as the New Living Translation follow the second. Most popular translations land somewhere between the two poles.

Even so, translation philosophies can lead to very different meanings. This is particularly the case when we mix in theological questions. For example, the two most popular modern translations of recent decades handle the Greek word *sarx* differently: the New Revised Standard Version renders it as "flesh," a fairly literal translation, while the New International Version often reads, "sinful nature." "Flesh" may be the more literal meaning, but what do biblical authors, especially Paul, mean when they use the word? The NIV translators, who happen to represent evangelical Protestant communities, believe Paul often means "sinful nature," making a theological judgment on behalf of their readers. What if Paul uses flesh simply to refer to natural things like a man's penis (he's often talking about circumcision when he uses the term) or kinship?[76] To take another example, the ancient world lacked a term that corresponded to the modern concept of homosexuality. But homosexuality represents the single most controversial issue among American Protestants today. No wonder, then, that the Common English Bible translates two notoriously difficult Greek terms in 1 Corinthians 6:9—one of the most hotly contested passages in such debates—as "both participants in same-sex intercourse," while we find a wild diversity of renderings in other translations. Historical research into the terminology behind these two words will not solve church debates, but at least it will enhance our understanding.[77] Both "flesh" and the terms in 1 Corinthians 6:9 challenge translators to take account of historical linguistics but also of literary context, argument structure, and their own theological considerations.

Inevitably, translations come up short. There's no way to offer a full rendering of the nuances of one language into another. In both Hebrew and Greek, for example, the same word groups can indicate justice and righteousness. Our translations tend to favor righteousness. Within the Bible these word groups occur with respect to legal proceedings, the character of individuals, and the status of mortals before God. At a strict dictionary level, that's no problem: justice and righteousness basically amount to fair dealing and integrity. But in popular English we tend to reserve righteousness for the spiritual realm. We do not like "self-righteous" people. Consider what a big difference there is between Jesus blessing "those who hunger and thirst for righteousness," as opposed to those who hunger and thirst for justice (Matt 5:6). English speakers will tend to associate the former with spiritual longing, but the latter with persons who are oppressed.

One fascinating translation problem occurs in the book of Job. After voicing all his complaints about God, Job undergoes a dramatic confrontation with the divine glory. The entire story has been building up to this point. Consider four major translations of Job 42:6.

- Therefore I retract, And I repent in dust and ashes. (New American Standard Bible)

---

76. Daniel Boyarin, *A Radical Jew: Paul and the Politics of Identity* (Berkeley: University of California Press, 1994), 68.

77. For discussion, with reference to other studies on the subject, see Loader, *The New Testament on Sexuality*, 326–32.

- Therefore I despise myself and repent in dust and ashes. (New International Version)
- ... therefore I despise myself, and repent in dust and ashes. (New Revised Standard Version)
- Therefore, I recant and relent, Being but dust and ashes. (Jewish Publication Society)

All of these translations basically portray Job as realizing that he has overstepped his bounds. Mere dust and ashes, who is he to confront God? But the Hebrew of Job 42:6 is notoriously ambiguous, lending itself to several possible meanings. One possible translation of Job 42:6 might read, "Therefore I retract my words, and I am comforted concerning dust and ashes."[78] In this reading Job indeed gives up his complaint against God—but not because he is persuaded. He is not. Instead, he accepts consolation for his losses and moves on.[79] Remarkably, better historical data will not resolve this translation problem. The Hebrew is well known; it's just ambiguous.

Our English Bibles reflect not only translation decisions but text-critical ones as well. We possess original copies of none of the biblical books. All we have are a few ancient copies, more for the New Testament than for the Jewish Scriptures, medieval copies, and ancient translations into languages like Syriac, Coptic, Ethiopic, and a host of other languages. Text criticism involves the study of these manuscripts and versions in an attempt to understand the history of the biblical text. Traditionally, text critics aimed to establish the most likely "original" version of the biblical books. Today most text critics are more skeptical of our ability to find an original text, with many even skeptical that an "original" ever existed. Nevertheless, the process of translation and biblical interpretation often involves discerning the text from which we work.

Some text-critical problems are well known, whether difficult to resolve or not. The medieval Masoretic Text of 1 Samuel 13:1 literally reads, "Saul was one year old when he began to reign; and he reigned two years over Israel."

One year old! Really? The New Revised Standard Version of 1 Samuel 13:1 reads,

---

78. Carol A. Newsom, "Job," *NIB* (Nashville: Abingdon, 1996), 4.629.
79. David J. A. Clines, *Job*, WBC 18B (Nashville: Thomas Nelson, 2011), 1207–11, 1218–24.

"Saul was . . . years old when he began to reign; and he reigned . . . and two years over Israel." The translation committee adds two footnotes to alert readers to the problem but does not attempt to resolve it.[80]

Two particularly famous text-critical problems appear in the New Testament. Although older translations of Mark include appearances of the risen Jesus to his disciples (16:9–20), modern manuscript finds reveal that—so far as we can tell—Mark originally ended after 16:8, with no encounters with the risen Jesus. Likewise, it seems that the famous story of Jesus and the adulterous woman, found at John 7:53–8:11, found its way into the narrative (and at places in Luke) well after the Gospel's composition.

Text-critical problems can bear significant implications for the interpretation of a passage or a book, but they also provide evidence for the history of interpretation. In Mark 1:40–45 Jesus encounters a leper who, kneeling before him, says, "If you choose, you can make me clean." Jesus does so, then "sternly" commands the man not to tell anyone. But the man spreads the news everywhere, so that crowds hound Jesus throughout the rest of Mark. The story includes two significant text problems, but attention has tended to focus on the one in verse 41: most ancient manuscripts describe Jesus as moved with compassion or pity, but a few describe him as angry.

The difference between a compassionate and an angry Jesus is quite wide, and it bears implications for Mark's Gospel as a whole. This passage provides our first glimpse into Jesus's state of mind. To this point Jesus can be forceful: he has issued orders to potential disciples (1:17) and commanded unclean spirits to be silent (1:25, 34). Later he will scold his disciples on multiple occasions and engage in arguments with his enemies. Mark's Jesus is hardly soft and cuddly. But angry with a victim of leprosy? That reaction seems excessive.

Some features of the story lend themselves to an angry Jesus. Without his anger, it's hard to explain why he "sternly" commands silence. The "touch" Jesus applies to the leper has a range of meanings, some of which are hostile. But the main problem boils down to pure logic. It's easy to explain why a copyist would change an angry Jesus into a compassionate one. But how does one explain the reverse? A growing number of scholars are beginning to regard the "angry" reading as earlier,

---

80. Emmanuel Tov, *Textual Criticism of the Hebrew Bible* (Minneapolis: Fortress, 1992), 10.

despite the fact that most of our best manuscripts describe Jesus as compassionate. The recent Common English Bible describes Jesus as "incensed."

Finding the most likely original meaning is important, but this example also has some things to teach us about early Christian history. Very quickly scribes corrected Mark to reflect a Jesus more in line with emerging Christian thought concerning his divinity. We see similar processes in many instances.[81] A sinless Jesus, much less a divine one, would not respond to human suffering with anger. We also note that Matthew and Luke both relate this same story from Mark, and both eliminate any reference to Jesus's emotional response. Again, this decision is much easier to explain if their copies of Mark had an angry rather than a compassionate Jesus. Indeed, Matthew and Luke *always* modify Mark when Mark describes Jesus as angry.[82] This text-critical problem opens the possibility for understanding how early Christian theology developed—and how some scribes felt about the Bible's role in that process.

THE LIMITS OF HISTORIOGRAPHY

Earlier we discussed complaints against historical criticism. Fundamentalists reject "higher criticism" on the grounds that it begins with a skeptical attitude toward faith. Some other theologically inclined interpreters reject *historicism*, a disposition that values historical considerations above all others. Just as dissection in the biology lab requires dead frogs, they say, historical-critical slicing and dicing removes the life from biblical literature. Most readers, however, value the insights generated by historical research even if the variety of proposals arouses a degree of skepticism.

Historical criticism, like every research discipline, has its limits. Introductory students routinely find themselves frustrated that the commentaries and other sources they read disagree on basic issues. The 1990s were a classic moment for confusion on major historical questions. Historians of ancient Israel could not agree as to when or how

---

81. Bart D. Ehrman, *The Orthodox Corruption of Scripture: The Effect of Early Christological Controversies on the New Testament* (New York: Oxford University Press, 1993).

82. The examples include Mark 3:5 (see Luke 6:10) and 10:14 (see Matthew 19:14; Luke 18:16). Bart D. Ehrman, *Misquoting Jesus: The Story behind Who Changed the Bible and Why* (San Francisco: HarperSanFrancisco, 2005), 133–39.

"Israel" actually appeared on the scene. And research into the historical Jesus amounted to a grand public debate concerning how Jewish and how apocalyptic was Jesus's outlook.

Until fairly recently, historians assumed that the biblical narratives provided a broad outline of Israel's history. They were suspicious of the patriarchal narratives in Genesis, just as historians of ancient Rome do not rely on the myth that Romulus and Remus, Rome's legendary founders, were raised by wolves. They realized the narratives of the exodus and the conquest of the land involved some sensationalism, but many agreed to the basic timeline from the book of the Judges forward.[83] But the 1980s and 1990s witnessed a divide between "maximalists," who tended to trust the broad outlines of the biblical narratives, and "minimalists," who regarded ancient Israel as a fiction developed by the biblical authors themselves.[84] The debate continues, perhaps with an emerging consensus that kings like David and Solomon actually existed but not exactly in the fashion we encounter in the biblical narratives.

Likewise, a near-consensus regarding Jesus seems to have held until the 1980s. The canonical Gospels are hardly historical chronicles, scholars reasoned; instead, they represent theological interpretations of Jesus's significance for early Christian readers. However, Matthew, Mark, and Luke basically got Jesus right: he was an apocalyptic prophet who proclaimed a gospel of repentance in preparation for God's last-days intervention. The emergence of the Jesus Seminar in 1985 changed the conversation. Combing through the Gospels for traces of historical authenticity, John Dominic Crossan and others argued that the Synoptics basically got Jesus wrong—more accurately, interpreted Jesus in a way he would not have recognized. Jesus was more of a popular sage, maybe a holy man, who built communities of solidarity and interdependence. He was not much concerned with religious details like prayer, much less with apocalyptic speculation. Early layers of Jesus

---

83. The once-standard textbooks on the subject reflect some uncertainty as to how far back from the monarchy one can trace meaningful history. See John Bright, *A History of Israel*, 3rd ed. (Philadelphia: Westminster, 1981); and, with less confidence, J. Maxwell Miller and John H. Hayes, *A History of Ancient Israel and Judah* (Philadelphia: Westminster, 1986).

84. For example, Philip R. Davies, *In Search of "Ancient Israel,"* JSOTSup 148; Sheffield: Sheffield Academic, 1992); and Nils Peter Lemche, *Ancient Israel: A New History of Israelite Society*, The Biblical Seminar (Sheffield: Sheffield Academic, 1988).

tradition—found in parts of Q and the Gospel of Thomas, especially—revealed this countercultural, non-apocalyptic Jesus.[85] Again intense debate ensued, but this time generating best-sellers. These debates transformed the conversation so that today, most interpreters have returned to the apocalyptic-Jesus view—but with a greatly chastened understanding of our ability to identify discrete bits of "authentic" sayings and deeds by Jesus.[86] Sharp debates and changing consensuses call into question the authority of historical research. After all, if even the experts can't agree, why should the rest of us follow them?

Not only do experts disagree; they also change their minds. One pillar of New Testament research held that the "Johannine community," the hypothetical group from which emerged the Gospel and letters of John, had experienced expulsion from the synagogues. This theory, most influentially developed by J. Louis Martyn, turned to passages such as John 9:22 and 16:2 (see 12:11 as well), which portray Jewish authorities banning Jesus believers from the synagogues. No such thing could have happened during Jesus's career, as synagogues were not central to Jewish identity in Galilee and Judea until quite later, nor were people confessing faith in Jesus as Messiah, so Martyn speculated that these passages reflected developments in the history of the Johannine community. He further traced the expulsion of Jesus people to a rabbinic action at Yavneh (Jamnia) in 85 CE. What had been an inner-synagogue group of *Christian Jews* now became—against its will—a separated community of *Jewish Christians*.[87]

This theory, first advanced in 1968, held sway for nearly three decades until it yielded to critical investigation. After the year 85, some Jews followed other messiahs—all without being expelled from Jewish communities. Moreover, first-century Judaism lacked the sort of cen-

---

85. Crossan, *Historical Jesus*.
86. E.g., Dale C. Allison Jr., *The Historical Christ and the Theological Jesus* (Grand Rapids: Eerdmans, 2009); and Anthony Le Donne, *Historical Jesus: What Can We Know and How Can We Know It?* (Grand Rapids: Eerdmans, 2011).
87. J. Louis Martyn, *History and Theology in the Fourth Gospel*, 2nd ed. (Nashville: Abingdon, 1979), 66, quoted in John Ashton, *Understanding the Fourth Gospel*, 2nd ed. (New York: Oxford University Press, 2007), 113. Martyn's *History and Theology in the Fourth Gospel* has appeared in three editions, the first in 1968 and the third in 2003. See Raymond E. Brown, *The Community of the Beloved Disciple* (New York: Paulist, 1979).

tralized leadership by which such an edict—if it ever functioned as Martyn interpreted it—could take effect. Today most interpreters hold a more modest view: John's Gospel reflects that *some rupture* occurred between one group of Jewish Jesus believers and their Jewish communities, but our sources do not allow us to know the precise nature of that traumatic process.[88] The expulsion hypothesis so dominated scholarship on the Fourth Gospel for a significant period of time, that my students still refer to it as "fact" in their papers. No wonder many readers express frustration at major changes in historical research.

Not only do historical proposals change over time; they also reflect the perspectives of the historians themselves. Many graduate programs offered their first doctorates to women in the 1970s or even later. The first African American woman to receive a doctorate in Hebrew Bible, Renita J. Weems, completed her degree in 1989. Not surprisingly, new scholars have produced fresh insights. If research on the historical Jesus has been dominated by white males, Elisabeth Schüssler Fiorenza's groundbreaking study, *In Memory of Her*, pursued a different line of inquiry. Schüssler Fiorenza was interested in Jesus, but she focused her attention upon the histories of women almost covered over in the Gospel narratives and New Testament epistles. Schüssler Fiorenza found that, whatever Jesus may have done or taught with respect to women, the early Jesus movement had a strong egalitarian impulse, and women played prominent roles in this "discipleship of equals."[89] Male scholarship had tended to reflect church debates about whether or not to authorize women for religious leadership, but feminist historians moved beyond seeking permission from Paul and other biblical writers, instead uncovering evidence for women's actual contributions to and leadership in the early churches.[90] And while many people assumed the

---

88. For an abbreviated account of this movement in scholarship, see Adele Reinhartz, "Judaism in the Gospel of John," *Int* 63 (2009): 382–93. Also, Reinhartz, "On Travel, Translation, and Ethnography: Johannine Scholarship at the Turn of the Century," in *"What Is John?"* vol. 2: *Literary and Social Readings of the Fourth Gospel*, ed. Fernando F. Segovia, SBLSymS 7 (Atlanta: Scholars, 1998), 111–38.

89. Elisabeth Schüssler Fiorenza, *In Memory of Her: A Feminist Theological Reconstruction of Christian Origins* (New York: Crossroad, 1983).

90. Classic studies include Antoinette Clark Wire, *The Corinthian Women Prophets: A Reconstruction through Paul's Rhetoric* (Minneapolis: Augsburg Fortress, 1990); Ross Shepard Kraemer and Mary Rose D'Angelo, eds., *Women and Christian Origins* (New York: Oxford University Press, 1999); and Carolyn Osiek and Margaret Y. MacDon-

absolute subjection of women in the ancient world, historians like Ross Shepard Kraemer uncovered countless examples of women's agency and leadership.[91] Similar research uncovered the lives of women in ancient Israel.[92] Christian New Testament scholarship had tended to characterize ancient Judaism in misleading and negative ways. Jewish feminist scholars such as Amy-Jill Levine, Paula Fredriksen, and Adele Reinhartz began correcting the record by uncovering the history of Jewish women and the polemical dimensions of early Christian literature.[93]

African American scholarship likewise critiqued European American historiography. One aspect of that research involved calling attention to Africa's role in the formation of Israel and its history and in the emergence of early Christianity. Egypt, Ethiopia (Nubia), and Libya had long been recognized as influential sources of early Christian thought and literature, but European American scholars had downplayed that significance. Moreover, they tended to the Hellenistic (Greek) and Mediterranean, as opposed to the African, dimensions of Egyptian and North African culture. Critics such as Charles Copher, Cain Hope Felder, and Randall C. Bailey began emphasizing "the black presence" in the Bible.[94] A more recent wave of scholarship, modeled by Gay L.

ald with Janet H. Tullock, *A Woman's Place: House Churches in Earliest Christianity* (Minneapolis: Fortress, 2006).

91. Ross Shepard Kraemer, *Her Share of the Blessings: Women's Religions among Pagans, Jews, and Christians in the Greco-Roman World* (New York: Oxford University Press, 1992); and *Maenads, Martyrs, Matrons, Monastics: A Sourcebook on Women's Religions in the Greco-Roman World* (Philadelphia: Fortress, 1988).

92. Tikva Frymer-Kensky, *In the Wake of the Goddesses: Women, Culture, and the Biblical Transformation of Pagan Myth* (New York: Fawcett Columbine, 1992); and Meyers, *Discovering Eve*.

93. For an entry into the discussion, with bibliographical references to a much wider body of scholarship, see Paula Fredriksen and Adele Reinhartz, eds., *Jesus, Judaism, and Christian Anti-Judaism: Reading the New Testament after the Holocaust* (Louisville: Westminster John Knox, 2002); Amy-Jill Levine, *The Misunderstood Jew: The Church and the Scandal of the Jewish Jesus* (New York: HarperOne, 2006); and Adele Reinhartz, *Befriending the Beloved Disciple* (New York: Continuum, 2001); see also Tal Ilan, *Jewish Women in Greco-Roman Palestine* (Peabody, MA: Hendrickson, 1996).

94. For a review of the scholarship, see Michael Joseph Brown, *Blackening of the Bible: The Aims of African American Religious Scholarship*, African American Religious Thought and Life (Harrisburg, PA: Trinity Press International, 2004), 24–68. Classic essays by Felder, Copher, and Bailey appear in Cain Hope Felder, ed., *Stony the Road*

Byron, explores the role of racial discourse, specifically "blackness," in early Christian literature.[95] Historians who emerge from underrepresented groups naturally pose challenges to the conventional wisdom of historical research, undermining the notion that historiography provides universal or permanent results.

Most readers do care about history and believe historical research is relevant, even essential, for biblical interpretation. The question involves the level of authority granted to historiography. Given that historians disagree with one another on essential questions, that today's consensus turns into tomorrow's outdated opinion, and that historical research inevitably reflects the life experiences—and limitations—of the researchers, should we grant historians ultimate say in the work of meaning-making?

One complaint against historical criticism is that it limits meaning to the past. If we tie a text's meaning to the moment of its composition, how can it prove relevant to contemporary readers? One classic model posited that interpreters should ask "what it meant" before dealing with "what it means,"[96] a relationship that has vexed philosophers and theologians through the centuries. At the most practical level, locating meaning in the past raises as many questions as it answers. Do we mean the intention of the author, who is not available for interview? For that matter, does the assumption of authorship "fit" texts that clearly evolved over time through the activity of multiple authors? Similar problems arise if we locate meaning in a text's ancient audience. How, exactly, do we identify the audience of Proverbs, which often addresses "my son," especially in chapters 1–10? Many biblical books come with complicated composition histories: Does every redactional layer generate its own level of meaning? Problems like this become particularly acute with cases such as Jesus's parables. One might interpret a parable's meaning at the level of Jesus's intention, in its usage and development in (hypothetical) early Christian communities, or in the received forms

---

We Trod: African American Biblical Interpretation (Minneapolis: Fortress, 1991): Felder, "Race, Racism, and the Biblical Narratives," 127–45; Copher, "The Black Presence in the Old Testament," 146–64; and Bailey, "Beyond Identification: The Use of Africans in Old Testament Poetry and Narratives," 165–84.

95. Gay L. Byron, *Symbolic Blackness and Ethnic Difference in Early Christian Literature* (New York: Routledge, 2002).

96. Krister Stendahl, "Biblical Theology, Contemporary," *IDB* (Nashville: Abingdon, 1962), 1.418–32.

of Matthew, Mark, and Luke. Even as I write, I'm consulting a major recent book that argues against tracing more than a handful of parables to Jesus himself.[97]

One might overstate the problem. We all know texts have a way of communicating beyond their moments of origin. Male undergraduates will continue to identify with Gilgamesh, Odysseus, and Socrates. And producers will go on staging Shakespeare's plays in contemporary settings. The question simply amounts to the level of authority we hand over to the past.

Readers turn to history for diverse reasons. Although most of my own scholarship has a theological cast, with historical perspectives contributing to my interpretation at every turn, I strongly relate to those who enjoy history for its own sake. Phenomena such as prophecy in the ancient Near East, the ways in which Jews and Christians invented a sense of identity such as "Jew" and "Christian," and the development of ideas like messianic expectation or the afterlife fascinate me. I would love to know how Jewish and Christian owners of enslaved people understood their relationships to their own enslaved people, along with the degree to which the religious convictions of those enslaved people may have fueled hope for emancipation. Some interpreters appeal to history in addressing contemporary cultural debates. Hardly theological in orientation, a work like Sarah Ruden's *Paul among the People* places Paul's letters in the context of other popular Greek and Roman literature of the day—with fascinating results. Paul was no modern egalitarian, but maybe his social outlook was more progressive than many think.[98] Paul may not say what some of us wish he would say, leaving us to weigh his own cultural context as part of our assessment. Theologically invested readers often appeal to history in seeking to understand a problem like the violent imagery in Nahum. Does it make sense to "blame" Israel's ruthless neighbors for the book's violent rhetoric, particularly its depiction of Nineveh as a violated woman?

> Because of the countless debaucheries of the prostitute, gracefully alluring, mistress of sorcery, who enslaves nations through her debaucheries, and peoples through her sorcery, I am against you, says the Lord of hosts, and

---

97. John P. Meier, *A Marginal Jew: Rethinking the Historical Jesus*, vol. 5: *Probing the Authenticity of the Parables*, AYBRL (New Haven: Yale University Press, 2016).
98. Ruden, *Paul among the People*.

will lift up your skirts over your face; and I will let nations look on your nakedness and kingdoms on your shame. (3:4–5)

While some reject Nahum, and others argue that the book exemplifies divine anger in response to injustice, Julia M. O'Brien recommends chastened imagination that at once honors the call for justice and attends to the implications of our metaphors.[99] Historical concerns contribute to O'Brien's assessment, but they do not settle the matter independently. Most readers follow a similar pragmatic approach. We value history, but it is not our only or final concern. Historical considerations may guide our reading, but often they do not determine its outcome.

---

99. Julia M. O'Brien, *Challenging Prophetic Metaphor: Theology and Ideology in the Prophets* (Louisville: Westminster John Knox, 2008), 110–24.

CHAPTER 3.

TELL ME A STORY: LITERARY MODES OF INTERPRETATION

The vast majority of the Bible consists of stories and poems. Our cultural heritage of treating the Bible as history, and debating its merits on that score, distances us from this point. Christians may refer to the Bible's first five books as "the Law" (the Hebrew *Torah* carries broader connotations), but even its large chunks of legal material are wrapped inside broader narratives. We may think of books like Jeremiah and Ezekiel as "prophetic," and rightly so, but the prophets blend poetic meter with narrative prose. Likewise, we may consider Job a "wisdom" book, but it wraps poetic dialogue within a story. The Bible indeed emerges from a historical distance, and its material carries historical significance, but most of the Bible amounts to narrative and poetry. Among other things, the Bible is literature, and it rewards literary study.

Reflecting on our propensity to value historical accuracy over literary artistry, John Dominic Crossan has observed that Jesus seems to have preferred parables—that is, fictions—as a primary teaching vehicle. If that is the case, Crossan reasons, why not assume that biblical writers conveyed their most important information through fiction as well? If Jesus had a special preference for parables about God, did the evangelists, or Gospel authors, have a special preference for parables about Jesus?[1]

By taking seriously the Bible's literary nature, we do not necessarily

---

1. John Dominic Crossan, *A Long Way from Tipperary: What a Former Irish Monk Discovered in His Search for the Truth* (San Francisco: HarperSanFrancisco, 2000), 165.

set aside its historical dimensions. We do, as Crossan suggests, add new sensitivities and expectations to the process.

- We open the space to savor the pleasure of literature well written.
- We set aside, if only for a moment, a preoccupation with "what really happened" or how the text came to be as it is.
- We imagine ourselves encountering the text for the first time. We experience irony, suspense, and surprise.
- We don't so much appreciate biblical figures as personalities to whom we attribute motives and character traits of our own devising, but greet them as characters mediated exclusively as the story presents them.
- We allow "gaps" in the story—those things unexplained—to remain unresolved.
- Our experience of the Bible includes our experiences of other stories and poems.

In short, a literary approach to biblical interpretation requires some things of *us*, the readers: specific sets of expectations, skills, and dispositions. It requires that we become "good readers" rather than simply cultural historians.[2] It also offers the promise that, just as we all enjoy a good story, play, or film, we might also delight in the experience of reading the Bible.

THE FICTION OF HISTORY

A reader might object that, yes, stories make up chunks of the Bible from Genesis through Chronicles (in a Protestant Bible) and Matthew through Acts, but that fact does not negate their historical relevance. Indeed, interpreters continue to grapple with how biblical stories, along with other literature, relate to historical developments. From the perspective of literary theory, however, the telling of history essentially involves a literary endeavor. Close inspection renders the line between historical narrative and literary fiction vanishingly thin.[3]

In profound ways every historical narrative reflects literary inven-

---

2. Judy Stack-Nelson, "Beyond Biblical Literacy: Developing Readerly Readers in Teaching Biblical Studies," *Dialog* 53 (2014): 293–303.
3. See Mary Ann Tolbert, "Writing History, Writing Culture, Writing Ourselves: Issues in Contemporary Biblical Interpretation," in Lozada and Carey, *Soundings in Cultural Criticism*, 17–30.

tion. Historical narratives require selection and emplotment. That is to say, even the most "factual" account requires an author to select some details as essential while leaving out others. It would be impossible to include everything. And for a story to make sense, its authors must construct a plot, a meaningful way of sequencing and building relationships among events. Every story could be told differently.

To take one example, the books of Samuel and Kings tell very different stories of David than does 1 Chronicles. In Samuel, David's interactions with his predecessor, Saul, contribute vital information for our impression of David's character. But Saul plays only a cameo role in Chronicles. After lengthy genealogies and a brief reference to Saul, the real story of Chronicles begins with David. The overall plot focuses upon Israel's decline and downfall from the glory that attended David's reign until the exile.

Thus, Saul is not particularly important to Chronicles' account. Before we encounter him, the Chronicler informs readers concerning the general plot line of the story: "Judah was taken into exile in Babylon because of their unfaithfulness" (1 Chr 9:1). All we really need to know about Saul is his death, briefly narrated in 1 Chronicles 10. Having established that "Saul died for his unfaithfulness" (10:13), the Chronicler proceeds to David's career as king.

If Saul is not important for Chronicles, neither are David's formative years. For example, we derive the impression of David as an instrumental musician from Samuel, not Chronicles. While Chronicles does associate the adult David with appointing musicians and perhaps composing lyrics (1 Chr 16:7–37; 25:1–31), it does not portray him as an instrumental musician.[4] Chronicles also omits any reference to David's misdeeds, especially his rape of Bathsheba and the murder of her husband, and to the chaos that consumed David's household after that point. Absalom's rebellion never occurs. Thus, not only does Chronicles select different material than does Samuel; it creates a very different plot with different points of tension. Taken as stories, the Samuel–Kings narrative and the Chronicles resemble historical fictions placed in almost identical settings and populated by many (but not all) of the same characters. Chronicles' David is a very different person—or *literary character*—than the David of Samuel and Kings.

---

4. Contrast this discussion with Philip R. Davies, *Scribes and Schools: The Canonization of the Hebrew Scriptures*, Library of Ancient Israel (Louisville: Westminster John Knox, 1998), 126–28.

The David accounts demonstrate how narrative requires selection, emplotment, and the building of characters. Skilled readers also know how to find significance in settings in place and time, as for example in the stories of Nicodemus and the Samaritan woman in John 3 and 4. These two stories occur very close together, and they draw upon a host of literary techniques. They juxtapose two characters, one of whom apparently departs baffled while the other becomes (it seems) a model disciple.[5] Both stories employ ambiguity, irony, and suspense: Jesus says things that can be understood in multiple ways, leading readers to speculate as to what he means, to judge the characters' understanding of Jesus, and to wonder how things will turn out. And both stories feature commentary by the narrator, the storytelling voice who informs us that Nicodemus is "a leader of the Jews" (3:1) and that Jews have nothing to do with Samaritans (4:9).

The literary settings of these stories, particularly that of the Samaritan woman, have drawn much discussion. Nicodemus comes to Jesus at night, and he apparently leaves the conversation "in the dark." In John's Gospel, light stands as a metaphor for revelation and understanding, darkness for resistance and confusion. Indeed, after Jesus concludes his conversation with Nicodemus, he or the narrator informs us that evildoers prefer the darkness over the light (3:19–20). This detail leads many commentators to conclude that Nicodemus just doesn't get it—at least not at this point in the story.

In contrast, the Samaritan woman encounters Jesus out in the open and at the middle of the day. Many commentators have understood this detail to reflect her tragic situation as either a misfit, a social loser, or a sinner. She has had, after all, five men or husbands (4:18). Indeed, the scene creates a bit of literary suspense: Are Jesus and the Samaritan flirting? The Bible includes several stories in which a protagonist encounters a woman in a foreign land: in every case, the meeting leads to a wedding.[6] In this light the back-and-forth dialogue between Jesus and the woman, leading to her declaration "I have no husband," invites inquiring minds to spin. Starting with assumptions about the woman, her sexual history, and her desires, and adding the detail that Mediter-

---

5. Endless are the scholarly debates concerning these two characters. I recommend the discussion by Susan E. Hylen, *Imperfect Believers: Ambiguous Characters in the Gospel of John* (Louisville: Westminster John Knox, 2009), 23–58, with extensive bibliography.
6. As noted by Alter, *Art of Biblical Narrative*, 47–62.

ranean women tend to draw water in the cool of the morning and the evening, many commentators have speculated that the Samaritan approaches the well at noon in order to avoid the crowd's prying eyes. As one interpreter puts it, "Her experiences with five husbands probably generated no small amount of gossip in a small village!"[7]

But what if the Samaritan woman comes to the well at noon not because of shame but for a literary purpose? What if she comes at noon "because" Nicodemus came at night? As many feminist commentators point out, the assumption that her noon appearance reflects her social alienation emerges from the imaginations of male interpreters who see her as a loser or a transgressor. A literary approach might work differently. In the words of Susan E. Hylen, "Just as 'night' may signal to the reader that Nicodemus will not entirely understand Jesus, so 'noon' may indicate that the woman will become one who 'walks in the light.'"[8] In this case a literary reading makes all the difference. Rather than speculating as to the characters' social histories and psychological motives, we may ask what literary purposes are served by the spatial and temporal settings in which these characters encounter Jesus. We'll likely never know how much history stands behind the stories of Nicodemus and the Samaritan woman, but we can benefit by attending to the literary techniques that link those accounts.

TREASURES OLD AND NEW

Jews and Christians have recognized the Bible's literary nature throughout their history, but the emphasis given to this dimension has waxed and waned.

As long as people have sung, recited, or performed, we have also debated the merit and significance of literary works.[9] In Western thought literary theory goes back all the way to the Greeks and Romans, including figures as significant as Plato and Aristotle. However, for most of Western history, literary theory has emphasized two questions: What is the *nature* of literature, and what should *authors* do? Following more contemporary literary theory, literary approaches to biblical interpretation tend to stress another question: how *readers*

---

7. Mark F. Whitters, "Discipleship in John: Four Profiles," *Word & World* 18 (1998): 424.
8. Hylen, Imperfect Believers, 43.
9. George A. Kennedy, *The Cambridge History of Literary Criticism*, vol. 1: *Classical Criticism* (Cambridge: Cambridge University Press, 1989), ix.

should read. This distinction oversimplifies things, but it does assist us in coming to terms with literary interpretation of the Bible today.

The ancient Greek poet Hesiod describes the Muses, daughters of Zeus, revealing the nature of poetic inspiration: "We know how to tell many lies that resemble the truth, but we also know how to tell the truth when we wish" (*Theogony* 1.27–28).[10] This question, the relationship between poetry and truth, occupies Plato's thought in sections of the *Republic*. Plato's attempt to examine the very nature of literature and to assess its value marks a turn from pre-Socratic criticism that tends to praise and blame particular performances.[11] Plato asked, Does poetry, or literature more generally, reflect the truth? Likewise, does poetry improve humankind? Plato held poetry in low esteem, regarding it as a kind of possession by the Muse that has nothing to do with reason. Even Homer and Hesiod, the great luminaries of Greek literature, composed falsehoods in Plato's view. From his ideal republic Plato excludes poetry and fiction because they distract from reality. Plato's disciple Aristotle, however, devoted a volume to analyzing poetry and instructing authors in composition. In his mind, poetry imitated reality by describing things as they typically are rather than in their particulars.[12]

Ancient Bible readers were less inclined to assess biblical texts in terms of their relative merit. They tended to do so only when defending the Bible against its critics. Philo, whose life overlapped with both Jesus and Paul, defended the laws of Moses in a cultural environment particularly hostile to Jews in Alexandria, among other things claiming Moses as the greatest of lawgivers and the source of Greek wisdom (*Life of Moses* 2.12–13). Not only was Moses the most perfect man ever to live (*Life of Moses* 1.1); even those who translated his work into Greek were prophets and priests who shared Moses's spirit (*Life of Moses* 2.40).[13]

---

10. In D. A. Russell and M. Winterbottom, *Ancient Literary Criticism: The Principal Texts in New Translations* (New York: Oxford University Press, 1972), 3.
11. Andrew Ford, *The Origins of Criticism: Literary Culture and Poetic Theory in Classical Greece* (Princeton: Princeton University Press, 2002), 19–22.
12. See the classic discussion by Robert Scholes and Robert Kellogg, *The Nature of Narrative* (New York: Oxford University Press, 1966), 117–21.
13. Quoted by Michael Satlow, *How the Bible Became Holy* (New Haven: Yale University Press, 2014), 153. See the treatment of Philo in Peder Borgen, "Philo of Alexandria," in *Jewish Writings in the Second Temple Period*, ed. Michael E. Stone, CRINT 2/2

Early Christian authors also defended the Bible's excellence against outside opposition, as Origen (ca. 185–234 CE) challenges his opponent Celsus to compare the ethical system of Moses to those of other ancient philosophers (*Against Celsus* 1.18). Otherwise, figures such as Philo, Origen, and Augustine moved away from the general tendencies to praise or blame biblical material, on the one hand, and to prescribe how literature should be composed, on the other, to assist people who sought to read the Bible faithfully.

Sometimes these ancient interpreters downplayed the literary dimensions of biblical narrative in favor of allegorical interpretation. A common method of reading in the ancient world, allegorical interpretation transposes characters, events, and literary techniques into spiritual meanings. Ancient Jews and Christians hardly invented allegory, but they did practice this kind of interpretation, as Paul famously does in Galatians 4:21–31. Philo called for both literal attention to the laws of Moses and sensitivity to their spiritual significance (*On the Migration of Abraham* 89–93). Origen, who in one instance argued that the Bible can be defended in literal terms (*Against Celsus* 4.45), also acknowledges that some passages make no literal sense at all and require moral and spiritual interpretations (*On First Principles* 4.12). In his view, over-literal reading lay at the heart of all scriptural misunderstanding (4.9). Augustine (354–430 CE), perhaps the most influential Christian thinker outside the canon, recalled being unimpressed by the Bible's literary artistry prior to his conversion (*Confessions* 3.5).[14] Augustine shared with Origen the sense that only a figural interpretation could make sense of some thorny passages (*Doctr. chr.* 3.17).[15] In the end, he counsels, interpreters must employ every available intellectual resource, but most importantly, they should pray for understanding (3.56).

With some notable exceptions, allegorical reading dominated Christian interpretation through the medieval period. Medieval rhetorical handbooks turned to the Bible for examples of literary artistry, but what we might today call literary interpretation had to wait a very long

---

(Philadephia: Fortress, 1984), 233–82; and Borgen, "Philo of Alexandria as Exegete," in Hauser and Watson, *History of Biblical Interpretation*, 1:114–43.
14. Cited in Richard A. Norris Jr., "Augustine and the Close of the Ancient Period," in Hauser and Watson, *History of Biblical Interpretation*, 1:382.
15. Norris, "Augustine and the Close," 391.

time.[16] Although Protestant Reformers like Martin Luther and John Calvin reemphasized the "plain meaning" of texts, attention to the artistic dimensions of biblical narrative and poetry remained largely dormant until the twentieth century.

Perhaps this neglect resulted in part from the polemical use of the Bible among competing Christian communions. Perhaps it reflects the fascination with history that marked the Enlightenment and created the context for biblical studies to emerge as an academic discipline. And perhaps "literary criticism" could not emerge in biblical studies until it had taken shape in academic departments of literature. By many accounts, modern literary criticism, focused upon the act of interpretation rather than assigning standards for literary excellence, emerged in the 1930s. We might locate this development within a larger cultural shift toward literature as an independent form of art, which creates an autonomous field of value and signification.[17] This point may at first seem tangential, but its significance will become clear quite soon. In any case, biblical literary scholarship as a recognizable movement began to take shape in the 1960s.

The trend received a strong assist from secular literary critics who, having recognized the Bible's influence on literature throughout history, began to examine biblical stories in concert with other ancient narratives. Erich Auerbach famously read the "binding of Isaac" story from Genesis 22 over against the *Odyssey*, and Mark's account of Peter's denial in conversation with passages from Petronius and Tacitus.[18] Moving to more modern parallels, Frank Kermode juxtaposed a parable in Kafka with biblical parables, and an obscure character from James Joyce's *Ulysses* with the young man who flees from Jesus's arrest naked, among other case studies.[19] One breakthrough moment occurred when Robert Alter, a professor of comparative literature, scolded biblical scholars for their failure to recognize the artistry of Hebrew narrative and poetry. Alter modeled his approach in a series of case studies, call-

16. E.g., George A. Kennedy, *Classical Rhetoric and Its Christian and Secular Tradition from Ancient to Modern Times* (Chapel Hill: University of North Carolina Press, 1980), 192.

17. Catherine Gallagher, "The History of Literary Criticism," *Daedalus* 126 (1997): 133–53.

18. Erich Auerbach, *Mimesis: The Literary Representation of Reality in Western Literature*, trans. Willard R. Trask (Princeton: Princeton University Press, 1953 [1946]), 3–49.

19. Frank Kermode, *The Genesis of Secrecy: On the Interpretation of Narrative* (Cambridge, MA: Harvard University Press, 1979), 23–73.

ing attention to features such as the strategic use of repetition and variation in Hebrew narrative and of emotional intensification in biblical poetry.[20] Alter's work provided a template for literary-sensitive reading among biblical scholars, one that omits or at least deemphasizes historical reconstruction.

Literary interpretation touched a sensitive nerve in theological circles—ironically, in opposed ways. As I suggested in the previous chapter, some critics have argued that historical criticism so dissects the Bible as to drain the life from it. Many readers welcomed a renewed appreciation of biblical poetry and storytelling, celebrating the power of artistry to shape consciousness.[21] A move toward literary and metaphorical theology rather than abstract speculation proved congenial to literary modes of biblical interpretation.[22] Moreover, in some theologically conservative circles, literary interpretation allowed readers to dodge difficult questions related to the historical development and accuracy of biblical accounts. Indeed, a counter-reaction among theological conservatives insists upon the necessity for historical reasoning in biblical interpretation. As one evangelical scholar puts it, "the Bible has been cast adrift from its [historical] moorings and left to float on a sea of modern relativity."[23] Although many readers pursue literary interpretation for its own interest and pleasure, for others the question raises significant theological stakes.

READING IN A LITERARY MODE

Literary reading of the Bible proliferated in the 1980s and continues in varied forms today. It initially drew heavily from a major movement in American literary scholarship, the "New Criticism." The New Criticism regarded stories and poems as self-contained icons. One might regard

---

20. Alter, *Art of Biblical Narrative*; and *Art of Biblical Poetry*.
21. A critical work in this movement is Hans Frei, *The Eclipse of Biblical Narrative: A Study in Eighteenth and Nineteenth Century Hermeneutics* (New Haven: Yale University Press, 1974).
22. See the collected essays in Stanley Hauerwas and L. Gregory Jones, eds., *Why Narrative? Readings in Narrative Theology* (Grand Rapids: Eerdmans, 1989); and Sallie McFague, *Speaking in Parables: A Study in Metaphor and Theology* (Philadelphia: Fortress, 1975).
23. Grant R. Osborne, *The Hermeneutical Spiral: A Comprehensive Introduction to Biblical Interpretation* (Downers Grove, IL: InterVarsity, 1991), 164.

a poem as a "well wrought urn," an object to be appreciated on its own merits.[24] External considerations such as a poem's historical context, the material conditions of its production, and even its author's biography and intentions are all set aside. For biblical interpreters, authorial intent posed a crucial problem. Biblical scholarship had long insisted upon identifying ancient authors' aims as a primary goal. The New Criticism rejected the possibility, even the desirability, of judging a work according to its author's intent. Even if we could interview the author, New Critics insisted, his or her work stands on its own. Likewise, New Critics rejected the desirability of guessing a text's impact upon its readers, another common move among biblical interpreters. ("Imagine the surprise in Corinth upon receiving Paul's letter.") The New Criticism's rejection of both the "intentional fallacy" and the "affective fallacy" pressed biblical interpreters to read in a new mode.

We can scarcely overestimate the New Criticism's influence upon Bible readers. For one thing, it democratizes biblical interpretation. Some of us may read more sensitively than others, but we all know how to appreciate a story or a poem. We need no specialized training to do so. We might have some friends who are more clever than we are. As we walk out of the theater their comments may include some detail or sophistication that lies beyond us. We might even argue with them over the details. But we need no specialized knowledge to join the conversation. With no special training, interpreters throughout the centuries have called attention to the weighty suspense and delicious irony that enliven the story of David taking (raping) Bathsheba and then being rebuked by the prophet Nathan: "*You* are the man!" (2 Sam 12:7).

For many, however, literary interpretation challenges familiar reading habits. Many readers, especially churchly ones, are used to reading the Bible in small units like individual verses or small passages. Churches and synagogues alike tend to read the Bible one passage at a time in worship. But narrative criticism emphasizes treating each biblical book as a literary whole (with the usual exception of the Psalms). Narrative criticism always takes the larger view: even if we're focusing upon a particular scene from, say, Genesis, we keep in mind its relationship to the entire story. When Laban tricks Jacob into marrying *both* his daughters, we remember that Jacob has it coming: he's been tricking

---

24. Appropriating the title of a classic work of New Criticism, Cleanth Brooks, *The Well Wrought Urn: Studies in the Structure of Poetry* (San Diego: Harcourt, Brace, 1947).

other people all along. He even tricks Laban again in retaliation. In bargaining for a reward for his labor, Jacob offers to take the striped and spotted goats from Laban's flock. They divide the goats, but Jacob continues to supervise Laban's flocks. Jacob then places striped sticks at the watering troughs visited by Laban's healthier goats during mating season, somehow resulting in Jacob acquiring even more striped and spotted goats—and the healthier ones to boot (30:25–43). (Don't bother to ask a biologist.) The motif of trickery shapes Jacob's entire story.

To be sure, it did not require narrative critics to discover the pattern of trickery in Jacob's story. Nor did it require professional biblical scholars. A long preaching tradition, especially in black churches, involves preachers summarizing the biblical story before arriving at the specific passage they will discuss. But narrative interpreters have also offered compelling fresh interpretations on many occasions. For our purposes at the moment, literary interpretation requires readers to take account of much larger contexts than they may have been accustomed to. Literary readers are always asking how one part of a story or poem relates to a larger whole.

Literary interpretation also challenges other conventional approaches by moving away from abstract ideas to the things of art: design, tone, and effect. A great deal of biblical interpretation inside both the church and the academy has focused upon the Bible's implications for doctrine or ethics. What does the Bible have to say about salvation? What theological beliefs did the apostle Paul express? Does the Bible offer a coherent teaching on what happens after we die?[25] Along with historical questions, such doctrinal investigations once dominated biblical studies. One problem with such idea-based interpretation is that it usually imposes *our* categories—whether they come from the Christian doctrinal development or from more contemporary concerns—onto ancient biblical texts that may not have shared just those concerns.

Similar problems arise when we scrutinize the Bible to answer our contemporary ethical questions. Ancient Jews and Christians certainly had morals, ways of valuing and behaving that were affirmed by their communities. But that is not the same as saying they were asking the

---

25. On salvation: Joel B. Green, *Salvation*, Understanding Biblical Themes (Nashville; Abingdon, 2003); on Paul's theology, in 808 pages, James D. G. Dunn, *The Theology of Paul the Apostle* (Grand Rapids: Eerdmans, 1998); on the afterlife, Jaime Clark-Soles, *Death and the Afterlife in the New Testament* (New York: T&T Clark, 2006).

same ethical questions we do. The past thirty years, for example, have featured endless attempts to apply the Bible to contemporary sexual ethics. But when it comes to sexuality, the biblical world would shock a modern visitor from the post-industrialized West. As we have seen, both biblical authors and modern readers share a general concept called adultery. But biblical adultery is defined in terms of women's marital status, not men's. Biblical adultery involves a married woman having sexual relations with a man other than her husband. In contrast, modern people judge adultery upon the marital status of either or both sexual partners. In the modern world a married man can commit adultery through intimate relations with a single woman. Not so in the biblical world.[26] The point is not that contemporary readers, especially Jewish and Christian ones, should avoid posing ethical questions of the Bible. It is simply to illustrate that doing so usually involves asking questions that biblical authors might not have considered—or might have conceived of very differently.

Narrative interpretation often sets aside those theological and ethical categories in favor of literary ones. The rules of modern literature differ significantly from ancient literary conventions. Most obviously, ancient texts were written to be "read" more with the ears than with the eyes. Literacy rates were quite low, with perhaps only 3 percent of the population able to read Genesis, a Psalm, or Luke. So texts were read *aloud* to their audiences. Even individual readers read aloud to themselves, however quietly. Doing so was necessary because ancient Hebrew, Greek, and Latin manuscripts lacked markers such as spaces between words and punctuation marks: How else could someone read an ancient text other than by sounding it out? Paul Achtemeier may have overstated the case, but only slightly, when he said that in the Greco-Roman world "*no* writing occurred that was not vocalized."[27] Thus Cyril of Jerusalem admonished women to read and pray "so that their lips may speak,

---

26. According to William Loader, adultery was understood as "wrong because it infringed upon the rights of another man." We do encounter exceptions to this rule, according to which an adulterous man also harms his own wife: *The New Testament on Sexuality*, 4, 5. For a brief treatment of biblical adultery, see Mary E. Shields, "Adultery," *NIDB* 1.57.

27. Paul Achtemeier, "*Omne verbum sonat:* The New Testament and the Oral Environment of Late Western Antiquity," *JBL* 109 (1990): 15. For a slight revision of Achtemeier's proposal, see Frank D. Gilliard, "More Silent Reading in Antiquity: *Non omne verbum sonabat*," *JBL* 112 (1993): 689–94.

but others may not hear" (*Catechetical Lectures* 1.14).[28] Not much later, Augustine famously marvels at the intelligence of his mentor Ambrose, who could read without moving his lips (*Confessions* 6.3)![29]

The experience of hearing a story, even one read aloud to oneself, is quite different than that of reading it only with the eyes. Hearing (or aural) audiences can easily become confused or distracted. Performances for the ear, therefore, place markers to keep the audience oriented and (hopefully) alert.[30] We are all familiar with speakers who enumerate their points: *first, second,* and *third*. Biblical storytellers do so as well, as when Genesis counts the days of creation (1:1–2:4a), when Luke reminds us that Pilate has judged Jesus innocent three times (23:22), and when John counts the first and second of Jesus's seven miraculous signs (2:11; 4:54). Patterns of repetition and contrast work especially well for aural audiences. Feeling threatened in foreign lands, Abraham twice passes off Sarah as his sister. Historical critics interpret this repetition as proof for the Documentary Hypothesis, one of many occasions in which we encounter multiple accounts of the same basic tale from the diverse literary sources that comprise the Torah. From a literary point of view, however, we might interpret this repetition in terms of Abraham's character: it is far from clear that the patriarch learns or grows as time progresses.

From a literary perspective, Abraham is just that: a character who develops as the story proceeds. He is not a moral exemplar, not a model of covenant or election, nor necessarily a clue to Israel's conception of its own geographic origins, as historical, critical, and doctrinal readers might conclude. His relationship with God is significant, understanding that God, too, functions as a literary character in Genesis. The most influential story related to Abraham may be the *Aqedah*, the binding of Isaac in Genesis 22. There God commands Abraham to sacrifice Isaac, "your only son, whom you love." Abraham simply does as he is told; we never hear of his reaction. He saddles up the donkey with chopped wood and takes along Isaac and two other young men. Dialogue is short.

28. *The Catechetical Lectures of S. Cyril, Archbishop of Jerusalem*, ed. John Henry Newman (Oxford: J. H. Parker, 1839). Cyril is cited and translated in Michael Slusser, "Reading Silently in Antiquity," *JBL* 111 (1992): 499.

29. Cited in Achtemeier, "*Omne verbum sonat*," 16–17.

30. Mary Ann Tolbert, *Sowing the Gospel: Mark's World in Literary-Historical Perspective* (Minneapolis: Fortress, 1989), esp. 43–47.

As Abraham and his son walk on alone to the place of sacrifice, Isaac calls out, "My father" (my translation). Abraham's reply echoes his reply to God in 22:1: "Here I am, my son."

"My father" and "Here I am, my son," intensify the drama of the story by reminding us that Isaac is Abraham's only son.

Isaac inquires, "The fire and the wood are here, but where is the lamb for a burnt offering?" (22:7).

Abraham replies: "God himself will provide the lamb for a burnt offering, my son" (22:8).

Again we are reminded of Isaac's identity.

God has promised Abraham that he will bring forth a great nation (12:3; 17:6). Isaac is his only son, the only living link to that promise. Yet Abraham binds Isaac and prepares to slaughter him. We see that Abraham is willing to follow through on God's grisly command. Readers might intuit his emotions. We might assume all kinds of feelings and even thoughts. We are prone to theologize the moment and attribute to Abraham faith or doubt. As a literary character, however, Abraham does directly what he is commanded, but he barely speaks. His promise that God will provide a lamb for the offering suggests faith, yet Abraham follows through in preparing to kill Isaac. Only when God intervenes, saying, "Now I know that you fear God" (22:12), does the story begin to interpret Abraham's character: he fears God. To read Abraham without reading "into" him our values and preoccupations requires enormous discipline.

To focus on the story does not require that we shut off our theological imaginations. But narrative interpretation can change the ways we read. By whatever name, God is the only character who remains present throughout Genesis. The Documentary Hypothesis teaches us to expect differing portrayals from J, E, and P. Narrative criticism generally ignores such source-critical considerations, but the diverse portrayals of God among these literary threads confront us with a question that runs throughout the Bible. It includes diverse, sometimes conflicting, interpretations of God. Put another way, within the Bible the deity appears as several distinct literary characters. What are we to say about God as a literary character in the *Aqedah*?

Theologically inclined readers routinely struggle with the portrayal of God in Genesis 22. The story begins by informing us of God's immediate motive: "God tested Abraham" (22:1). Christian readers immediately recall the testing of Jesus in the Synoptic Gospels, and indeed

Greek versions of Genesis employ the same verb that the Gospels do. The Hebrew verb *nasah* can be understood in non-troubling ways. Testing can amount to simple assessment, or it may refer to intentional training as in Exodus 20:20: "Moses said to the people: 'Do not be afraid; for God has come only to test you and to put the fear of him upon you so that you do not sin.'"

As the story develops, the first explanation gains weight. Only after Abraham truly puts Isaac's life on the line does the angel say, "Now I know that you fear God" (22:12). So we have a God who seems somewhat fickle, even cruel—a God who makes great promises to Abraham then threatens to destroy them. Moreover, this God is not quite omniscient, needing reassurance of Abraham's fidelity. A narrative reader might appeal to larger patterns of God's consistency in Genesis, but this scene undermines such theologically conventional readings.

Among theological commentators on the Hebrew Bible, Walter Brueggemann may be the most influential of his generation. He recognizes the challenge of Abraham's sacrifice and the "aversion immediately felt for a God who will command the murder of a son." In a sense, however, Brueggemann refuses to pass a final judgment on the story, describing it as "not a tale of origins, but a story of anguished faith."[31] The story seems to contradict itself by depicting God both testing Abraham and offering provision for the test.[32] In the end, Brueggemann escapes the world of the story by turning to the crucifixion (testing) and resurrection (provision) of Jesus as a model that demonstrates the mystery and the dialectic of God's ways with mortals.[33]

Brueggemann's example shows us that literary analysis of a story like the *Aqedah* may not provide the kind of theological consistency many readers desire. Brueggemann cannot make theological sense out of Genesis without layering another narrative, the story of Jesus, on top of it. But suppose we were reading another story with a human character, "Fred," who behaves as God does toward Abraham and Isaac. Fred makes and repeats promises to Abraham and protects him from time to time, but Fred delays in fulfilling those promises. When hope arrives, Fred tests Abraham to see if he *really* believes—and tests Abraham in a most severe way. The test places poor Isaac in a horrible situation:

---

31. Walter Brueggemann, *Genesis*. Interpretation (Atlanta: John Knox, 1982), 185.
32. Brueggemann, *Genesis*, 188–92.
33. Brueggemann, *Genesis*, 192–94.

Isaac will always know that his father was prepared to kill him. The poet Jaha Zainabu imagines asking Isaac, "Did you flinch for years after, every time he called you son?"[34] Now satisfied, Fred calls off the whole experiment, sending Abraham and Isaac home for lives that must be defined as "before" and "after" this grisly test. Indeed, many commentators have noted Isaac's relative passivity as an adult in comparison with Abraham and Jacob.[35] Abraham's wife Sarah dies almost immediately (23:1–2), and Abraham negotiates her burial plot and arranges a marriage for Isaac, but Abraham is essentially done as a major player in the story. Readers would indeed acknowledge the contradictions in Fred's character, but we would not need to resolve them into a consistent, likable Fred. Most of us know a few individuals so conflicted. The literary analysis would then move on to the effects of Fred's character upon the rest of the narrative.

Narrative interpretation can stretch conventional religious ways of reading, such as the compulsion to justify God's behavior with respect to the binding of Isaac. It can also challenge familiar interpretations that smooth over rough parts in the biblical narrative. For example, Matthew and Mark relate a scene in which Jesus refuses to heal a Gentile woman's daughter by saying, "It is not fair to take the children's food and throw it to the dogs" (Mark 7:27; Matt 15:26). Many readers reasonably infer that Jesus has just insulted this woman by calling her and her daughter dogs. I've also encountered many readers who rationalize Jesus's behavior. Surely Jesus would not have been so cruel, they reason. He was just "testing the woman's faith."

I'm not sure what it means to test a person's faith. We've just encountered one such story involving Abraham and Isaac. In Matthew the Holy Spirit sends Jesus into the wilderness to face temptation from the devil, but we do not know exactly why (4:1). From a literary point of view, however, nothing in the story suggests that Jesus's insult functioned as a test. In Matthew, but not Mark, he does congratulate the woman for her faith (15:28), but the text says nothing about a test. The "testing her faith" interpretation injects an element foreign to the story in order to remove its potential offense.

Every story has what literary critics call "gaps"—unexplained ele-

---

34. Jaha Zainabu, "Dear Isaac," April 6, 2013, https://www.youtube.com/watch?v=eftmI_m6sRc.
35. Mark McEntire, *Portraits of an Immature God* (Minneapolis: Fortress, 2013), 56.

ments that invite a measure of curiosity on the part of the reader. Throughout history Jewish and Christian readers have ingeniously filled in those gaps with other material, sometimes consciously and often less so. Ancient Jewish interpreters sought to explain why God would seek to kill Moses in Exodus 4:24–26—and how Zipporah could convince God otherwise. It must have been an angel rather than God, many reasoned. Contemporary interpreters scarcely do better.[36]

Some literary characters invite curiosity to a degree readers simply can't resist. The Gospels mention a Mary Magdalene who visits Jesus's empty tomb. In John's Gospel she is the first person to encounter the risen Jesus. Among the Gospels only Luke adds the detail that Mary was a key supporter of Jesus's ministry and that Jesus had exorcised seven demons from her (8:1–3). In the popular imagination, however, Mary's story grows. Many people assume Mary was a former prostitute—the Gospels never say that—and a legend has circulated that Jesus and Mary were lovers, perhaps even married. As someone who speaks in churches and other public settings, even bars on occasion, I'm often asked what's up with the Jesus-Mary hookup.

It's not difficult to explain how Christians turned Mary into a prostitute, although the transition to Jesus's lover requires more of a stretch. Luke's reference to Mary and other significant women occurs immediately after the story of Jesus's encounter with a sinful woman (7:36–50). The woman, identified as a sinner three times within the story—"her sins ... were many," Jesus says (7:47)—anoints Jesus's feet with ointment and dries them with her hair. Countless interpreters have judged her behavior as that of a prostitute. One colleague, a gay man no less, remarked of her action, "I don't care who you are; that's sexy." Evocative as it is, the scene led many Christian readers, who for centuries were generally celibate clergy, to regard the sinful woman of Luke 7 as a prostitute and then identify her with formerly possessed Mary of Luke 8.

As an expression of the New Criticism in literary studies, narrative criticism requires readers to discipline themselves. They are to withhold judgment regarding gaps in the stories. Rather than figure out who is the naked young man of Mark 14:51–52 or divine the identity of John's "beloved disciple," "virtuous" readers refrain from speculation, allowing the story to provide its own information and no more. This

---

36. James L. Kugel, *The Bible as It Was* (Cambridge, MA: Belknap/Harvard, 1997), 305–6.

requirement is controversial, as we shall see, but it can also prove highly productive. At a minimum, it encourages a peculiar humility in readers who allow stories to keep their secrets.

Narrative interpretation may rein in speculation, but it has also generated helpful insights. By attempting a literary interpretation of Mark's Christology, or interpretation of Jesus, Elizabeth Struthers Malbon offers one particularly ambitious example.[37] Mark's understanding of Jesus has long vexed interpreters. Mark introduces Jesus as the Messiah (1:1),[38] and heavenly voices declare him God's Son (1:11; 9:7), a confession apparently shared by a centurion at the moment of Jesus's death (15:39). But Jesus never refers to himself as Son of God or as Messiah, nor does he even acknowledge others who do. When Peter identifies Jesus as the Messiah (8:29), Jesus turns the conversation to one about the Son of Man, who will suffer humiliation and death prior to his resurrection. Peter, for one, perceives a conflict between his confession of Jesus as Messiah and Jesus's own saying regarding the Son of Man and rebukes Jesus for getting things wrong. In turn, Jesus rebukes Peter (8:31–33). How can it be that Mark's Gospel identifies Jesus as Messiah and Son of God, but Jesus himself (as a character within the story) rejects both labels and refers to himself as Son of Man? That question hounds Markan interpreters to this day.

Messiah, *Son of God*, and *Son of Man*: these "titles," as they have come to be known, have often defined the conversation concerning Mark's Christology. Scholars have sought to understand what these terms meant in their historical contexts. They have asked how Mark uses these titles, which almost surely varies from our other ancient sources. (Prior to Jesus, no ancient source links suffering to the concept of a messiah.) And they have sought to understand how these key concepts relate to one another within Mark's Gospel. It's easy to understand why interpreters would focus upon these titles and their relationships: they occur at critical moments in Mark's story, including the very first verse, at Jesus's baptism, at the first reference to Jesus's death and resurrection, during Jesus's trial, and at the very moment of his death.

Because she focuses on Mark as a *story*, Malbon gives the titles a rel-

---

37. Elizabeth Struthers Malbon, *Mark's Jesus: Characterization as Narrative Christology* (Waco, TX: Baylor University Press, 2009).
38. Some manuscripts of Mark identify Jesus as God's Son from the very beginning (1:1), but significant manuscripts do not.

ative demotion. She regards titles as abstract concepts, which only take meaning in the flow of Mark's story, in the give-and-take among characters and their actions. Mark's Christology is attached to a literary character: Jesus, as he is presented within the narrative and as he interacts with other characters. Borrowing from another scholar, Robert Tannehill, Malbon seeks Mark's "narrative christology." In the end, Malbon argues that Jesus's *identity* and *essence*—what is a Messiah or Christ, after all?—are less important than his *influence*. Despite the narrator's proclamation of "Jesus Christ, the Son of God," Mark's Jesus deflects the focus away from himself and toward the kingdom of God. Jesus "proclaims and participates in the in-breaking of the kingdom of God" by bringing healing to those who need it, serving the most lowly, and even risking his own life for this vision of God's will.[39] Fundamentally, Mark's Jesus provokes people into active engagement with the mystery of God. Only in the responses of "fallible" characters, like the disciples, and in a couple of exemplary characters whom Jesus heals does Mark reveal what it means for Jesus to be the Christ.

ENTER THE READER: MAP VS. GPS

While the New Criticism focused upon a story's internal components like plot, character development, setting, and modes of narration, it largely set aside the experiences of readers. Literary approaches that emphasize a text's effect upon its readers, actual or imaginary, fall under the umbrella of reader-response criticism.

The New Criticism came over to biblical criticism from university literary departments. Other modes of literary scholarship were already flourishing, but the New Criticism shaped the most influential early ventures into literary interpretation. The New Criticism's insistence upon the text as a world unto itself excluded any attempt to assess the actual or potential reactions of readers, what critics called "the affective fallacy." Readers experience literary works *in time*, not as static representations. We encounter anticipation and redundancy, suspense and surprise. The New Criticism, and narrative approaches to biblical interpretation, treat texts as JPEG rather than MPEG files. They tend to freeze the story into a snapshot to the neglect of readers' experiences.

Following literary theorist Seymour Chatman, narrative critics locate the reader as a factor *within* the text rather than as an actor beyond it.

---

39. Malbon, *Mark's Jesus*, 55, 215–17.

A common model analyzes levels of discourse within biblical stories.[40] On the one hand, actual authors communicate through stories with actual readers. But those real readers have no access to the real authors apart from the story. The story itself "suggests" an implied author, the sort of person whose point of view comes through in the work. At a secondary level of discourse the story creates an implied reader, the imaginary reader who is capable of following the story from beginning to end. This implied reader knows only what the story reveals—and what is required in order to understand it. For example, the implied reader of 1 and 2 Samuel knows Hebrew, along with the geography presupposed by the story. This point is critical: the implied reader is "real" only as a means of talking about the story. Embedded within this secondary level of discourse are other levels of discourse, in which narrators share the action with narratees. The primary narrator provides the speaking voice we encounter in, say, Esther or Acts, but other narrators speak within the stories too. Consider, for example, the poor soldier who informs David that Saul and Jonathan have died. According to this soldier—and we have no way of knowing whether or not to trust him—he killed Saul at the king's own request. We, the readers, hear the story through the primary narrator, but David (as a narratee) receives the report from the soldier (2 Sam 1:2–15). Thus, real authors create stories that suggest idealized, or "implied," authors. Those implied authors speak through various narrators who inform narratees concerning the story. Real readers encounter the stories indirectly, through the interaction between those implied authors and readers.

Fig. 3.1
Levels of Narration

---

40. Seymour Chatman, *Story and Discourse: Narrative Structure in Fiction and Film* (Ithaca, NY: Cornell University Press, 1978).

It's complicated, and we have generally avoided wading into the technicalities of this model. One key point, however, involves this ideal reader. Narrative criticism, following the New Criticism, tended to set the implied reader aside, but both secular literary students and, soon after, biblical scholars devoted increasing attention to this ideal reader. Might the implied reader's experience, albeit imaginary, lend insight to the work of interpretation? As Wolfgang Iser once proposed, it's precisely the implied reader's fictional status that makes the concept helpful.[41] Thus reader-response criticism was born.

Reader-response criticism comes in two basic flavors: implied readers and actual readers.[42] The first, grounded in the New Criticism, focuses upon the implied reader as a theoretical but useful construct. Fancy word alert: we might call the implied reader a "heuristic" construct, in that the implied reader exists only in our minds and our conversations but lends insight to the process of interpretation. The search for an *implied* reader naturally arouses our interest in *actual* readers: how individuals and groups respond to literary texts. We turn to those actual, flesh-and-blood readers, later. These two basic flavors, predictably, include a wide range of variations. We will follow a simple approach, adding nuance when necessary.

Literary critics have described the implied reader as an ideal reader; in fact, the terms sometimes function interchangeably. We identify this reader by asking what sort of reader is necessary for full appreciation of a literary text. Some of the requirements are immediately obvious: Daniel requires a reader who understands Hebrew and Aramaic and recognizes the places Babylon and Persia. (This ideal reader might or might not need to forget some historical details, since the story values historical accuracy lightly.) In contrast, an ideal reader does not need to know that "according to the law of the Medes and the Persians" (6:8) the king's edicts cannot be revoked. That may be a good thing, since no such custom actually existed among the Persians or the Medes.[43] Indeed, the story *implies* a reader who lacks this information; after all, why relate the custom otherwise? In other words, the implied reader

---

41. Wolfgang Iser, *The Act of Reading: A Theory of Aesthetic Response* (Baltimore: Johns Hopkins University Press, 1978), 29.
42. Iser already perceived these two ways of understanding readers: see *Act of Reading*, 27–30.
43. Carol A. Newsom, *Daniel*, OTL (Louisville: Westminster John Knox, 2014), 196.

must be familiar with a text's historical and cultural allusions—and willing to believe what the story claims regardless of its facticity. (We do this all the time when we read science fiction and fantasy literature.)

Nothing earth-shattering there: biblical critics have long reconstructed the audiences of biblical books by relying on precisely this kind of information. When Mark's Gospel explains Jewish customs—for example, how Pharisees "and all the Jews" thoroughly wash their hands before eating (7:3)—we reasonably conclude that Mark's audience includes Gentiles. After all, Jews already possess such information.

But reader-response criticism is not an exercise in historical investigation. It aims to imagine the effect of a piece of literature upon a plausible audience. Reader-oriented interpretation exercises its power by describing this process of reading over time.[44] The implied reader understands and remembers everything she sees and hears. In so doing, she acquires values and expectations. She learns which characters to trust and others to regard with suspicion. She notices when patterns are reinforced and when they're reversed. She reads sequentially.

I often compare our attention to sequential reading with the difference between using a paper road map, which I usually did until about 2007, with relying upon GPS navigation. Both processes have their advantages. Without question, today's GPS navigation is more helpful in getting us to our precise destinations than are old-fashioned maps. But the maps had their advantages. Whenever I moved to a new town, I'd look over a road map to get a sense of the bigger picture. Having learned the major roads and their directions, I could drive around town, intentionally getting myself lost from time to time because I knew that eventually I'd find one of those major roads. Yes, sometimes, I'd get *too* lost, and I'd have to pull out the road map. But over time, I'd largely grow independent of the map because I would form a mental picture of my environment. Drivers who only use GPS take longer to develop that big-picture perspective because the GPS only informs us of our very next turn.

But road maps also give us previews of our future destinations. GPS drivers experience the same sort of surprise we encounter when we read a short story or watch a movie. Bible readers often approach a nar-

---

44. Robert M. Fowler, *Let the Reader Understand: Reader-Response Criticism and the Gospel of Mark* (Minneapolis: Fortress, 1991), 1–58, a foundational example of reader-oriented biblical scholarship, outlines this theory base in detail.

rative already knowing the plot line. For that reason, we can struggle to appreciate the kinds of suspense and surprise a first-time reader might enjoy.

To take one example, imagine Mark's disciples when Jesus tells them:

> To you has been given the secret of the kingdom of God, but for those outside, everything comes in parables; in order that
> "they may indeed look, but not perceive,
> and may indeed listen, but not understand;
> so that they may not turn again and be forgiven." (Mark 4:11–12)

The implied reader now distinguishes between those insiders, the disciples, and the masses who fail to perceive and to understand.

But my, how things change. Jesus twice feeds massive crowds with just a few fish and loaves of bread (6:30–44; 8:1–10). Immediately after the second feeding miracle, the disciples misunderstand Jesus. When he tells them to "beware of the yeast of the Pharisees and the yeast of Herod," they think he's concerned that they haven't taken bread on their journey (8:15–16). The implied reader notes a lack of perception on the part of these supposed insiders. After two feeding miracles, they should know bread presents no challenge to Jesus. Jesus then drives the point home. In chapter 4 his description of "those outside" is quoted explicitly from Isaiah 6:9–10. Presumably, an ideal reader recognizes quotations and allusions from the Hebrew Scriptures. Now, rather than congratulating the disciples, Jesus scolds them using language from that same quotation.

> Do you still not perceive or understand? Are your hearts hardened? Do you have eyes, and fail to see? Do you have ears, and fail to hear? (Mark 8:17–18)

Who are the outsiders now?

This case study in reader-response interpretation relies entirely upon the sequential experience of reading. Its reader is generic, having no identifiable characteristics apart from those required of her by Mark's story. But the reader's early appreciation for the disciples, first formed in their remarkable response of following Jesus (2:13–17) and confirmed by Jesus's pointed praise (4:11–12), has been called into question from time to time. They've shown a lack of faith (4:40) and have failed to understand Jesus's first feeding miracle (6:52). Already challenged and even undermined, the implied reader's initial reaction is now under serious pressure—if it hasn't collapsed altogether.

But so what? How much do we care if the implied reader's estimation of the disciples is descending? To our abstract and anonymous reader, many interpreters add an element of interest: Mark's implied reader must be a believer. We receive a strong hint of this possibility at Mark 15:21. There a bystander is conscripted to carry Jesus's cross, and the narrator injects a direct comment to the reader: "It was Simon of Cyrene, the father of Alexander and Rufus." Our implied reader is somehow familiar with Alexander and Rufus. The simplest explanation is that these two men are known within early Christian circles.

With respect to the Bible, then, reader-response criticism carries religious freight. In one formative example of biblical reader-oriented reading, R. Alan Culpepper asserts:

> In John the ideal narrative audience adopts the narrator's ideological point of view, penetrates the misunderstandings, appreciates the irony, and is moved to fresh appreciations of transcendent mystery through the gospel's symbolism.... We can concentrate, therefore, on the gospel's definition of its authorial audience and the work of the contemporary reader in adopting the perspective of that audience.[45]

For Culpepper and many other interpreters, successful reading entails replicating the ideal reader's experience, "adopting" that reader's perspective. In this mode—and this is not the only possible way to pursue reader-focused interpretation—reading is sacramental. It provides a means of religious conversion.

Without question, authors imagine the audiences they address. Likewise, most of us would agree that individual texts require certain competencies on the part of their readers. At a minimum, a competent reader will understand the story's language and its historical and cultural allusions. In high school I loved Arthur Conan Doyle's Sherlock Holmes stories, and I found myself frustrated when details of Victorian culture escaped me. Studying Shakespeare in school certainly taught me how much I needed supplemental help. Imagine my shock when I took a course on William Faulkner, an author from my own part of the country who died only three years before I was born, and I found an author

---

45. R. Alan Culpepper, *Anatomy of the Fourth Gospel: A Study in Literary Design* (Philadelphia: Fortress, 1983), 208.

with a style so complex I could scarcely keep up! If stories imply their readers, or if they require ideal readers, we're asking a great deal.

Decades ago the literary theorist Terry Eagleton acknowledged that "a reader is already included within the very act of writing itself."[46] But he also observed that the kind of reader-response criticism we've been exploring inevitably turns back upon itself. Its logic is necessarily circular. We imagine an implied reader who helps us interpret a story—but the very act of constructing that ideal reader requires that we've already interpreted the text. In other words, we tend to imagine an implied reader who will read just as we are likely to read on our own. We craft an implied reader in our own image.

We observe this tendency in authors who tell us how the reader *should* respond to a text. Certain kinds of reader-response criticism rely upon submissive readers who do what (these interpreters say) the text requires of them. Let us return to Culpepper, whose work I greatly admire. Here Culpepper is describing opposition to Jesus in the Gospel of John.

> The reader is led to accept the evangelist's view of Jesus before the antithetical point of view is given more than passing reference. *It is hardly possible* after these chapters for the reader to be persuaded by another view of Jesus.[47] (emphasis mine)

This sort of conclusion is hardly rare among biblical interpreters. Culpepper posits a submissive reader who believes as she is told. In the process he also imagines what I characterize "the success of the author." Biblical scholars, perhaps more than other kinds of literary critics, are prone to favor interpretation that celebrates the brilliance of the author or of the text. If we're honest with ourselves, what we're celebrating is the brilliance of our own interpretations. After all, is it not abundantly clear that real readers, unlike our implied readers, interpret these texts in all sorts of ways? In the end, our claims about the implied reader function to discredit those other readers who read differently than we do.

Yet the implied-reader concept remains helpful for interpretation. Its primary contribution involves the reminder that reading is a process, since stories develop in time. It's one thing, having read a story, to

---

46. Terry Eagleton, *Literary Theory: An Introduction* (Minneapolis: University of Minnesota Press, 1983), 84.
47. Culpepper, *Anatomy of the Fourth Gospel*, 91.

look down upon it from a bird's-eye view. Time after time Saul tries to kill David, but David is Israel's chosen king. Even the implied reader anticipates David's rise. Yahweh has already condemned Saul's reign: "I have rejected him from being king over Israel. . . . I will send you to Jesse the Bethlehemite, for I have provided for myself a king among his sons" (1 Sam 16:1). But when David flees and hides in a cave along with his little army, and Saul enters—alone—to relieve himself (1 Sam 24), we attribute suspense to our imaginary reader. It's like a James Bond movie: in the end, we know David will be fine, but the fun lies in *how* the future will reach safety. David's ploy, cutting a fragment from Saul's king garments while the king figuratively has his pants down, is particularly delightful. Forgive me if I've just controlled my implied reader and celebrated the implied author's success, but suspense like this marks good storytelling.

Despite its value, Eagleton and countless other literary theorists have pointed out that ideal readers could not and would not exhaust the story of reading. The problem isn't simply the circular logic that usually marks that style of interpretation. As it has usually been practiced among biblical scholars, reader-oriented reading assumes a universal and objective reader.[48] By positing the reader as a *quality of the text*, interpreters felt emboldened to define correct interpretations—or at least, a correct range of possible interpretations. The bald fact that *real* readers read differently from one another undermines such confidence, to put it mildly. To press the point even further, conventional reader-response interpretation of the Bible makes no room for *resistant* readers, *playful* readers, or even readers who celebrate the specific concerns they bring to the text. Enter the question of actual, embodied readers.

This book is about you, an actual, embodied interpreter of the Bible. It is about the resources, perspectives, and questions you bring to the process of biblical interpretation. In later chapters, however, we will focus our attention on real readers in two ways. In chapter 4 we will discuss whether certain character traits are especially desirable for readers of the Bible. And in chapter 5 we will explore the diverse identities and practices of actual biblical interpreters.

---

48. Stephen D. Moore noted that New Testament reader-response criticism "is a more narrowly focused and more unified phenomenon than its nonbiblical counterpart" (*Literary Criticism and the Gospels: The Theoretical Challenge* [New Haven: Yale University Press, 1989], 72).

RHETORIC, OLD AND NEW

Upon hearing the word *rhetoric*, most folks pinch their nostrils and turn away, for rhetoric has a bad reputation. We choose words like "empty," "false," or "misleading" as prefixes for *rhetoric*. Writing this chapter a heated presidential election, I feel people's pain. There's a lot of nasty rhetoric out there. (See, I did it myself!) People of my generation may recall John Belushi's impassioned speech in the film *Animal House*: "Was it over when the Germans bombed Pearl Harbor?" Checking in with his frat brother, one asks, "Germans?"

"Forget it. He's rolling." The persuasive speaker, we suspect, employs charisma and guile to deceive the public. But I should stop. It's an election year.

But speakers in every society have found their own ways of winning people's agreement, moving them to action, and promoting certain values over others. That art of persuasion—for this is what rhetoric is, the art of persuasion—is a universal human phenomenon. *How* we do it varies from culture to culture. *That* we persuade is universal.

In *Things Fall Apart*, Chinua Achebe sketches a fascinating portrait of precolonial Ibo culture, in which the agile use of proverb and analogy wins the day in public deliberation. A marital dispute between families revolves around whether the husband routinely abuses his runaway wife. He claims she ran away to visit a lover while she was pregnant. Then an ancestral spirit retorts, "What kind of lover sleeps with a pregnant woman?" That logic may not persuade many in contemporary North America, but it wins assent from the public assembly.[49] In private negotiations the protagonist Okonkwo appeals to a proverb: "As our people say, a man who pays respect to the great paves the way for his own greatness. I have come to pay you my respects and also to ask a favor."[50] Many West African cultures trade in the rhetoric of proverb and parable.

Ancient Hebrews, Greeks, and Romans developed their own rhetorical conventions, and rhetorical criticism involves identifying the persuasive elements in biblical texts. The Greeks and Romans thought systematically about rhetoric to the point of producing textbooks and exercises for students. Elite boys learned rhetoric at what would cor-

---

49. Chinua Achebe, *Things Fall Apart* (New York: Anchor, 1994 [1959]), 91.
50. Achebe, *Things*, 19.

respond to our middle-school level of education. Hebrew rhetoric is a little more challenging to pin down because we do not have similar examples of self-conscious reflection on the work of persuasion.

Ancient Hebrew rhetoric emerged in the context of ancient Near Eastern scribal activity.[51] Modern rhetorical analysis of the Hebrew Bible began in the 1960s, with an overemphasis upon style rather than upon persuasive design and effect.[52] For example, Hebrew poetry relies heavily upon the repetition of individual words and the composition of parallel lines that reinforce one another in various ways. Psalm 54 begins: "Save me, O God, by your name, / and vindicate me by your might" (54:1). But Hebrew rhetoric proves far more sophisticated than simple stylistic adornment. Indeed, it sometimes resembles the rhetoric we encounter in *Things Fall Apart*, with aphorisms, rhetorical questions, and parables carrying the message. Consider the account of Rehoboam, who succeeds Solomon on Israel's throne (1 Kings 12:1–20). But another man, Jeroboam, has rebelled against Solomon and still wants to be king. Jeroboam and representatives from all over Israel pledge their loyalty to Rehoboam on one condition: that he relieve the pressure, or yoke, Solomon had imposed upon the people. Rehoboam seeks advice from his counselors. His older, and wiser, counselors suggest Rehoboam should respond to the people's grievance, but his younger counselors offer two aphorisms, condensed statements of his position.

"My little finger is thicker than my father's loins." (12:10)

And:

"My father disciplined you with whips, but I will discipline you with scorpions." (12:11, 14)

Rehoboam ignores the older sages and adopts his friends' advice. Not surprisingly, civil war ensues and Rehoboam loses most of his territory. The people respond with a rhetorical question: "What share do we have in David?" (12:16). And they resume the rebellion. The Deuteronomistic historian puts it this way: "So Israel has been in rebellion against the house of David to this day" (12:19).

---

51. Jack R. Lundbom, "Hebrew Rhetoric," in *Encyclopedia of Rhetoric*, ed. Thomas O. Sloane (New York: Oxford University Press, 2001), 325.

52. Phyllis Trible, *Rhetorical Criticism: Context, Method, and the Book of Jonah*, Guides to Scholarship (Minneapolis: Fortress, 1994), 48.

The Hebrew Bible's most famous use of parable involves the prophet Nathan (2 Sam 12:1–15). David has taken Bathsheba for his own sexual use, and she has become pregnant. In order to cover up the crime, David brings Bathsheba's husband Uriah home from war—hoping his visit will explain Bathsheba's pregnancy. But Uriah refuses the pleasure of sexual intercourse while his fellow soldiers fight for their lives. David sets up Uriah's death, and the prophet comes to confront the king. Perhaps because it's dangerous to call out a king directly, Nathan resorts to parable (Hebrew: *mashal*). In the parable a rich man, who has livestock of his own, seizes a poor man's beloved lamb and slaughters it for a guest. Enraged, David pronounces judgment and a fine upon the rich man: "The man who has done this deserves to die, . . . because he had no pity" (12:5–6). Only then does Nathan turn the tables on David: "You are the man!" (12:7). And Nathan pronounces God's judgment against the king. In this case the parable cushions the prophet from speaking out against the king directly, and it persuades the king to assent to his own condemnation.

Without question, writers of Hebrew developed certain stylistic features, including parallelism and acrostic poetry. (Each line of an acrostic poem begins with a new letter of the alphabet.) But a self-conscious rhetorical tradition seems not to have developed. This is perhaps surprising in that the Hebrew Scriptures include several allusions to lawsuits, a primary site of public persuasion. "And now, inhabitants of Jerusalem and people of Judah, judge between me and my vineyard," presses Isaiah (5:3). The prophet's case begins with an exposition of the past, what the Greeks and Romans would have called a narrative: after careful cultivation, the vineyard has produced only sour grapes. He presses forward with rhetorical questions: "What more was there to do for my vineyard that I have not done in it? When I expected it to yield grapes, why did it yield wild grapes?" (5:4). Significant portions of Job feature Job's accusation that God has treated him unjustly—God has allowed Job to suffer gravely although Job has done nothing to deserve it—and another passage articulates the deity's response (38:1–42:6). Job laments that no umpire will step in and judge between him and God; if only God would stand before him as an equal, Job would prosecute his case (9:32–35). Likewise, God has no ordinary address, making it impossible for Job to go to God's dwelling, "fill my mouth with arguments," and hear God's reply (23:3–5).[53] According to many commentators, Job holds his own. God's response may overwhelm the mortal, but it does not address his questions directly. Apart from filling his mouth with arguments, Job offers no direct indication of rhetorical instruction.

Some Mesopotamian cultures educated scribes in creating fictional debates, which would presumably require rhetorical self-consciousness. And the Egyptians seem to have cultivated both an appreciation for eloquence and something of a rhetorical tradition based upon the *ethos*, or character, of the speaker, but no tradition of rhetorical analysis survives from the ancient Near East.[54] No wonder, then, that our knowledge of Hebrew rhetoric requires the sort of inductive observations I have suggested. We have no textbooks and no evidence of formal rhetorical education.

We know much more about Greek and Roman than Hebrew rhetoric. All New Testament authors were capable of writing extended literature in Greek. That does not necessarily mean these authors all enjoyed sophisticated education in rhetoric, but it does mean they had surely overheard public speeches and encountered the popular conventions of Greek and Roman rhetoric. Because Greek and Roman men might find themselves arguing their cases in a public assembly, rhetoric provided a fundamental element of an elite Greek man's education. Quite a few ancient handbooks and workbooks on rhetoric have survived, so that interpreters began to ask how various New Testament documents, or parts of documents, may have been shaped by the popular rhetorical strategies.[55] As a result, New Testament rhetorical criticism has grown

---

53. See Wilda C. Gafney, "Suing God," June 24, 2012, http://www.wilgafney.com/2012/06/24/suing–god/.
54. George A. Kennedy, *Comparative Rhetoric: An Historical and Cross-Cultural Introduction* (New York: Oxford University Press, 1998), 115–40; Michael V. Fox, "Ancient Egyptian Rhetoric," *Rhetorica* 1 (1983): 9–22; David Hutto, "Ancient Egyptian Rhetoric in the Old and Middle Kingdoms," *Rhetorica* 20 (2002): 213–34; Carol S. Lipson, "It All Comes Down to *Maat*: Ancient Egyptian Rhetoric," in *Rhetoric before and beyond the Greeks*, ed. Carol S. Lipson and Roberta A. Binkley (Albany: State University of New York Press, 2004), 79–98.
55. Mikeal C. Parsons and Michael Wade Martin, *Ancient Rhetoric and the New Testament: The Influence of Elementary Greek Composition* (Waco, TX: Baylor University Press, 2018).

more detailed and perhaps more sophisticated than its Hebrew Bible counterpart.

In Romans, Paul relies heavily upon a fascinating rhetorical technique, the *diatribe*. The diatribe pits the author's voice over against an imaginary, usually resistant, audience. It's as if we're hearing a back-and-forth conversation, as the author/speaker "makes frequent use of imaginary opponents, hypothetical objections, and false conclusions."[56] Paul uses this technique in other letters as well, but it provides the skeleton for large chunks of Romans, perhaps even for most of the letter. To select just a few examples:

- Therefore you have no excuse, whoever you are, when you judge others; for in passing judgment on another you condemn yourself, because you, the judge, are doing the very same things. (2:1)
- Then what advantage has the Jew? Or what is the value of circumcision? Much, in every way. (3:1–2)
- What then are we to say was gained by Abraham, our ancestor according to the flesh? (4:1)
- What then? Should we sin because we are not under law but under grace? By no means! (6:15)
- What then should we say? That the law is sin? By no means! (7:7)
- You will say to me then, "Why then does he still find fault? For who can resist his will?" But who indeed are you, a human being, to argue with God? (9:19–20)
- I ask, then, has God rejected his people? By no means! I myself am an Israelite, a descendant of Abraham, a member of the tribe of Benjamin. (11:1)

The diatribe encourages an audience to join in the conversation, but it has the potential to backfire. Paul raises potential objections to or misunderstandings of his own argument, then dismisses them quickly. What if the first hearers of Romans aren't so easily dissuaded?

But the diatribe also raises questions for contemporary interpreters. What is Paul's larger aim in choosing this technique? According to one school of thought, Paul is a master teacher, using the diatribe to help his hearers follow his argument. But Paul uses the diatribe heavily in Romans—addressed to a group of churches he has never met. Perhaps, some interpreters suggest, Paul is taking a defensive position, like a

---

56. David E. Aune, *The Westminster Dictionary of New Testament and Early Christian Literature and Rhetoric* (Louisville: Westminster John Knox, 2003), 128.

fencer preparing to fend off an opponent's blows. Having concluded his initial greeting to the Romans, Paul launches his argument on this note: "For I am not ashamed of the gospel; it is the power of God for salvation to everyone who has faith, to the Jew first and also to the Greek" (1:16).

Of all the choices available to Paul, "I am not ashamed" is a remarkable way to begin. It sounds defensive—*apologetic*, not in the sense of saying "I'm sorry" but in the way of asserting one's own innocence. Some interpreters see a link between this opening gambit and the diatribe. Suppose Paul has heard that many in Rome are suspicious of him and may have distorted his message. If he wants to visit them (1:13–15; 15:22–24), perhaps he needs to clean up these misperceptions. The diatribe would make a promising tool for the work of defense.

Understanding Romans this way, we should approach it not just as a set of ideas. We need a rhetorical approach, seeing the letter as dialogical. And this can confuse modern readers. For example, Paul asks, "Should we continue in sin so that grace may abound?" (6:1). In other words, if God graciously forgives our sins, why not sin all the more and multiply God's grace? "Of course not!" Paul replies. Paul isn't really worried that the Roman Christians are looking for opportunities to sin. That's not the point at all. Instead, he's answering his potential opponents. They have heard that Paul welcomes Gentile believers into the church without requiring their conversion to Judaism. If Paul's gospel emphasizes grace but does not require adherence to the law of Israel, Paul's opponents may wonder, on what basis should these believers live righteously? Why not sin all the more? Paul's approach isn't to discourage people from sinning—no one is looking for a reason to do that. He's defending himself against an accusation. Many modern readers, failing to understand Paul's rhetorical strategy, think he's addressing a problem that's not even in play.

Some examples of rhetorical interpretation begin with a standard category from ancient rhetoric and investigate how it plays out in a biblical text. George A. Parsenios observes how often John's Gospel relies upon ancient lawsuit motifs, a trait John shares with Greek drama. According to Parsenios, John's language of judgment, witnessing, evidence, and seeking serves to demonstrate both Jesus's innocence and his identity as God's Son. People are constantly "seeking" Jesus—the language ancients used to describe the pursuit of a fugitive—and sometimes Jesus sneakily eludes their grasp (6:15; 7:10–11; 8:21, 37, 40).[57] Meanwhile, John's Jesus expects people to accept his heavenly identity on the basis of testimony: sometimes from other people (4:39), sometimes from the Scriptures (5:39), sometimes from God (5:31–38; 8:18), and sometimes from Jesus himself (5:36; 8:14, 18).

Biblical rhetorical criticism has developed beyond the constraints of ancient categories to encompass contemporary approaches to ancient realities. Vernon K. Robbins and others have cultivated an interdisciplinary approach called socio-rhetorical criticism. This framework includes attention to rhetography, the verbal presentation of visual elements for persuasive effect.[58] Without explicitly following Robbins's lead, Davina C. Lopez performs sophisticated analysis of Roman imperial rhetoric in the form of sculpture. The Romans depict themselves as defeating "the nations," often rendering the nations as naked and vulnerable, usually women, or barbaric. In contrast to these images, Lopez interprets Paul as an apostle "to the nations." (Translations usually render the Greek word *ethnoi* as "Gentiles." Lopez uses "nations.") Paul creates a counter-rhetoric to Roman propaganda. Instead of subjecting "the nations" to his will and depicting them as savages, as the Romans do, Paul meets the nations where they live and builds communities of solidarity among them.[59]

Rhetorical interpretation conveys several benefits. It helps us understand how ancient people sought to persuade one another, allowing us to read biblical texts according to the conventions of ancient communication. Perhaps more importantly, it reminds us that early Christians wrote not simply to convey ideas but also to influence thoughts, attitudes, and behaviors.

---

57. George A. Parsenios, *Rhetoric and Drama in the Johannine Lawsuit Motif*, WUNT 258 (Tübingen: Mohr Siebeck, 2010).

58. Vernon K. Robbins, "Rhetography: A New Way of Seeing the Familiar Text," in *Words Well Spoken: George Kennedy's Rhetoric of the New Testament*, ed. C. Clifton Black and Duane F. Watson (SRR 8; Waco, TX: Baylor University Press, 2008), 81–106. For socio-rhetorical interpretation, see *The Tapestry of Early Christian Discourse: Rhetoric, Society, and Ideology* (New York: Routledge, 1996); and *The Invention of Christian Discourse*, vol. 1: *From Wisdom to Apocalyptic*, Rhetoric of Religious Antiquity 1 (Brussels: Deo, 2008).

59. Davina C. Lopez, *Apostle to the Conquered: Reimaging Paul's Mission*. Paul in Critical Contexts (Minneapolis: Fortress, 2008).

CONCLUSION

Everybody loves a good story—and most of us like poems. Literary interpretation promises to make the Bible more accessible to non-specialists, since most of the Bible amounts to those two literary forms. Few people have the time to acquire intimate familiarity with the cultures that produced the biblical books, fewer still with the historical processes by which the biblical texts came to be or with the biblical languages.

The turn to literary interpretation also sets us free to enjoy the Bible's many examples of literary artistry. Narrowly pursued, sometimes historical approaches can reduce a text to the processes behind it, diverting our attention from the story (or poetry) itself. This process can splinter the text into its constituent parts. The parable of the Good Samaritan (Luke 10:25–37) stands among the Bible's most familiar and beloved passages, but biblical scholars have picked apart the process of its composition. Mark includes two stories that sound somewhat like the conversation in which the Good Samaritan appears. In each, Jesus encounters a potential disciple. First, a rich man asks, "Good Teacher, what must I do to inherit eternal life?" (Mark 10:17). Luke shares its own version of this story (18:18–30). Second, a scribe asks, "Which commandment is the first of all?" (Mark 12:28), but Luke does not relate that story. Luke cuts that story from its context in Mark 12:28–34, substitutes the question, "Teacher, what must I do to inherit eternal life?" (10:25), and then uses the parable to resolve the back-and-forth between Jesus and the lawyer. If the parable came from Jesus, it's likely he didn't deliver it in response to a confrontation with a lawyer who asked, "Who is my neighbor?"

Surely we don't need all that information to appreciate Jesus's parable and Luke's story. Historical reconstruction might help us understand Luke's working methods, but the story does just fine as a story. Lots of readers would find the preceding source- and redaction-critical insights more distracting than helpful.

As we have seen, some interpreters turned to literary approaches as a sort of escape. Historical criticism raises some tough problems, especially for theologically conservative readers. It calls into question the historicity of most biblical narratives. Not least, historical criticism questions the reliability of the Gospels, complicating our access to the historical Jesus. A turn to story shifts authority from the speculations of historical critics and toward the stories themselves.

But as literary interpretation evolved, it raised questions and problems of its own. Biblical literary interpreters followed the progress of their counterparts in university departments of literature. By the 1970s literary studies were abandoning the guarantee of certainty. As if it were not obvious, they "discovered" that no interpretive system can control what people draw from a text.[60] As literary theorists waded into postmodern continental philosophy, the hope of authoritative interpretation stretched vanishingly thin. Once, people grounded their interpretations in an author's likely intentions, but when they realized that authors could not control the texts they produced, interpreters turned toward the formal features of the text themselves. Now, chastened by philosophers like Jacques Derrida and theorists like Paul de Man, they concluded that even texts themselves are unstable. Every literary artifact amounts to webs of allusion, contrast, and inference—so much so that when interpreters pull on a literary thread, the whole text begins to unravel. Interpretation undermines itself. The result is a literary movement known as deconstruction.[61]

If such textual instability strains our comprehension, let's consider an example. Stephen D. Moore, one of the first biblical scholars to practice deconstruction, examined a classic metaphor in John's Gospel—water.[62] There Jesus appears as the source of living water that never runs out (4:10–14). When a Roman soldier stabs the crucified

---

60. For the classic argument, see Stanley Fish, *Is There a Text in This Class? The Authority of Interpretive Communities* (Cambridge, MA: Harvard University Press, 1992).

61. For deconstruction in biblical scholarship, see David W. Odell-Scott, "Deconstruction," in Adam, *Handbook of Postmodern Biblical Interpretation*, 55–61; Yvonne Sherwood, "Derrida," in Adam, *Handbook of Postmodern Biblical Interpretation*, 69–75; A. K. M. Adam, *What Is Postmodern Biblical Criticism?* Guides to Biblical Scholarship (Minneapolis: Fortress, 1995); and Stephen D. Moore, *Literary Criticism and the Gospels*. See also Jacques Derrida, *A Derrida Reader: Behind the Blinds*, ed. Peggy Kamuf (New York: Columbia University Press, 1991); and Paul de Man, *Blindness and Insight: Essays in the Rhetoric of Contemporary Criticism*, 2nd ed. Theory and History of Literature 7 (Minneapolis: University of Minnesota Press, 1983). And for a readable introduction to deconstruction, see Jonathan Culler, *On Deconstruction: Theory and Criticism after Structuralism* (Ithaca, NY; Cornell University Press, 1982).

62. Stephen D. Moore, "Are There Impurities in the Living Water That the Johannine Jesus Dispenses? Deconstruction, Feminism, and the Samaritan Woman," *BibInt* 1 (1993): 207–27.

Jesus, water flows out along with Jesus's blood (19:34). Jesus is also the bread of life. John's Gospel insists that Jesus provides sustenance—bread (6:33–58) and water—for all who believe. He even has access to food his disciples don't know about (4:32). John's Gospel presents Jesus as the source of sustenance and vitality.

But Moore asks: If Jesus is the eternal source of food and water, and if he has access to secret food, why does he still hunger? And why does he thirst? Jesus asks the Samaritan woman for water, but he does not confess to thirst (4:7). Moore first establishes that Jesus has desires of his own: What Jesus longs for from this woman, even more than delicious spring water, is that *she* crave the living water that *he* longs to give *her*. Jesus thirsts to arouse *her* thirst.[63]

At the end of the Gospel, Jesus hangs on the cross. In what appears to be his extremity, he utters, "I thirst" (19:28). Lest we rush ahead and conclude that Jesus "needs" something to drink, the narrator intervenes: Jesus only says this "in order to fulfill the scripture." But that intervention leaves the textual thread exposed. John assures us that Jesus, by promising to quench the thirst of anyone who comes to him to supply their bellies with "rivers of living water," is referring to the gift of the Holy Spirit (7:37–39). But having voiced his own thirst, Jesus pronounces, "It is finished," and yields up that same Spirit (19:30). Jesus, it appears, supplies the living water precisely by running out of that same life-giving resource. John's aqueous metaphor doesn't hold its own water.

Authors can't be trusted. Once we release a text to the public, we cannot control it—and let's be honest, every author wishes we could change something about everything we've written. Readers never could be trusted, as they rarely agree on much. Even the text itself can't be trusted to hold its integrity in the face of careful scrutiny. Perhaps, many biblical scholars have concluded, there's no way to protect the Bible from the vagaries of interpreters and interpretation.

More likely, most biblical scholars still proceed as if interpretation can be controlled. (It can't.) In any case, almost all biblical scholars recognize the value of literary insights. Narrative, reader-response, and rhetorical criticism constitute essential resources for contemporary interpretation.

---

63. Moore, "Impurities," 208.

CHAPTER 4.

THE VIRTUOUS READER

In 2019 Joel B. Green ignited a social media brushfire by writing that the "best" biblical scholars love the Bible and engage in ongoing practices of discipleship and worship.[1] Immediately other scholars rose up to criticize Green for being narrow, sectarian, and self-serving in promoting his own flavor of interpretation with an implicit criticism of those who practice interpretation differently. No one should have been surprised by Green's words: he's a prominent biblical scholar, and his comments echo things he's published before.[2] The barbs whipped back and forth, indicating that Green had placed his finger on two most sensitive issues. Are some people better suited for public interpretation than others? Likewise, can we identify particular virtues that mark excellent biblical interpretation? Whether one agrees with Green or not (I mostly don't), both questions are important. And they are rarely discussed.

The world of biblical interpretation includes all kinds of people. Real people. Many adhere to some expression of Judaism or Christianity, but many do not. People also practice interpretation in diverse settings. For example, academic biblical scholars work in public, secular, and church-related colleges and universities. Some work specifically in theological schools that serve various religious bodies. Others work outside academic campuses, sometimes within religious organizations and

---

1. "Joel B. Green on 'What Makes a Good Biblical Scholar,'" TheLAB: The Logos Academic Blog, ed. Tavis Bollinger, March 6, 2019, https://tinyurl.com/t2bt285.
2. See especially Joel B. Green, *Seized by Truth: Reading the Bible as Scripture* (Nashville: Abingdon, 2007); and *Practicing Theological Interpretation: Engaging Biblical Texts for Faith and Formation* (Grand Rapids: Baker Academic, 2011).

sometimes far removed from them. Some even work in divinity schools located within secular universities. Collectively these settings relate to the Bible and its interpretation in diverse ways. And that's just academics.

One major fault line among professional interpreters involves whether faith commitments should or should not play a role in public biblical interpretation. Particularly among Christians, some argue that helpful interpretation requires religious belief and dispositions. Among Jews, some hold that critical interpretation, especially of the historical variety, has nothing to do with faith, but the more common view seeks to integrate critical interpretation into their practice and understanding.[3] This contemporary diversity reflects the distinctions among Jewish movements—Orthodox, Conservative, Reform, and Reconstructionist—and the ways in which they negotiate the relationship between ancient faith and modernity.[4] Thus in Jewish tradition it makes a difference whether one does or does not read from a faith perspective, but most Jewish biblical scholars do not perceive a contradiction between academic and faith-oriented interpretation.[5] Meanwhile, some secular scholars maintain that theologically driven interpretation is uncritical or unscholarly. Some argue that religious bias skews the potential for critical interpretation.

Some academic societies, such as the Society of Biblical Literature, adopt a pluralist approach to the question. These pluralist organizations welcome all kinds of interpretation so long as they are both critical and nonsectarian. By *critical* we mean subject to the common standards of academic research; by *nonsectarian,* that conversations are open to persons from all perspectives.[6] Other organizations, such as the Catholic Biblical Association and the Evangelical Theological Society,

---

3. Mark Zvi Brettler, "My Bible: A Jew's Perspective," in Brettler, Enns, and Harrington, *The Bible and the Believer,* 21–66.

4. Karin Heder Zetterholm, *Jewish Interpretation of the Bible: Ancient and Contemporary* (Minneapolis: Fortress, 2012 [2008]), 145–88.

5. The term *theological interpretation* circulates among Christians. As doctrine plays a much larger role in Christian life than in Judaism, the term rarely occurs among Jewish interpreters.

6. Though see the critiques by Jacques Berlinerblau, "What's Wrong with the Society of Biblical Literature," *Chronicle of Higher Education* 53/12 (November 10, 2006): B13; and Stephen D. Moore and Yvonne Sherwood, *The Invention of the Biblical Scholar: A Critical Manifesto* (Minneapolis: Fortress, 2013), esp. 49–81.

welcome faith-based inquiry. Purely secular biblical scholarship owns no academic society of similar scale, though its practitioners are many.

The question of personal investment does not confine itself to the matter of religion. A second space of conversation involves readers' personal and social investments. Factors such as class, race, ethnicity, gender identity, sexual orientation, ability and disability, and nationality enter the picture. We'll take up the matter of "flesh-and-blood" readers in the next chapter; in this chapter, we'll consider the matter of ethics. Should biblical interpreters argue for what they believe is good and right?

A FAITHFUL READER?

Students sometimes ask about the authors of the texts I assign for class: Are they Christians? I've fielded this question in a church-related college, a state university, and a theological seminary. Not all students have this question, but some do. I can't speak for them, but the question tends to come from devoted Christian students. I suppose it reflects a question of trust: some religious people believe they can trust authors who share their convictions. Perhaps some also feel that secular interpreters or interpreters from non-Christian religious traditions might present ideas that somehow undermine their own faith. Some religious circles hold academic scholarship in suspicion, after all.

This question is hardly new. Augustine of Hippo stands among the most influential voices in the history of Western Christianity. His stature is all the more elevated among Protestants due to his influence upon Martin Luther, who was of course an Augustinian monk, while Eastern Orthodox Christians hold some of Augustine's opinions against him. Luther eventually departed from Augustine's interpretation of grace and its relationship to justification, Luther's most revolutionary doctrinal innovation, but he remained in conversation with Augustine his entire life.[7] An adult convert, Augustine eventually was made a priest involuntarily in 391, then served as bishop of Hippo on the Algerian coast from 395 until his death in 430.[8] His writings range

---

7. Stephen J. Chester, *Reading Paul with the Reformers: Reconciling Old and New Perspectives* (Grand Rapids: Eerdmans, 2017), 95–101.
8. Richard A. Norris Jr., "Augustine and the Close of the Ancient Period," in Hauser and Watson, *History of Biblical Interpretation*, 1:385.

widely, but he also left a profound impression through his active participation in a series of church controversies.

Augustine's classic *On Christian Doctrine* (*Doctr. chr.*) presents a sort of handbook for biblical interpretation and teaching. Augustine was not the first to compose such a project. Historians routinely sketch a conflict between third-century hermeneutical circles in Alexandria, most prominently Origen, and their fourth-century critics in Antioch: Origen promoted spiritual and allegorical meanings for biblical texts, whereas the Antiochenes complained that Origen too quickly abandoned their narrative contexts and textual specifics. Origen argued that faithful interpreters exercise humility: they must admit their own ignorance of Scripture's mystical meanings (*Princ.* 4.9). Aware of those earlier debates, Augustine does not discard spiritual meaning, particularly when passages evoke logical or philosophical challenges. In comparison with Origen, however, Augustine places greater emphasis upon the character, or virtue, of the interpreter and on the presuppositions that should guide interpretation.

Augustine measured interpreters according to their theological orthodoxy and charitable behavior. Two rules provided the criteria for interpretation: the rule of love and the rule of faith. If interpretation does not contribute to greater love of God and of one's neighbor, and if interpretation strays from the fundamental tenets of Christian orthodoxy, Augustine judged, the interpreter stands in error (*Doctr. chr.* 1.86). An interpreter should be "a defender of right faith and an enemy of error" (4.4).[9] The interpreter's virtue is so important that even accurate understanding of the Bible can prove harmful: interpreters who speak wisely but live wickedly, Augustine warned, may benefit students but will harm their own souls (4.27).

Advocates for faithful submission as a criterion of interpretation often ground their position in arguments concerning the nature or purpose of Scripture. If we approach the Bible as a document of faith, it seems intuitive that participants in that same faith tradition would be most sensitive to its message. And if we assign to the Bible a religious purpose, to promote the knowledge and love of God, then attunement to that purpose will reward the reader. This line of thinking boasts an ancient pedigree. Augustine described the "end," or purpose, of the

---

9. Augustine of Hippo, *On Christian Doctrine*, trans. D. W. Robertson Jr., Library of Liberal Arts (New York: Macmillan, 1958).

Scriptures as the love of a being who is to be enjoyed and can share that enjoyment with human beings (*Doctr. chr.* 1.35).[10]

One particularly innovative attempt to sketch the virtue of faithful interpretation comes from Richard S. Briggs. Drawing from a series of examples from the Hebrew Scriptures/Old Testament, Briggs argues that each case study brings forth a virtue appropriate to faithful interpretation. In other words, the Bible can teach its own readers how to become more faithful and more wise. To this end Briggs digs into the story of Ruth and that of Elisha's interaction with the Aramean general Naaman. Both stories require moments of discernment and decision from their heroes, and both heroes interpret their interactions with other people charitably. Ruth's love for Naomi shows that love occurs in community and before God, while Elisha blesses Naaman without requiring the general to become anything other than who he is, a non-Israelite. With this example and others, Briggs argues that the virtues we encounter in these characters are virtues we should exercise as readers of the Bible. Without his commitment to reading the Hebrew texts from a position of faith, Briggs would not have arrived at these provocative interpretations.[11]

The contemporary Theological Interpretation of Scripture movement provides a splendid case study for thinking through the role of faith in public biblical interpretation. Notice the capitalization. The movement echoes Augustine's argument directly. Lots of people interpret the Bible in ways they and we believe are theologically oriented; that is, many interpret the Bible as part of the larger quest for religious meaning. Capitalized, *Theological Interpretation of Scripture* indicates a movement guided by a specific set of commitments regarding how theological interpretation (not capitalized) should be done.

The Theological Interpretation movement begins with understanding the Bible as God's loving self-disclosure to humankind.[12] Some even speak of the Bible as if it were a person "yearning" to shape readers' self-

---

10. See the discussion in Darren Sarisky, *Reading the Bible Theologically*, Current Issues in Theology (New York: Cambridge University Press, 2019), 75–104.

11. Richard S. Briggs, *The Virtuous Reader: Old Testament Narrative and Interpretive Virtue*, Studies in Theological Interpretation (Grand Rapids: Baker Academic, 2010), esp. 135–66.

12. Fowl, *Theological Interpretation of Scripture*, 6, citing John Webster, *Holy Scripture: A Dogmatic Sketch*, Current Issues in Theology (Cambridge: Cambridge University Press, 2003), 5–41; see Green, *Seized by Truth*, 11.

understanding.[13] Thus, the proper aim of interpretation should be to love God more fully. To that end, the interpreter's personal virtues are all the more important, marked by particular "habits, dispositions, and practices."[14] L. Gregory Jones encourages the church to seek guidance from "saintly readers," *saintly* not necessarily meaning those who have been canonized but those whose lives have been shaped by "the grace and holiness of God" in ways that illumine their readings of Scripture.[15] In interpreting the Bible, many maintain, spiritual virtue and spiritual intentions lead to spiritual growth. One of those values is *trust* in the Bible's capacity to attain this end.[16] Another involves commitment to theological orthodoxy.[17]

If God ultimately stands as the Bible's author, and if God designed the Bible to help people love God and neighbor, the Bible will especially reward obedient and submissive readers. Jones, for example, calls Christian readers to imitate their "saintly exemplars."[18] Joel B. Green highlights "a yielding, an obedience, a willingness to accept these notes as the right notes, this pattern as the true pattern."[19] Peter Leithart describes theological interpretation as "a form of piety" that should not be divorced from worship and prayer.[20] And Darren Sarisky maintains that "when the Bible is understood positively, as in Christian communities, and brought within a reader's framework of beliefs, its imperatives must be . . . enacted."[21] If biblical interpreters begin with piety and emulate saintly readers, how do these readers respond to ethical and

---

13. Joel B. Green, *Why Salvation?* Reframing New Testament Theology (Nashville: Abingdon, 2014), 57.
14. Fowl, *Theological Interpretation of Scripture*, 13–14.
15. L. Gregory Jones, "Embodying Scripture in the Community of Faith," in Davis and Hays, *The Art of Reading Scripture*, 147–18.
16. Patricia D. Fosarelli and Michael J. Gorman, "The Bible and Spiritual Growth," in Gorman, *Scripture: An Ecumenical Introduction*, 232–34.
17. Fowl, "Theological and Ideological Strategies of Biblical Interpretation," in Gorman, *Scripture: An Ecumenical Introduction*, 169–71.
18. Jones, "Embodying Scripture," 156–59.
19. Green, *Seized by Truth*, 11.
20. Peter Leithart, *Athanasius*, Foundations of Theological Exegesis and Christian Spirituality (Grand Rapids: Baker, 2011), 28. Cited in W. David Buschart and Kent Eilers, *Theology as Retrieval: Receiving the Past, Renewing the Church* (Downers Grove, IL: InterVarsity, 2015), 49–50.
21. Sarisky, *Reading the Bible Theologically*, 285.

theological problems raised by the Bible? Does theological interpretation, as promoted by many, rule out critique, protest, and reconfiguration? In Theological Interpretation of Scripture circles, the weight of discussion falls upon trust rather than suspicion or protest. Acknowledging that the Bible was produced by human beings, reflecting the limited perspectives and oppressive structures endemic to our condition, Michael Gorman nevertheless commends a disposition of trust over a hermeneutic of suspicion. Texts are polyvalent, he argues, with multiple levels of meaning; Christian interpreters should seek out a fresh and life-giving message from the Bible's messy pages.[22] Submissive readers will labor to preserve the Bible's authority from generation to generation.[23]

Theological Interpretation of Scripture advocates also maintain that faithful interpretation conforms to the rule of faith. The rule of faith need not represent a narrow or sectarian construal of Christianity. Instead, it embraces only the commonly held essentials of Christian confession.[24] Admittedly, that modest claim opens lots of wiggle room: one community's commonly held essentials may differ from another's in both their extent and their contents. But for Theological Interpretation advocates, interpretations "that do not cohere with the Rule of Faith are not Christian readings of the Scriptures."[25]

Predictably, many disagree with the prescription that only a certain kind of reader—a Christian who believes the right things and owns a trusting disposition—is best suited to read the Bible. Significant contributions come from all kinds of interpreters: people of all sorts of faith and of no faith, and people from all sorts of backgrounds. Moreover, it makes lots of sense to assume that faithfully motivated interpreters will address the concerns common among believing communities. We don't have to pose things as an either/or dichotomy. Therefore, we need to refine our questions in more focused and helpful ways. What values

---

22. Michael J. Gorman, "The Interpretation of the Bible in Protestant Churches," in Gorman, *Scripture: An Ecumenical Introduction*, 186–87.

23. R. W. L. Moberly, *The Bible, Theology, and Faith: A Study of Abraham and Jesus*, Cambridge Studies in Christian Doctrine (Cambridge: Cambridge University Press, 2000), 43.

24. Kathryn Greene-McCreight, "Rule of Faith," in *Dictionary for Theological Interpretation of the Bible*, ed. Kevin J. Vanhoozer et al. (Grand Rapids: Baker, 2005), 703–4.

25. Green, *Practicing Theological Interpretation*, 80.

derive from privileging believing and trusting interpreters, and what gets lost when people do so?

When we pose our questions in these more focused ways, the matter grows more complicated. I regard the commitments and the interests that real readers bring to the Bible not as obstacles to objectivity but as catalysts for insight. This claim applies to all sorts of readers, not just to those who fit a particular definition. We might begin by acknowledging how theologically driven interpreters can produce remarkably creative readings. These readings can enrich faith communities, and may also prove helpful to interpreters who do not share their assumptions. Bruce L. McCormack, a systematic theologian and not a professional biblical scholar, has argued that beginning with a dogmatic Christology will "help to make better sense of the Christological commitments of the writer to the Hebrews than does the work of even the best of our exegetes today."[26] McCormack's approach runs in precisely the opposite direction of most biblical interpretation. In asking theological questions, most interpreters refrain from imposing their own theological convictions upon the text. In so doing, they aim to avoid overpowering the voice of the text itself. According to McCormack, Hebrews makes better sense if we assume something the book does not say on its own, certainly not explicitly: that Jesus bears a divine-human identity. Only in this light do we fully understand how the book describes Jesus as submitting to God, "learning" obedience, being made perfect, and being appointed by God as a high priest (5:5–10)—all while Jesus is proclaimed as God's Son, "the reflection of God's glory and the exact imprint of God's very being" (1:1–3).[27] This doctrinal stance, McCormack argues, will inform all readers of Hebrews, not just Christian believers.

On the other hand, narrowly confessional interpretation can produce deleterious side effects. It is unfortunate that Theological Interpretation of Scripture advocates rarely encourage listening to interpreters beyond their faith communities. The problem shows its fangs when it comes to theological interpretation of the Jewish Scriptures, or (for Christians) the Old Testament, a common topic in Theological Inter-

---

26. Bruce L. McCormack, "'With Loud Cries and Tears': The Humanity of the Son in the Epistle to the Hebrews," in *The Epistle to the Hebrews and Christian Theology*, ed. Richard Bauckham, Daniel R. Driver, Trevor A. Hart, and Nathan MacDonald (Grand Rapids: Eerdmans, 2009), 37.

27. McCormack, "'With Loud Cries and Tears,'" 64–67.

pretation circles. The danger consists of supersessionism, the notion that Christianity displaces Judaism in the economy of divine favor. Often supersessionism expresses itself by reading the Jewish Scriptures as if they are "about" Jesus—a move that occludes their significance for their historical audiences and for Jewish communities today.

Let's not paint with too broad a brush: contributors to the movement are aware of the problem and its complications. Stephen E. Fowl helpfully recommends that Christian interpreters "can and should engage" with Jewish and secular interpreters of these scriptures.[28] He also argues that, while Christian readers naturally find Christian meanings in the Old Testament, the notion of finding "Christ" in those Scriptures neither exhausts the meaning of those texts nor shows that there is "someone [namely, Jesus] lying hidden beneath the surface of the OT."[29] And R. W. L. Moberly recognizes that, while Christians will find Christian meanings in Israel's Scriptures, pre-Christian meanings remain relevant and instructive.[30]

However, particular trends in the Theological Interpretation movement tend to favor supersessionist reading. The movement tends to minimize the relevance of historical criticism: historical interpretation moves meaning away from theological engagement and into the speculative reconstructions of scholars. As Green argues, historical investigation of early Christianity in the light of Acts is not the same process as theological interpretation of the same book.[31] But historical criticism reminds us of the historical specificity of biblical texts, that the Hebrew prophetic books addressed real people and concrete concerns that bear ongoing relevance for Jewish communities. Historical critics further remind us that Jews have not misunderstood their own Scriptures by failing to find Jesus in them. Despite these factors, it's not rare to find Theological Interpretation practitioners arguing that "Israel's Scriptures testify to the Christ (and none other) who first inspired them," not because Christians find Jesus when they read those Scriptures but because Jesus is inherently present in them.[32]

28. Fowl, *Theological Interpretation of Scripture*, 56.
29. Fowl, *Theological Interpretation of Scripture*, 57.
30. R. W. L. Moberly, "Theological Interpretation, Second Naiveté, and the Rediscovery of the Old Testament," *ATR* 99 (2017): 661–62.
31. Green, *Practicing Theological Interpretation*, 56–70.
32. Green, *Seized by Faith*, 38–39.

Theological Interpretation devotees also tend to talk about the Bible's overall unity. This, essentially, reduces the Jewish Scriptures to secondary status. If themes from the Jewish Bible find themselves "addressed and reshaped by the NT writers,"[33] a unitary view of the Bible leads Christian readers to subsume the voice of the Jewish Scriptures under Christian theology. In 2001 the Pontifical Biblical Commission warned against such marginalization of Israel's Scriptures. The commission maintains that Jewish interpretation of the Bible is legitimate in its own right, apart from a Christian overlay. Moreover, it acknowledges that the New Testament's appropriation of those Scriptures to witness to Jesus is "retrospective." That is, while early Christians believed that the Jewish Scriptures attested to Jesus, the Hebrew prophets were originally tasked to interpret the times in which they and their audiences lived. They did not "predict" Jesus in any literal sense. We should not expect Christians to interpret the Bible as Jews do, the Commission argued, but Jewish and Christian interpretation can and should inform one another.[34]

The notion of biblical unity is highly contested, requiring readers to supply a grand rubric that accounts for the whole of what's contained within the canon. Theological Interpretation practitioners embrace a degree of diversity within the Bible, but only in a restricted sense. Moreover, consider how Jewish readers might respond to this assessment of biblical unity:

> Old and New Testaments join in their singular witness to the God of Abraham and Sarah, the God who raised Jesus from the dead.[35]

One wonders if a Christian scholar would say this aloud, knowing that a rabbi was sitting in the front row. If this is how Christian readers describe the Bible's unity, the potential for genuine dialogue between Christians and Jews is very small. Even when Christian interpreters work very hard to avoid reducing the Jewish Bible to the status of back-

---

33. David A. Leiter, "The Character and Composition of the Books of the Old Testament," in Gorman, *Scripture: An Ecumenical Introduction*, 68.
34. Pontifical Biblical Commission, "The Jewish People and Their Sacred Scriptures in the Christian Bible," https://tinyurl.com/mt3e. Cited and summarized by Marc Brettler and Amy-Jill Levine, "Isaiah's Suffering Servant: Before and After Christianity," *Interpretation* 73 (2019): 159.
35. Green, *Seized by Truth*, 60.

ground for Jesus, they often struggle to articulate an independent role for Israel's Scriptures.[36]

The question of unity and diversity within the Bible transcends the distinction between Jewish and Christian Scriptures. Readers have "always" recognized diversity within the canon. To a significant degree, however, that diversity provides one of the key motivations for the rise of modern biblical scholarship since the Enlightenment. Where Theological Interpretation advocates account for the diversity among biblical accounts as "extremely limited," especially in comparison with the diversity among other ancient texts,[37] that same diversity within the Torah led to the Documentary Hypothesis, the idea that we can identify distinctive literary traditions, each with their own worldview, ideological commitments, and cultural contexts. The God who creates simply by speaking in Genesis 1, then declaring all things good, differs markedly from Yahweh as described in Genesis 2–3, the deity who tries out new ideas and regrets earlier decisions. Likewise, students can identify each of the four canonical Gospels according to their distinctive stylistic and thematic traits.

Beyond the conversation about the Theological Interpretation movement, all readers benefit from dialogue and diversity. Christian readers are scarcely an exception. For example, a Christian scholar named David A. deSilva has set out to demonstrate the Jewishness of earliest Christianity. The point might seem obvious: Jesus was, after all, Jewish, as were all (or almost all) of his followers. But deSilva correctly identifies a problem: Christian scholars, preachers, and laypeople have long sought to distance Jesus from Judaism, often contrasting Jesus with his own native culture. This sort of argumentation has too often accompanied anti-Semitism. With case study after case study, deSilva's book demonstrates how the Gospels and other New Testament literature reflect the influence of the Hebrew Scriptures and especially non-canonical ancient Jewish literature.[38]

However pure deSilva's intentions, he received a sharp rebuke from Eva Mroczek, who grew up Roman Catholic and now identifies most

---

36. As in Fowl, *Theological Interpretation of Scripture*, 34–35.
37. Richard Bauckham, "Reading Scripture as a Coherent Story," in Davis and Hays, *The Art of Reading Scripture*, 43.
38. David A. deSilva, *The Jewish Teachers of Jesus, James, and Jude: What Earliest Christianity Learned from the Apocrypha and Pseudepigrapha* (New York: Oxford University Press, 2012).

closely with Jewish tradition.[39] First, Mroczek points out that the work of foregrounding Jesus's Jewishness has long ago been accomplished, and by the *Jewish* scholar Geza Vermes. DeSilva doesn't cite Vermes at all but tends to engage other Christian scholars.[40] Second, Mroczek critiques deSilva for writing about Jewish *influence* on Jesus rather than Jesus's *participation* in Jewish culture. What a difference a word makes: "influence" distances Jesus from Judaism, while "participation" underscores his full Jewish identity. Although Mroczek lays out other concerns, this influence-versus-participation weighs heavily. DeSilva usually cannot show direct lines of literary influence between ancient Jewish literature and Jesus (or James or Jude), but he can show how the early Christian texts are drinking from a common stream. In other words, he's describing not influence but cultural participation. Third, deSilva treats Judaism in a monolithic manner, as if there were a single thing called "Judaism" that influenced Jesus. But the texts deSilva engages are wildly diverse.

In the end, Mroczek argues, deSilva winds up committing the sin he seeks to avoid. By comparing Jesus to individual Jewish sources, deSilva sets up a pattern that will show how Jesus supposedly conforms to Jewish values and diverges from them. Judaism is a single thing, so whenever Jesus differs from an ancient Jewish text, he comes across as a reformer of "Judaism." Participation in a complex cultural stew is scarcely an option. Mroczek's take:

> This kind of flattening is inherent in the method. When Jesus is compared individually to specific texts in terms of influence and innovation, the old division between Judaism and Christianity becomes re-entrenched, and far too early. This Jesus does not participate in a larger matrix of diverse traditions as one of its representatives, but is influenced by and departs from Jewish materials.[41]

As a participant-reformer of Judaism, this Jesus plays into an ancient script. He introduces a Christianity that is supposedly more spiritual and more inclusive than the supposedly (again) ritualistic and boundary-oriented Judaism from which he emerges.

39. Eva Mroczek, "Jesus vs. Judaism . . . Again," *Marginalia*, April 15, 2014, https://tinyurl.com/swvsnua.

40. Geza Vermes, *Jesus the Jew: A Historian's Reading of the Gospels* (Minneapolis: Fortress, 1981 [1973]).

41. Mroczek, "Jesus vs. Judaism . . . Again."

→ We all benefit from interactions with readers whose questions and commitments differ from our own. I have received criticism very similar to the ones Mroczek weighs against deSilva. Marvin A. Sweeney points out that my survey of ancient Jewish and Christian apocalyptic literature cuts off the conversation at the period when the first Christian literary apocalypses emerged—about the time when the book of Revelation was composed. Yes, my work discusses Jewish as well as Christian apocalypses of the period, but the narrative I construct suggests that's the end of things, as if all that other literature, especially Jewish literature, is primarily helpful for understanding Revelation. My book shows little curiosity about the ongoing phenomena of Jewish and Christian apocalypticism. Ouch.[42]

→ Those who differ from us can hold us accountable for our own narrow perspectives. But in public interpretation, we cannot assume good faith on everyone's part. Quite a few biblical scholars have played very public roles in calling to account abuses on the part of the Museum of the Bible, a purportedly nonsectarian institution that exists "to invite all people to engage with the Bible."[43] One set of concerns involves how the Museum acquires its materials. Scholars treat antiquities with great care: if we don't know an artifact's pedigree, there's a good chance it has been stolen, smuggled, or forged. Unfortunately, the sponsors of the Museum were forced to pay $3 million in damages for acquiring such goods—and perhaps for disguising their true nature. Biblical scholars Candida R. Moss and Joel S. Baden brought this story to broad public attention. If such offenses were committed by amateur enthusiasts, that would be one thing, but the Museum of the Bible sponsors have signed on dozens of highly recognized biblical scholars to lend authenticity to their project—and some of those scholars have been implicated in instances of deception.[44]

The Museum has also attracted criticism for deception in its purportedly nonsectarian self-presentation. Along with a team of colleagues, Jill Hicks-Keeton has published a series of studies regarding the

---

42. Marvin A. Sweeney, "Review of Greg Carey, *Ultimate Things: An Introduction to Jewish and Christian Apocalyptic Literature*," *Religious Studies Review* 33, no. 1 (January 2007): 62.

43. Museum of the Bible, Washington, DC, https://museumofthebible.org/museum/about-us.

44. Candida R. Moss and Joel S. Baden, *Bible Nation: The United States of Hobby Lobby* (Princeton: Princeton University Press, 2017), esp. 22–61.

Museum.[45] One could explain away an inherent Protestant bias to the complex reality of cultural Christianity. The Museum was founded by evangelical Christians. Naturally, they think of the Bible in terms of the Protestant Bible, as opposed to the Jewish Bible or the Bibles of other Christian communions. Nor is it surprising that the Museum portrays the Bible as a single story in which the Jewish Scriptures eventually point to Jesus Christ, an example of supersessionism. Before excusing these realities too quickly, we should remember the massive amount of scholarly consultation the Museum receives.[46]

Religious institutions are entitled to understand the Bible as they see fit, whether we agree with them or not. But Hicks-Keeton stumbled across something more troubling. In January 2018 Hicks-Keeton visited an Oklahoma City Baptist church, where Museum of the Bible director of Bible engagement Michael McAfee offered a display of artifacts. The preacher that Sunday was Jeremiah Johnston of Houston Baptist University, founder of the university's Christian Thinkers Society and an advocate of apologetics, the public defense of Christianity. McAfee devoted his time to defending the Bible's historical trustworthiness against the positions of a popularly published biblical scholar, while Johnston presented the case for the physical resurrection of Jesus and for the Bible's historical reliability in general. Hicks-Keeton diagnosed the trouble at an institutional level: Why would a nonsectarian museum be promoting very sectarian views in an Oklahoma church? And why would it be partnering with an institution committed to Christian apologetics? Responding to Hicks-Keeton, Museum director of communications Jeremy Burton stated that the Museum had only a "pre-marketing" arrangement with Johnston's center that began in November 2017. But Hicks-Keeton found a press release from Houston Baptist University from June of that year promoting the partnership, with promotional materials displaying the Museum's logo. Steve Green, the Museum's founder, has even written the foreword to one of Johnston's books. Once Hicks-Keeton published her experience, references to the Museum were scrubbed from the Christian Thinkers Society's website. Hicks-Keeton concludes:

---

45. Jill Hicks-Keeton and Cavin Concannon, eds., *The Museum of the Bible: A Critical Introduction* (Lanham, MD: Lexington Books, 2019).
46. Jill Hicks-Keeton, "Christian Supersessionism and the Problem of Diversity at the Museum of the Bible," in *Museum of the Bible*, 49–70.

What we are left with is a museum pretending to be something it's not, an evangelical wolf in scholarly sheep's clothing—whose officials are more than happy to stand by, and even encourage, slippage around what the aims and claims of biblical scholarship actually are. It is not a pretty picture.[47]

Public biblical interpretation requires that informed persons monitor public spaces for this kind of deception.

In a more constructive vein, those of us who do read the Bible theologically might take a hint from within the Bible itself, particularly from the apostle Paul. Paul wrote at a time when important questions were up for grabs. Rarely could Paul settle the disputes in the churches he addressed by appealing to a fixed "rule of faith" or creedal standard. Indeed, it appears that Paul often did not anticipate the conflicts he encountered, so he was forced to improvise his theological responses. Even when Paul cites Jewish Scripture, he often spins it with an innovative interpretation. For example, when Paul defends his proclamation that God justifies human beings through faith rather than through observance of the Torah, he provides a novel interpretation of the Abraham story: because Genesis declares Abram/Abraham righteous on account of his faith (15:6)—and *before* he submits to circumcision—Abraham shows the power of faith apart from works of the law (Gal 3:6–14; Rom 4:1–25). Paul advances such innovative arguments all the time. It appears Paul reasoned with a set of core convictions, applying those convictions to issues as they rose up from within the churches.

Interpreters have frequently mined Paul's letters for theological nuggets, fashioning those components into expositions of Paul's theology.[48] That process is necessary, as Christian readers naturally seek to bring their theological outlooks into conversation with that of Paul. But theologically invested interpreters might follow Paul's example differently. Calvin Roetzel, an eminent interpreter of Paul, suggested that we talk about Paul's *theologizing* rather than Paul's *theology*. Theologizing is an activity, whereas theology often connotes a fixed content of doctrinal beliefs. In Roetzel's view, "Paul scarcely had in mind a developed

---

47. Jill Hicks-Keeton, "What the Museum of the Bible Conveys about Biblical Scholarship behind Church Doors," *Religion and Politics*, March 13, 2018, https://tinyurl.com/qt22mv6.

48. See the massive treatments by Dunn, *Theology of Paul the Apostle*; and N. T. Wright, *Paul and the Faithfulness of God*, 2 vols. (Minneapolis: Fortress, 2013).

theology from the beginning, and in some cases he appears not to have known what he thought about a given issue until he worked it through as he composed a letter."[49]

We observe this process at work when Paul addresses a problem in Corinth: whether it's permissible to eat "idol-food," that is, meat that's been associated with one of the many religious cults that permeated everyday life. This question may seem distant from contemporary readers, but it appears to have constituted a major sticking point in early Christian assemblies, appearing not only in 1 Corinthians 8:1–13 but also in Romans 14:1–15:13 and Revelation 2:14, 20. The question involved far more than religious purity: almost every social meal from trade guilds to family gatherings involved religious observances, and most of the meat sold at public markets had previously been sacrificed—that is, cooked—in one of the many temples. In other words, believers who abstained from "idol-food" alienated themselves from basic social networks that provided their security. Many interpreters believe the argument likely reflected social divisions that were already present among the Corinthians: more affluent people could afford meat, and they had more to gain or lose in the debate. Some early Jesus followers abstained from eating meat because they wanted to avoid all contamination from idolatry. Others argued that, since the many pagan deities didn't really exist, they could eat whatever they wanted. We see both positions reflected in 1 Corinthians.

It appears that some of the Corinthians sought Paul's intervention on the matter. Rather than laying out a direct theological argument for what they should do, Paul acknowledges both sides of the issue, showing that he appreciates what's at stake for everyone involved. Instead of arguing that one side is theologically correct, however, Paul shifts his focus to community life. Perhaps it is okay to eat idol-food, but believers who exercise that freedom may injure the consciences of their "weaker" colleagues. Paul interjects a remarkable theological principle: believers should avoid injuring a brother or sister "for whom Christ died" (8:11). Indeed, Paul appeals to Jesus's crucifixion at several key points in 1 Corinthians. On the cross Jesus yielded his own prerogatives for the welfare of humankind (see Phil 2:1–11); believers should follow his example. This is true when some believers think they have attained

---

49. Calvin Roetzel, *Paul: The Man and the Myth*, Studies on Personalities of the New Testament (Minneapolis: Fortress, 1999 [1997]), 94.

superior wisdom (1 Cor 1:18–2:5), it applies when they're divided into factions (1:10–13; 4:16), it applies when believers are in conflict (6:7–8), and it even applies to Paul when he could require financial contributions from the Corinthians (9:12–23). In 1 Corinthians Paul takes one of his core convictions, that Jesus's crucifixion reveals how God works in the world (1:18–25), and creatively applies it to a host of issues presented by the Corinthians.

Theologically invested readers might emulate Paul. That is, we bring our convictions and expectations to the work of interpretation. We have no choice but to do so. As Donald H. Juel once wrote, "Some preconception has always been necessary to open the Scriptures."[50] At the same time, the process of theological interpretation remains distinctly fluid, dialogical, and even improvisational. Our questions and expectations change from one interpretive moment to another. We bring them to the work of interpretation without knowing whether the biblical texts will speak to those questions and expectations directly, transform them into new levels of investment, or challenge us to ditch those questions and expectations in exchange for others. Given the messiness of this process, it's best that we pursue such interpretation in community rather than in isolation, as Paul found himself required to do.

AN OBJECTIVE READER?

In large part modern biblical studies emerged as a reaction to dogmatic interpretation of the Bible. The Protestant Reformation and, later, the Enlightenment both involved revolts against religious authority, though in different ways. The Protestant Reformers and their more radical contemporaries insisted that people could interpret the Bible without necessarily submitting to Rome's magisterial authority. That is not to say that the Reformers welcomed anything resembling pure objectivity in biblical interpretation, but they did claim to understand the Bible on its own terms, and they did make the Bible available to non-clerical readers in their own vernacular languages. The Enlightenment pressed further, advocating absolute freedom in the pursuit of critical understanding, including the rejection of church authority altogether. With the rise of the modern research university, especially

---

50. Donald H. Juel, *Shaping the Scriptural Imagination: Truth, Meaning, and the Theological Interpretation of the Bible*, ed. Shane Berg and Matthew L. Skinner (Waco, TX: Baylor University Press, 2011), 101.

in Germany, biblical scholarship adopted an identity as *Wissenschaft*. Although some mistakenly identify *Wissenschaft* with our English conception of science, we should conceive of the term more broadly as relating to any rational, critical, and disciplined pursuit of understanding. Reason, rather than faithfulness, defined the discourse of critical biblical scholarship.

In chapter 1 we introduced the common distinction between *exegesis* and *eisegesis*. No one has ever seriously argued that interpreters can achieve pure, unbiased objectivity. However, in many corners that sort of objectivity became a criterion for critical interpretation. For example, a classic treatment of the history of modern New Testament interpretation acknowledges that the Reformers did well in seeking a literal understanding of the New Testament but failed to achieve an unbiased historical perspective, the outlook accomplished by critical scholarship.

> The new insight of the Reformers that the Bible must be understood in a literal sense and that it is to be explained by itself could not lead to a strictly historical view of the New Testament so long as interpreters failed to recognize the historical character of the New Testament and the consequent necessity of investigating it historically and without prejudice.[51]

Twenty-first-century readers, as attuned to cultural diversity and multiple perspectives as we are, may struggle to understand this mind-set. For over a century scholars elevated exegesis as disciplined, open-minded inquiry, whereas they regarded eisegesis as the biased imposition of one's values and assumptions upon the biblical text. In this spirit an interpreter could reject widely held views as products of eisegesis, reading broader theological assumptions into a text where those assumptions are instead absent.[52] If exegesis brings out meaning from the text, eisegesis infects the text with alien presuppositions. Back in 1937, G. Ernest Wright, one of the leading interpreters of his time, defined the issue in this way: the "conflict" between exegesis and eisegesis occurs "between what a text actually says and what one hopes or

---

51. Werner Georg Kümmel, *The New Testament: The History of the Investigation of Its Problems*, trans. S. MacLean Gilmour and Howard Clark Kee (Nashville: Abingdon, 1972 [1970]), 31.
52. For example, Urban C. von Wahlde, "Faith and Works in John VI 28–29: Exegesis or Eisegesis?" *NovT* 4 (1980): 304–15.

feels it should say."⁵³ A problem arises because eisegesis has contributed to highly effective preaching, often with edifying results, while exegesis owns no religious agenda. By 1937, Wright argues, exegetical and scientific objectivity had won the day. There could be no retreat from them. Modern believers will have to embrace exegesis in order to discern "what the real religious and authoritative values of the Bible are."⁵⁴

Many theologically oriented interpreters complied with the exegesis-over-eisegesis framework. Some still do, of course. The classic example might be Krister Stendahl's reference article, in which he defined the task of biblical theology as discerning "what it meant and what it means."⁵⁵ That is, Stendahl proposed that exegesis could establish the historical meaning of a biblical text, while a more constructive process builds bridges between ancient meaning and contemporary significance. Stendahl construed the exegetical task as "descriptive" while comparing the work of theological appropriation to "translation." Stendahl's essay constitutes Exhibit A regarding the ethos of objectivist biblical scholarship. His categories empowered theological interpreters to see themselves as "rational" historians with theological interests—as if we could separate one process from the other.⁵⁶

This basic story is easily oversimplified. Even at the high point of biblical criticism, scholars were composing major works on the art of interpretation. Rudolf Bultmann, the most influential biblical interpreter of the twentieth century, engaged the sophisticated contemporary literature on philosophical hermeneutics, the study of interpretation. He concluded that "exegesis without presuppositions" is possible only if we mean "without presupposing the results" of interpretation. But he also maintained that *all* interpretation requires presuppositions as interpreters necessarily bring a "life-relation" to the work they study.⁵⁷

---

53. G. Ernest Wright, "Exegesis and Eisegesis in the Interpretation of Scripture," *ExpTim* 48 (1937): 353.
54. Wright, "Exegesis and Eisegesis," 357.
55. Stendahl, "Biblical Theology, Contemporary."
56. Robert Morgan with John Barton, *Biblical Interpretation*, Oxford Bible Series (New York: Oxford University Press, 1988).
57. Rudolf Bultmann, *New Testament and Mythology and Other Basic Writings*, trans. Schubert M. Ogden (Philadelphia: Fortress, 1984 [1957]), 145–53; quoted and summarized in David Congdon, "The Word as Event: Barth and Bultmann on Scripture," in *The Sacred Text: Excavating the Texts, Exploring the Interpretations, and Engaging the*

By asserting that every student has a vested interest in the object of study, Bultmann echoed classic hermeneutical thinkers like Martin Heidegger and Hans-Georg Gadamer, who were contemporaries of his, but he also anticipated Jürgen Habermas. Habermas argues that these vested interests, or biases, are not obstacles to the process of learning; rather, they make learning possible in the first place. This phenomenon applies to all fields of knowledge: we study because there's something we want—a product, an outcome, or a value. Whether we wish to accomplish something through technical research or to understand ourselves and one another through the human sciences (like biblical interpretation), those aims pull us into the process of learning.[58]

Objectivity was never possible, nor does it constitute a desirable aim. The appeal to objectivity originated as an exercise in freedom, an antidote to control by church authorities. But people also seek objectivity as a filter against unchecked bias. Biases can indeed overpower our critical faculties. For example, most people experience self-serving bias, the notion that we are more skilled or more moral than the average person. Obviously, *most* of us can't be better than *most* other people—but at least we can think we are. In fact, most of us also believe we are less biased than everyone else.[59]

In place of objectivity, perhaps we could cultivate some more appropriate, even more helpful virtues. First, the twin values of *open-mindedness* and *curiosity* point in the same general direction as objectivity, the possibility that we might learn or change our minds concerning the objects of our attention. We might find ourselves surprised. Curiosity is scarcely controversial, though perhaps less common than we might assume. Curious interpreters aim to learn: the outcome of interpretation remains open to them. In contrast, an authentic discussion of open-mindedness forces us into controversial territory, where real talk is essential. Because biblical interpretation often brushes against things that matter, we often come to the process hoping for particular outcomes.

It is difficult to know whether *we* are open-minded, while spotting

---

Theologies of the Christian Scriptures, ed. Michael Bird and Michael Pahl, Gorgias Précis Folios 7 (Piscataway, NJ: Gorgias, 2010), 254–55.

58. Jürgen Habermas, *Knowledge and Human Interests* (Boston: Beacon, 1971 [1968]).

59. Jonathan Haidt, *The Happiness Hypothesis: Finding Modern Truth in Ancient Wisdom* (New York: Basic, 2006), 66–71.

"clobber verses"

closed-mindedness in others is fairly easy. For example, a fair number of biblical scholars work in settings that require them to believe certain things, usually due to their religious affiliations. Their religious communities may place a high value on the Bible's historical reliability: topics such as the historicity of Moses, the accuracy of the Gospels and Acts, or the authorship of epistles attributed to Paul, Peter, James, and John fall under this tent. When scholars with such affiliations defend the historical accuracy of the exodus accounts, we may justifiably approach their contributions with a measure of skepticism. Likewise, some institutional settings condemn LGBTQ persons or promote the spiritual authority of men over women: we know what to expect when interpreters are affiliated with those communities.

It's more challenging to assess our own open-mindedness. Those of us who hold social-justice commitments may struggle to find good news in our work; sometimes it seems that good news, like good love, is hard to find. I've experienced this process at work in my own advocacy for LGBTQ equality in churches. I had devoted little attention to the issue until around 2000, when students requested advocacy from some of the faculty at my school. They wanted some of us to address what are called the "clobber passages," biblical passages often used to condemn same-sex sex and the people who engage in it. Early on, I did what many LGBTQ-affirming scholars have done: I tried to explain away the vexing passages by appealing to their literary and cultural contexts. Maybe these passages don't mean what they seem to mean, I'd argue. But at a certain point I began to find myself unconvinced by my own arguments. The Bible does include passages that condemn sex between men, along with one that condemns sex between women, and they resist being explained away. (There may still be some surprising passages that affirm same-sex love, but I'm not sure.) What good does it do to pretend otherwise? In the long run, people need not rationalizations, but integrity. I began to turn my attention toward the cultural logics various parts of the Bible devote to human sexuality, eventually coming to the conclusion that gender, marriage, and sexuality in ancient biblical cultures have very little to do with our contemporary concerns. Explaining why I believe this would take a book of its own, one others have written already.[60] In the end, I now lead discussions about con-

60. For example, James V. Brownson, *Bible, Gender, Sexuality: Reframing the Church's Debate on Same-Sex Relationships* (Grand Rapids: Eerdmans, 2013); Michael Coogan, *God and Sex: What the Bible Really Says* (New York: Twelve, 2010); Jennifer Wright

sistency in how we understand the Bible: Do we apply the Bible to a question like sexuality in ways that are consistent with other important topics? Do we apply the Bible to straight people in the ways that we do to the lives of sexual minorities? The short answer to both questions is no.

Second, a commitment to *fairness* involves basic civility. We know we will disagree with one another. We demonstrate fairness by accurately representing positions with which we disagree. In public space most (unfortunately, not all) disagreements involve people who have thought through their opinions and provide reasons for them. Public biblical interpretation calls us to disagree where appropriate and to spell out our own reasoning while acknowledging the logic of others as best we can. Surprisingly, fairness also applies when we agree with someone else. We give credit to others who have influenced our line of thought, and we acknowledge people who express an idea before we do—even when their work did not influence our own. Most often, fairness applies in those muddy areas in which we experience general agreement but wish to advance our own distinctive contributions. There's a human tendency to promote our own ideas as great advances, implicitly minimizing the wisdom we've gleaned from other people. Public scholarship surely isn't immune to that vice, but fairness calls us to show appreciation rather than posture ourselves as superior.

Thoroughness constitutes a third virtue for public interpretation. Thorough interpreters take account of as much information as is reasonably possible, given their contexts. When dealing with biblical texts, we consider the broader literary and thematic characteristics of that body of literature, what we can ascertain about its historical and literary contexts, problems of text and translation, and the general range of opinion concerning its significance, among other considerations. The more factors we consider, the more likely our interpretations are to persuade other people.

Thoroughness means different things in different contexts. The standards are high for professional interpreters, although no one ever "finishes" with the information-gathering process. The past few decades have produced such an explosion of scholarly publication that even doctoral students can't be completely up to date in their areas of spe-

Knust, *Unprotected Texts: The Bible's Surprising Contradictions about Sex and Desire* (New York: HarperOne, 2011); and Ruden, *Paul among the People*.

cialization. Professional interpreters are expected to account for all the major lines of opinion in our work. A 1,000-word piece of online commentary may not reflect that standard, but articles and books should. When I was in graduate school, a visiting scholar presented some of her work to our gathered community. In passing, she mentioned a book by another prominent scholar that would be published in the coming months. The exclamation "Oh, shit!" broke up the somber academic gathering as a graduate student realized she would have to take account of this new book in writing her dissertation. Teachers, preachers, and other public interpreters who handle biblical texts weekly and daily can scarcely devote all their waking hours to library research, so a different standard applies. Nevertheless, I treasure my childhood memories of my grandfather Curvis Akin and uncle Norman Summers devoting a chunk of their Saturdays to preparation to teach adult Sunday school in their churches. Neither had received a college education, but each did his best to be thorough.

In recent years we have learned to regard *diversity* as a hallmark of excellence. Research has shown that working groups composed of diverse people tend to make better decisions than homogenous groups. They tend to pay better attention to the facts at hand, process their information more carefully, and work more creatively.[61] These factors don't even begin to account for the value of having diverse cultural perspectives and habits of thinking as part of a group's deliberations.

It's always a good idea for public interpretation to occur in social settings, but the truth is, we often work alone. Moreover, our immediate social circles are limited. In biblical interpretation, attending to diversity can mean cultivating a range of perspectives. If we're working on a particular question or text, it's well worth the time to search out at least one or two perspectives very different from our own, whether theologically or culturally so. More basically, we can build our own competence by acquiring familiarity with a wide range of interpretive perspectives, as we'll discuss in the following chapter. In interpersonal relationships we acquire new knowledge and skills from a wide range of friends. By reading broadly in, for example, feminist, South Asian, and Latinx hermeneutics, we can also broaden our capacity to ask productive questions and to observe fresh details.

---

61. David Rock and Heidi Grant, "Why Diverse Teams Are Smarter," *Harvard Business Review*, November 4, 2016, https://hbr.org/2016/11/why-diverse-teams-are-smarter.

By naming diversity as a virtue that interpreters should cultivate, we acknowledge that the practice of honoring diversity requires another virtue: humility. Every person inhabits a limited perspective, and engagement with diverse perspectives extends our competence. We might also consider diversity as an expression of another virtue: love. As Jacob D. Myers puts it,

> We who would seek to love our neighbor as ourselves in and through scripture must open ourselves to readings that emerge from different cultural spaces. We must expand our interpretive worldview, so to speak.[62]

Myers's language reflects a specifically Christian orientation, one I admittedly share. But his argument is accessible to readers of other religious and nonreligious orientations. The commitment to engage diverse perspectives is a commitment to respect people from every walk of life.

A fifth virtue for us to cultivate is *transparency*. As a classroom teacher, I practice accountability by letting students know what kind of perspectives they're receiving from me. In an introductory class, most of what they encounter amounts to common knowledge—almost any expert would tell you many of the same things: Joshua and Judges offer different accounts for how Israel emerged as a nation; Pharisees and Sadducees disagreed about the resurrection; and the same person probably wrote Luke and Acts. Other issues attract a diversity of opinion, sometimes split in near 50/50 proportions. Students have a right to know when we're discussing those kinds of ideas. And yes, sometimes I'm sharing what I call my own nutty opinion: a take on things that may be in the minority or that I haven't vetted with other scholars. Transparency of this kind holds us accountable, builds trust with our conversation partners, and opens space for productive conversation.

Transparency also bears upon the question of value, or relevance. Like everything else we do, interpretation has implications, whether moral, social, or theological. Interpersonally, we all know the experience of being factually correct but relationally wrong: we can tell the truth in hurtful ways just as easily as we can in helpful ones. The same applies to interpretation. Public interpreters show transparency by being open about the value we ascribe to our work, our motives in

---

62. Jacob D. Myers, *Making Love with Scripture: Why the Bible Doesn't Mean How You Think It Means* (Minneapolis: Fortress, 2015), 46.

pursuing it and in sharing the results, and the ethical and theological implications of our choices.

Pure objectivity is never possible, and the attempt to be truly objective may limit interpretation. Our true aim is to train our biases so that they will be as productive as possible in helping us to attain insight, while holding ourselves accountable to alternative perspectives. Virtues such as open-mindedness and curiosity, fairness, thoroughness, diversity, and transparency provide our best path to achieving those ends. In my view, the surest sign of virtuous interpretation occurs when we find ourselves surprised.

AN ETHICAL READER?

Some Christian interpreters insist upon the desirability of a "faithful" reader: one who expects to encounter God's voice through the Bible, who adheres to the rule of faith and desires to practice the rule of love. But if we grant theological concerns priority over other issues,[63] who defines what counts as theological? Is violence a theological question? What about misogyny? Poverty and inequality? If we believe in God, does God care less about those questions than about matters of doctrine? Should we?

We might begin by reflecting upon what we mean when we toss around words like *ethics* and *ethical*. The ethics courses I took in college and seminary looked this way. We'd begin the course with an introduction to ethical theory: ontological ethics started with norms or rules that are universally valid, while teleological ethics emphasized the outcomes of our moral choices. Then we'd move on to various sets of ethical issues: the obligation to help someone in need; war; capital punishment; euthanasia; abortion; and so forth. But during those years a sea change was underway in ethical thought, a move away from topical and decision-making ethics to an emphasis on the formation of character.[64] In essence this transition hearkened back to the ancient ethics of Aristotle, who elevated training in character above the rationality of decision making in moments of crisis. As one team of writers puts it, character ethics aims not so much at good decisions as at the good life. And the good life is achieved when we

---

63. Fowl, *Theological Interpretation of Scripture*, 15–24.
64. The watershed work is Alasdair MacIntyre, *After Virtue: A Study in Moral Theory* (South Bend, IN: University of Notre Dame Press, 1981).

choose the qualities that mark the good person and the good society and internalize these as the habits of heart, soul, and mind. When habitual, these qualities express who we are; they exhibit our moral identity and drive our actions. They create the good society from the inside out, as the outcome of the kind of persons we are and strive to be. The focus is on moral agents, from whom actions flow as water from a spring.[65]

That sort of training requires communities and traditions, not just collections of individuals with disembodied rational minds. As I am contemplating ethical readers and ethical interpretation, I have in mind readers who are committed to being good and to doing good in the world and for whom those commitments abide at the top of their priorities list.

In psychological terms, we are more likely to create ethical outcomes by devoting our energies to the formation of character than by building intellectual rubrics for sorting our way through ethical and moral dilemmas. Human beings are experts at rationalization: we decide what we desire, and we reason our way through our desires while we are in the midst of pursuing them. When it comes to our capacity to make good moral decisions, psychological research is extraordinarily discouraging, for it shows how profoundly we deceive ourselves. What we experience, and what we remember, as the agonizing process of making moral decisions in fact occurs *after* the decision has been made. Our internal struggles simply reflect the process by which we convince ourselves that our course is good and right. We were headed there already.[66] If we want to develop our moral capacity, that takes not the right thought system but systematic training.

Ethical reading is complicated by our diverse motivations for reading the Bible. Most studies of biblical ethics derive from Jewish and Christian religious communities, as authors seek to shape those communities' attitudes and behaviors. In other words, their aims are *normative*: they seek to guide people in righteous paths. But secular readers also have ethical interests. Often their aims are *descriptive*, seeking to understand the habits and values of biblical peoples as a humanist project, valuable as a point of curiosity or even for building cultural wisdom.

But secular critics also can take on advocacy roles quite effectively.

---

65. Bruce C. Birch, Jacqueline E. Lapsley, Cynthia Moe-Lobeda, and Larry L. Rasmussen, *Bible and Ethics in the Christian Life: A New Conversation* (Minneapolis: Fortress, 2018), 183.
66. Haidt, *Happiness Hypothesis*, esp. 1–24, 155–60.

Hector Avalos, an atheist, seeks to delegitimize the common appeal to the Bible in public ethics. Avalos begins by noting that in Christian ethics *"Jesus never does anything wrong."*[67] When writing on ethics, Christian scholars usually begin by giving Jesus a central role in ethical reflection. Avalos regards the Bible as an entirely inappropriate authority for moral formation, and he proceeds by arguing for a "bad Jesus." On issue after issue, from a flawed love ethic to slavery to gender to environmental concerns, Avalos shows how the teaching and behavior of Jesus make bad examples and do not reflect the ethics of modern persons.

Avalos has a point in zeroing in on the appeal to Jesus as a moral example. Jesus's centrality for Christian ethics is axiomatic, with major works in Christian ethics grounding themselves in Jesus.[68] Jesus's ethics lurk at a deeper level, in the formation of biblical studies, particularly New Testament studies, as an academic discipline. Although historical criticism quickly unraveled the traditional (Christian) assumption that the Bible simply describes things as they occurred, scholars deflected historical investigation to a search for authentic Israelite and Christian origins: the emergence of Israelite religion, the authentic voice of the prophets, the preaching and practice of the early church, and the authentic (there's that word again) teaching of Jesus. None of these efforts went as expected, leading neither to historical certainty nor to consensus regarding the essential nature of any of these subjects. So biblical scholars turned from history to ethics, especially the search for ethical, social, and theological good news in the Bible. That tendency persists, argue Stephen D. Moore and Yvonne Sherwood, and it shapes the ethos of biblical studies as an academic discipline.[69]

Scholarship devoted to ethical engagement with the Bible takes many forms. One approach is to begin from principles. Charles H. Cosgrove, for example, lays out five hermeneutical rules for bringing the Bible

---

67. Hector Avalos, *The Bad Jesus: The Ethics of New Testament Ethics*, BMW 68 (Sheffield: Sheffield Phoenix Press, 2015), 1. (Italics his.)

68. Howard Thurman, *Jesus and the Disinherited* (Nashville: Abingdon, 1949); John Howard Yoder, *The Politics of Jesus*, rev. ed. (Grand Rapids: Eerdmans, 1994 [1972]); Obery M. Hendricks Jr., *The Politics of Jesus: Rediscovering the True Revolutionary Nature of Jesus' Teachings and How They Have Been Corrupted* (New York: Doubleday, 2006); Richard A. Burridge, *Imitating Jesus: An Inclusive Approach to New Testament Ethics* (Grand Rapids: Eerdmans, 2007).

69. Moore and Sherwood, *The Invention of the Biblical Scholar*.

into ethical conversations. One involves assessing the ancient *purpose* of a biblical teaching: the teaching itself may not pertain to our current dilemmas because it reflects cultural logics that simply do not carry to our situations. A second and related rule appeals to *analogy*: we should ask whether biblical teachings "fit" the situations and dilemmas we face today. Third, Cosgrove posits that the Bible tends to favor a *countercultural witness*, speaking truth to power and reforming the status quo. (Not everyone would agree, to put it mildly.) Fourth, Cosgrove maintains the Bible's *nonscientific scope*: we recognize that biblical authors were not operating from a modern scientific mind-set, nor were they providing answers to scientific questions in ways modern people do. Fifth, and quite vexing, is the matter of *moral-theological adjudication*: here we appeal to broader principles, even ones that relate to our interpretation of the Bible, and apply them to the biblical evidence. The rule of love would constitute a good example. I would argue that countercultural witness, Cosgrove's third rule, provides a criterion for moral-theological adjudication: after all, countercultural witness is both a moral and a theological value assumption applied to interpretation.[70]

Any reconstruction of biblical ethics, whether of the whole Bible, on a given topic, or on a section of the Bible, invites interpreters to lay out their assumptions. Some pass by this step, attempting to deal with the Bible's complexity on its own terms without imposing a theoretical and methodological framework.[71] But the biblical material is diverse, and "describing" what the Bible approves and doesn't approve results in diverse piles of conflicting and ambiguous material. Richard B. Hays recalls his grandmother saying, "The Devil can cite Scripture to his purpose," as he introduces a massive set of reflections concerning how to make moral sense out of the New Testament.[72] Among Jewish and Christian interpreters, for whom the Bible provides a fundamental resource and sometimes the ultimate authority for ethical reflection,

---

70. Charles H. Cosgrove, *Appealing to Scripture in Moral Debate: Five Hermeneutical Rules* (Grand Rapids: Eerdmans, 2002).

71. For example, John Barton, *Ethics and the Old Testament*, 2nd ed. (London: SCM, 2002); though see the same author's "The Basis of Ethics in the Hebrew Bible," *Semeia* 66 (1994): 11–22.

72. Richard B. Hays, *The Moral Vision of the New Testament: A Contemporary Introduction to New Testament Ethics* (New York: HarperCollins, 1996), 1.

simply listing what the Bible "says" and trying to "obey" it inevitably prove inadequate.[73]

A second approach to ethical interpretation foregrounds transparency. Interpreters occasionally acknowledge how ethical considerations shape their judgment. Charles H. Cosgrove mentions Lloyd Gaston, who wrote a great deal about the presentation of Jews and Judaism in the New Testament. Gaston argues that it is possible to interpret Paul as affirming both Israel and the Torah—and that in the wake of the Holocaust, "it is necessary to do so."[74] Brian K. Blount offers a similar assessment of Paul regarding other ethical issues. African American Christians have tended to neglect Paul, largely because owners of enslaved people and their preachers proclaimed that Paul admonished enslaved people to be obedient. But, Blount argues, "the liberative benefits that can be gleaned from [Paul's] counsel are legion."[75] According to Blount, Paul's logic on matters like gender and sexuality, slavery, and church-state relations is so conflicted that it is possible to read Paul optimistically. Blount therefore calls upon African American readers to interpret Paul with freedom and creativity.[76]

Ethical transparency lends itself to what we might call advocacy interpretations. Interpreters use all sorts of language for these ways of reading, but we might identify advocacy interpretations by their common characteristic: readers begin with ethical commitments, which they then apply to the process of interpretation. Brian Blount's study begins with "where African American theology and, indeed, the African American church itself began: with the African American slave."[77] His investigation of New Testament ethics consistently builds connections with values and practices reflected in those of enslaved African Americans. One might readily envision ethical approaches grounded in the perspectives, experiences, and interests of diverse communities, whether they define themselves in terms such as feminist, queer, postcolonial, or of particular racial and ethnic identities. Beyond advocacy

---

73. Birch, Lapsley, Moe-Lobeda, and Rasmussen, *Bible and Ethics*, esp. 69–87.
74. Lloyd Gaston, *Paul and the Torah* (Vancouver: University of British Columbia Press, 1987), 34; cited in Cosgrove, *Appealing to Scripture*, 154.
75. Brian K. Blount, *Then the Whisper Put on Flesh: New Testament Ethics in African American Context* (Nashville: Abingdon, 2001), 156.
76. Blount, *Then the Whisper Put on Flesh*, 119–57.
77. Blount, *Then the Whisper Put on Flesh*, 23.

for groups of people, we might also consider advocacy interpretation focused on key issues such as environmental concerns or peacemaking. One might even conceive of a broader commitment to "emancipatory" interpretation at the intersection of such diverse interests.[78]

Both within and outside of religious communities, the Bible is routinely invoked as a source of moral authority. For that reason, some interpreters see the ethical task as exposing the drawbacks of using the Bible in that way. This happens outside church and synagogue, as we see in the example of Hector Avalos, but it happens within religious communities as well. Some readers call for direct confrontation with dangerous or incorrect aspects of the Bible. For example, stories portraying Israel's annihilation of its neighbors undermine the capacity of religious communities to reject nationalism and ethnic cleansing, while the New Testament expectation of Jesus's imminent return tends to diminish reliance on human agency to improve the world. In addition to the need for basic intellectual and spiritual integrity, religious communities can learn from the Bible's counter-example.[79] Attempts to rationalize our way out of the Bible's complications, however sophisticated, ultimately cut short ethical and interpretive accountability.[80] That reality, perhaps more than any other, weighs in favor of ethically committed and ethically mature interpreters.

CONCLUSION

In this chapter we have asked whether certain kinds of people hold an advantage in biblical interpretation: religiously faithful people, critically objective people, and ethically committed people. It doesn't surprise us that these are all contested questions. Each one opens the path to further questions. For example, maybe we don't buy the notion that religiously observant interpreters are somehow more qualified to read the Bible than are secular and resistant readers, but we might grant that "faithful" readers serve their own faith communities in distinctive ways. I argued that pure objectivity is not only unattainable but

---

78. Elisabeth Schüssler Fiorenza, *Democratizing Biblical Studies: Toward an Emancipatory Educational Space* (Louisville: Westminster John Knox, 2009), 104–6.
79. Thom Stark, *The Human Faces of God: What Scripture Reveals When It Gets God Wrong (and Why Inerrancy Tries to Hide It)* (Eugene, OR: Wipf & Stock, 2011).
80. Eryl W. Davies, *The Immoral Bible: Approaches to Biblical Ethics* (New York: T&T Clark, 2010).

undesirable, but I also suggested that virtues like open-mindedness and curiosity, fairness, thoroughness, diversity, and transparency can hold public interpreters accountable. Perhaps no one would object to a preference for ethical readers; however, once we reflect on what it means to read the Bible ethically, all sorts of complications pop up.

Having weighed all these complications, we might grow cynical. Every attempt to specify what a virtuous reader looks like amounts to a power grab. We like readers who ask *our* questions and serve *our* interests; other interpreters we call "biased." To be clear: we should be suspicious of interpretive power grabs.

I would suggest a different conclusion. Although I would resist any generalizations that one kind of reader is more competent than others, I would also call attention to what we learn by asking these questions. For example, I believe there's a place for interpreters who serve particular religious communities—and I am convinced those same communities benefit greatly by attending to the views of readers beyond their boundaries. A critique of objectivity leads us to appreciate the passions and investments that energize interpretation—and to the need for accountability to a broad public. And the question of ethics confronts us with the question "*Whose* ethics?" That question leads us to explore not theoretical readers but real, "flesh-and-blood" readers and how we relate to one another.[81]

---

81. Fernando F. Segovia, "'And They Began to Speak in Other Tongues': Competing Modes of Discourse in Contemporary Biblical Criticism," in Segovia and Tolbert, *Reading from This Place*, 1:20; Segovia, "Hermeneutics of the Diaspora," in Segovia and Tolbert, *Reading from This Place*, 1:57.

CHAPTER 5.

FLESH AND BLOOD

At points in this book I have referred to the "flesh-and-blood reader," a category introduced by Fernando F. Segovia about twenty-five years ago.[1] Biblical scholars often discuss how a biblical text addresses its "reader." We all recognize that this reader is a hypothetical figure, a shorthand way of imagining how ancient or contemporary readers would interact with texts. Nevertheless, this language conveys a host of assumptions, all of them questionable: (1) that texts influence their audiences in predictable ways; (2) that we can discern both an author's intentions *and* a text's effects upon real people; and (3) that authors generally succeed in guiding readers to adopt specific points of view.

Let's be real: our hypothetical reader amounts to a projection of our own interpretive decisions.

Isn't it remarkable that when commentators tell us how "the reader" responds to a text, those same commentators are usually promoting novel interpretations? In other words, *real* readers have generally *not* responded to the text in the ways the commentator proposes. Flesh-and-blood readers respond to the Bible in complex and often unpredictable ways, and for reasons that generally go unstated.

In chapter 2 we discussed reception history, the process of assessing the history of the Bible's reception or influence. This field aligns closely with religious history, as it requires expertise in the diverse moments of human culture as much as it does with biblical texts and their historical contexts. Biblical scholars and historians alike conduct research in reception history, sometimes collaboratively. It is rare for a biblical

---

1. Segovia, "'And They Began to Speak in Other Tongues,'" and "Hermeneutics of the Diaspora," in Segovia and Tolbert, *Reading from This Place*, 1:20 and 1:57 respectively.

scholar to develop the kind of expertise we expect from cultural historians, just as it is challenging for cultural historians to gain fluency in the questions, methods, and conversations that define biblical scholarship. When all these things come together, the results are remarkable.[2] This chapter focuses not so much upon studies in reception history as upon *ways of reading*, particularly among readers who own distinctive cultural perspectives and affinities.

As we discussed in the previous chapter, for a very long time, biblical scholarship valorized objectivity in interpretation, pitting exegesis over against eisegesis. In this chapter, however, we're emphasizing interpreters who *foreground* the contributions of culture, faith, and identity toward the work of interpretation. In the objectivist, exegesis-oriented mode of interpretation, readers try to set aside the influence of factors like race, ethnicity, nationality, global positioning, gender, class, sexual orientation, and physical ability. But the turn toward real flesh-and-blood readers brings these dimensions of human experience to the forefront. In this chapter we consider significant movements in contemporary interpretation that do precisely that. *I propose that public biblical interpretation should account for globally diverse approaches to the Bible*, a criterion that is appreciated far too rarely in textbooks and other literature.

As the chapter concludes, we'll consider one category of interpreters that has generally avoided the role of culture and identity in interpretation: white interpreters. Modern academic biblical interpretation has been dominated by Northern Europeans and North Americans, the same group that originally promoted objectivist exegesis. Because white interpreters have so long resided at the center of public interpretation, we (I'm white) have rarely felt the need to subject our assumptions and methods to critical scrutiny; instead, we've assumed those assumptions and methods *are* critical and objective. We'll look into attempts to specify what "white" interpretation looks like. It would be just as valuable to study "male" or "heterosexual" interpretation; indeed, I'm sure we'd encounter significant overlap among these categories. It is my hope that critical reflection on the role of whiteness in interpreta-

---

2. See chapter 2's discussion of Sawyer, *The Fifth Gospel*. Other examples from biblical scholars include: Timothy Beal, *The Book of Revelation: A Biography*, Lives of Great Religious Books (Princeton: Princeton University Press, 2018); Boxall, *Patmos in the Reception History*; and Chester, *Reading Paul with the Reformers*.

tion will open a path toward greater understanding of what public biblical interpretation means for all of us.

A LIBERATIONIST IMPULSE

Until quite recently, public biblical interpretation largely occurred only among professional clergy and other highly educated persons. Rabbinical schools, monasteries, and universities provided the institutional homes for learned engagement with Scripture. Critics of Judaism and Christianity also participated, especially in the ancient world and during the Enlightenment. Nevertheless, access to libraries and to the means of publication reserved public interpretation for relatively few classes of people.

The point can be overstated, of course. For example, significant research has uncovered how enslaved persons in North America developed distinctive interpretive practices, even when laws prohibited teaching enslaved persons how to read.[3] Literacy itself provided a means of amplifying one's public voice while demonstrating one's "own membership in the human community."[4] The interpretations of the enslaved may not often have been literate, but they certainly took account of real-life conditions and traditions of interpretation. Meanwhile, literate African American abolitionists, whether clergy or not, also appropriated the Bible for liberation.[5] Maintaining that the God revealed in the Bible loves all people and created none of them for enslavement, "early African American interpreters attempted to demonstrate the discontinuity between slave ideology, enslavement, and the biblical witness."[6]

Frederick Douglass, for example, started a Sunday Bible class for enslaved persons with the sharp recognition that owners of enslaved

---

3. See especially Emerson B. Powery and Rodney S. Sadler Jr., *The Genesis of Liberation: Biblical Interpretation in the Antebellum Narratives of the Enslaved* (Louisville: Westminster John Knox, 2016); and Martin, "'Somebody Done Hoodoo'd the Hoodoo Man.'"
4. Powery and Sadler, *Genesis of Liberation*, 60, quoting Henry Louis Gates Jr.
5. John Saillant, "Origins of African American Biblical Hermeneutics in Eighteenth-Century Black Opposition to the Slave Trade and Slavery," in *African Americans and the Bible: Sacred Texts and Social Textures*, ed. Vincent L. Wimbush (New York: Continuum, 2001), 236–50; Margaret P. Aymer, *First Pure, Then Peaceable: Frederick Douglass Reads James*, LNTS 379 (New York: T&T Clark, 2007).
6. Mitzi J. Smith, *Insights from African American Interpretation*, Reading the Bible in the 21st Century (Minneapolis: Fortress, 2017), 11.

people were likely to suppress the work, as they eventually did. Sterling Stuckey quotes Douglass's recollection at several points.

> Our pious masters at St. Michaels must not know that a few of their dusky brothers were learning to read the word of God, lest they should come down with lash and chain.

The masters' fear derived from a recognition that enslaved persons might extract an emancipatory message from the Bible. Douglass continued:

> If slaves learned to read they would learn something more and something worse. The peace of slavery would be disturbed. Slave rule would be endangered. I do not dispute the soundness of the reasoning. If slavery were right, Sabbath-schools for teaching slaves to read were wrong, and ought to have been put down. These Christian class-leaders were, to this extent, consistent. They had settled the question that slavery was right, and by that standard they determined that Sabbath-schools were wrong.[7]

Feminists in the United States also claimed authority to engage in public biblical interpretation. During the women's suffrage movement Elizabeth Cady Stanton and a team of feminist colleagues composed and collected commentary on biblical passages of concern to women. Their two-volume *The Woman's Bible*, published in 1895 and 1898, included lay and ordained women, mostly from the United States but also from Europe.[8] The authors' comments called attention to neglected or controversial passages, but they also openly critiqued patriarchy where they found it necessary. We can trace this balance in two passages treated by Stanton. First, she takes the story of Esther, who wins a contest to become queen to the Persian ruler Ahasuerus by "pleasing him" and thus displaces Vashti, who displeases the king by refusing to appear so that he can display her beauty to the public. Esther uses her position as queen to save the Jews in Susa from annihilation, while Vashti disappears from the story altogether. Stanton chooses to place the spotlight on Vashti rather than on the eponymous Esther,

---

7. Sterling Stuckey, "'My Burden Lightened': Frederick Douglass, the Bible, and Slave Culture," in Wimbush, *African Americans and the Bible*, 259; from Douglass, *Life and Times of Frederick Douglass, Written by Himself* (New York: Collier, 1892), 187–88. I have filled in some of Douglass's words where Stuckey has summarized the contents.

8. Elizabeth Cady Stanton, *The Woman's Bible*, rpt. (Salem, NH: Ayer Company, 1988). See Kathi Kern, *Mrs. Stanton's Bible* (Ithaca, NY: Cornell University Press, 2001).

adding detail to the story. Vashti refuses to put her beauty on display because "dignity and modesty alike forbid" it. Thus she "stands out a sublime representative of self-centered womanhood." Stanton concludes:

> I have always regretted that the historian allowed Vashti to drop out of sight so suddenly. Perhaps she was doomed to some menial service, or to entire sequestration in her own apartments.[9]

In this balanced spirit Stanton recommends charity toward the apostle Paul when he passes judgment on women's "adornment," while she also suggests he suffered from a narrowly patriarchal perspective.

> It is perhaps not fair to judge Paul by the strict letter of the word. We are not well informed of the habits of women in his time in regard to personal adornment.... The Apostles all appeared to be much exercised by the ornaments and the braided hair of the women.... But women had other reasons for braiding their hair beside attracting men. A compact braid was much more comfortable than individual hairs free to be blown about with every breeze.[10]

In view of non-professional antecedents like African Americans and feminists in previous centuries, we should show caution before assigning public biblical interpretation only to the academic class of interpreters. At the same time, the second half of the twentieth century brought about a massive expansion in access to specialized education and to publication. Liberationist movements blossomed on a global scale, addressing concerns regarding economic justice and human rights; gender and sexuality; and race, ethnicity, and culture. Although still marginalized with reference to the field's white, male, and Christian center, interpreters whose voices had largely been muffled began to own public space. These developments reflect the same transformations that were occurring on a global scale, transforming public conversations, in just about every field of inquiry.

Latin American liberation theology marks a critical movement in public biblical interpretation—interpretation in an explicitly advocacy-oriented mode. The movement seems to have begun in the 1960s, gaining increasing levels of attention over the next two decades until its influence reconfigured theological work and education in both the

---

9. Stanton, *The Woman's Bible*, 2:84–90.
10. Stanton, *The Woman's Bible*, 2:161.

Northern and the Southern Hemispheres. Understanding interpretation as *producing* meaning, rather than as extracting already-existing meanings embedded in biblical texts, liberation thinkers argued that *praxis*—the work of pursuing justice—should determine the shape of interpretation. Thus "hopes and struggles of the oppressed" mark the critical starting point for Latin American liberationist hermeneutics.[11]

Latin American liberationist interpretation is very much concerned with things of the spirit, but material concerns come first. Liberationist readers practice a "preferential option" for the poor. Although the biblical authors themselves did not identify as oppressed, the experiences they describe—such as the exodus of enslaved Israelites—are those of suffering and liberation. For this reason, the Bible belongs first to the poor because, in the words of J. Severino Croatto, their "horizon of understanding" corresponds to that of the biblical material.[12]

The grassroots nature of liberationist practice moves interpretation out of the academy and the monastery into the communities of poor people. As with Cardenal's transcription of Bible study sessions among peasants in Solentiname, which we mentioned in chapter 2, "base community" Bible study and common life provide a locus for public interpretation.[13] Often a more professional reader, a priest or an academic, works as a consultant in such settings, but interpretation stays close to disenfranchised people.

These shifts in social location and in presuppositions lead to provocative interpretations that, upon reflection, will inform more privileged readers. Students in a class I teach read a *Solentiname* study on the Lord's Supper as it is presented in Mark 14:12–25. An artist visiting the Solentiname community begins the study by observing, "It seems to have been a clandestine supper." Another recalls that one of Jesus's disciples was armed, as he wounds a member of the party that arrests Jesus only verses later (14:47). Cardenal, the priest who convened the studies and recorded the conversations, added that Passover began as a liberation festival among *campesinos*, or peasant farmers. Later on, members of the community maintain that people who oppress

---

11. J. Severino Croatto, *Biblical Hermeneutics: Toward a Theory of Reading as the Production of Meaning* (Maryknoll, NY: Orbis, 1987), 51.

12. Croatto, *Biblical Hermeneutics*, 63.

13. See Carlos Mesters, *Defenseless Flower: A New Reading of the Bible* (Maryknoll, NY: Orbis, 1989), 55–155.

the poor are forbidden from participating in the Eucharist.[14] Almost all students find these interpretations surprising, as they typically think of the Lord's Supper in spiritual rather than sociopolitical terms. We then discuss evidence that supports the Solentiname interpretations. For example, Jesus seems to pre-arrange the supper: finding the man with a water jar and having already secured a guest room suggest a clandestine arrangement (14:13–15). And Passover is indeed a liberation festival, as it celebrates freedom from enslavement. People in Jesus's day, not least the Roman authorities, were aware of that. Our students find themselves instructed by this circle of professional and nonprofessional interpreters.

To take another example, the Greek word *diké* has to do with justice. It also forms the root of many New Testament terms that are translated in other ways: "righteousness" and "justification." In church circles those terms receive spiritual meanings. Righteousness has to do with right behavior or with a status God imparts to people: they are "righteous" in relation to God. And justification involves the process by which God imparts that status. Paul's teaching on justification provides one of the most controversial—some would say, overworked—topics in biblical interpretation. As with the Lord's Supper, these theological conversations typically locate righteousness and justification in the realm of doctrine and spirituality. Furthermore, righteousness and justification pertain to individuals rather than to societies or to the world.[15] In contrast, Mexican liberation theologian Elsa Tamez challenges interpreters to ground righteousness, justification, and other Pauline terms in their most basic use: relations of justice and injustice. Paul conceives of sin not in terms of individual misdemeanors but as oppression of the powerless by the powerful.[16] God's justice involves not merely forgiveness but empowerment to live justly.[17] Justification,

---

14. Cardenal, *The Gospel in Solentiname*, 533–43.

15. Though see, for example, Beverly Roberts Gaventa, *When in Romans: An Invitation to Linger with the Gospel according to Paul*, Theological Explorations for the Church Catholic (Waco, TX: Baylor University Press, 2016); and Neil Elliott, *The Arrogance of Nations: Reading Romans in the Shadow of Empire*, Paul in Critical Contexts (Minneapolis: Fortress, 2008), 59–86.

16. Elsa Tamez, *The Amnesty of Grace: Justification by Faith from a Latin American Perspective* (Nashville: Abingdon, 1993), 115.

17. Tamez, *Amnesty of Grace*, 126.

according to Tamez, involves making things right, a classic understanding of Paul's vocabulary.

It may be a mistake to credit Latin American liberation theology with similar movements in other global contexts. We can observe that white North American and European scholars appreciated the challenges presented by liberationist interpretation and found ways to promote it in their own settings, with enormous influence especially in theological education.[18] In the 1980s and 1990s, publishers took the hint and published collections of essays authored by scholars from diverse global settings. In 1991 R. S. Sugirtharajah's *Voices from the Margin* included authors from all around the world, including Native American and Palestinian authors,[19] while in the mid-1990s Fernando F. Segovia and Mary Ann Tolbert released two volumes of essays, the first from North American scholars and the second global in reach.[20] Among other purposes, such volumes exposed masses of readers to the diverse interests and interpretive strategies that mark global biblical interpretation. In the ensuing decades others have updated the project by providing similar collections, some focused on individual texts and others more general.[21]

Whatever its origins, liberationist interpretation emerged in its own ways in other global settings. Under South Korea's military regime, Ahn Byung-Mu fostered *minjung* theology, adopting a term that refers to the oppressed masses of people. His study of the crowds in Mark led him to see Jesus as siding with the minjung. Though Jesus never calls for armed revolt, Mark depicts the authorities as being afraid of the crowds as an unpredictable and restless force. Jesus's proclamation of God's reign offers a theology and a social vision that empower these oppressed masses.[22]

---

18. For example, Christopher Rowland and Mark Corner, *Liberating Exegesis: The Challenge of Liberation Theology to Biblical Studies* (Louisville: Westminster John Knox, 1989); and Norman Gottwald and Richard H. Horsley, eds., *The Bible and Liberation: Political and Social Hermeneutics*, rev. ed. (Maryknoll, NY: Orbis, 1993).
19. Sugirtharajah, *Voices from the Margin*.
20. Segovia and Tolbert, eds., *Reading from This Place*, 2 vols.
21. See Lozada and Carey, eds., *Soundings in Cultural Criticism*.
22. Ahn Byung-Mu, *Minjung Theology: People as the Subjects of History* (Maryknoll, NY: Orbis, 1981). For contemporary assessments, see Yung Suk Kim and Jin-Ho Kim, eds., *Reading Minjung Theology in the Twenty-First Century* (Eugene, OR: Pickwick, 2013).

Liberationist interpretation also manifested itself in Apartheid South Africa. Allan A. Boesak found the critique of Roman imperial oppression in Revelation a resource for resistance.[23] Working from a more explicitly Marxist perspective, Itumeleng J. Mosala critiqued the common view that Luke stands out for its advocacy for the poor. Mosala countered that it does no good to call attention to the Bible's liberating motifs while neglecting those threads that undermine the liberationist impulse. Luke may emphasize the poor, but he introduces Jesus to an elite reader, Theophilus, and presents Jesus within the structures of elite society: in a family of means with priestly connections. Luke presents Jesus not as revolutionary but as "acceptable" to the rich and powerful—and, Mosala insists, to middle-class interpreters promote Luke's agenda in the present day.[24] In these black South African interpreters of the 1980s we hear liberationist interpretation in multiple voices, one almost entirely affirming the Bible's potential for liberation and the other more skeptical.

Liberation theology emerged out of concerns with poverty and economic oppression. Over time liberationist interpretation expanded from this material base to engage cultural concerns. Interpreters recognized that economic and political oppression legitimate themselves through cultural exploitation. Colonial powers invest enormous energy in the process of cultural representation, the power to describe, analyze, and categorize the societies they dominate. This process occurs in literature, through the establishment of academic disciplines and museums, through reportage, and in countless other cultural settings. The postcolonial project, which we discussed in chapter 2, asserts the power of colonized and formerly colonized people to "talk back" to empire by representing themselves and their colonizers.

Cultural interpretation in a liberationist mode is practically infinite in scope. Since colonial authorities exercise power through language and translation, those issues manifest themselves in biblical interpretation.[25] It can manifest itself in the representation of indigenous spiritu-

---

23. Boesak, *Comfort and Protest*.
24. Itumeleng J. Mosala, *Biblical Hermeneutics and Black Theology in South Africa* (Grand Rapids: Eerdmans, 1989).
25. For example, Ekaputra Tupamahu, "Language Politics and the Constitution of Racialized Subjects in the Corinthian Church," *JSNT* 41 (2018): 223–45; Johnson Kiriaku Kinyua, "A Postcolonial Analysis of Bible Translation and Its Effectiveness

ality, as when Zimbabwean biblical scholar Temba L. J. Mafico suggests reading the Hebrew term *elohim*, which is plural, not as a proper name for "God" but as "gods," with Israelites worshipping Yahweh as senior among the deities.[26] It can involve reading a biblical narrative, such as Mary's conception of Jesus, through the experiences of Indian surrogate mothers.[27] When readers bring their own cultural resources to bear upon the process of interpretation, the horizons of interpretation expand indefinitely.

A WHOLE WIDE WORLD

Historians remember the 1960s as a period of intense cultural change—and conflict—in North America and Europe. In the United States the Civil Rights Movement attained its most dramatic legal accomplishments, while liberation movements among feminists, Latinx persons, and the LGBTQ community blossomed. The United States' military involvement in Vietnam led to sharp social divisions and raised questions about the Cold War and its relationship to colonialism. Mass protests broke out not only in the US but also in Poland, France, Mexico, Italy, and what were then Czechoslovakia and West Germany. These trends all contributed to a sea change in public biblical interpretation, as liberation movements adapted and responded to the Bible in manifold ways.

Neither feminist nor African American interpretation began in the 1960s. The first independent African American churches emerged in the 1810s, inheriting already established interpretive practices from free and enslaved African Americans. As early as 1819 Jarena Lee was authorized to preach in the African Methodist Episcopal (AME) church, perhaps the first woman authorized to preach beyond a local congregation in the United States but one of several notable African American women preachers in the nineteenth century.[28] Among white feminists,

---

in Shaping and Enhancing the Discourse of Colonialism and the Discourse of Resistance: The Gĩkũyũ New Testament—A Case Study," *Black Theology* 11 (2013): 58–95.

26. Temba L. J. Mafico, "The Divine Name Yahweh 'Ĕlōhîˆm from an African Perspective," in Segovia and Tolbert, *Reading from This Place*, 2:21–32.

27. Jacob, *Reading Mary alongside Indian Surrogate Mothers*.

28. Nyasha Junior, *An Introduction to Womanist Biblical Interpretation* (Louisville: Westminster John Knox, 2015), 48–50; Nancy A. Hardesty, *Women Called to Witness: Evangelical Feminism in the 19th Century* (Nashville: Abingdon, 1984), 96. See Chanta M.

Elizabeth Cady Stanton's *Woman's Bible* was preceded by Antoinette Brown, ordained in 1853, and by the Grimké sisters, Sarah and Angelina, who combined feminism with abolitionism. Although the Grimkés were not preachers, they received intense criticism for speaking before audiences that included men as well as women, and each sister wrote tracts specifically critiquing slavery in biblical and theological terms. Angelina Grimké, who married the prominent abolitionist Theodore Weld, wrote to a friend that "the rights of the slave and woman blend like the colors of the rainbow."[29] Feminist and abolitionist concerns often shared the same platforms: following upon the 1848 Seneca Falls Convention, in which Frederick Douglass spoke, the annual Women's Rights Conventions from 1850 through 1860 featured both pro-feminist and anti-slavery messages.

FEMINIST INTERPRETATION

Contemporary feminist interpretation grew from the resurgence of the American feminist movement in the 1960s. Remarkably, women's participation in the Society of Biblical Literature, the world's largest academic society devoted to biblical studies, *declined steadily* from 1920 until 1970, from over 10 percent of the SBL's membership to about 3.5 percent.[30] That pattern reversed in 1970, though women constituted only 23.93 percent of the SBL membership as of 2018.[31] It is common to characterize the broader feminist movement in waves: a first wave in the nineteenth and early twentieth centuries devoted to women's equality, especially under the law; a second wave appearing in the 1960s seeking nondiscrimination and equal opportunity; and a third wave beginning in the 1980s that looks beyond the concerns of heterosexual white women to the intersections of gender, sexuality, race, class,

---

Haywood, "Prophesying Daughters: Nineteenth-Century Black Religious Women, the Bible, and Black Literary History," in Wimbush, *African Americans and the Bible*, 355–66; and Karen Baker-Fletcher, "Anna Julia Cooper and Sojourner Truth: Two Nineteenth-Century Black Feminist Interpreters of Scripture," in Schüssler Fiorenza, *Searching the Scriptures*, 2 vols., 41–51.

29. Hardesty, *Women Called to Witness*, 121.
30. Susanne Scholz, *The Bible as Political Artifact: On the Feminist Study of the Hebrew Bible* (Minneapolis: Fortress, 2017), 196 n. 9, citing Dorothy C. Bass, "Women's Studies and Biblical Studies," *JSOT* 22 (1982): 6–12.
31. Society of Biblical Literature, 2019 SBL Membership Data, https://tinyurl.com/ucfl7dk.

and ethnicity.[32] Second-wave feminist scholars "began the process of placing feminist questions within the framework of professional biblical scholarship."[33] But because feminist biblical scholarship has *always* included diverse points of view, it may be better to identify several trajectories within the movement, with individual authors often participating in multiple trajectories.[34]

One impulse of feminist criticism has been to *reclaim* the Bible as including good news for women. Reclaiming the Bible sometimes requires *correcting* misguided patriarchal readings. We encounter this move in the work of a first-generation academic feminist, Phyllis Trible. Describing Genesis 2–3 as "a love story gone awry," Trible points out how traditional interpretations regard the story as legitimating male superiority and pit Eve as the troublemaker who deceives Adam. Trible repeatedly shows how such patriarchal readings misconstrue the narrative dynamics of the story.[35] We might also consider popular takes on the sinful woman who anoints Jesus's feet (Luke 7:36–50) or the Samaritan woman who encounters Jesus at a well (John 4:4–42): many suppose that the first woman is a prostitute and the second is sexually immoral, assumptions neither story provides. Those interpretations emerged in the imaginations of male interpreters a long time ago.[36]

32. The three articles on "Feminism" in O'Brien et al., *Oxford Encyclopedia* reflect this structure: Claudia Setzer, "First-Wave Feminism," 1:234–42; Susanne Scholz, "Second-Wave Feminism," 1:242–51, and Surekha Nelavala, "Third-Wave Feminism," 1:251–55.

33. Pamela J. Milne, "Toward Feminist Companionship: The Future of Feminist Biblical Studies and Feminism," in *A Feminist Companion to Reading the Bible: Approaches, Methods and Strategies*, ed. (Athalya Brenner and Carole Fontaine (Sheffield: Sheffield Academic Press, 1997), 41.

34. Elisabeth Schüssler Fiorenza identifies nine feminist interpretive practices, integrating them in a tenth, what she calls "a critical feminist rhetorical model": *But She Said: Feminist Practices of Biblical Interpretation* (Boston: Beacon, 1992), 21–50.

35. Phyllis Trible, *God and the Rhetoric of Sexuality* (Philadelphia: Fortress, 1978), 72–143.

36. Three contemporary resources abound in feminist readings of contested passages: Carol A. Newsom, Sharon H. Ringe, and Jacqueline E. Lapsley, eds., *Women's Bible Commentary*, 3rd ed. (Louisville: Westminster John Knox, 2012); Carol Meyers, ed., *Women in Scripture: Dictionary of Named and Unnamed Women in the Hebrew Bible, the Apocryphal/Deuterocanonical Books, and the New Testament* (Grand Rapids: Eerdmans, 2000); and Elisabeth Schüssler Fiorenza, ed., *Searching the Scriptures*, 2 vols. (New York: Crossroad, 1993–94).

Another mode for reclaiming the Bible involves *uncovering* women's history in and around biblical texts. Sometimes the Bible minimizes or covers over women's actual contributions; on other occasions those histories lie hidden in plain sight. A good measure of energy has gone into documenting the lives and contributions of women in ancient Israelite society.[37] Likewise, we might investigate the presence of women prophets in early Israel.[38] As early as 1976 Elisabeth Schüssler Fiorenza, perhaps the most influential feminist biblical scholar to date, recommended that readers "unearth traces of a genuine 'her-story' of women in the Bible,"[39] a project she continued in writing a classic treatment of women's early Christian her-story. Schüssler Fiorenza retold the story of emergent Christianity as a general decline from its beginnings, when Christians practiced "a discipleship of equals," to the movement's broad attempt to accommodate its patriarchal environment. Among other things, Schüssler Fiorenza points to the women whom Paul references as missionary partners rather than as subordinates.[40]

Ever since Elizabeth Cady Stanton's *Woman's Bible*, feminists have also acknowledged that the Bible both participates in and contributes to the patriarchy of its cultural contexts. *Critiquing* those layers of patriarchy plays an essential role in feminist interpretation. Susanne Scholz has undertaken this process with respect to Deuteronomy 21:10–14, a law that authorizes Israelites to "marry" women they capture in warfare. Scholz lays out case studies in which male and female scholars interpret the passage in terms of marriage values rather than in terms of coercion, specifically rape. The passage allows captive women time to mourn their lost families, but it addresses the captured woman's will only when the captor rejects her: then she is free to find her own way, albeit in a hostile society and with no resources of her own.[41] Likewise, Jouette M. Bassler brings into painful relief the underlying logic

---

37. Meyers, *Discovering Eve*.
38. Wilda Gafney, *Daughters of Miriam: Women Prophets in Ancient Israel* (Minneapolis: Fortress, 2008).
39. Elisabeth Schüssler Fiorenza, "Interpreting Patriarchal Traditions," in *The Liberating Word: A Guide to Nonsexist Interpretation of the Bible*, ed. Letty M. Russell (Philadelphia: Westminster, 1976), 60.
40. Schüssler Fiorenza, *In Memory of Her*.
41. Scholz, *Bible as Political Artifact*, 96–100.

by which Paul enjoins Corinthian men to avoid prostitutes. Her example is instructive:

> Paul focuses exclusively on the actions of men. Reflecting the prevailing view of his culture, he assumes women are merely passive objects of men's desires. Moreover, the women in question here—prostitutes—are (presumably) outside the community of faith. Thus Paul does not have—nor does he take—the opportunity to reflect on the implications of a woman's mystical union with Christ.[42]

Paul, who in another case demonstrates concern for women's sexuality (1 Cor 7:3–4), shows no concern for the prostitute, only for her potential john.[43]

Feminist interpretation calls for both imagination and discernment. The biblical texts are themselves complicated. Although profoundly patriarchal, they sometimes show concern for women's welfare, acknowledge women's pain, tell women's stories, and emphasize women's contributions, even leadership. Through cracks in the patriarchal flooring, feminist interpreters can glimpse spaces for women's freedom, dignity, and authority.

AFRICAN AMERICAN INTERPRETATION

Contemporary African American biblical scholarship emerged from the call for black liberation as reflected in the early work of James H. Cone in 1969 and 1970.[44] Howard Thurman's classic *Jesus and the Disinherited*, published in 1949, had already presented Jesus as a poor person from a minoritized group whose teachings and practices offered a path for survival and nonviolent resistance.[45] In their different ways Cone and Thurman both called for interpretive practices that advocate for racial justice while also fostering the dignity of African Americans and black culture. Prominent streams in African American interpretation include interpretation grounded in African American cultural resources; research into African American biblical interpretation

---

42. Jouette M. Bassler, "1 Corinthians," in Newsom, Ringe, and Lapsley, *Women's Bible Commentary*, 558.
43. Gail Corrington Streete, *The Strange Woman: Power and Sex in the Bible* (Louisville: Westminster John Knox, 1997), 129–30.
44. James H. Cone, *Black Theology and Black Power* (New York: Harper & Row, 1969); and *A Black Theology of Liberation* (Philadelphia and New York: Lippincott, 1970).
45. Thurman, *Jesus and the Disinherited* (Nashville: Abingdon, 1949).

among nonprofessional readers, including the enslaved; interest in African places and people as reflected in the Bible; exploration of biblical topics like slavery and ethnicity; and the quest for freedom and dignity.[46]

Several of these motifs manifest themselves in the work of Brian K. Blount. Blount opens his interpretation of Mark's Gospel with the legendary figure of High John de Conquer, as related by Zora Neale Hurston.[47] Recognized only by black people during the days of slavery, High John was a heavenly figure who walked among mortals and would arrive suddenly to inspire hope and comfort them in their distress. High John was a messianic figure who would arrive in the future to deliver his people. Blount compares High John to the symbol of the kingdom of God in Mark's Gospel, representing "a future possibility of freedom and respect that did not exist in the present" and "a piece of that freedom" in the here and now.[48] Blount uses High John as an analogy that helps modern readers appreciate the potency of an ancient, abstract symbol like the kingdom of God.

Blount moves on to explore how the kingdom of God works through Mark's depiction of Jesus's ministry. One key aspect of Jesus's ministry is what Blount calls "boundary breaking." Jesus's ministry, according to Blount, particularly touches people who are marginalized in his own society: a leper, a bleeding woman, a demoniac, and a Gentile woman. Blount likely overstates his case by interpreting Jesus as violating the law of Israel, but his point is that Jesus brings God's reign in a way that overcomes the boundaries that exclude and oppress people. The challenge, for the black church in particular but for all of Jesus's followers, is to practice the same liberating pattern.[49]

---

46. The first major collection of African American interpretation is Felder, *Stony the Road We Trod*. More currently, Smith, *Insights from African American Interpretation*; and Brown, *Blackening of the Bible*. Two one-volume commentaries relevant to the discussion are: Hugh R. Page Jr. et al., eds., *The Africana Bible: Reading Israel's Scriptures from Africa and the African Diaspora* (Minneapolis: Fortress, 2010); and Brian K. Blount et al., eds., *True to Our Native Land: An African American New Testament Commentary* (Minneapolis: Fortress, 2007).

47. Zora Neale Hurston, "High John de Conquer," *The American Mercury* 57 (1943): 450–58.

48. Brian K. Blount, *Go Preach! Mark's Kingdom Message and the Black Church Today*, The Bible and Liberation (Maryknoll, NY: Orbis, 1998), 3.

49. Similar practices emerge in other examples of Blount's work, such as *Then the Whis-*

Sometimes the work of liberation entails identifying good news that's generally overlooked. And sometimes liberation requires calling out aspects of the Bible that prove problematic. This sort of ambivalence marks African American interpretation and many other streams of scholarship. For example, while owners of enslaved people may have extended the Sabbath to enslaved African Americans, they did so out of self-interest. In time, enslaved and free African Americans adapted the Sabbath toward opportunities for education and community development, even for escape.[50]

African American interpretation may find good news where it can; where the news is more complicated, ambivalent reading ensues. I grew up hearing white Southerners deploy the book of Ezra to make the case against interracial marriage. Ezra comes into Yehud and leads the male inhabitants to cast out their non-Israelite wives and even their offspring. Cheryl B. Anderson sorts through the problems inherent in Ezra's decree. Anderson argues that while African Americans will reject exclusionary policies ancient or modern, African Americans may also draw contemporary lessons from Ezra. Ezra's politics, for example, affect race/ethnicity, but they also wield power through the politics of gender (men decide what to do with women) and class (Ezra is concerned with Yehud's elite class). Ezra, then, provides a lesson in intersectionality, how issues that involve race intertwine with other power relationships.[51]

Alternatively, the verdict could be that the message amounts to bad news. Mitzi J. Smith critiques the Gospels' language of the kingdom of God, specifically Matthew's "kingdom of the heavens." Smith observes that several of Matthew's kingdom parables feature enslaved characters—and not necessarily in empowering roles. Smith identifies three consecutive parables in which enslaved persons do not behave as their masters desire and thus receive punishment: the parables of the faithful and unfaithful enslaved people (Matt 24:45–51); the ten bridesmaids, whom Smith reads as enslaved brides for the bridegroom (25.1–13);

per Put on Flesh, referenced in chapter 4; and *Can I Get a Witness? Reading Revelation through African American Culture* (Louisville: Westminster John Knox, 2005).

50. Powery and Sadler, *Genesis of Liberation*, 63–81.
51. Cheryl B. Anderson, "Reflections in an Interethnic/racial Era on Interethnic/racial Marriage in Ezra," in *They Were All Together in One Place? Toward Minority Biblical Criticism*, ed. Randall C. Bailey, Tat-siong Benny Liew, and Fernando F. Segovia, SemeiaSt 57 (Atlanta: Society of Biblical Literature, 2009), 47–64.

and the talents (25:14–30). These parables play on stereotypes that dehumanize enslaved persons. In the end, Smith judges,

> The social reality of systemic oppression signified by slave parables baptized in kingdom-of-the-heavens rhetoric promotes stereotypical slave behavior and oppressive relationships as ideals worthy of imitation and transcending time and space.[52]

LATINX INTERPRETATION

Every socially grounded mode of interpretation reflects the distinctive concerns of the communities that give it birth. The experience of slavery in the United States formed an either/or racial logic: although countless Americans are multiracial to some degree, slavery and segregation divided the population into two categories: black and white. Latinx interpreters share with African Americans an interest in economic and social oppression, but Latinx interpreters tend to emphasize racial, ethnic, and linguistic hybridity—indeed, fluidity across a host of categories.[53]

For most Latinx persons, those whose ancestors did not live in the parts of the United States that once belonged to Mexico, questions of diaspora, identity, and belonging figure prominently in interpretation. Justo L. González's classic exposition of Latinx interpretation sets forth five primary categories, three of which involve identity and belonging. In addition to poverty and solidarity, González foregrounds marginality, *mestizaje* (in his words, being "mixed-breeds"), and exile (or being

---

52. Smith, *Insights from African American Interpretation*, 94.
53. A major recent anthology on Latino/a hermeneutics testifies to this sense of fluidity, as multiple authors contest whether Latino/a interpretation has an essential nature: Francisco Lozada Jr. and Fernando F. Segovia, eds., *Latino/a Biblical Hermeneutics: Problematics, Objectives, Strategies*, SemeiaSt 68 (Atlanta: SBL Press, 2014). On hybridity and Latinx identity, see Jacqueline Hidalgo, "Reading from No Place: Toward a Hybrid and Ambivalent Study of Scriptures," in that volume, 165–86. The term *Latinx* denotes descendants of Latin Americans who live in the United States. The term is admittedly contested and fairly recent. It represents an attempt to escape the binary gender assumptions of "Latino" and "Latina," and it functions as an alternative to "Hispanic," which includes only descendants of Spanish-speaking Latin Americans. See Francisco Lozada Jr., *Toward a Latino/a Biblical Interpretation*, RBS 91 (Atlanta: SBL Press, 2017), 23–30.

aliens).⁵⁴ To be Latinx, according to González, involves living outside one's cultural home and belonging to no single ethnic or social category.

As I am writing, a Mexican-American presidential candidate is responding to criticism that he does not speak Spanish as well as other candidates (not all of them Latinx) do. The threat is that people would not perceive Julián Castro as authentically Latinx. Defending himself, he relates that he is still seeking to improve his Spanish, but Spanish was rarely spoken in his home.

> In my grandparents' time . . . Spanish was looked down upon. You were punished in school if you spoke Spanish. You were not allowed to speak it. People, I think, internalized this oppression about it and basically wanted their kids first to be able to speak English.⁵⁵

Castro's account reveals the elusiveness of a singular authentic Latinx identity.

Echoing González, Francisco Lozada Jr. foregrounds identity as a preoccupation of Latinx interpretation and reminds us that Latinx hermeneutics implicitly invites participants to join in solidarity with one another. The diverse people who pursue Latinx interpretation, and their diverse, sometimes conflicting, interests, challenge interpreters to account for intersectionality. Latinx hybridity opens space for interpretation that encompasses sexuality, gender, and class along with race and identity.⁵⁶

What if biblical authors also conceived of ethnic identity in fluid and plural, rather than fixed, categories? This question animates the ongoing research of Eric D. Barreto.⁵⁷ According to Barreto, Acts values diverse racial identities, even hybrid ones. Acts celebrates the baptism of an Ethiopian, dwelling intensely upon what the audience of Acts would perceive as his exotic identity. Timothy is the child of a "Greek"

---

54. Justo L. González, *Santa Biblia: The Bible through Hispanic Eyes* (Nashville: Abingdon, 1996).
55. For video of this interview, see https://tinyurl.com/rq6ffuv.
56. Lozada, *Toward a Latino/a Biblical Interpretation*, 113–17.
57. For example, Eric D. Barreto, *Ethnic Negotiations: The Function of Race and Ethnicity in Acts 16*, WUNT 2:294 (Tübingen: Mohr Siebeck, 2010); "Reexamining Ethnicity: Latina/os, Race, and the Bible," in Lozada and Segovia, *Latino/a Biblical Hermeneutics*, 73–93; and "Negotiating Difference: Theology and Ethnicity in the Acts of the Apostles," in Lozada and Carey, *Soundings in Cultural Criticism*, 97–106.

father and a "Jewish" mother. Paul identifies as a Jew—and as a Roman citizen and as a native of Tarsus in Roman Asia. Acts, Barreto maintains, "forwards a powerful theological argument that faithful unity and ethnic diversity are neither at odds nor mutually exclusive."[58]

WOMANIST AND *MUJERISTA* INTERPRETATION

Many African American and Latinx women relate to the concerns of feminist, African American, and Latinx interpretation. Yet they have also raised critiques of those movements: of feminism, for failing to account for race, ethnicity, language, culture, and sexuality in adequate ways; and of African American and Latinx interpretation for failing to account for the experiences of women and sexual minorities. The resulting movements, womanist and *mujerista* interpretation, have emerged in response to these deficiencies. They have done so in sophisticated but not identical ways.

The term *womanist* derives from the novelist Alice Walker, who offered several definitions of the term. Part of one definition reads, "Womanist is to feminist as purple is to lavender," emphasizing not only a more fulsome experience of color but also a degree of intensity. Womanism operates at the intersections of gender, race, ethnicity, class, and sexuality. It begins with the experiences and concerns of black women, but it insists on the wholeness of human beings. In contrast to white feminism, which sought to demonstrate women's capacity to work and inhabit public spaces, womanism recognizes that black women have always assumed they could bear enormous burdens and make a way for themselves, their families, their communities, and others.[59] Rooted in the lives of African American women, womanism commits itself to their welfare and to the welfare of other people as well.

Womanist theology first surfaced among James Cone's graduate students, who were

> the first to begin to express new black liberationist theology that was also inclusive of their particular experiences of sexism and racism in the academy and the church, perpetuated even by their own black male colleagues.[60]

---

58. Barreto, "Negotiating Difference," 105.
59. Junior, *Introduction to Womanist Biblical Interpretation*, xiii, xvi–xvii.
60. Gay L. Byron and Vanessa Lovelace, "Introduction: Methods and the Making of Womanist Biblical Hermeneutics," in *Womanist Interpretations of the Bible: Expanding*

Womanist theology first impacted my own interpretive practices when I was working with Matthew's story of Jesus and the Canaanite woman (15:21–28). The woman, a non-Israelite, comes to Jesus seeking her daughter's liberation from demonic possession. First, she *cries out*, "Have mercy on me, Lord, Son of David; my daughter is tormented by a demon." The disciples ask Jesus to shoo her away, and Jesus remarks, "I was sent only to the lost sheep of the house of Israel." Next she *kneels* and prays, recognizing Jesus's true identity: "Lord, help me." But Jesus calls her a "dog," not a child worthy of people food. Finally, the woman bests Jesus in the argument: "Yes, Lord, yet even the dogs eat the crumbs that fall from their masters' table." Then Jesus commends the woman's faith and heals her daughter.

Interpreters routinely find this passage troubling. Not only does Jesus insult the woman—some interpreters minimize the insult—but we observe the woman's agency diminishing as the story progresses: from standing and shouting, to kneeling and praying, to accepting a dog's status. Some interpreters regard the woman as a hero, the only character in the Bible to win an argument with Jesus. Others see her as a victim who endures humiliation. Faced with this dilemma, I was looking for another way.

At that point I recalled womanist ethics. Katie Geneva Cannon, one of the first womanist theologians, argues that black women's ethical lives defy the analysis of conventional—what she calls "dominant"—ethics.

> Black women live out a moral wisdom in their real-lived context that does not appeal to the fixed rules or absolute principles of the white-oriented, male-structured society. Black women's analysis and appraisal of what is right or wrong and good or bad develops out of the various coping mechanisms related to the conditions of their own cultural circumstances. Black women have justly regarded survival against tyrannical systems of triple oppression as a true sphere of moral life.[61]

Cannon's insight transformed my approach to the Canaanite woman through an indirect path. Although I am white, I was raised by a single mother. In order to make a path for our survival, my mom endured

---

the Discourse, ed. Gay L. Byron and Vanessa Lovelace, SemeiaSt 85 (Atlanta: SBL Press, 2016), 3.

61. Katie Geneva Cannon, *Black Womanist Ethics*, AAR Academy Series 60 (Atlanta: Scholars Press, 1988), 4.

all sorts of degrading behavior from men who held power over her, whether colleagues at work, landlords, or my coaches. I began to see the Canaanite as more than a hero and a victim but as a mother who endured attacks on her dignity in order for her daughter to thrive.

It should not surprise us that womanist interpretation takes many forms. Stephanie Buckhanon Crowder begins by interpreting motherhood as experienced among African American women, then introduces womanist interpretation. With this framework in place, Crowder interprets the stories of six biblical mothers, one of whom is the Canaanite. Crowder describes the Canaanite as "relentless," which she surely is, and then uses her story to reflect upon the lives of African American professional women. Crowder calls attention to an aspect of the story I certainly had not considered: in seeking Jesus's aid, the Canaanite leaves her unwell daughter at home. The story raises questions about how African American women manage career and family and about paying public attention to children's welfare.[62]

Wilda C. Gafney takes a different path, embracing the Jewish interpretive technique called *midrash*. Gafney observes that rabbinic interpretation makes much of textual details, even the letters of words. They see these details "as potential revelatory spaces; [rabbinic readings] reimagine often dominant narratival readings while crafting new ones to stand alongside—not replace—former readings."[63]

Gafney imaginatively rereads the stories of women in the Torah and women with royal associations in the books of Samuel and Kings. Sometimes Gafney offers incisive commentary on a given story or passage. For example, addressing the command that both partners in an adulterous relationship should be executed (Lev 20:10), Gafney observes that Israelite men were free to impose themselves sexually upon women they enslave and may frequent prostitutes: neither of those behaviors constitutes adultery in the Torah. Israelite women do not have the same freedom. Then Gafney points out that it appears this law never functioned in Israelite life, citing several examples of adulterous people in which the biblical texts never mention capital punishment. If the commandments against adultery "were widely known and

---

62. Stephanie Buckhanon Crowder, *When Momma Speaks: The Bible and Motherhood from a Womanist Perspective* (Louisville: Westminster John Knox, 2016), esp. 84–91.
63. Wilda C. Gafney, *Womanist Midrash: A Reintroduction to the Women of the Torah and the Throne* (Louisville: Westminster John Knox, 2017), 3.

available," she concludes, it appears that "the Israelites heard and understood their own Scriptures with nuance rather than literalism."[64]

In addition to commentary, Gafney uses her "sanctified imagination" to offer retellings of the biblical accounts. She conjures a scene in which Shiphrah and Puah, the birthing women who refuse to obey Pharaoh's commandment to execute Israelite boys at birth, gather a "convocation" of other birthing women. Speaking prophetically, both Shiphrah and Puah spread the word to defy Pharaoh and "deliver the deliverer," Moses. Gafney concludes with commentary on the biblical account: Israel's liberation starts with Shiphrah and Puah, "the first deliverers in the book of deliverance."[65]

The conversation surrounding womanist criticism has expanded beyond the African American experience to include other women who interpret the Bible in womanist ways.[66] Reading the Bible at the complicated intersection of gender, race, ethnicity, class, and sexuality can take place in many contexts. Among Latinx women, *mujerista* interpretation, drawn from the Spanish word for "woman," represents one such movement. Ada María Isasi-Díaz, a Cuban American theologian, coined the term *mujerista theology* as a mode of theology that begins with and accounts for "the reality of Latina grassroots women."[67] That reality features *mestizaje* not only as the given experience of Latinx women but also as "an ethical choice," a commitment to resist racism and its effects.[68] And it turns biblical interpretation toward the end of building a "preferred future," starting from survival and leading toward flourishing.[69]

What does *mujerista* interpretation look like in practice? First, Latinx women have diverse experiences with the Bible, some in religious communities where Bible reading is rare and others in communities where

---

64. Gafney, *Womanist Midrash*, 122.

65. Gafney, *Womanist Midrash*, 89–91.

66. See the essays collected in Byron and Lovelace, eds., *Womanist Interpretations of the Bible*.

67. Ada-María Isasi-Díaz, *Mujerista Theology* (Maryknoll, NY: Orbis, 1997), 149–50. See Leticia A. Guardiola-Sáenz, "From the Pulpit to the Academy—Latinx Scriptural Hermeneutics," *Lexington Theological Quarterly* 48 (2018): 21–24.

68. Rodolfo J. Hernandez-Díaz, "Mujerista Theology: Strategies for Social Change," *Feminist Theology* 20 (2011): 48.

69. Isasi-Díaz, *Mujerista Theology*, 150–51.

Bible reading is a daily devotional practice. Isasi-Díaz recognized that most Latinx women were used to individualistic and pietistic ways of understanding the Bible, a useful starting place that must be transcended in order for biblical interpretation to address structural sin and oppression.[70] In such contexts the Bible must function as an "interpretive key," a starting point from which readers perceive their own world with fresh and critical sensitivity. Isasi-Díaz turns to the story of Shiphrah and Puah, the case study we selected from Wilda Gafney's womanist midrash project. But Isasi-Díaz notices different details, such as the midwives' ambiguous ethnic identity, even as she, like Gafney, points to the necessary role Shiphrah and Puah play in Israel's liberation. In the end, Isasi-Díaz brings from the story not a focused interpretation but a series of questions for Latinx women, such as how people oppressed by unjust systems may yet remain faithful to God.[71]

It would be very, very misleading to suggest that what goes on among academic interpreters in African American and Latinx communities represents the Bible's popular appropriation among black and brown readers in the United States. Professional scholars often lament the Bible's reception in religious communities. This issue is universal, applying to every category of person, but African American scholars and theologians have addressed it most directly. African American interpretation has always included diverse strategies.[72] But where scholarly interpretation tends to focus upon public issues such as race and power, reflecting an ambivalent disposition toward the Bible's helpfulness, many black churches emphasize individual piety and personal deliverance without questioning biblical authority.[73]

---

70. Isasi-Díaz, *Mujerista Theology*, 151–53, 160.

71. Isasi-Díaz, *Mujerista Theology*, 162–65.

72. In addition to Wimbush, ed., *African Americans and the Bible*, see Wimbush, *The Bible and African Americans: A Brief History*, Facets (Minneapolis: Fortress, 2003); and Allan Dwight Callahan, "'Brother Saul': An Ambivalent Witness to Freedom," *Semeia* 83/84 (1998): 235–50.

73. Wimbush, *Bible and African Americans*, 63–75; see Raphael G. Warnock, *The Divided Mind of the Black Church: Theology, Piety, and Public Witness*, Religion, Race, and Ethnicity (New York: New York University Press, 2014).

GLOBAL SCOPE: ASIAN AND ASIAN AMERICAN INTERPRETATION AS A CASE STUDY

Every reading community bears its distinctive resources as it confronts its own challenges. Asian and Asian American interpreters represent an enormous range of cultural resources and social interests, yet they also manage to stay in conversation with one another on key points. Perhaps this is so because many scholars who identify as Asian American themselves grew up in Asia and maintain relationships in Asia, while others grew up several generations removed from the process of immigration.[74]

Jin Young Choi has reflected specifically upon the complexities of interpreting the Bible as a Korean immigrant to the United States. Describing her project as "Asian and Asian American," she brings to Mark's Gospel a Korean spirituality that is "based on spiritual experience, embodiment, and relationality." Meanwhile Choi argues, as many others do, that Asian Americans experience a distinctive variety of racism: they are regarded as religious Others because of their cultural backgrounds, while they, women and men alike, are feminized in American culture. "As a result," she writes, they remain invisible, silent, and absent" in US culture.[75] Tat-siong Benny Liew confirms this analysis: because racial discourse in the US is overdetermined in terms of "black" and "white," Asian Americans often deal with cultural invisibility.[76]

Choi brings Korean and Korean American sensibilities to a prominent issue in the interpretation of Mark: discipleship. Interpreters have long noted that in comparison to the other Gospels, Mark presents the disciples in a relatively negative light. The problem, according to conventional (whitestream) wisdom, is that the disciples so often fail to understand who Jesus is. Choi counters with *phronesis*, an embodied wisdom that characterizes Asian and Asian American feminist consciousness: "not merely the employment of an abstract theory for an individual's interpretation but . . . a recognition, and enactment, of

---

74. See Tat-siong Benny Liew, "On Asian/Asian North American Scholarship and Feminism: Twenty-Eight Years Later," *Journal of Feminist Studies in Religion* 31 (2015): 127–31.

75. Jin Young Choi, *Postcolonial Discipleship of Embodiment*. Postcolonialism and Religions (New York: Palgrave Macmillan, 2015), 2.

76. Liew, "On Asian/Asian North American Scholarship and Feminism," 127.

meaning making in which power is involved."[77] Jesus, whose own body would endure mutilation, engages with disciples in corporeal ways and calls them to participate in his life-giving work.

Some Asian American interpreters emphasize the peculiar status of Asian Americans in US society. Conversations about race often fixate on black-white dynamics and perhaps include Latinx people, then include Asian Americans as the "model minority," the group that assimilates and achieves academic and financial success. The model-minority motif pits Asian Americans against other minoritized groups and does not grant them full access to a white-dominated society. The model minority also lives as a "perpetual foreigner." Gale A. Yee reads the story of Ruth according to this rubric: through hard work and family loyalty, Ruth achieves security and a measure of inclusion—yet she is always "Ruth the Moabite."[78] In later work Yee adapts the concept of "racial melancholia," a "psychic condition" of perpetual dissatisfaction in which the dominant culture welcomes racialized groups into its midst but cannot/will not fully assimilate them. Ruth remains "both the familial and female Other," making "it impossible for her to become fully Israelite herself." Ruth never achieves full belonging.[79]

A classic 2006 anthology of Asian American interpretation includes essays with titles like "Neither Here nor There," "The *Realpolitik* of Liminality," "Betwixt and Between," and "Constructing Hybridity and Heterogeneity."[80] In this light Hagar, the enslaved mother of Abraham's first son, "represents not only herself, but also her people. As a repre-

---

77. Choi, *Postcolonial Discipleship*, 31.

78. Gale A. Yee, "'She Stood in Tears amid the Alien Corn': Ruth, the Perpetual Foreigner and Model Minority," in Bailey, Liew, and Segovia, *They Were All Together in One Place?*, 119–40.

79. Gale A. Yee, "Racial Melancholia and the Book of Ruth," in *The Five Scrolls*, ed. Athalya Brenner-Idan, Gale A. Yee, and Archie C. C. Lee, Texts@Contexts 6 (New York: T&T Clark, 2018), 68.

80. The anthology is Mary F. Foskett and Jeffrey Kah-Jin Kuan, eds., *Ways of Being, Ways of Reading: Asian American Biblical Interpretation* (St. Louis: Chalice, 2006). The essays include: Lai Ling Elizabeth Ngan, "Neither Here nor There: Boundary and Identity in the Hagar Story," 70–83; Uriah Yong-Hwan Kim, "The *Realpolitik* of Liminality in Josiah's Kingdom and Asian America," 84–98; Sze-kar Wan, "Betwixt and Between: Towards a Hermeneutics of Hyphenation," 137–51; and Frank M. Yamada, "Constructing Hybridity and Heterogeneity: Asian American Biblical Interpretation from a Third-Generation Perspective," 164–77.

sentative of the significant Other, she is the focus of envy and hate."[81] Josiah's reform, often construed as a purification of Judah's religious life, can be read as establishing a nationalistic culture that brings into relief the liminal status Asian Americans experience, having perhaps grown up in Decatur, Georgia, or San Diego but always subject to being asked, "Where are you from?"[82] Reading as a third-generation Japanese American, Frank M. Yamada reads the Adam and Eve story in terms of "untidy human survival in the midst of adversity." What is most surprising about the story is not that Eve and Adam eat the forbidden fruit, nor is it that they are cast out of Eden; it is that they do not die.[83] When Asian American scholars attain "a place at the table" of public biblical interpretation, Sze-kar Wan points out, a painful irony accompanies the invitation to speak explicitly as marginalized persons by interpreting from an explicitly Asian American perspective.[84]

Asian cultures and histories vary dramatically. It is not surprising that interpreters from different regions of Asia bring diverse questions and cultural resources to the work of interpretation. Biblical studies are largely a Jewish and Christian endeavor, and most Asian biblical scholars emerge from Christian communities; Christianity is a minority religion in most Asian cultures. Therefore, questions of interreligious dialogue figure prominently in Asian interpretation, as does recourse to Asian cultural resources, often sacred texts. Especially in societies with colonial legacies, postcolonial criticism figures prominently, and in many contexts interpretation turns toward economic justice.[85]

Asian, Asian American, and African interpreters bring a host of cultural resources and questions to the process of interpretation. Tat-siong Benny Liew frequently reads biblical narratives in conversation with Chinese American fiction. Noting how American popular culture fix-

---

81. Ngan, "Neither Here nor There," 79.
82. Kim, "*Realpolitik*."
83. Yamada, "Constructing Hybridity and Heterogeneity," 176–77.
84. Wan, "Betwixt and Between."
85. These generalizations apply across a significant body of literature and are reflected in several essays in Foskett and Kuan, eds., *Ways of Being, Ways of Reading*; Devadasan N. Premnath, "Biblical Interpretation in India: History and Issues," 1–16; John Yueh-Han Yieh, "Chinese Biblical Interpretation: History and Issues," 17–30; Samuel Cheon, "Biblical Interpretation in Korea: History and Issues," 31–44; and Philip P. Chia, "Differences and Difficulties: Biblical Interpretation in the Southeast Asian Context," 45–59.

ates upon the eyes of Chinese people, Liew takes up Amy Tan's novel *The Hundred Secret Senses* and the Chinese notion of people with "yin yang eyes"—the capacity to see not only living people but the dead. Liew notes that other Chinese American scholars have developed the same metaphor—but differently. For Liew, reading the Bible with yin yang eyes entails seeing both the life-giving and the oppressive dimensions of the Bible and its appropriations. It also means refusing to "whitewash" the problems readers encounter, a willingness to resist biblical narratives where necessary.[86]

If particular cultural resources fuel interpretation, so can questions that emerge from specific global contexts. Mary F. Foskett examines the scholarly search for origins in conversation with the experience of Chinese girls adopted by American parents. A great deal of scholarship has been devoted to the origins of Israel, the life of Jesus, and the emergence of Christianity in order to shape an authorized story of identity. As a feminist, Foskett notes how often early Christian sources, such as Luke's Gospel, minimize and obscure the contributions of women to the early Christian movement. Feminist historical research calls into question malestream ways of imagining earliest Christianity, offering alternative accounts of women and their participation. Likewise, Chinese adoptees may choose to look beyond the stories their American parents tell of their adoptions. They may never arrive at definitive histories of their own birth families, but they may address their sense of cultural dislocation by understanding the social and cultural circumstances that brought about the adoption of Chinese girls by North Americans.[87]

AFRICAN BIBLICAL INTERPRETATION

Many of the dynamics we encounter in Asian and Asian American interpretation apply in other global contexts, though each setting generates its own questions and its own unique interpretive perspectives. In Africa, where many countries are majority Christian, the legacy of Christian missions and imperialism looms large. Botswanan scholar Musa W. Dube applies a feminist postcolonial reading strategy to

---

86. Tat-siong Benny Liew, *What Is Asian American Biblical Hermeneutics? Reading the New Testament* (Honolulu: University of Hawaii Press, 2008), 18–33.

87. Mary F. Foskett, "Obscured Beginnings: Lessons from the Study of Christian Origins," in Foskett and Kuan, *Ways of Being, Ways of Reading*, 178–91.

Matthew's Gospel, with particular attention to the Canaanite woman (15:21–28), who receives so much attention in global feminist interpretation. Matthew, Dube argues, does not critique Roman imperialism. Instead, it imagines a gospel mission characterized by travel to distant lands and condemns Gentile ways. That the Canaanite submits to Jesus calling her a dog augurs poorly for Matthew's vision of mission to "others." Moreover, Dube critiques middle-class Western interpreters for reading alongside Matthew rather than resisting its empire-friendly tendencies. Dube intervenes by researching interpretations of the Canaanite's story among women in African Independent Churches, whose interpretive values honor inclusivity and relational healing. The women Dube and her colleagues surveyed also reject the imposition of Christianity by one group upon another.[88]

Indeed, attention to ordinary readers and their interpretations figures prominently in African biblical scholarship. Dube's work with African Independent Church readers provides a primary case study, as does the work of white South African scholar Gerald O. West. West and a colleague, Jonathan A. Draper, investigated a familiar passage, Jesus's encounter with a rich man in Matthew 19:16–26, with various study groups in South Africa. For many readers the crux of the passage occurs when Jesus instructs the would-be disciple, "If you wish to be perfect, go, sell your possessions, and give the money to the poor, and you will have treasure in heaven; then come, follow me" (19:21). The young man departs, "grieving, for he had many possessions" (19:22). West and Draper found that most readers applied the passage to individual sin, the sin of prioritizing possessions over following Jesus. But particularly in "groups from poor and marginalized communities, there was some discussion of 'structural sin,'" inequities that result from social patterns more than from individual choices.[89] One's choice of reading partners makes all the difference, West observes. This approach, when professional scholars attend to what we sometimes call "ordinary readers," has found its way from Central American, African, and other contexts into North America, as when Bob Ekblad reports Bible studies he has con-

---

88. Dube, *Postcolonial Feminist Interpretation*, esp. 127–95.
89. Gerald O. West, *The Academy of the Poor: Towards a Dialogical Reading of the Bible* (Interventions 2; Sheffield: Sheffield Academic, 1999), 25. See West, *Biblical Hermeneutics of Liberation*.

ducted among prisoners and undocumented immigrants in the United States.[90]

African context and cultural resources energize biblical interpretation. The Nigerian interpreter Justin S. Ukpong takes up the "notorious" parable of the dishonest manager (Luke 16:1–13) through West African lenses.[91] The parable is notorious because it has a scoundrel for its hero: A corrupt middle manager faces unemployment for his mismanagement, and he rescues himself by conspiring with his master's debtors to reduce their loan obligations. In this way he will receive hospitality after his firing. Ukpong reads the parable not from the perspective of the manager, nor that of his master, but from alongside the indebted peasants. Writing in 1996, Ukpong observes that "most ordinary West Africans are peasant farmers" who "live by the worldview" that "there should be no exploitation of fellow human beings."[92] Yet the farmers are exploited, many of them carrying debt burdens. In Ukpong's interpretation, the peasants receive no favor from the manager when he reduces their debts. Those debts are already exploitative, and their reduction is an act of justice. "The manager's action is restitutive and is an action of self-criticism."[93] It reflects his awareness that he has participated in an unjust financial arrangement and repairs the injustice, at least partially. Only the rich landowner considers the manager's behavior unjust.[94] As the Ghanaian theologian John S. Pobee observes, African societies often feature more communitarian sensibilities than do those in the "North."[95] Rather than privileging the rich landowner's absolute right to his own property, Ukpong's interpretation reflects the sense of human interrelatedness.

---

90. Bob Ekblad, *Reading the Bible with the Damned* (Louisville: Westminster John Knox, 2005).
91. Justin S. Ukpong, "The Parable of the Shrewd Manager (Luke 16:1–13): An Essay in Inculturation Biblical Hermeneutics," *Semeia* 73 (1996): 189.
92. Ukpong, "Parable of the Shrewd Manager," 192.
93. Ukpong, "Parable of the Shrewd Manager," 205.
94. Ukpong, "Parable of the Shrewd Manager," 206.
95. John S. Pobee, "Bible Study in Africa: A Passover of Language," *Semeia* 73 (1996): 166.

QUEER INTERPRETATION

June 28, 1969, is often treated as the beginning of the gay liberation movement. Having endured police suppression on a routine basis, on that particular night LGBTQ persons fought back against a police raid of the Stonewall Inn in New York. A series of confrontations ensued that led to a new age of activism toward civil rights for sexual and gender minorities. In some ways, LGBTQ advocacy resembles that of African American and feminist interpretation. For one thing, the Bible has often functioned to legitimate the marginalization of all these groups. Just as people used the Bible to defend slavery and segregation and to enforce women's subordination, many believe the Bible blesses only heterosexual love and conventional gender-conforming behavior. Thus, one dimension of LGBTQ-affirming interpretation involves developing arguments to counter religiously based discrimination. But African American and feminist hermeneutics, like Latinx hermeneutics, also developed culturally grounded practices of interpretation distinctive to their own communities. The emergence of queer interpretation, not simply interpretation of the Bible oriented toward social equality—there's a lot of that too—but practices of interpretation that emerge from the experiences of nonconformity and resistance, occurred first in secular literary and cultural criticism, then moved into queer theology and queer biblical hermeneutics.

Some readers and students may object to the term *queer* because it has often been deployed as a slur against sexual and gender minorities. Nevertheless, queer theorists have appropriated this term once used against them and turned it into a rallying point. As Laurel C. Schneider describes it, "Queer theory seeks to disrupt modernist notions of fixed sexuality and gender . . . by appropriating post-structuralist critiques of 'natural' identities."[96] That definition comes loaded with technical language, but Schneider helpfully underscores how queer theory turns the marginalized dimensions of LGBTQ experience into powerful interpretive resources. Many straight people my age grew up imagining that humankind divided into the categories of male and female, that men and women possessed gender-based characteristics that varied but basically held steady in predictable ways, and that sexual attraction occurred between men and women rather than between men and

---

96. Laurel C. Schneider, "Queer Theory," in Adam, *Handbook of Postmodern Biblical Interpretation*, 206.

men or women and women. Human behavior that did not fit that model we considered abnormal—if not wrong, then at least strange, or "queer." Drawing upon deep philosophical resources, queer theory flips that script on its head: as the rock band Living Colour pointed out in a song about bisexuality, "Everybody's fucked up with their sexuality."[97] Where we assumed gender and sexuality were "natural," queer interpretation unravels these stable categories. In other words, queer life becomes an interpretive resource.

Reflecting on a collection of essays devoted to queer interpretation of Paul and his letters, Lynn R. Huber offers a metaphor for how we might imagine queer interpreters.

> I wonder if we might imagine the queer biblical interpreter as an assemblage. The queerness of this interpreter does not reside within a gay/lesbian/bi/trans/intersex/asexual/gender fluid/aromantic/asexual/et cetera identity; rather, this queerness emerges out of the interpreter's willingness to move nimbly and nonlinearly across time and location, to embrace difference in terms of sex, gender, sexuality and desire.[98]

Or as Joseph A. Marchal suggests,

> Queer is less an identity and more a disposition, a mode of examining the processes that cast certain people and practices into categories of normal and abnormal than of interrogating the effects of such processes.[99]

Queer interpreters relish the opportunity to draw meaning from marginal elements in a biblical text—and, conversely, to undermine what seems given or obvious. Let's consider examples of each practice.

Manuel Villalobos Mendoza shares elements of his experience growing up queer in Mexico and living as a member of the Mexican diaspora in the United States. He uses the metaphor *del otro lado*, "from the other side," to denote queer experience. In Mark's account of the Last Supper Jesus instructs two disciples to find a man carrying a water jar. Other interpreters have suggested that Jesus arranged things in this

---

97. Living Colour, "Bi," by Vernon Reid and Will Calhoun, *Stain*, Epic Records, 1992.
98. Lynn R. Huber, "Interpreting as Queer or Interpreting Queerly?" in *Bodies on the Verge: Queering Pauline Epistles*, ed. Joseph A. Marchal, SemeiaSt 93 (Atlanta: SBL Press, 2019), 320.
99. Joseph A. Marchal, "Queer Approaches: Improper Relations with Pauline Letters," in *Studying Paul's Letters: Contemporary Perspectives and Methods*, ed. Joseph A. Marchal (Minneapolis: Fortress, 2012), 210.

way because women did the water carrying in Jesus's day: the disciples would easily spot a man carrying water. Villalobos Mendoza presses this detail further. He calls the man Nachito *el machito* after a gay man forced to flee his Mexican village due to his sexuality. Nachito's queer behavior would have suggested something about his master and his household. Indeed, Jesus chooses Nachito and his household precisely to establish a new community of such marginalized persons. Villalobos Mendoza writes:

> For those of us who have been punished, excluded, tormented in useless therapies, obligated to go to our prostitute sisters, and forced to learn how to do our gender correctly, the story of Nachito *el machito* is a sign of hope and redemption.[100]

Villalobos Mendoza turns queer interpretation toward liberation and inclusion. Not all queer interpreters seek to use the Bible in that way. Paul's epistle to the Galatians invests deeply in flesh, specifically in the question of whether the Galatian men will circumcise their penises. Along the way Paul reflects on other kinds of flesh, including his own diseased body. Valérie Nicolet begins by reflecting on monsters, creatures that reside outside the boundaries of normalcy. Monsters signify the boundary between the human and the other, and they remind us just how fragile the boundary really is. In writing to the Galatians, Paul wishes his opponents would literally cut themselves off; that is, he hopes that during circumcision the knife would slip and cause a greater injury (5:12). Paul also disfigures his own body, depicting himself as a woman in the pains of childbirth (4:19). Paul appeals to his infirmity (4:13) and to the scars on his body (6:17). In one of the epistle's most elevated passages (3:28), Paul imagines the Galatians as a "new hybrid and created body," one that transcends even the distinction between male and female. In short, Paul's language takes nonconforming and imperfect, or "monstrous," bodies and integrates them into his vision of a redeemed community. The Galatians even welcome "the deformed, maternal, and stigmatized body of Paul 'like an angel' (4:14)." Nicolet concludes that monsters, such as the redeemed monsters of Galatians, "encourage us to work toward stitched-up communities that skillfully

---

100. Manuel Villalobos Mendoza, *Abject Bodies in the Gospel of Mark* (BMW 45; Sheffield: Sheffield Phoenix, 2012), 75.

disassemble and reassemble various bits of the identities that Paul desperately seeks to bound [sic] together."[101]

Queer interpretation pays attention to bodies, especially to bodies that conform to social convention in imperfect ways. It appeals to language in similar ways, especially to language that may seem natural but doesn't really hold together as neatly as we might imagine. Returning to Matthew's account of Jesus's encounter with the Canaanite woman (15:21–28), Stephen D. Moore fixes upon the boundary between the human and the animal: Jesus calls the woman a dog. Jesus warns disciples not to give holy things to dogs (7:6). If we begin to contrast her dog-nature with Jesus's human nature, we're confronted by Jesus's status as Son of Man, which isn't quite so human. After all, Mark's "Son of Man" language draws upon the "one like a human being" (or "like a son of man") in Daniel 7:13. And unlike animals, the Son of Man has nowhere to lay his head (8:20). In this respect Jesus, Moore judges, "is more animal-like than a fox, more creaturely even than a bird."[102] By the story's end, Jesus's slaughter sets the terms for the final holy meal. Before we're done, the boundaries between Jesus and the Canaanite have begun to crumble, as does even the boundary between the human and the animal.

Queer criticism's distinctive gifts include that capacity to explore the gaps and margins in biblical texts and to playfully create meaning from things that go unsaid. Queer interpreters also expose the fragility of distinctions that interpreters have assumed for decades, even centuries. Where, for example, Paul might write about prostitution as a problem *external* to the Corinthian assembly, queer interpreters remind us that those same assemblies included quite a few enslaved persons—and that many, if not most, prostitutes were themselves enslaved.[103] In short, queer interpretation poses a welcome threat to our stable interpretive habits.

---

101. Valérie Nicolet, "Monstrous Bodies in Paul's Letter to the Galatians," in Marchal, *Bodies on the Verge*, 137.

102. Stephen D. Moore, "The Dog-Woman of Canaan and Other Animal Tales from the Gospel of Matthew," in Lozada and Carey, *Soundings in Cultural Criticism*, 64.

103. Midori E. Hartman, "A Little Porneia Leavens the Whole: Queer(ing) Limits of Community in 1 Corinthians 5," in Marchal, *Bodies on the Verge*, 143–63.

A GLOBAL FUTURE

Our survey of contextually aware biblical interpretation has only brushed the surface of feminist, African American, Latinx, womanist and *mujerista*, Asian and Asian American, African, and queer interpretation. Moreover, space has not permitted us to appreciate interpretive practices from countless other settings and perspectives.[104]

So far this chapter has worked toward two purposes. First, it has introduced a variety of significant interpretive perspectives, briefly outlining some of their distinctive outlooks, resources, and questions. We have encountered overlap from one perspective to another. Many context-aware interpreters address the problem of oppression in its many forms: economic, political, gendered and sexualized, racial and ethnic, and cultural. Many interpreters appropriate their own cultural perspectives to lend insight into biblical texts. Some investigate how the Bible has been used in harmful ways, while others turn to the wisdom of ordinary, nonprofessional interpreters in their own contexts.

Second, this chapter aims to demonstrate the value of attention to actual flesh-and-blood readers who bring diverse outlooks and resources to the process of interpretation. For this reason, we have sampled specific cases in which attention to the context of interpretation generates profound insight. It is not the case that I agree with all the interpretations we have sampled here, but all of them are instructive to me. We all bring unique gifts to the work of interpretation, just as we come with the limitations of our own cultural histories and perspectives. That is why educating ourselves in diverse modes of biblical interpretation is helpful to us. The qualifications for public biblical interpretation include historical and literary skills and knowledge, and they may include personal virtues. Unfortunately, many interpreters fail to recognize that global awareness is just as essential for public interpretation as any other resource. As our world grows smaller through travel and technology, informed readers will continue to develop global competence.[105]

---

104. For helpful teaching resources filled with samples of global interpretation, see Mark Roncace and Joseph Weaver, eds., *Global Perspectives on the Bible* (Upper Saddle River, NJ: Pearson, 2013); and Daniel Patte et al., eds., *Global Bible Commentary* (Nashville: Abingdon, 2004).

105. Kwok Pui-lan, "Geopolitical Hermeneutics," in Lozada and Carey, *Soundings in Cultural Criticism*, 165–76.

MULTIDISCIPLINARY CULTURAL STUDIES

People relate to the Bible in all sorts of ways. Attending to the ways in which actual readers understand and appropriate biblical texts requires a formidable amount of work. In addition to familiarity with the Bible and its interpretation, we must come to know multiple cultural and historical contexts. This approach situates the Bible in the flow of human culture, including the struggle to interpret our lives, legitimate our aspirations, and shape the imaginations of others. When we take the Bible out of its ancient contexts and examine it in the innumerable contexts of human use, we participate in cultural-studies approaches to biblical interpretation.[106]

We've encountered multiple examples of cultural criticism already. John F. A. Sawyer shows how early Christians appropriated the prophet Isaiah's message as Christian proclamation, a pattern that has resounded through the centuries.[107] Emerson B. Powery and Rodney S. Sadler Jr. dug into the interpretive work of enslaved and other African Americans prior to the Civil War.[108] When scholars such as Musa W. Dube and Gerald O. West research popular interpretation among readers in southern Africa, they too are contributing to cultural studies.[109] We could go on and on.

I have chosen one example of cultural interpretation for our reflection. David A. Sánchez begins with the Woman Clothed with the Sun in Revelation 12.[110] In the vision a Dragon chases the Woman, who receives divine protection and gives birth to the Messiah. Sánchez first argues that the Woman adapts an ancient Mediterranean symbol: the Romans appropriated an even more ancient Dragon Slayer myth as a means of depicting how their empire subjugated chaos and established an age of peace and prosperity. Sánchez judges that Jews adapted this myth as a means of resistance: the Woman and her messianic offspring

---

106. Fernando F. Segovia, "Cultural Studies and Contemporary Biblical Criticism: Ideological Criticism as a Mode of Discourse," in Segovia and Tolbert, *Reading from This Place*, 2:1–17; Lozada and Carey, *Soundings in Cultural Criticism*.
107. Sawyer, *The Fifth Gospel*.
108. Powery and Sadler, *Genesis of Liberation*.
109. Dube, *Postcolonial Feminist Interpretation*; West, *Academy of the Poor*; and *Biblical Hermeneutics of Liberation*.
110. David A. Sánchez, *From Patmos to the Barrio: Subverting Imperial Myths* (Minneapolis: Fortress, 2008).

displace the Roman emperor. Revelation 12, a Christian text, takes this Jewish paradigm and applies it to Jesus, the messianic offspring who will defeat the Dragon and the Beast.

Most Revelation commentators would agree with Sánchez to this point. However, Sánchez adds two critical observations. First, imperial myths "can be used both to justify and deconstruct claims to power"; in other words, the same mythical power can both enforce and resist imperial authority.[111] And second, people living on the margins of power, especially those who find themselves in imperial, colonial, and neocolonial contexts, will challenge centers of power in patterned ways across both time and culture.[112]

This is where the cultural-studies piece kicks in. Sánchez moves from early Christianity's ancient Mediterranean setting to seventeenth-century Mexico and then to twentieth-century Los Angeles. Devotion to the Virgin Mary draws upon Revelation 12's vision of a woman giving birth to the Messiah. In seventeenth-century Mexico two centers of Mary devotion emerged: Spaniards tended to the Virgin in Remedios, while creole and indigenous Mexicans favored Guadalupe. In other words, veneration of Mary takes place in the midst of conflict over empire and colonization. By the twentieth and twenty-first centuries the Virgin of Guadalupe functions as a symbol of independence in Los Angeles, a sort of "flag" for the Chicano liberation movement in the United States.[113] The overall project demonstrates how one cultural motif, passing through Roman, Jewish, Christian, Spanish, Mexican, and Chicano communities, can work both for and against cultural domination.

Let's take a minute to ponder the scope of Sánchez's project. Sánchez handles conventional biblical-studies material, like Roman imperial propaganda, Jewish apocalyptic literature, and the book of Revelation. But his discussions of seventeenth-century Mexico and contemporary Los Angeles are just as detailed. Typically, we expect experts to cover each of these subjects independently. Sure enough, Sánchez relies heavily upon the work of those experts, citing secondary sources perhaps more than doing his own primary investigations.

I have experienced the same limitations on occasion. Once I was

---

111. Sánchez, *From Patmos to the Barrio*, 2.
112. Sánchez, *From Patmos to the Barrio*, 45.
113. Sánchez, *From Patmos to the Barrio*, 111.

offering a presentation on Clarence Jordan, a white Georgian who founded a racially integrated farming community in 1942. Over the years Jordan and that community endured persecution ranging from being expelled from their church to having shots fired into their houses and dynamite applied to their roadside produce stands. (That community gave rise to Habitat for Humanity and the Fuller Center for Housing.) I'm scarcely a historian of Southern religious history, but at some point I realized that Jordan, a Baptist minister, "must" have been reading a theologian named Walter Rauschenbusch while he was in seminary. While I didn't include that insight in my paper, I did offer it during my oral presentation.[114] Afterward I ran into an actual historian, Charles Marsh, and asked him about my hunch.

Marsh: "Yes, they were reading Rauschenbusch at Southern Seminary."

Me: "It seemed like they must have. How do you know?"

Marsh: "Well, I went to the archives and looked at the syllabi."

That interaction indicates the difference between a true specialist and those of us who try our hands outside our range of expertise. I had a hunch, and it happened to be correct. Marsh *knew* because he knew how to pursue the question and took the time to do so.

Cultural-studies projects like that of Sánchez confront us with a dilemma. Rare is the interpreter who expertly assesses cultural core samples that range over multiple centuries, languages, and cultures. For that reason, we might take a topic and parcel out the pieces to various experts.[115] Instead, Sánchez shows us the insight that comes when an individual or a small team works on a problem and arrives at a synthetic point of view. Sánchez shows us how a motif that shows up in the Bible can work its way through centuries and across time, while somehow consistent patterns persist. In the case of the Woman Clothed with the Sun, that pattern reveals the ongoing struggle between the powerful and those who resist them to appropriate sacred symbols for their own purposes. A team could not have written with the focus and insight Sánchez contributes as an individual. In my view the risks, formidable as they are, are worth it.

---

114. I *almost* express the thought in the essay: "Clarence Jordan as a (White) Interpreter of the Bible," in *Roots in the Cotton Patch*, vol. 1: *The Clarence Jordan Symposium 2012*, ed. Kirk Lyman-Barner and Cori Lyman Barner (Eugene, OR: Cascade, 2014), 36–39.

115. See Wimbush, *African Americans and the Bible*, for a classic example.

WHITEWASH: WHITENESS IN THE INTERPRETIVE ENTERPRISE

Whether liberationist, feminist, African American, Latinx, womanist or *mujerista*, Asian American or Asian, African, or queer, all the interpreters we've discussed in this chapter foreground their motivations and aims in biblical interpretation. They reflect on how their cultural histories and commitments shape the work they do, integrating those factors into the process of interpreting the Bible.

We should be clear, however: that these sorts of advocacy interpretations, and others, exist does not mean that *all* women, people of color, and queer folk participate in such self-consciously "located" reading. Countless people of all backgrounds and identities read the Bible without taking account of factors like culture and identity. By no means should we assume that the discussion in this chapter describes every Latinx or Asian American interpreter or every act of interpretation performed by people who identify with those categories. Our discussion has covered *only* those who foreground culture and identity in their interpretive work.

Generally speaking, white interpreters have rarely reflected upon how culture and identity shape their own interpretive work. Feminists may speak to gender. Sexual minorities may speak from a perspective of queerness. But only occasionally do white interpreters grapple with their own race and ethnicity in public ways. Jewish interpreters, categorized as white in American society, sometimes situate their responses to the New Testament as responses to Christian anti-Judaism.[116] By way of memoir, John Dominic Crossan shares that his Irish background, defined by the reality of British occupation and Irish resistance, guided him to understand Jesus's relationship as a Judean peasant to the Roman Empire.[117] These cases feature interpreters engaging their identities through the lens of legitimate marginalization. Whiteness does not function as an operative category.

Less common is work like that of Jeffrey L. Staley, who reflects on his background as a child of white missionaries who worked among the Navajo on an Arizona reservation. Staley narrates how, during his childhood, his Navajo classmates associated him with white cru-

---

116. Reinhartz, *Befriending the Beloved Disciple*; Amy-Jill Levine, *The Misunderstood Jew*.

117. *A Long Way from Tipperary: What a Former Irish Monk Discovered in His Search for Truth* (New York: HarperSanFrancisco, 2000), 47–52.

elty—and how he came to discover that his own ancestors participated in murder and exploitation of Native Peoples. On one occasion local Navajos drove Staley and his brother away from their swimming spot. Staley would later learn that the Navajo believed his white skin might infect the sheep who watered themselves there. Staley first found himself in a white-majority environment when he entered high school. One day, as he and some white friends sat together, "four or five Hispanic students walked by."

> Without any exchange of words or looks I instantly felt my friends' temperatures rising. Suddenly I could taste their sticky-sweet whiteness. It oozed from their pores and ran in little rivulets down the steps that we were sitting on, toward the Mexican kids who were hurrying past us. In that revelatory moment I discovered that the white epidermis could indeed infect and destroy other living things.[118]

As an adult, a professional biblical scholar, Staley examines how his childhood experiences and his family background have shaped his approach to biblical interpretation. Staley's childhood intercultural experiences cause him, a descendant of European Protestants, to reassess the assumptions about the Bible his ancestors passed down to him. For them "scriptural meaning was always simple and crystal clear," but his experience with cultural difference taught him to value diversity in interpretation and to promote critical self-awareness among his students.[119]

Staley moves the conversation forward by including his whiteness as a factor in interpretation. We still wonder, however, what *characterizes* white interpretation. One might characterize whiteness as a sort of void: because white voices have shaped and dominated public discourse, we do not ask white interpreters to justify their interests or assumptions. Indeed, white people often speak about race and ethnicity as it applies to other people.[120] Gale A. Yee, a Chinese American scholar, describes being asked during a job interview how her race and ethnicity

---

118. Jeffrey L. Staley, *Reading with a Passion: Rhetoric, Autobiography, and the American West in the Gospel of John* (New York: Continuum, 1995), 171.
119. Staley, *Reading with a Passion*, 191.
120. Denise Kimber Buell, "Anachronistic Whiteness and the Ethics of Interpretation," in Hockey and Horrell, *Ethnicity, Race, Religion*, 150.

"made any difference" in her scholarly work.[121] The question betrayed a key assumption, a white norm: no one would ask a white scholar the same question because "white" cannot mean "different" in that way of imagining the world. White presumably means "normal." Yee invites scholars of color to "make whiteness transparent as a culturally constructed and racialized category," to show what a difference whiteness makes.[122]

Another path might tease out the origins and functions of whiteness. J. Kameron Carter traces whiteness back to an ancient struggle to define a singular Christian identity over against Judaism. When European Christianity encountered cultural difference through Christian mission, it racialized the differences between European Christian cultures and the diversity encountered through new contacts. That difference, of course, was interpreted as inferiority: to be white came to be identified with being Christian.[123] Students of early Christian discourse such as Gay L. Byron point out that ancient Christians often interpreted blackness, along with Egyptian and Ethiopian identity, as a sign of wickedness. Is whiteness, then, a by-product of how white people describe other people? Is it the remainder left over from what makes everyone else different?[124]

In my view, confluence of two streams still feeds the ethos of white interpretation in the United States: the philosophy of common-sense realism and the struggle to defend or criticize the legitimacy of slavery.[125] Common-sense realism dominated Protestant American intel-

---

121. Gale A. Yee, "Yin/Yang Is Not Me: An Exploration into Asian American Biblical Hermeneutics," in Foskett and Kuan, *Ways of Being, Ways of Reading*, 152–53.

122. Yee, "Yin/Yang Is Not Me," 162.

123. Kameron J. Carter, *Race: A Theological Account* (New York: Oxford University Press, 2008). Denise Kimber Buell identifies this trend in Christian characterizations of Judaism, where Christianity is represented as "universal" as opposed to "particularistic" Judaism: *Why This New Race: Ethnic Reasoning in Early Christianity* (New York: Columbia University Press, 2005), esp. 21–29. Also: Willie James Jennings, *The Christian Imagination: Theology and the Origins of Race* (New Haven: Yale University Press, 2010), 58–64.

124. See the discussion in Stephanie Y. Mitchem, *Race, Religion, and Politics: Toward Human Rights in the United States* (Lanham, MD: Rowman & Littlefield, 2019), 43.

125. I suggested this line of thought in Greg Carey, "Introduction and a Proposal: Culture, Power, and Identity in White New Testament Studies," in Lozada and Carey, *Soundings in Cultural Criticism*, 1–13.

lectual life in the nineteenth century. Protestants have always foregrounded the Bible's authority over Christian theology and moral life, but we often underestimate an important dimension of Protestantism's relationship to the Bible. Protestants have tended to argue for the ordinary believer's direct access to the Bible's meaning through common-sense reasoning, a doctrine called the perspicuity (or clarity) of Scripture.[126] Joined to common-sense realism, a movement that emerged in seventeenth-century Scottish philosophy, the notion of Scripture's clarity turned ballistic.[127] Common-sense realism rejected the idealism posed by David Hume, John Locke, and George Berkeley, all of whom radically questioned the link between human perception and objective reality. In other words, common-sense realism maintained that our perceptions of the world may be faulty but are grounded in reality. The nineteenth-century Southern Baptist theologian John Leadley Dagg expressed high confidence that Christians could know God's will because God created the world and authored the Bible: "The Author of the Bible is the maker of the world, and the author of all truth; and his works and his word must harmonize, for Truth is always consistent."[128]

Common-sense realism fueled a particular approach to the Bible that still shapes popular American religion. As historian of religion E. Brooks Holifield observed, "Religious conservatism in the Old South was always as much a matter of philosophical as of Biblical considerations."[129] His insight does not apply simply to the American South. Whenever people refer to the Bible as an "instruction manual for life" or a "road map," they assume that we can know what the Bible means and that what we "find" in it applies directly to our contemporary questions.[130] After all, common-sense realism "was nothing if not democra-

126. Michael C. Legaspi argues that while the perspicuity of Scripture functioned as a critical Protestant doctrine, it eventually—and ironically—led to biblical studies as an academic endeavor to be performed only by experts: *The Death of Scripture and the Rise of Biblical Studies*, Oxford Studies in Historical Theology (New York: Oxford University Press, 2010).

127. For a classic discussion of this phenomenon in American culture, see E. Brooks Holifield, *The Gentlemen Theologians: American Theology in Southern Culture, 1795–1860* (Durham, NC: Duke University Press, 1978), esp. 110–26.

128. Quoted in Holifield, *Gentlemen Theologians*, 124.

129. Holifield, *Gentlemen Theologians*, 125.

130. A similar logic underlies the Bible prophecy movement, which treats the Bible as

tic."[131] *Anyone* could pick up the Bible, interpret it independently, and apply it to the topics of their choosing.

Common-sense realist biblical interpretation stamped American slavery debates. As we saw in chapter 1, slavery's advocates could collect Bible verses and passages to legislate and regulate slavery, as well as those that exhort owners of enslaved people and enslaved persons to behave in particular ways and that argue that slavery was God's will. Opponents of slavery attempted to rise to the occasion, building arguments of their own, but they confronted an uphill struggle. Biblical cultures were slaveholding cultures, and slavery's advocates had more verses and passages on their side than did their opponents. Remarkably, enslaved and free African Americans developed a diverse array of interpretive strategies to resist the dehumanizing messages of their owners and to appropriate the Bible as a source of healing. They could read themselves into the exodus story, God's liberation of Israel from enslavement. They could interpret the passages often enlisted by slavery's advocates differently. They could outright reject the preaching supplied by masters of enslaved people. The opponents of slavery likewise sought alternatives to the biblical practice of stockpiling verses. Nevertheless, common-sense biblicism continues to shape public conversations on controversial issues from gender to sexuality to immigration.

I suspect this legacy resides in the DNA of white biblical interpretation. Common-sense biblicism assumes that the Bible speaks with one voice and that its meanings should be clear to everyone. If whiteness means anything in biblical interpretation, it has something to do with universalism, the notion that everyone should be able to see the Bible in the same way. If we simply approach the Bible with the tools of reason, our best interpretive methods, we should all come to agreement. For whiteness does not perceive itself as a perspective.[132] Interlaced with

---

predicting the final history of the world. See George M. Marsden, *Fundamentalism and American Culture: The Shaping of Twentieth-Century Evangelicalism: 1870–1925* (New York: Oxford University Press, 1980), 212–21.

131. Randall Balmer, "Casting Aside the Ballast of History and Tradition: White Protestants and the Bible in the Antebellum Period," in Wimbush, *African Americans and the Bible*, 198.

132. Wei Hsien Wan, "Re-examining the Master's Tools: Considerations on Biblical Studies' Race Problem," in Hockey and Horrell, *Ethnicity, Race, Religion*, 225–26.

common-sense realism, whiteness observes all things with a universal perspective—or claims to.

Here we encounter a profound irony. J. Kameron Carter traces whiteness to the early Christians' attempts to distinguish themselves from Jews. Modern biblical scholarship has often classified early Christianity as universalistic, as opposed to a supposedly exclusive and inward-looking Judaism.[133] This practice frequently manifests itself when Christians, even nonwhite Christians, have advocated for social justice. Denise Kimber Buell argues:

> Assertions that Christianity has had from its beginnings a universalizing, racially inclusive mandate have been central to both mainstream academic scholars and to marginalized voices seeking social, political, and religious reform. For mainstream scholars, race has served as the primary criteria by which one can classify Christianity as a special kind of religion, not linked to race. . . . The mainstream approach makes race an out-of-bounds topic for Christianness.[134]

The irony: Christianity's claim to transcend race animates its attempts, ancient and modern, to establish a (false) superiority over against Judaism. Whiteness has something to do with the attempt to transcend race and perspectivalism. This whitewashing universalism resists our attempts to pin down, describe, or analyze whiteness.

On occasion, however, scholars have spotted whiteness in action. Like photographs of Sasquatch, the images are blurry and indistinct. But they do exist. For example, Shawn Kelley has shown how the aesthetic values that shaped Nazi ideology still resound in biblical scholarship. Those of us (I've been one!) who described Jesus's parables in terms of "immediacy, authenticity, primordiality, organicity, and metaphoricity" are echoing the values set forth by Martin Heidegger as distinctively German. Heidegger's profoundly influential aesthetics (I read Heidegger in graduate school) provided a means of buttressing the German *Volk*. While Kelley does not accuse contemporary biblical scholars of complicity with Nazism, he points out how this Nazi discourse yet influences the field. Without question, one common feature in parables scholarship involves a comparison between Jesus's parables

---

133. Jonathan Z. Smith, *Drudgery Divine: On the Comparison of Early Christianities and the Religions of Late Antiquity* (Chicago: University of Chicago Press, 1990).
134. Buell, *Why This New Race*, 157.

and those of the rabbis. Jesus comes across as unique, his parables more imaginative, more radical than were those of the rabbis.[135]

Perhaps our best chances of photographing Sasquatch do not involve searching all over the woods but finding watering holes where the creature is likely to visit. And perhaps an optimal approach to identifying white biblical interpretation is to find case studies where white scholars engage questions like race and ethnicity in biblical texts. One accessible drinking spot would involve homing in on an individual white interpreter, or a group of them. We might ferret out intuitively how whiteness shapes this interpreter's point of view.

Ekaputra Tupamahu, an Indonesian immigrant to the United States, provides an admirable case of this process. Tupamahu is interested in the intersections of language, ethnicity, and power in society, and he focuses much of his work on *glossolalia*, or speaking in tongues, in 1 Corinthians. Most interpreters believe Paul is writing about mystical or heavenly language, but Tupamahu stands in the minority: in his opinion, the tongues in 1 Corinthians are actually the native languages of immigrants to Corinth. White interpreters, Tupamahu observes, do not take this possibility into account. A white scholar who describes these Corinthians as Greek-speaking immigrants accidentally gives away their white perspective. By describing them as "Greek-speaking," we erase their distinctive identities as immigrants from *somewhere.* Immigrants to the United States would not call themselves "English-speaking" immigrants; instead, Tupamahu describes himself as "a *bahasa Indonesia*-speaking immigrant who happens to speak English." Although he speaks English, Tupamahu writes, "I do not identify myself with the English language."[136]

Likewise, we might consider someone like Clarence Jordan, whom I mentioned earlier. A white Southern radical, Jordan resisted segregation in multiple ways. His Koinonia Farm practiced integration when it was dangerous to do so, and he collaborated with people beyond his immediate circle to promote integration. Jordan held a PhD in New Testament Greek; indeed, his translation of much of the New Testament into colloquial Southern is still in print and forms the basis of the

---

135. Kelley, *Racializing Jesus*; further developed in Kelley, "Race, Aesthetics, and Gospel Scholarship," 191–209.
136. Ekaputra Tupamahu, "'I Don't Want to Hear Your Language!': White Social Imagination and the Demography of Roman Corinth," unpublished paper. I understand that this paper has been accepted for publication.

musical *Cotton Patch Gospel*.[137] Jordan's interpretations of the New Testament often address issues related to race. For example, his iteration of the Good Samaritan parable (Luke 10:25–37) renders the Samaritan as "a black man." In this way Jordan communicates the shock that Jesus would include a Samaritan as the story's hero while confronting white audiences by presenting that hero as an African American. Jordan also characterizes Jesus's crucifixion as a lynching, "stringing him up," reminding his audiences of racist violence.

Although I do not question Jordan's desire to foster racial justice or his courage in doing just that, something troubles me about these interpretations. I strongly suspect that black preachers well before Jordan (a white man, recall) appealed to the Good Samaritan parable in precisely the same way Jordan did.[138] In the 1940s Howard Thurman began an argument for racial justice by referencing this parable.[139] I am certain African American interpreters had observed the parallels between lynching and crucifixion long before Jordan made the association.[140] Jordan does not credit African American interpreters for these insights, something we might excuse in that his translations are not accompanied by footnotes and other scholarly apparatus. Perhaps he felt that making such connections clear would have undermined his persuasiveness among white audiences. But it is also the case that Jordan chose not to support many of the Civil Rights Movement's methods, arguing that the movement used nonviolence as a tactic rather than as a commitment of positive love.[141]

It is scarcely surprising that a white interpreter would fail to credit the agency of nonwhite people. I've been confronted with the same error in my own writing. While making a point about insiders and out-

---

137. Clarence Jordan, *Cotton Patch Gospel: The Complete Collection* (Macon, GA: Smyth & Helwys, 2012).
138. Henry H. Mitchell makes precisely this connection in his 1990 *Black Preaching: The Recovery of a Powerful Art* (Nashville: Abingdon, 1990), 60, in an example that suggests his audience would have recognized the interpretation as conventional.
139. Thurman, *Jesus and the Disinherited*, 89.
140. Recently classically expressed by James H. Cone, *The Cross and the Lynching Tree* (Maryknoll, NY: Orbis, 2011), though Cone does not explicitly refer to a tradition of interpretation along these lines.
141. Tracy Elaine K'Meyer, *Interracialism and Christian Community in the Postwar South: The Story of Koinonia Farm* (Charlottesville: University of Virginia Press, 1997), 156–57; see Carey, "Clarence Jordan."

siders, I referenced a scene in the classic film *To Kill a Mockingbird*. We might note that the movie and the novel upon which it is based revolve around the threat of racial violence in the American South, lynching. Both foreground a white male hero, Atticus Finch, with African Americans largely helpless. Lots of people have pointed out the motif of white heroes saving black people in American art, and I must confess I did not escape the appeal of that trope. At one point in the film the African American domestic worker Calpurnia scolds one of Atticus's children for mocking a poorer classmate's table manners. I describe the scene, quoting Calpurnia's speech. But imagine my embarrassment when a student confronted me with a cold fact: I attributed Calpurnia's speech to Atticus.[142] I wish I could name that student, and I desperately wish I could change my description of that scene—more than I'd like to change anything else I've ever written. But that's how whiteness works.

David G. Horrell likewise investigates case studies for clues of whiteness. He surveys commentary on Galatians 3:28, a passage that foregrounds ethnicity explicitly, specifically Paul's claim that in Christ "there is no longer Jew or Greek." Horrell begins by noting, "It has come to strike me that I have spent the last twenty years as a New Testament scholar without ever reflecting on how my racial or ethnic identity shapes what I do, what I see, what I ask and do not ask."[143]

Horrell finds that interpretations of this passage vary over time. White commentators once saw Paul "abolishing" human distinctions, eliminating the significance of race and ethnicity in human relations. But the "New Perspective" on Paul, which began to take hold around 1980, transformed how many interpreters understood Paul's relationship to his own Jewish identity: simply, Paul was and never ceased to be Jewish. Although still inclined to contrast Paul's view of ethnic difference with those of most of his Jewish contemporaries, more recent commentators tend to view Paul as honoring diversity within a larger unity.

Horrell presses further, noting that Christian commentators rarely reflect on how their religious commitments shape their commentary, a reality we might compare with how rarely we engage the question

---

142. Greg Carey, *Sinners: Jesus and His Earliest Followers* (Waco, TX: Baylor University Press, 2009), 172.

143. David G. Horrell, "Paul, Inclusion and Whiteness: Particularizing Interpretation," *JSNT* 40 (2017): 124.

of our own whiteness. When commentators celebrate unity in Christ, have they considered that many people do not count this vision as "hopeful and inspiring"?[144] Moreover, Christian interpreters continue to set Paul over against the exclusionary views of his Jewish contemporaries, failing to investigate the positive value of particularity for ancient Jews, modern Jews, or anyone else. Nor do commentators discuss the "widespread appeal of Jewish customs and practices to outsiders" in Paul's day.[145] Horrell discerns an intersection between the Christian identity that shapes commentary on Galatians and whiteness that exempts itself from holding particular biases and points of view: each assumes the possibility of unity that requires conformity from others.

Quoting the Sri Lankan scholar R. S. Sugirtharajah (who has spent his career in England), Horrell observes that mainstream (white) interpretation continues to present itself as normative, "labelling the enterprise of others—'Asian', 'African', and so on, or in gender and ethnic terms."[146] Horrell argues that if we expect, for example, African American interpreters to perceive relevance in their own identity and experience, "so too those of us raced as white should equally expect that our ethnic or racial identity constitutes part of the package of factors that shapes our reading."[147] That indeed is the challenge of public interpretation for everyone, even and especially white readers.

---

144. Horrell, "Paul, Inclusion and Whiteness," 134.

145. Horrell, "Paul, Inclusion and Whiteness," 135.

146. R. S. Sugirtharajah, "Muddling Along at the Margins," in *Still at the Margins: Biblical Scholarship Fifteen Years after Voices from the Margin*, ed. R. S. Sugirtharajah (London: T&T Clark, 2008), 8, quoted in Horrell, "Paul, Inclusion and Whiteness," 139.

147. Horrell, "Paul, Inclusion and Whiteness," 141.

CHAPTER 6.

BRINGING IT HOME, TAKING IT OUTSIDE

I was sitting in a graduate seminar devoted to the Gospel of John. We were discussing a highly influential study of John's Gospel by R. Alan Culpepper.[1] Fernando F. Segovia, who would become my doctoral advisor and lifelong mentor, singled me out.

"Greg, does this interpretation seem Baptist to you?"

It was a complete deer-in-the-headlights moment. Culpepper's book, then ten years old, was a landmark in literary interpretation of the Bible. It had never crossed my mind to assign the book to a particular category of interpretation apart from that—literary criticism. But I knew why Fernando was asking the question. I, like Culpepper, was a Baptist. In fact, I had just graduated from the seminary where Culpepper had taught, although he left before I had the opportunity to sit in one of his classes. But how could Culpepper's book be "Baptist"? It never mentions Christian denominationalism in any way.

Culpepper argues that John aims to bring the "ideal narrative audience" to share the Gospel's point of view. Meanwhile, Culpepper aims to help *real* readers to "adopt the perspective of that audience."[2] I didn't realize it twenty-five or so years ago, but that sounds a lot like evangelism, doesn't it? Moreover, Culpepper's work defines faith in terms of individual comprehension. Notice both parts: *individual* and *comprehension*. Baptists tend to emphasize individual believers' voluntary response to the Gospel.

That perspective makes sense of many parts of John's Gospel. But I had overlooked other aspects of John. For example, Jesus uses the

1. Culpepper, *Anatomy of the Fourth Gospel*.
2. Culpepper, *Anatomy of the Fourth Gospel*, 208.

metaphor of a vine in chapter 15, instructing his disciples, "Abide in me as I abide in you" (15:4). As a Baptist, I'd been taught to apply that verse to my individual spiritual life: I would relate to Jesus on a one-to-one, mystical basis. I had not considered that the passage uses communal language: Jesus speaks to the disciples in the second-person *plural*, something English translations struggle to capture since we use "you" for the singular *and* the plural, and the vine/branches imagery suggests a community hanging together rather than an individual relationship. Jesus, addressing disciples who will likely endure persecution (15:18), is telling them he dwells *among* them.

Culpepper's interpretation of John seemed perfectly natural to me until Fernando called it into question. I'd rarely encountered forms of Christianity that read John differently, nor could I without building new relationships. To be clear, Fernando respected Culpepper's work highly; that's why we were reading it. But it was essential to my education that I engage questions and perspectives that were foreign to me.

There's no way to keep up with all the ways the Bible is being used and read. That's far too much to ask from anyone. But public interpretation requires that we interact with readers who do not share our assumptions and find ways to communicate. We develop the capacity to understand their ways of interpreting the Bible, open to the possibility that we may learn something in the process, and to explain our own point of view in ways most people can understand. Along the way we grow in self-understanding. In the same way that we learn about ourselves when we encounter cultures that are new to us, we also see our interpretive assumptions and habits differently when we interact with interpreters who work differently.

BRINGING IT HOME: THE WORK WE NEED TO DO

The work of public interpretation calls us to cultivate knowledge and habits that we already practice, but also to develop them in ways appropriate to the biblical materials. The historical dimension of biblical interpretation requires us to think like detectives and social scientists. We appreciate how greatly biblical cultures differ from our own, and often from one another, and gather cultural information that helps us understand biblical texts in fresh ways.

For example, at one point I was taken aback by the polemic we encounter in parts of the New Testament, particularly in Revelation and in parts of Paul's letters. The language is intense indeed: in Revelation John imagines a competing prophet thrown upon a bed while Christ strikes her children dead (Rev 2:20–23), a fantasy of sexualized violence,[3] while Paul relishes the thought of his opponents castrating themselves (Gal 5:12). Paul curses those opponents in the same letter (1:8)—and in case we wonder whether he really means it, he doubles down: "As we have said before, so now I repeat, if anyone proclaims to you a gospel contrary to what you received, let that one be accursed!" (1:9). I doubt many of us would appropriate such language in contemporary contexts, but how would John and Paul have come across in their own cultural context? I find it helpful to learn about the intensity of ancient polemical language. Consider how Cicero, considered the greatest Roman orator of all, attacks his enemy Catiline, albeit in a genuine public crisis:

> What brand of domestic baseness is not stamped upon your life? What disgraceful circumstance is wanting to your infamy in your private affairs? From what licentiousness have your eyes, from what atrocity have your hands, from what iniquity has your whole body ever abstained? Is there one youth, when you have once entangled him in the temptations of your corruption, to whom you have not held out a sword for audacious crime, or a torch for licentious wickedness? (*Against Catiline* 1.6)[4]

Cicero's inflamed rhetoric does not excuse that of John and Paul, but it does provide a context against which to understand what ancient audiences expected in moments of conflict. Apparently ancient audiences were accustomed to higher levels of intensity than we are today.[5] Who knows how the rhetoric of Twitter wars, reality TV, and our current politics will affect our contemporary standards?

As public interpreters we also sharpen our skills in literary interpretation. Appreciating that most of the Bible consists of narrative and poetry, we consider the artistic shaping of biblical texts. In chapter 3 we briefly mentioned Robert Alter, one of the modern pioneers of Hebrew Bible literary interpretation, and his insight that patterns of repetition

---

3. I would describe this as a "clear" example of sexualized violence, but many commentators interpret the bed as a sickbed.
4. Translation by Charles Duke Yonge, *Cicero's Orations*, Dover Thrift Editions (Mineola, NY: Dover, 2018).
5. See Luke Timothy Johnson, "The New Testament's Anti-Jewish Slander and the Conventions of Ancient Polemic," *JBL* 108 (1989): 419–41.

and variation can shape readers' encounters with biblical stories. Alter calls our attention to Westerns, the film genre that often features male heroes with superior shooting skills. In film after film, the hero draws his pistol with astonishing speed and shoots his enemies with unfailing accuracy. But what would audiences make of a hero whose right arm is withered and who fights with a rifle he keeps slung over his back? After watching, say, eleven films featuring hyper-reflexive sheriffs, the twelfth sheriff stands out by contrast.

> Here is a sheriff who seems to lack the expected equipment for his role, but we note the daring assertion of manly will against almost impossible odds in the hero's learning to make do with what he has, training his left arm to whip his rifle into firing position with a swiftness that makes it a match for the quickest draw in the West.[6]

In other words, once a literary pattern is set, deviations from the pattern prove especially meaningful.

Alter goes on to examine a biblical type-scene with a pattern: when an Israelite man encounters a woman at a well in a foreign land, a betrothal ensues. The pattern occurs three times (Gen 24:10–61; 29:1–20; and Exod 2:15b–21). Alter emphasizes the specific ways each story differs from the common script, arguing that those deviations reveal something about the character of the protagonist. The third example involves Moses, who stands out from the other stories by fighting off hostile shepherds, then drawing water himself. In Exodus, Alter points out, Moses is indeed a man of conflict. Moreover, the association with Moses and water includes the midwives who hide Moses on the river (2:1–10), Moses's leadership of the Israelites through the Red Sea (14:10–31), and Moses's capacity to transform bitter water into sweet water (15:25) and to produce a spring of water from a rock (17:1–7).[7] Moses's well encounter not only leads to his marriage; it contributes to his overall characterization.

Alter has much more to say about the well type-scene, but his attention is devoted to the Hebrew Bible. The Gospel of John also includes a scene in which an Israelite man passes through a foreign country and meets a woman at a well: the famous story of the Samaritan woman (4:1–42). Most readers do not expect flirtation in this encounter. But if we imagine that John's Gospel expects its audience to recognize scrip-

---

6. Alter, *Art of Biblical Narrative*, 49.
7. Alter, *Art of Biblical Narrative*, 47–62.

tural allusions, Jesus's arrival at the well sets the scene for a bit of flirtation. After all, do not Jesus and the unnamed woman banter back and forth? And doesn't the tone change when Jesus instructs the woman to bring her husband—prompting her denial that she even has a husband? (Instead, she's living with a man who is not her husband.) John's Gospel is full of double-entendre, cases where speech carries multiple levels of potential significance: Don't the Hebrew Scriptures employ water as a euphemism for women's sexuality?[8] John presents Jesus as teasing the woman concerning his true intentions, leaving readers to evaluate the goings-on. Reading the Torah and John with a literary perspective helps us appreciate such literary strategies.

In chapter 4, I argued that public interpretation involves far more than our rational faculties. Some suggest that because the Bible is a sacred text for Christians and Jews, religious believers are its most insightful interpreters. It's likely that faith communities need interpreters who share their values and speak their language—but faith communities also suffer when they ignore the wisdom of interpreters who bring different values and ask different questions. Moreover, public interpretation is, well, public: it necessarily speaks to readers who hold all kinds of religious and nonreligious outlooks, and it should take account of their concerns and insights. In my view, we all suffer when we allow some readers to set the rules that should guide interpretation for everyone else.

Modern biblical scholarship traces its roots to the Enlightenment, which elevated reason above traditional sources of authority, such as the church. The field cultivated a scientific ethos that elevated objectivity as a primary virtue in interpretation. Pure objectivity is, of course, impossible: our biases and commitments generally run much deeper than we realize, a factor that applies especially to people of privilege. Moreover, we have learned that those biases and commitments are both necessary and productive. They draw our attention to the objects we study and provide frameworks by which we make sense of them. Before we abandon objectivity altogether, we might consider the reasons our predecessors attached such value to it. They desired freedom from institutional constraints and space for public dialogue where no position enjoyed special privilege over others. Those are important val-

---

8. Lyle Eslinger, "The Wooing of the Woman at the Well: Jesus, the Reader and Reader-Response Criticism," *Journal of Literature and Theology* 1 (1987): 167–83.

ues. Perhaps other values help us attain similar ends: I propose that open-mindedness and curiosity, fairness, thoroughness, diversity, and transparency make a good start.

The conversation about which virtues distinguish excellent public interpretation also pushes us toward taking account of real, flesh-and-blood readers. None of us can attain competence with respect to every interpretive movement. Nevertheless, I maintain that public interpretation requires that we stretch our imaginations and understandings through deep encounters with reading communities on a global scale. Thirty years ago many professional scholars would have mocked this claim, but I see it as essential. In the long run, interpreters who interact only with those who look and sound like them forfeit the opportunity to broaden their audiences and, more importantly, their understandings.

GOING PUBLIC: HOW IT MATTERS

The Bible's public role won't submit to simple characterization. Most people rarely open a Bible, though in theory many defer to its authority. Others couldn't care less. Still others read the Bible every day, usually with prayer, and think through the issues of their lives in biblical categories. And many enjoy the Bible as a cultural resource, interacting with it for literary pleasure or out of historical interest. Some activists magnify the Bible as a foundation for civilization, some are more concerned by the Bible's use for evil ends, and still others can readily imagine history turning out about the same without the Bible. There are lots of reasons to interpret the Bible—and lots of reasons people avoid it.

Public interpretation comes in precisely because people interact with the Bible in so many ways. It happens most regularly in Jewish and Christian religious settings, where professionals and volunteers interpret the Bible in order to shape spiritual life and values in religious communities. Biblical interpretation matters in these settings. Some religious communities regard the outside world as a hostile place, while others are far more optimistic concerning the interface between spirituality and culture. Specific biblical understandings shape both outlooks. Religious bodies appeal to the Bible in determining their organization and practices: a common denominational dividing line involves whether women may be authorized as leaders of those communities, and the controversy concerning the role of LGBTQ persons in church life continues to divide Christian denominations.

People who provide spiritual care know how profoundly people's understandings of the Bible shape their spiritual lives. What a person makes of the Bible often reflects their own character. Religious believers necessarily weave the Bible into their own self-understandings, their responses to stress and trauma, and their interactions with other people. While writing this chapter, I asked several pastoral leaders to share how biblical understandings influence people's spiritual lives. Several noted that people who emphasize a judgmental, punishing deity often struggle to accept themselves and others as they are. The fear of judgment fosters disillusionment and bitterness, alienating many people from God and from one another. This is especially the case when people interpret their present suffering as punishment for past behavior. Another observed that people who believe that the "Fall" of Adam and Eve corrupted human nature may be inclined to deny their true selves rather than trusting that their own passions and inclinations may lead to flourishing. On the other hand, several leaders offered that many people experience blessing and reconciliation through their understandings of the Bible, which free them to pursue life and growth.

To take one example, the issue of prayer vexes many people. First, there are the intellectual problems: Why should God respond to our prayers if God knows all things and is always working for good? Why should prayer make any difference? But people also voice spiritual problems: Does prayer depend on how firmly we believe? On the particular words we say? Are some ways of praying better than others? A third set of questions involves praying for ourselves: Is it selfish to do so?

One prominent stream in American (and global) Christianity is known as the prosperity gospel. According to the prosperity gospel, God wants people to flourish in every way. So if people live righteously and pray faithfully, they should avoid illness, financial distress, and personal problems. Some Christians express this view quite explicitly. More common is the unspoken assumption that we should overcome our suffering with *just. enough. faith.* How sadly ironic, then, that Kate Bowler, a divinity school professor who researched the prosperity gospel, should face a devastating medical diagnosis. Just thirty-five years old, with a husband, a child, and a promising career, she learned she had terminal cancer. Still living with cancer as of this writing,

Bowler questions the spirituality of the prosperity gospel. If you ask some people how they're doing, they'll reply, "I'm blessed"—no matter what they're going through. The prosperity gospel, Bowler argues, does not allow people to express their suffering or their concern for one another in authentic ways. "The prosperity gospel," she writes, "popularized a Christian explanation for why some people make it and some do not. They revolutionized prayer as an instrument for getting God always to say 'yes.'" Bowler considers examples in which prosperity-gospel adherents simply could not face grim reality and concludes:

> There is no graceful death, no *ars moriendi*, in the prosperity gospel. There are only jarring disappointments after fevered attempts to deny its inevitability.[9]

If the prosperity gospel makes for easy ridicule, the problem of forgiveness is far more complex. I once had a student who disappeared from my class for weeks, lied about the reason, and expected a passing grade because I should forgive him. More seriously, we've seen compelling examples of forgiveness. In Lancaster County, Pennsylvania, where I live, a man walked into a one-room Amish schoolhouse, told the male students to leave, and shot ten girls there, killing five, before taking his own life. The Amish community rapidly expressed forgiveness to the shooter and his family and included them all in their prayers.

The Lancaster County Amish communities who practiced forgiveness after this shooting make for a remarkable example. Many Christians regard forgiveness as a moral obligation, citing the Lord's Prayer (Matt 6:12: "Forgive us our debts, as we also have forgiven our debtors.") and Jesus's command that his disciples forgive one another's sins (Matt 18:21–22). But is obligatory forgiveness healthy? Is it even possible? Maria Mayo argues that biblical forgiveness is often conditional, expecting repentance and amendment on the part of the offender (as in Matt 18:15–20). Moreover, she maintains, requiring forgiveness from individuals can add to victims' trauma or expose them to danger, as can happen to domestic violence victims. Mayo points to the example of Jesus in Luke. On the cross, Jesus prays, "Father, forgive them; for they do not know what they are doing" (23:34).[10] Following this example,

---

9. Kate Bowler, "Death, the Prosperity Gospel and Me," *New York Times*, February 13, 2016. https://tinyurl.com/gu88lem.

10. Luke 23:34 presents a difficult text-critical problem, as it is absent from important ancient manuscripts.

people can leave forgiveness to God rather than accepting the burden of forgiveness themselves.[11]

Biblical interpretation bears not just upon our personal spiritualities but on our public life as well. In the United States in particular, what happens in religious communities can strongly affect public policy, but the broader culture likewise influences how synagogues and churches understand the Bible. For example, Protestant teachings on divorce have changed dramatically since the late nineteenth century. Until about a century ago, it was extremely rare for Protestant churches to have divorced pastors. Many prohibited pastors from performing weddings for divorced persons, except for persons who had divorced on account of adultery committed by their previous spouse. In 1932 United Methodists modified their policy: persons divorced due to adultery or its "full moral equivalent" could remarry. And by 1960 they allowed remarriage for divorced persons who had undergone appropriate counseling. In 1972 the denomination affirmed the right of divorced persons to remarry without qualification.[12] One suspects that Protestant churches would not have amended their policies without feeling pressure to adapt to a rapidly changing culture.

One need not hold an interest in the Bible to care how other people interpret it. On issue after issue biblical understandings shape political attitudes and therefore public policy. If someone thinks God prefers families in which husbands do the bread winning and wives do the nurturing, that will affect their support for women's equality in the workplace. If someone believes a human life is just as sacred at the moment of conception as it is several months later because the Bible says, "Before I formed you in the womb I knew you, and before you were born I consecrated you" (Jer 1:5), that will affect their opinions on reproductive rights. People who interpret the crucifixion as Jesus substituting himself for the punishment people deserve for their sin are more likely to support capital punishment than are other people.[13]

11. Maria Mayo, *The Limits of Forgiveness: Case Studies in the Distortion of a Biblical Ideal* (Minneapolis: Fortress, 2015).

12. Rex D. Matthews, "Divorce and Remarriage in American Methodism: The Evolution of Church Positions from 1884 to 2012," *The United Methodist Reporter*, April 28, 2016. Online: https://tinyurl.com/redj823.

13. Greg Carey, "Mass Incarceration, Capital Punishment, and Penal Atonement Theories: Correlation or Something More?" in *Thinking Theologically about Mass Incarceration: Biblical Foundations and Justice Imperatives*, ed. Antonios Kireopoulos, Mitzi J.

There's no denying that US policy toward Israeli-Palestinian issues is profoundly shaped by the Bible prophecy movement, where Christian preachers link support for the nation of Israel with being on God's side in the great final conflict. End-time expectation influences the politics on other issues as well. Bible prophecy believers believe the world is headed toward more, not less, conflict, so they resist most international and interdenominational cooperation. And if people believe the world will end in a massive military conflagration, and *soon*, they're far less likely to concern themselves with the climate crisis.

As I'm writing, immigration policy constitutes perhaps the most pressing, painful, and divisive issue in American life, with tension escalating under the Trump Administration's policy of separating migrant children from their families. It appears that religious teachings influence public opinion. According to an October 2018 Public Religion Institute study, white evangelical Christians are the only religious group in which a majority regards immigrants as a threat to society (57 percent) and supports a ban on refugees entering the country (51 percent).[14] Race seems to play a greater role in public opinion than does religious identity, as white mainline Protestants are only slightly less likely to hold these views than are white evangelicals, but differences among religious groups remain significant.

In the face of such a contentious issue, research suggests that, at least in Christian circles, religious instruction affects churchgoers' opinions. For example, positive messages about immigrants from their pastors measurably influence people's opinions concerning whether unauthorized immigrants should have a legal path to citizenship and whether immigrants pose a threat to society. Members of churches that emphasize Romans 13:1–7, commonly appropriated to support submission to government authority, tend to oppose comprehensive immigration reform. Since the Bible enjoins Christians to obey the law, some reason, they should not support people who enter or remain in the country ille-

---

Budde, and Matthew D. Lundberg. National Council of Churches Faith and Order Commission Theological Series (Mahwah, NJ: Paulist Press, 2017), 205–16.

14. Robert P. Jones, et al., *Partisan Polarization Dominates Trump Era: Findings from the 2018 American Values Survey* (New York: PRRI, 2018), 31–40, https://tinyurl.com/rhpz3fd. See Ulrike Elisabeth Stockhausen, "Evangelicals and Immigration: A Conflicted History," *Process: A Blog for American History*, March 18, 2019, https://tinyurl.com/uny4m42.

gally.[15] Given the political and religious polarization in current American life, attitudes toward immigration likely reflect factors other than religion, such as political and racial identity. For example, white evangelicals are more likely to identify as politically conservative than are any other major religious group. Nevertheless, the evidence suggests that public biblical interpretation, as practiced in religious communities, can contribute to shaping opinion on social and political issues. Public interpretation matters.[16]

The immigration conversation plays differently among those directly impacted. Speculative opinions about policy come from those who judge whom to let in or leave out, whom to help or abandon. Many people, especially but not only white readers, can regard immigration from an abstract or theoretical point of view. Immigrants and their families know migration as a lived experience. Their points of contact with the Bible may not all be the same, but they will be inflected by questions of "migration, exile, and diaspora."[17] It's one thing to come to the Bible while living the experience of immigration, quite another to do so from a distance.[18]

Meanwhile, the theme of migration fills the Bible literally from beginning to end. Adam and Eve leave the garden. Having murdered his brother, their son Cain lives as a vulnerable fugitive, protected only by God (Gen 4:11–16). In response to a divine promise, Abraham takes his household on a journey, and having settled among the Canaanites, he journeys out from the land due to famine. Abraham's migrations expose him to vulnerability: fearing powerful people will murder him to take his wife Sarah, he twice passes her off as his sister (12:10–20; 20:1–18). His son Isaac does the same (26:6–11). Famine forces Jacob, now called

---

15. Ruth M. Melkonian-Hoover, "Better Late Than Never? Evangelicals and Comprehensive Immigration Reform," in *Is the Good Book Good Enough? Evangelical Perspectives on Public Policy*, ed. David K. Ryden (Lanham, MD: Lexington, 2011), 105.

16. Ruth M. Melkonian-Hoover and Lyman A. Kellstedt, *Evangelicals and Immigration: Fault Lines among the Faithful*, Palgrave Studies in Religion, Politics, and Policy (Cham, Switzerland: Palgrave Macmillan, 2019), 145–49.

17. See Efraín Agosto and Jacqueline M. Hidalgo, "Introduction: Reading the Bible and Latinx Migrations/the Bible as Text(s) of Migration," in *Latinxs, the Bible, and Migration*, ed. Efraín Agosto and Jacqueline M. Hidalgo. The Bible and Cultural Studies (Cham, Switzerland: Palgrave Macmillan, 2018), 1–2.

18. See Safwat Marzouk, *Intercultural Church: A Biblical Image for an Age of Migration*. Word & World (Minneapolis: Fortress, 2019), 45–80.

Israel, and his family to journey to Egypt, where their descendants become enslaved. We could continue the narrative, including the people Israel's exodus out of Egypt and conquest of Canaan, to the exile of Judahites at the hands of the Babylonians and a later return to the land under the Persians, and the story of Ruth the Moabite, who migrates to Israel in hope of survival. We might rehearse Israel's laws that command kindness to strangers, or "aliens," because "you were aliens in the land of Egypt" (see Lev 19:9–10, 33–34). We might remember the migration of Jesus's parents Mary and Joseph who fled wicked Herod and sojourned with their son in Egypt, the conversion of visitors to Jerusalem in Acts 2 and 8, the travels of Paul and other apostles around the Mediterranean world, or 1 Peter's address to believers to see themselves as "exiles and aliens" (2:11; see 1:1). Revelation concludes with "the nations" entering the New Jerusalem and contributing to its life (21:24). We might also recall biblical examples in which outsiders receive harsh treatment: Ezra's command that the Judahites expel their foreign wives (chapters 9–10), Jesus's dismissive comments about "the Gentiles" in Matthew (5:47; 6:7, 32; 18:17; 20:25), and even the odd ethnic joke in Acts (14:8–18). If we think of the Bible as a single book with two covers, stories about migrants—including the dangers that force people to move and the vulnerabilities they suffer—run from one cover to the other.

The questions we bring to the Bible matter. The book of Ruth plays many roles in the popular imagination. It's often part of wedding celebrations, where ministers recite Ruth's pledge to Naomi:

> Where you go, I will go;
>   where you lodge, I will lodge:
> your people shall be my people,
>   and your God my God. (1:16)

Ruth's words have nothing directly to do with marriage: Ruth and Naomi have no intention of marrying one another. But the words seem apt for the high level of commitment marriage entails. Ruth is often taken as a love story, celebrating the relationship between Ruth and her eventual husband Boaz. Upon close reading, however, we might be tempted to ask, "What's love got to do with it?" After all, the book's only reference to love involves Ruth and Naomi, not Ruth and Boaz (4:15).

Instead, Ruth has everything to do with the question of belonging. Ancient Judahites debated the legitimacy of intermarriage—that is, marriage between Judahites and foreign women. For example, Ezra 9–10 plays this theme in a most dramatic way: the Israelites (as the story calls them) expel the women they have married and their children. The story shows no interest in what becomes of these women and children. By contrast, the book of Ruth commemorates how a non-Israelite, specifically a Moabite, woman demonstrates faithfulness to her Israelite mother-in-law, marries a prominent man in Israel, and eventually becomes the great-grandmother of David, Israel's greatest king.[19]

What happens if we read the story of Ruth with immigration in mind, remembering the Bible's extensive interest in stories of migration? Several factors may jump to attention when we read a book like Ruth with a specific question in mind.

First, we might notice that the book dramatizes the motives for immigration. In the book's first six verses we learn that a famine drives Naomi and her husband Elimelech to leave Judah and migrate to Moab—and that Naomi returns to Judah because her husband and sons have died, leaving her with slim chances of survival in Moab.

Second, close attention reveals the dangers that come with immigration, especially for women and children. Four times the story indicates the likelihood that Ruth may be sexually assaulted even in Judah. Boaz warns his workers not to "touch" Ruth (2:9), not to "humiliate" her (2:15), and not to "corrupt" her (2:16).[20] For her part, Naomi knows that Ruth would be unsafe working in other fields, since Ruth might be assaulted without protection from Boaz (2:22). Modern English trans-

---

19. Gale A. Yee, "Ruth," in *Fortress Commentary on the Bible: The Old Testament and Apocrypha*, ed. Gale A. Yee, Hugh R. Page Jr., and Matthew J. M. Coomber (Minneapolis: Fortress, 2014), 351. See the discussions in Jennifer L. Koosed, *Gleaning Ruth: A Biblical Heroine and Her Afterlives*, Studies on Personalities of the Old Testament (Columbia: University of South Carolina Press, 2011), 18–20; and Alice L. Laffey and Mahri Leonard-Fleckman, *Ruth*, Wisdom Commentary 8 (Collegeville, MN: Liturgical Press, 2017), lix–lxii.

20. For the Hebrew verb (*ng'*) that appears in Ruth 2:9 and 22, see Gen 26:11. For the verb (*klm*) that appears in 2:15, see Jer 3:3; Ezek 16:27, 63. For the verb (*g'r*) that appears in 2:16, see Mal 2:3. Many commentators understand the verbs in 2:15 and 2:16 to indicate verbal scolding rather than the threat of assault. On the danger Ruth faces and the translation issues in these verses, see Dana Nolan Fewell and David Miller Gunn, *Compromising Redemption: Relating Characters in the Book of Ruth*, Literary Currents in Biblical Interpretation (Louisville: Westminster/John Knox, 1990), 76–77.

lations don't convey this well, but the Hebrew is quite clear. When people immigrate to new lands, they're vulnerable to being taken advantage of. Sex trafficking and child enslavement are scarcely modern developments.

Third, we might remember Gale A. Yee's insight into Ruth, mentioned in chapter 5. Ruth wins admiration and inclusion in Judahite society. But Yee also observes that Ruth remains "Ruth the Moabite" throughout the story, even to the end (4:10). As with many immigrants, Ruth's status remains perpetually hyphenated, her outsider status always marked.[21]

Rarely, if ever, is it a good idea to snatch biblical passages, even whole books, and stitch them together to build contemporary ethical or political positions. Like strip-mining, that process levels off the diverse perspectives we find within the Bible itself. It also minimizes the vast cultural differences between biblical cultures and our own. This is no less the case with immigration than it is with issues such as civil government, finance, or family life. Nevertheless, when we bring our contemporary questions to the Bible, a story like Ruth's can draw our attention, even our emotions, to aspects of the immigration experience—the factors that compel people to move, the grief people experience in separating from people and places they love, the vulnerability migrants experience all over the world, and the challenges of finding a place in a new culture. And Ruth presents us with the often unappreciated contributions immigrants bring to their new homes. We also learn from the insights of readers, like Gale Yee, who bring to the work of interpretation perspectives that may be new to us.

At its best, public biblical interpretation draws us to see ourselves and the world in fresh, life-giving ways.

---

21. Yee, "'She Stood in Tears amid the Alien Corn,'" 119–40.

BIBLIOGRAPHY

Achebe, Chinua. *Things Fall Apart.* New York: Anchor, 1994 (1959).
Achtemeier, Paul. "*Omne verbum sonat:* The New Testament and the Oral Environment of Late Western Antiquity." *JBL* 109 (1990): 3–27.
Adam, A. K. M., ed. *Handbook of Postmodern Biblical Interpretation.* St. Louis: Chalice, 2000.
———. *What Is Postmodern Biblical Criticism?* Guides to Biblical Scholarship. Minneapolis: Fortress, 1995.
Agosto, Efraín, and Jacqueline M. Hidalgo. "Introduction: Reading the Bible and Latinx Migrations/the Bible as Text(s) of Migration." In *Latinxs, the Bible, and Migration*, edited by Efraín Agosto and Jacqueline M. Hidalgo, 1–20. The Bible and Cultural Studies. Cham, Switzerland: Palgrave Macmillan, 2018.
Allison, Dale C. Jr. *The Historical Christ and the Theological Jesus.* Grand Rapids: Eerdmans, 2009.
———. *The Jesus Tradition in* Q. Harrisburg, PA: Trinity Press International, 1997.
Alter, Robert. *The Art of Biblical Narrative.* New York: Basic Books, 1981.
———. *The Art of Biblical Poetry.* New York: Basic Books, 1985.
Anderson, Cheryl B. "Reflections in an Interethnic/racial Era on Interethnic/racial Marriage in Ezra." In Bailey, Liew, and Segovia, *They Were All Together in One Place?*, 47–64.
Ashcroft, Bill, Gareth Griffiths, and Helen Tiffin, eds. *The Empire Writes Back: Theory and Practice in Post-Colonial Literatures.* London: Routledge, 1989.
Ashton, John. *Understanding the Fourth Gospel.* 2nd ed. New York: Oxford University Press, 2007.
Ateek, Naim S. "A Palestinian Perspective: Biblical Perspectives on the Land." In Sugirtharajah, *Voices from the Margin*, 267–76.
Auerbach, Erich. *Mimesis: The Literary Representation of Reality in Western Litera-*

ture. Translated by Willard R. Trask. Princeton: Princeton University Press, 1953 (1946).

Augustine of Hippo. *On Christian Doctrine*. Translated by D. W. Robertson Jr. Library of Liberal Arts. New York: Macmillan, 1958.

Aune, David E. *The Westminster Dictionary of New Testament and Early Christian Literature and Rhetoric*. Louisville: Westminster John Knox, 2003.

Avalos, Hector. *The Bad Jesus: The Ethics of New Testament Ethics*. BMW 68; Sheffield: Sheffield Phoenix Press, 2015.

Aymer, Margaret P. *First Pure, Then Peaceable: Frederick Douglass Reads James*. LNTS 379; New York: T&T Clark, 2007.

Azzoni, Annalisa. "Marriage and Divorce: Hebrew Bible." In O'Brien et al., *Oxford Encyclopedia*, 1:483–88.

Baden, Joel. *The Composition of the Pentateuch: Renewing the Documentary Hypothesis*. AYBRL. New Haven: Yale University Press, 2012.

Baden, Joel, and Candida Moss. "The Curious Case of Jesus's Wife." *The Atlantic*, December 2014. https://tinyurl.com/sddu79z.

Bailey, Randall C. "Beyond Identification: The Use of Africans in Old Testament Poetry and Narratives." In Felder, *Stony the Road We Trod*, 165–84.

Bailey, Randall C., Tat-siong Benny Liew, and Fernando F. Segovia, eds. *They Were All Together in One Place? Toward Minority Biblical Criticism*. SemeiaSt 57. Atlanta: Society of Biblical Literature, 2009.

Baker-Fletcher, Karen. "Anna Julia Cooper and Sojourner Truth: Two Nineteenth-Century Black Feminist Interpreters of Scripture." In Schüssler Fiorenza, *Searching the Scriptures*, 1:41–51.

Balmer, Randall. "Casting Aside the Ballast of History and Tradition: White Protestants and the Bible in the Antebellum Period." In Wimbush, *African Americans and the Bible*, 193–200.

Barreto, Eric D. *Ethnic Negotiations: The Function of Race and Ethnicity in Acts 16*. WUNT 2:294. Tübingen: Mohr Siebeck, 2010.

———. "Negotiating Difference: Theology and Ethnicity in the Acts of the Apostles." In Lozada and Carey, *Soundings in Cultural Criticism*, 97–106.

———. "Reexamining Ethnicity: Latina/os, Race, and the Bible." In Lozada and Segovia, *Latino/a Biblical Hermeneutics*, 73–93.

Barrios, Richard. *Screened Out: Playing Gay in Hollywood from Edison to Stonewall*. New York: Routledge, 2003.

Barton, John. "The Basis of Ethics in the Hebrew Bible." *Semeia* 66 (1994): 11–22.

———. *Ethics and the Old Testament*. 2nd ed. London: SCM, 2002.

Bass, Dorothy C. "Women's Studies and Biblical Studies." *JSOT* 22 (1982): 6–12.

Bassler, Jouette M. "1 Corinthians." In Newsom, Ringe, and Lapsley, *Women's Bible Commentary*, 557–65.

———. *Navigating Paul: An Introduction to Key Theological Concepts.* Louisville: Westminster John Knox, 2007.

Bauckham, Richard. "Reading Scripture as a Coherent Story." In Davis and Hays, *The Art of Reading Scripture*, 38–53.

Beal, Timothy. *The Book of Revelation: A Biography.* Lives of Great Religious Books. Princeton: Princeton University Press, 2018.

Berlinerblau, Jacques. "What's Wrong with the Society of Biblical Literature." *Chronicle of Higher Education* 53, no. 12 (November 10, 2006): B13.

Bernhard, Andrew. "The End of the Gospel of Jesus' Wife Forgery Debate." *NT Blog.* September 8, 2015. https://tinyurl.com/rt5v26z.

Bhabha, Homi. *The Location of Culture.* New York: Routledge, 1994.

Birch, Bruce C., Jacqueline E. Lapsley, Cynthia Moe-Lobeda, and Larry L. Rasmussen. *Bible and Ethics in the Christian Life: A New Conversation.* Minneapolis: Fortress, 2018.

Blount, Brian K. *Can I Get a Witness? Reading Revelation through African American Culture.* Louisville: Westminster John Knox, 2005.

———. *Go Preach! Mark's Kingdom Message and the Black Church Today.* The Bible and Liberation. Maryknoll, NY: Orbis, 1998.

———. *Then the Whisper Put on Flesh: New Testament Ethics in African American Context.* Nashville: Abingdon, 2001.

Blount, Brian K. et al., eds. *True to Our Native Land: An African American New Testament Commentary.* Minneapolis: Fortress, 2007.

Boesak, Allan A. *Comfort and Protest: The Apocalypse from a South African Perspective.* Philadelphia: Westminster, 1987.

Boin, Douglas. *Coming Out Christian in the Roman World: How the Followers of Jesus Made a Place in Caesar's Empire.* New York: Bloomsbury, 2014.

Borg, Marcus J., and John Dominic Crossan. *The First Paul: Reclaiming the Radical Visionary behind the Church's Conservative Icon.* San Francisco: HarperOne, 2009.

Borgen, Peder. "Philo of Alexandria." *Jewish Writings in the Second Temple Period*, edited by Michael E. Stone, CRINT 2, no. 2: 233–82. Philadelphia: Fortress, 1984.

———. "Philo of Alexandria as Exegete." In Hauser and Watson, *History of Biblical Interpretation*, 1:114–43.

Bowler, Kate. "Death, the Prosperity Gospel and Me." *New York Times*, February 13, 2016. https://tinyurl.com/gu88lem.

Boxall, Ian. *Patmos in the Reception History of the Apocalypse*. Oxford Theology and Religion Monographs. New York: Oxford University Press, 2013.

Boyarin, Daniel. *A Radical Jew: Paul and the Politics of Identity*. Berkeley: University of California Press, 1994.

Brasher, Brenda. *Godly Women: Fundamentalism and Female Power*. New Brunswick, NJ: Rutgers University Press, 1998.

Braun, Willi. "Sociology, Christian Growth, and the Obscurum of Christianity's Imperial Formation in Rodney Stark's *The Rise of Christianity*." *RSN* 25, no. 2 (April 1999): 128–32.

Brettler, Marc Zvi. "My Bible: A Jew's Perspective." In Brettler, Enns, and Harrington, *The Bible and the Believer*, 21–66.

Brettler, Marc Zvi, Peter Enns, and Daniel J. Harrington, S.J., *The Bible and the Believer: How to Read the Bible Critically and Religiously*. New York: Oxford University Press, 2012.

Brettler, Marc, and Amy-Jill Levine. "Isaiah's Suffering Servant: Before and After Christianity." *Interpretation* 73 (2019): 158–73.

Briggs, Richard S. *The Virtuous Reader: Old Testament Narrative and Interpretive Virtue*. Studies in Theological Interpretation. Grand Rapids: Baker Academic, 2010.

Bright, John. *A History of Israel*. 3rd ed. Philadelphia: Westminster, 1981.

Brooks, Cleanth. *The Well Wrought Urn: Studies in the Structure of Poetry*. San Diego: Harcourt, Brace, 1947.

Brown, Michael Joseph. *Blackening of the Bible: The Aims of African American Biblical Scholarship*. African American Religious Thought and Life. Harrisburg, PA: Trinity Press International, 1994.

Brown, Raymond E. *The Community of the Beloved Disciple*. New York: Paulist, 1979.

Brownson, James V. *Bible, Gender, Sexuality: Reframing the Church's Debate on Same-Sex Relationships*. Grand Rapids: Eerdmans, 2013.

Brueggemann, Walter. *Genesis*. Interpretation. Atlanta: John Knox, 1982.

Brueggemann, Walter, and William H. Bellinger Jr. *Psalms*. NCBC. New York: Cambridge University Press, 2014.

Buell, Denise Kimber. "Anachronistic Whiteness and the Ethics of Interpretation." In Hockey and Horrell, *Ethnicity, Race, Religion*, 149–67.

———. *Why This New Race: Ethnic Reasoning in Early Christianity*. New York: Columbia University Press, 2005.

Bultmann, Rudolf. *New Testament and Mythology and Other Basic Writings*. Translated by Schubert M. Ogden. Philadelphia: Fortress, 1984 (1957).

Burridge, Richard A. *Imitating Jesus: An Inclusive Approach to New Testament Ethics*. Grand Rapids: Eerdmans, 2007.

Buschart, W. David, and Kent Eilers. *Theology as Retrieval: Receiving the Past, Renewing the Church*. Downers Grove, IL: InterVarsity, 2015.

Byron, Gay L. *Symbolic Blackness and Ethnic Difference in Early Christian Literature*. New York: Routledge, 2002.

Byron, Gay L., and Vanessa Lovelace. "Introduction: Methods and the Making of Womanist Biblical Hermeneutics." In Byron and Lovelace, *Womanist Interpretations of the Bible*, 1–18.

———, eds. *Womanist Interpretations of the Bible: Expanding the Discourse*. SemeiaSt 85. Atlanta: SBL Press, 2016.

Byung-Mu, Ahn. *Minjung Theology: People as the Subjects of History*. Maryknoll, NY: Orbis, 1981.

Callahan, Allan Dwight. "'Brother Saul': An Ambivalent Witness to Freedom." *Semeia* 83/84 (1998): 235–50.

Cannon, Katie Geneva. *Black Womanist Ethics*. AAR Academy Series 60. Atlanta: Scholars Press, 1988.

Cardenal, Ernesto. *The Gospel in Solentiname*. Maryknoll, NY: Orbis, 2010 (1975, 1977).

Carey, Greg. "Clarence Jordan as a (White) Interpreter of the Bible." In *Roots in the Cotton Patch*. Vol. 1: *The Clarence Jordan Symposium 2012*, edited by Kirk Lyman-Barner and Cori Lyman Barner, 33–43. Eugene, OR: Cascade, 2014.

———. "Early Christianity and the Roman Empire." In *The State of New Testament Studies*, 9–34. Edited by Scot McKnight and Nijay K. Gupta. Grand Rapids: Baker Academic, 2019.

———. "Introduction and a Proposal: Culture, Power, and Identity in White New Testament Studies." In Lozada and Carey, *Soundings in Cultural Criticism*, 1–13.

———. "Mass Incarceration, Capital Punishment, and Penal Atonement Theories: Correlation or Something More?" In *Thinking Theologically about Mass Incarceration: Biblical Foundations and Justice Imperatives*, edited by Antonios Kireopoulos, Mitzi J. Budde, and Matthew D. Lundberg, 205–16. National Council of Churches Faith and Order Commission Theological Series. Mahwah, NJ: Paulist, 2017.

———. *Sinners: Jesus and His Earliest Followers*. Waco, TX: Baylor University Press, 2009.

Carter, J. Kameron. *Race: A Theological Account*. New York: Oxford University Press, 2008.

Carter, Warren. *John and Empire: Initial Explorations*. New York: T&T Clark, 2008.

———. *Matthew and Empire: Initial Explorations*. Harrisburg, PA: Trinity Press International, 2001.

———. *The Roman Empire and the New Testament: An Essential Guide*. Essential Guides. Nashville: Abingdon, 2006.

Case, Shirley Jackson. *Jesus: A New Biography*. Chicago: University of Chicago Press, 1927.

Chatman, Seymour. *Story and Discourse: Narrative Structure in Fiction and Film*. Ithaca, NY: Cornell University Press, 1978.

Cheon, Samuel. "Biblical Interpretation in Korea: History and Issues." In Foskett and Kuan, *Ways of Being, Ways of Reading*, 31–44.

Chester, Stephen J. *Reading Paul with the Reformers: Reconciling Old and New Perspectives*. Grand Rapids: Eerdmans, 2017.

Chia, Philip P. "Differences and Difficulties: Biblical Interpretation in the Southeast Asian Context." In Foskett and Kuan, *Ways of Being, Ways of Reading*, 45–59.

Choi, Jin Young. *Postcolonial Discipleship of Embodiment*. Postcolonialism and Religions. New York: Palgrave Macmillan, 2015.

Clark-Soles, Jaime. *Death and the Afterlife in the New Testament*. New York: T&T Clark, 2006.

Clines, David J. A. *Job*. WBC 18B. Nashville: Thomas Nelson, 2011.

Cone, James H. *Black Theology and Black Power*. New York: Harper & Row, 1969.

———. *A Black Theology of Liberation*. Philadelphia and New York: Lippincott, 1970.

———. *The Cross and the Lynching Tree*. Maryknoll, NY: Orbis, 2011.

Congdon, David. "The Word as Event: Barth and Bultmann on Scripture." In *The Sacred Text: Excavating the Texts, Exploring the Interpretations, and Engaging the Theologies of the Christian Scriptures*, edited by Michael Bird and Michael Pahl. Gorgias Précis Folios 7. Piscataway, NJ: Gorgias, 2010, 241–65.

Coogan, Michael. *God and Sex: What the Bible Really Says*. New York: Twelve, 2010.

Cooper, Kate. *Band of Angels: The Forgotten World of Early Christian Women*. New York: The Overlook Press, 2013.

Copher, Charles B. "The Black Presence in the Old Testament." In Felder, *Stony the Road We Trod*, 146–64.

Cosgrove, Charles. H. *Appealing to Scripture in Moral Debate: Five Hermeneutical Rules*. Grand Rapids: Eerdmans, 2002.

Croatto, J. Severino. *Biblical Hermeneutics: Toward a Theory of Reading as the Production of Meaning.* Maryknoll, NY: Orbis, 1987.

Crossan, John Dominic. *The Historical Jesus: The Life of a Mediterranean Jewish Peasant.* San Francisco: HarperCollins, 1993.

———. *A Long Way from Tipperary: What a Former Irish Monk Discovered in His Search for Truth.* New York: HarperSanFrancisco, 2000.

Crowder, Stephanie Buckhanon. *When Momma Speaks: The Bible and Motherhood from a Womanist Perspective.* Louisville: Westminster John Knox, 2016.

Culler, Jonathan. *On Deconstruction: Theory and Criticism after Structuralism.* Ithaca, NY: Cornell University Press, 1982.

Culpepper, R. Alan. *Anatomy of the Fourth Gospel: A Study in Literary Design.* Philadelphia: Fortress, 1983.

Cyril of Jerusalem. *The Catechetical Lectures of S. Cyril, Archbishop of Jerusalem*, ed. John Henry Newman. Oxford: J. H. Parker, 1839.

Davies, Eryl W. *The Immoral Bible: Approaches to Biblical Ethics.* New York: T&T Clark, 2010.

Davies, Philip R. *In Search of "Ancient Israel."* JSOTSup 148. Sheffield: Sheffield Academic, 1992.

———. *Scribes and Schools: The Canonization of the Hebrew Scriptures.* Library of Ancient Israel. Louisville: Westminster John Knox, 1998.

Davis, Ellen F. "Teaching the Bible Confessionally in the Church." In Davis and Hays, *The Art of Reading Scripture*, 9–26.

Davis, Ellen F., and Richard B. Hays, eds. *The Art of Reading Scripture.* Grand Rapids: Eerdmans, 2003.

Davis, Thomas W. *Shifting Sands: The Rise and Fall of Biblical Archaeology.* New York: Oxford University Press, 2004.

DeBerg, Betty A. *Ungodly Women: Gender and the First Wave of American Fundamentalism.* Macon, GA: Mercer University Press, 2000 (1990).

DeConick, April. "The Gospel of Thomas." In *The Non-Canonical Gospels*, edited by Paul Foster, 13–29. London: T&T Clark, 2008.

de Man, Paul. *Blindness and Insight: Essays in the Rhetoric of Contemporary Criticism.* 2nd ed. Theory and History of Literature 7. Minneapolis: University of Minnesota Press, 1983.

Derrida, Jacques. *A Derrida Reader: Behind the Blinds*, edited by Peggy Kamuf. New York: Columbia University Press, 1991.

deSilva, David A. *The Jewish Teachers of Jesus, James, and Jude: What Earliest Christianity Learned from the Apocrypha and Pseudepigrapha.* New York: Oxford University Press, 2012.

Douglass, Frederick. *Life and Times of Frederick Douglass, Written by Himself.* New York: Collier, 1892.

Dube, Musa W. "Decolonizing the Darkness: Bible Readers and the Colonial Cultural Archive." In Lozada and Carey, *Soundings in Cultural Criticism*, 31–44.

———. *Postcolonial Feminist Interpretation of the Bible.* St. Louis: Chalice, 2000.

Dunn, James D. G. *The Theology of Paul the Apostle.* Grand Rapids: Eerdmans, 1998.

Eagleton, Terry. *Literary Theory: An Introduction.* Minneapolis: University of Minnesota Press, 1983.

Ehrman, Bart D. *Misquoting Jesus: The Story behind Who Changed the Bible and Why.* San Francisco: HarperSanFrancisco, 2005.

———. *The Orthodox Corruption of Scripture: The Effect of Early Christological Controversies on the New Testament.* New York: Oxford University Press, 1993.

Ekblad, Bob. *Reading the Bible with the Damned.* Louisville: Westminster John Knox, 2005.

Elgvin, Torleif. "Jewish Christian Editing of the Old Testament Pseudepigrapha." In *Jewish Believers in Jesus: The Early Centuries*, edited by Oskar Skarsaune and Reidar Hvalvik, 278–304. Peabody, MA: Hendrickson, 2007.

Elliott, John H. *What Is Social Scientific Criticism?* Guides to Biblical Scholarship. Minneapolis: Fortress, 1993.

Elliott, Neil. *The Arrogance of Nations: Reading Romans in the Shadow of Empire.* Paul in Critical Contexts. Minneapolis: Fortress, 2008.

———. *Liberating Paul: The Justice of God and the Politics of the Apostle.* Minneapolis: Fortress, 2006 (1994).

Enns, Peter. *Inspiration and Incarnation: Evangelicals and Incarnation: Evangelicals and the Problem of the Old Testament.* 2nd ed. Grand Rapids: Baker Academic, 2015.

Eslinger, Lyle. "The Wooing of the Woman at the Well: Jesus, the Reader and Reader-Response Criticism." *Journal of Literature and Theology* 1 (1987): 167–83.

Felder, Cain Hope. "Race, Racism, and the Biblical Narratives." In Felder, *Stony the Road We Trod*, 127–45.

———, ed. *Stony the Road We Trod: African American Biblical Interpretation.* Minneapolis: Fortress, 1991.

Fewell, Dana Nolan, and David Miller Gunn. *Compromising Redemption: Relating Characters in the Book of Ruth.* Literary Currents in Biblical Interpretation. Louisville: Westminster/John Knox, 1990.

Fish, Stanley. *Is There a Text in This Class? The Authority of Interpretive Communities.* Cambridge, MA: Harvard University Press, 1992.

Ford, Andrew. *The Origins of Criticism: Literary Culture and Poetic Theory in Classical Greece.* Princeton: Princeton University Press, 2002.

Fosarelli, Patricia D., and Michael J. Gorman. "The Bible and Spiritual Growth." In Gorman, *Scripture: An Ecumenical Introduction to the Bible and Its Interpretation,* 229–38.

Foskett, Mary F. "Obscured Beginnings: Lessons from the Study of Christian Origins." In Foskett and Kuan, *Ways of Being, Ways of Reading,* 178–91.

Foskett, Mary F., and Jeffrey Kah-Jin Kuan. *Ways of Being, Ways of Reading: Asian American Biblical Interpretation.* St. Louis: Chalice, 2006.

Fowl, Stephen. "Theological and Ideological Strategies of Biblical Interpretation." In *Scripture: An Ecumenical Introduction to the Bible and Its Interpretation,* edited by Michael J. Gorman, 163–75. Peabody, MA: Hendrickson, 2005.

———. *Theological Interpretation of Scripture.* Cascade Companions. Eugene, OR: Cascade, 2009.

Fowler, Robert M. *Let the Reader Understand: Reader-Response Criticism and the Gospel of Mark.* Minneapolis: Fortress, 1991.

Fox, Michael V. "Ancient Egyptian Rhetoric." *Rhetorica* 1 (1983): 9–22.

Fredriksen, Paula, and Adele Reinhartz, eds. *Jesus, Judaism, and Christian Anti-Judaism: Reading the New Testament after the Holocaust.* Louisville: Westminster John Knox, 2002.

Frei, Hans. *The Eclipse of Biblical Narrative: A Study in Eighteenth and Nineteenth Century Hermeneutics.* New Haven: Yale University Press, 1974.

Friedman, Richard Elliott. *Who Wrote the Bible?* Englewood Cliffs, NJ: Prentice Hall, 1987.

Frymer-Kensky, Tikva. *In the Wake of the Goddesses: Women, Culture, and the Biblical Transformation of Pagan Myth.* New York: Fawcett Columbine, 1992.

Gafney, Wilda C. *Daughters of Miriam: Women Prophets in Ancient Israel.* Minneapolis: Fortress, 2008.

———. "Suing God." June 24, 2012. http://www.wilgafney.com/2012/06/24/suing-god/.

———. *Womanist Midrash: A Reintroduction to the Women of the Torah and the Throne.* Louisville: Westminster John Knox, 2017.

Gallagher, Catherine. "The History of Literary Criticism." *Daedalus* 126 (1997): 133–53.

Gallagher, Sally. *Evangelical Identity and Gendered Family Life.* New Brunswick, NJ: Rutgers University Press, 2003.

Gaston, Lloyd. *Paul and the Torah.* Vancouver: University of British Columbia Press, 1987.

Gaventa, Beverly Roberts. *When in Romans: An Invitation to Linger with the Gospel according to Paul.* Theological Explorations for the Church Catholic. Waco, TX: Baylor University Press, 2016.

Gilliard, Frank D. "More Silent Reading in Antiquity: *Non omne verbum sonabat.*" *JBL* 112 (1993): 689–94.

González, Justo. *Santa Biblia: The Bible through Hispanic Eyes.* Nashville: Abingdon, 1996.

Goodacre, Mark. *The Case against Q: Studies in Markan Priority and the Synoptic Problem.* Harrisburg, PA: Trinity Press International, 2002.

———. *Thomas and the Synoptics: The Case for Thomas's Familiarity with the Synoptics.* Grand Rapids: Eerdmans, 2012.

Gorman, Michael J. "The Interpretation of the Bible in Protestant Churches." In *Scripture: An Ecumenical Introduction*, 177–93.

———, ed. *Scripture: An Ecumenical Introduction to the Bible and Its Interpretation.* Peabody, MA: Hendrickson, 2005.

Gottwald, Norman, and Richard H. Horsley, eds. *The Bible and Liberation: Political and Social Hermeneutics.* Rev. ed. Maryknoll, NY: Orbis, 1993.

Gowler, David B. *What Are They Saying about the Parables?* Mahwah, NJ: Paulist, 2000.

Grant, Robert M., and David Tracy. *A Short History of the Interpretation of the Bible.* 2nd ed. Minneapolis: Fortress, 1984.

Green, Joel B. "Joel B. Green on 'What Makes a Good Biblical Scholar.'" TheLAB: The Logos Academic Blog. Edited by Tavis Bollinger. March 6, 2019: https://tinyurl.com/t2bt285.

———. *Practicing Theological Interpretation: Engaging Biblical Texts for Faith and Formation.* Grand Rapids: Baker Academic, 2011.

———. *Salvation.* Understanding Biblical Themes. Nashville: Abingdon, 2003.

———. *Seized by Truth: Reading the Bible as Scripture.* Nashville: Abingdon, 2007.

———. *Why Salvation?* Reframing New Testament Theology. Nashville: Abingdon, 2014.

Greene-McCreight, Kathryn. "Rule of Faith." In Vanhoozer et al., *Dictionary for Theological Interpretation of the Bible*, 703–4.

Guardiola-Sáenz, Leticia A. "From the Pulpit to the Academy—Latinx Scriptural Hermeneutics." *Lexington Theological Quarterly* 48 (2018): 11–34.

Gundry-Volf, Judith M. "Celibate Pneumatics and Social Power: On the Motivations for Sexual Asceticism in Corinth." *USQR* 48, no. 3–4 (1994): 105–26.

Habermas, Jürgen. *Knowledge and Human Interests.* Boston: Beacon, 1971 (1968).

Haidt, Jonathan. *The Happiness Hypothesis: Finding Modern Truth in Ancient Wisdom.* New York: Basic, 2006.

Hammett, Dashiell. *The Maltese Falcon.* New York: Alfred A. Knopf, 1930.

Hardesty, Nancy A. *Women Called to Witness: Evangelical Feminism in the 19th Century.* Nashville: Abingdon, 1984.

Harrill, James Albert. *The Manumission of Slaves in Early Christianity.* HUT 32. Tübingen: Mohr Siebeck, 1995.

———. *Slaves in the New Testament: Literary, Social, and Moral Dimensions.* Minneapolis: Fortress, 2006.

Harris, Robert A. "Medieval Jewish Biblical Exegesis." In Hauser and Watson, *History of Biblical Interpretation*, 2: 141–71.

Hartman, Midori E. "A Little Porneia Leavens the Whole: Queer(ing) Limits of Community in 1 Corinthians 5." In Marchal, *Bodies on the Verge*, 143–63.

Harvard University, "Gospel of Jesus's Wife." http://gospelofjesusswife.hds.harvard.edu/.

Hauerwas, Stanley, and L. Gregory Jones, eds. *Why Narrative? Readings in Narrative Theology.* Grand Rapids: Eerdmans, 1989.

Hauser, Alan J., and Duane F. Watson, eds. *A History of Biblical Interpretation.* 2 vols. Grand Rapids: Eerdmans, 2003–2009.

Haynes, Stephen R. *Noah's Curse: The Biblical Justification of American Slavery.* Religion in America. New York: Oxford University Press, 2007.

Hays, Richard B. *The Moral Vision of the New Testament: A Contemporary Introduction to New Testament Ethics.* New York: HarperCollins, 1996.

Haywood, Chanta M. "Prophesying Daughters: Nineteenth-Century Black Religious Women, the Bible, and Black Literary History." In Wimbush, *African Americans and the Bible*, 355–66.

Heidel, Alexander. *The Babylonian Genesis.* 2nd ed. Chicago: University of Chicago Press, 1951.

Hendricks, Obery M. Jr., *The Politics of Jesus: Rediscovering the True Revolutionary Nature of Jesus' Teachings and How They Have Been Corrupted.* New York: Doubleday, 2006.

Hernandez-Díaz, Rodolfo J. "Mujerista Theology: Strategies for Social Change." *Feminist Theology* 20 (2011): 45–53.

Herzog, William R. *Parables as Subversive Speech: Jesus as Pedagogue of the Oppressed.* Louisville: Westminster John Knox, 1994.

Hicks-Keeton, Jill. "Christian Supersessionism and the Problem of Diversity at the Museum of the Bible." In *The Museum of the Bible: A Critical Introduction*, edited by Jill Hicks-Keeton and Cavin Concannon, 49–70. Lanham, MD: Lexington Books, 2019.

———. "What the Museum of the Bible Conveys about Biblical Scholarship behind Church Doors." *Religion and Politics*, March 13, 2018. https://tinyurl.com/qt22mv6.

Hicks-Keeton, Jill, and Cavin Concannon, eds. *The Museum of the Bible: A Critical Introduction.* Lanham, MD: Lexington Books, 2019.

Hidalgo, Jacqueline. "Reading from No Place: Toward a Hybrid and Ambivalent Study of Scriptures." In Lozada and Segovia, *Latino/a Biblical Hermeneutics*, 165–86.

Hockey, Katherine M., and David G. Horrell, eds. *Ethnicity, Race, Religion: Identities and Ideologies in Early Jewish and Christian Texts, and in Modern Biblical Interpretation.* New York: T&T Clark, 2018.

Hogan, Michael J. "The Enola Gay Controversy: History, Memory, and the Politics of Presentation." In *Hiroshima in History and Memory*, edited by Michael J. Hogan, 200–232. New York: Cambridge University Press, 1996.

Holifield, E. Brooks. *The Gentlemen Theologians: American Theology in Southern Culture, 1795–1860.* Durham, NC: Duke University Press, 1978.

Horrell, David G. "Paul, Inclusion and Whiteness: Particularizing Interpretation." *JSNT* 40 (2017): 123–47.

Horsley, Richard A. *In the Shadow of Empire: Reclaiming the Bible as a History of Faithful Resistance.* Louisville: Westminster John Knox, 2008.

———. *Jesus and Empire: The Kingdom of God and the New World Disorder.* Minneapolis: Fortress, 2003.

———. "Paul and Slavery: A Critical Alternative to Recent Readings." *Semeia* 83/84 (1998): 153–200.

Huber, Lynn R. "Interpreting as Queer or Interpreting Queerly?" In Marchal, *Bodies on the Verge*, 311–21.

Hurston, Zora Neale. "High John de Conquer." *The American Mercury* 57 (1943): 450–58.

Hutto, David. "Ancient Egyptian Rhetoric in the Old and Middle Kingdoms." *Rhetorica* 20 (2002): 213–34.

Hylen, Susan E. *Imperfect Believers: Ambiguous Characters in the Gospel of John.* Louisville: Westminster John Knox, 2009.

Ilan, Tal. *Jewish Women in Greco-Roman Palestine.* Peabody, MA: Hendrickson, 1996.

Isasi-Díaz, Ada-María. *Mujerista Theology.* Maryknoll, NY: Orbis, 1997.

Iser, Wolfgang. *The Act of Reading: A Theory of Aesthetic Response.* Baltimore: Johns Hopkins University Press, 1978.

Jacob, Sharon. *Reading Mary alongside Indian Surrogate Mothers: Violent Love, Oppressive Liberation, and Infancy Narratives.* The Bible and Cultural Studies. New York: Palgrave Macmillan, 2015.

Jennings, Willie James. *The Christian Imagination: Theology and the Origins of Race.* New Haven: Yale University Press, 2010.

Johnson, Luke Timothy. "The New Testament's Anti-Jewish Slander and the Conventions of Ancient Polemic." *JBL* 108 (1989): 419–41.

Johnson, Thomas Cary. *The Life and Letters of Robert Lewis Dabney.* Richmond, VA: Presbyterian Committee of Publication, 1903.

Jones, L. Gregory. "Embodying Scripture in the Community of Faith." In Davis and Hays, *The Art of Reading Scripture*, 143–59.

Jones, Robert P. et al., *Partisan Polarization Dominates Trump Era: Findings from the 2018 American Values Survey.* New York: PRRI, 2018. https://tinyurl.com/rhpz3fd.

Jordan, Clarence. *Cotton Patch Gospel: The Complete Collection.* Macon, GA: Smyth & Helwys, 2012.

Juel, Donald H. *Shaping the Scriptural Imagination: Truth, Meaning, and the Theological Interpretation of the Bible.* Edited by Shane Berg and Matthew L. Skinner. Waco, TX: Baylor University Press, 2011.

Junior, Nyasha. *An Introduction to Womanist Biblical Interpretation.* Louisville: Westminster John Knox, 2015.

Kagan, Dion. "Representing Queer Sexualities." In *The Routledge Companion to the Media, Sex and Sexuality*, edited by Clarissa Smith and Fiona Attwood with Brian McNair, 91–103. New York: Routledge, 2018.

Katz, Ben Zion. "Irrevocability of Persian Law in the Scroll of Esther." *JBQ* 31 (2003): 94–96.

Keith, Chris, and Anthony Le Donne, eds. *Jesus, Criteria, and the Demise of Authenticity.* New York: T&T Clark, 2012.

Kelley, Shawn. "Race, Aesthetics, and Gospel Scholarship: Embracing and Subverting the Aesthetic Ideology." In *Prejudice and Christian Beginnings: Investigating Race, Gender, and Ethnicity in Early Christian Studies*, edited by Laura Nasrallah and Elisabeth Schüssler Fiorenza, 191–209. Minneapolis: Fortress, 2009.

———. *Racializing Jesus: Race, Ideology and the Formation of Modern Biblical Scholarship.* London: Routledge, 2002.

Kennedy, George A. *The Cambridge History of Literary Criticism.* Vol. 1: *Classical Criticism.* Cambridge: Cambridge University Press, 1989.

———. *Classical Rhetoric and Its Christian and Secular Tradition from Ancient to Modern Times.* Chapel Hill: University of North Carolina Press, 1980.

———. *Comparative Rhetoric: An Historical and Cross-Cultural Introduction.* New York: Oxford University Press, 1998.

Kermode, Frank. *The Genesis of Secrecy: On the Interpretation of Narrative.* Cambridge, MA: Harvard University Press, 1979.

Kern, Kathi. *Mrs. Stanton's Bible.* Ithaca, NY: Cornell University Press, 2000.

Kim, Uriah Yong-Hwan. "The *Realpolitik* of Liminality in Josiah's Kingdom and Asian America." In Foskett and Kuan, *Ways of Being, Ways of Reading*, 84–98.

Kim, Yung Suk, and Jin-Ho Kim, eds. *Reading Minjung Theology in the Twenty-First Century.* Eugene, OR: Pickwick, 2013.

Kinyua, Johnson Kiriaku. "A Postcolonial Analysis of Bible Translation and Its Effectiveness in Shaping and Enhancing the Discourse of Colonialism and the Discourse of Resistance: The Gĩkũyũ New Testament—A Case Study." *Black Theology* 11 (2013): 58–95.

Kloppenborg, John S. *The Formation of Q: Trajectories in Ancient Wisdom Collections.* Studies in Antiquity and Christianity. Minneapolis: Fortress, 1987.

K'Meyer, Tracy Elaine. *Interracialism and Christian Community in the Postwar South: The Story of Koinonia Farm.* Charlottesville: University of Virginia Press, 1997.

Knust, Jennifer Wright. *Unprotected Texts: The Bible's Surprising Contradictions about Sex and Desire.* New York: HarperOne, 2011.

Koosed, Jennifer L. *Gleaning Ruth: A Biblical Heroine and Her Afterlives.* Studies on Personalities of the Old Testament. Columbia: University of South Carolina Press, 2011.

Kraemer, Ross Shepard. *Her Share of the Blessings: Women's Religions among Pagans, Jews, and Christians in the Greco-Roman World.* New York: Oxford University Press, 1992.

———. *Maenads, Martyrs, Matrons, Monastics: A Sourcebook on Women's Religions in the Greco-Roman World.* Philadelphia: Fortress, 1988.

Kraemer, Ross Shepard, and Mary Rose D'Angelo, eds. *Women and Christian Origins.* New York: Oxford University Press, 1999.

Kugel, James L. *The Bible as It Was.* Cambridge, MA: Belknap/Harvard, 1997.

Kümmel, Werner Georg. *The New Testament: The History of the Investigation of Its Problems.* Translated by S. MacLean Gilmour and Howard Clark Kee. Nashville: Abingdon, 1972 (1970).

Laffey, Alice L., and Mahri Leonard-Fleckman. *Ruth.* Wisdom Commentary 8. Collegeville, MN: Liturgical Press, 2017.

Le Donne, Anthony. *Historical Jesus: What Can We Know and How Can We Know It?* Grand Rapids: Eerdmans, 2011.

Legaspi, Michael C. *The Death of Scripture and the Rise of Biblical Studies.* Oxford Studies in Historical Theology. New York: Oxford University Press, 2010.

Leiter, David A. "The Character and Composition of the Books of the Old Testament." In Gorman, *Scripture: An Ecumenical Introduction*, 45–69.

Leithart, Peter. *Athanasius.* Foundations of Theological Exegesis and Christian Spirituality. Grand Rapids: Baker, 2011.

Lemche, Nils Peter. *Ancient Israel: A New History of Israelite Society.* The Biblical Seminar. Sheffield: Sheffield Academic, 1988.

Levine, Amy-Jill. *The Misunderstood Jew: The Church and the Scandal of the Jewish Jesus.* New York: HarperOne, 2006.

Lieu, Judith M., and J. W. Rogerson, eds. *The Oxford Handbook of Biblical Studies.* New York: Oxford University Press, 2008.

Liew, Tat-siong Benny. "On Asian/Asian North American Scholarship and Feminism: Twenty-Eight Years Later." *Journal of Feminist Studies in Religion* 31 (2015): 127–31.

———. "Tyranny, Boundary and Might: Colonial Mimicry in Mark's Gospel." *JSNT* 73 (1999): 7–31.

———. *What Is Asian American Biblical Hermeneutics? Reading the New Testament.* Honolulu: University of Hawaii Press, 2008.

Liew, Tat-siong Benny, and Fernando F. Segovia, eds. *Colonialism and the Bible: Contemporary Reflections from the Global South.* Lanham, MD: Lexington Books, 2018.

Linenthal, Edward T. "Anatomy of a Controversy." In *History Wars: The Enola Gay and Other Battles for the American Past*, edited by Edward T. Linenthal and Tom Engelhardt, 35–62. New York: Henry Holt, 1996.

Lipka, Michael. "More White Evangelicals Than American Jews Say God Gave Israel to the Jewish People," Pew Research Center. October 3, 2013. https://tinyurl.com/u9xbjmr.

Lipson, Carol S. "It All Comes Down to *Maat*: Ancient Egyptian Rhetoric." In *Rhetoric before and beyond the Greeks*, edited by Carol S. Lipson and Roberta A. Binkley, 79–98. Albany: State University of New York Press, 2004.

Loader, William. *The New Testament on Sexuality.* Grand Rapids: Eerdmans, 2012.

Lopez, Davina C. *Apostle to the Conquered: Reimaging Paul's Mission.* Paul in Critical Contexts. Minneapolis: Fortress, 2008.

Lozada, Francisco Jr., *Toward a Latino/a Biblical Interpretation.* RBS 91. Atlanta: SBL Press, 2017.

Lozada, Francisco Jr., and Greg Carey, eds. *Soundings in Cultural Criticism: Culture, Power, and Identity in the New Testament.* Minneapolis: Fortress, 2015.

Lozada, Francisco Jr., and Fernando F. Segovia, eds. *Latino/a Biblical Hermeneutics: Problematics, Objectives, Strategies.* SemeiaSt 68. Atlanta: SBL Press, 2014.

Lundbom, Jack R. "Hebrew Rhetoric." In *Encyclopedia of Rhetoric*, edited by Thomas O. Sloane, 325–28. New York: Oxford University Press, 2001.

MacIntyre, Alasdair. *After Virtue: A Study in Moral Theory.* South Bend, IN: University of Notre Dame Press, 1981.

Mafico, Temba L. J. "The Divine Name Yahweh ʾĔlōhîˆm from an African Perspective." In Segovia and Tolbert, *Reading from This Place*, 2:21–32.

Malbon, Elizabeth Struthers. *Mark's Jesus: Characterization as Narrative Christology.* Waco, TX: Baylor University Press, 2009.

Marchal, Joseph A., ed. *Bodies on the Verge: Queering Pauline Epistles.* SemeiaSt 93. Atlanta: SBL Press, 2019.

———. "Queer Approaches: Improper Relations with Pauline Letters." In *Studying Paul's Letters: Contemporary Perspectives and Methods*, edited by Joseph A. Marchal (Minneapolis: Fortress, 2012), 209–27.

Marsden, George M. *Fundamentalism and American Culture: The Shaping of Twentieth-Century Evangelicalism: 1870–1925.* New York: Oxford University Press, 1980.

Martin, Clarice J. "'Somebody Done Hoodoo'd the Hoodoo Man': Language, Power, Resistance, and the Effective History of Pauline Texts in American Slavery." *Semeia* 83/84 (1998): 203–33.

Martyn, J. Louis. *History and Theology in the Fourth Gospel.* 2nd ed. Nashville: Abingdon, 1979.

Marzouk, Safwat. *Intercultural Church: A Biblical Image for an Age of Migration.* Word & World. Minneapolis: Fortress, 2019.

Mathews, Shailer. *The Social Teachings of Jesus: An Essay in Christian Sociology.* New York: Macmillan, 1897.

Matthews, Rex D. "Divorce and Remarriage in American Methodism: The Evolution of Church Positions from 1884 to 2012." *The United Methodist Reporter*, April 28, 2016. https://tinyurl.com/redj823.

Matthews, Victor H. "The Unwanted Gift: Implications of Obligatory Gift Giving in Ancient Israel." *Semeia* 87 (1999): 91–104.

Mayo, Maria. *The Limits of Forgiveness: Case Studies in the Distortion of a Biblical Ideal.* Minneapolis: Fortress, 2015.

McCormack, Bruce L. "'With Loud Cries and Tears': The Humanity of the Son in the Epistle to the Hebrews." In *The Epistle to the Hebrews and Christian Theology*, edited by Richard Bauckham, Daniel R. Driver, Trevor A. Hart, and Nathan MacDonald, 37–68. Grand Rapids: Eerdmans, 2009.

McEntire, Mark. *Portraits of an Immature God*. Minneapolis: Fortress, 2013.

McFague, Sallie. *Speaking in Parables: A Study in Metaphor and Theology*. Philadelphia: Fortress, 1975.

McGuckin, John Anthony. "Recent Biblical Hermeneutics in Patristic Perspective: The Tradition of Orthodoxy." *Greek Orthodox Theological Review* 47 (2002): 295–326.

Meeks, Wayne A. *The First Urban Christians: The Social World of the Apostle Paul*. 2nd ed. New Haven: Yale University Press, 2003 (1983).

Meier, John P. *A Marginal Jew: Rethinking the Historical Jesus*. Vol. 5: *Probing the Authenticity of the Parables*. AYBRL. New Haven: Yale University Press, 2016.

Melkonian-Hoover, Ruth M. "Better Late Than Never? Evangelicals and Comprehensive Immigration Reform." In *Is the Good Book Good Enough? Evangelical Perspectives on Public Policy*, edited by David K. Ryden, 95–111. Lanham, MD: Lexington, 2011.

Melkonian-Hoover, Ruth M., and Lyman A. Kellstedt. *Evangelicals and Immigration: Fault Lines among the Faithful*. Palgrave Studies in Religion, Politics, and Policy. Cham, Switzerland: Palgrave Macmillan, 2019.

Mendoza, Manuel Villalobos. *Abject Bodies in the Gospel of Mark*. BMW 45; Sheffield: Sheffield Phoenix, 2012.

Mesters, Carlos. *Defenseless Flower: A New Reading of the Bible*. Maryknoll, NY: Orbis, 1989.

Meyers, Carol. *Discovering Eve: Ancient Israelite Women in Context*. New York: Oxford University Press, 1988.

———. *Rediscovering Eve: Ancient Israelite Women in Context*. New York: Oxford University Press, 2013.

———, ed. *Women in Scripture: Dictionary of Named and Unnamed Women in the Hebrew Bible, the Apocryphal/Deuterocanonical Books, and the New Testament*. Grand Rapids: Eerdmans, 2000.

Meyers, Eric M., and Mark A. Chancey. *Alexander to Constantine*. Vol. 3: *Archaeology of the Land of the Bible*. AYBRL. New Haven: Yale University Press, 2012.

Míguez, Néstor. "Apocalyptic and the Economy: A Reading of Revelation 18 from the Experience of Economic Exclusion." In Segovia and Tolbert, *Reading from This Place*, 2:250–62.

Miller, J. Maxwell, and John H. Hayes. *A History of Ancient Israel and Judah*. Philadelphia: Westminster, 1986.

Milne, Pamela J. "Toward Feminist Companionship: The Future of Feminist Biblical Studies and Feminism." In *A Feminist Companion to Reading the Bible:*

Approaches, Methods and Strategies, edited by Athalya Brenner and Carole Fontaine, 39–60. Sheffield: Sheffield Academic, 1997.

Mitchell, Henry H. *Black Preaching: The Recovery of a Powerful Art*. Nashville: Abingdon, 1990.

Mitchem, Stephanie Y. *Race, Religion, and Politics: Toward Human Rights in the United States*. Lanham, MD: Rowman & Littlefield, 2019.

Moberly, R. W. L. *The Bible, Theology, and Faith: A Study of Abraham and Jesus*. Cambridge Studies in Christian Doctrine. Cambridge: Cambridge University Press, 2000.

———. "Theological Interpretation, Second Naiveté, and the Rediscovery of the Old Testament." *ATR* 99 (2017): 651–70.

Moore, Stephen D. "Are There Impurities in the Living Water That the Johannine Jesus Dispenses? Deconstruction, Feminism, and the Samaritan Woman." *BibInt* 1 (1993): 207–27.

———. "The Dog-Woman of Canaan and Other Animal Tales from the Gospel of Matthew." In Lozada and Carey, *Soundings in Cultural Criticism*, 57–71.

———. *Literary Criticism and the Gospels: The Theoretical Challenge*. New Haven: Yale University Press, 1989.

———. "Postcolonialism." In Adam, *Handbook of Postmodern Biblical Interpretation*, 182–88.

Moore, Stephen D., and Fernando F. Segovia, eds. *Postcolonial Biblical Criticism: Interdisciplinary Intersections*. The Bible and Postcolonialism. New York: T&T Clark, 2005.

Moore, Stephen D., and Yvonne Sherwood, *The Invention of the Biblical Scholar: A Critical Manifesto*. Minneapolis: Fortress, 2013.

Morgan, Robert, with John Barton. *Biblical Interpretation*. Oxford Bible Series. New York: Oxford University Press, 1988.

Mosala, Itumeleng J. *Biblical Hermeneutics and Black Theology in South Africa*. Grand Rapids: Eerdmans, 1989.

Moss, Candida. *The Myth of Persecution: How Early Christians Invented a Story of Martyrdom*. San Francisco: HarperOne, 2013.

Moss, Candida R., and Joel S. Baden. *Bible Nation: The United States of Hobby Lobby*. Princeton: Princeton University Press, 2017.

Mroczek, Eva. "The Hegemony of the Biblical in the Study of Second Temple Literature." *JAJ* 6 (2015): 2–35.

———. "Jesus vs. Judaism . . . Again," *Marginalia*, April 15, 2014. https://tinyurl.com/swvsnua.

Myers, Ched. *Binding the Strong Man: A Political Reading of Mark's Story of Jesus*. Maryknoll, NY: Orbis, 1988.

Myers, Jacob D. *Making Love with Scripture: Why the Bible Doesn't Mean How You Think It Means.* Minneapolis: Fortress, 2015.

Negri, Antonio, and Michael Hardt. *Empire.* Cambridge, MA: Harvard University Press, 2001.

Nelavala, Surekha. "Third-Wave Feminism." In O'Brien et al., *Oxford Encyclopedia,* 1:251–55.

Newsom, Carol A. *Daniel.* OTL. Louisville: Westminster John Knox, 2014.

———. "Job," *NIB* (Nashville: Abingdon, 1996), 4:317–638.

Newsom, Carol A., Sharon H. Ringe, and Jacqueline E. Lapsley, eds. *Women's Bible Commentary.* 3rd ed. Louisville: Westminster John Knox, 2012.

Neyrey, Jerome H. *Paul, in Other Words: A Cultural Reading of His Letters.* Louisville: Westminster John Knox, 1990.

Ngan, Lai Ling Elizabeth. "Neither Here nor There: Boundary and Identity in the Hagar Story." In Foskett and Kuan, *Ways of Being, Ways of Reading,* 70–83.

Nicolet, Valérie. "Monstrous Bodies in Paul's Letter to the Galatians." In Marchal, *Bodies on the Verge,* 111–37.

Noll, Mark A. *The Civil War as a Theological Crisis.* Chapel Hill: University of North Carolina Press, 2006.

Norris, Richard A. Jr., "Augustine and the Close of the Ancient Period." In Hauser and Watson, *History of Biblical Interpretation*: 1:380–408.

O'Brien, Julia M. *Challenging Prophetic Metaphor: Theology and Ideology in the Prophets.* Louisville: Westminster John Knox, 2008.

———. "The Economics of Family: Changing Biblical Norms." *Biblical Archaeology Review* 36, no. 5 (Sept–Oct 2010): 30, 76.

O'Brien, Julia M. et al., eds. *The Oxford Encyclopedia of the Bible and Gender Studies.* 2 vols. New York: Oxford University Press, 2014.

Odell-Scott, David W. "Deconstruction." In Adam, *Handbook of Postmodern Biblical Interpretation,* 55–61.

Osborne, Grant R. *The Hermeneutical Spiral: A Comprehensive Introduction to Biblical Interpretation.* Downers Grove, IL: InterVarsity, 1991.

Osiek, Carolyn, and David L. Balch. *Families in the New Testament World: Households and House Churches.* Family, Religion, and Culture. Louisville: Westminster John Knox, 1997.

Osiek, Carolyn, and Margaret Y. MacDonald with Janet H. Tullock. *A Woman's Place: House Churches in Earliest Christianity.* Minneapolis: Fortress, 2006.

Page, Hugh R. Jr. et al., eds. *The Africana Bible: Reading Israel's Scriptures from Africa and the African Diaspora.* Minneapolis: Fortress, 2010.

Parsenios, George A. *Rhetoric and Drama in the Johannine Lawsuit Motif.* WUNT 258. Tübingen: Mohr Siebeck, 2010.

Parsons, Mikeal C., and Michael Wade Martin. *Ancient Rhetoric and the New Testament: The Influence of Elementary Greek Composition.* Waco, TX: Baylor University Press, 2018.

Paterson, Katherine. *Bridge to Terabithia.* New York: HarperCollins, 1977.

Patte, Daniel et al., eds. *Global Bible Commentary.* Nashville: Abingdon, 2004.

Paul, Shalom M. "The Mesopotamian Background of Daniel 1–6." In *The Book of Daniel,* vol. 1: *Composition and Reception,* edited by John J. Collins and Peter W. Flint, 55–68. Boston: Brill Academic, 2002.

Pippin, Tina. "'And I Will Strike Her Children Dead': Death and the Deconstruction of Social Location." In Segovia and Tolbert, *Reading from This Place,* 1:191–98.

Pobee, John S. "Bible Study in Africa: A Passover of Language." *Semeia* 73 (1996): 161–79.

Polaski, Sandra Hack. *A Feminist Introduction to Paul.* St. Louis: Chalice, 2005.

Pontifical Biblical Commission. "The Interpretation of the Bible in the Church." In *The Scripture Documents: An Anthology of Official Catholic Teachings,* edited by Dean P. Béchard, 244–316. Collegeville, MN: Liturgical Press, 2002.

———. "The Jewish People and Their Sacred Scriptures in the Christian Bible." https://tinyurl.com/mt3e.

Porton, Gary G. "Rabbinic Midrash." In Hauser and Watson, *History of Biblical Interpretation,* 1:198–224.

Powell, Mark Allan. *Introducing the New Testament: A Historical, Literary, and Theological Survey.* Minneapolis: Fortress, 2009.

Powery, Emerson B., and Rodney S. Sadler Jr. *The Genesis of Liberation: Biblical Interpretation in the Antebellum Narratives of the Enslaved.* Louisville: Westminster John Knox, 2016.

Premnath, Devadasan N. "Biblical Interpretation in India: History and Issues." In Foskett and Kuan, *Ways of Being, Ways of Reading,* 1–16.

Pui-lan, Kwok. "Geopolitical Hermeneutics." In Lozada and Carey, *Soundings in Cultural Criticism,* 165–76.

Reinhartz, Adele. *Befriending the Beloved Disciple: A Jewish Reading of the Gospel of John.* New York: Continuum, 2001.

———. "Judaism in the Gospel of John." *Int* 63 (2009): 382–93.

———. "On Travel, Translation, and Ethnography: Johannine Scholarship at the Turn of the Century." In *"What Is John?"* Vol. 2: *Literary and Social Readings of the Fourth Gospel,* edited by Fernando F. Segovia, 111–38. SBLSymS 7. Atlanta: Scholars, 1998.

Robbins, Vernon K. *The Invention of Christian Discourse*. Vol. 1: *From Wisdom to Apocalyptic*. Rhetoric of Religious Antiquity 1. Brussels: Deo, 2008.

———. "Rhetography: A New Way of Seeing the Familiar Text." In *Words Well Spoken: George Kennedy's Rhetoric of the New Testament*, edited by C. Clifton Black and Duane F. Watson, 81–106. SRR 8. Waco, TX: Baylor University Press, 2008.

———. *The Tapestry of Early Christian Discourse: Rhetoric, Society, and Ideology*. New York: Routledge, 1996.

Rock, David, and Heidi Grant. "Why Diverse Teams Are Smarter." *Harvard Business Review*, November 4, 2016. https://hbr.org/2016/11/why-diverse-teams-are-smarter.

Rodriguez, Rafael. *Structuring Early Christian Memory: Jesus in Tradition, Performance, and Text*. LNTS. New York: T&T Clark, 2010.

Roetzel, Calvin. *Paul: The Man and the Myth*. Studies on Personalities of the New Testament. Minneapolis: Fortress, 1999 (1997).

Roncace, Mark, and Joseph Weaver, eds. *Global Perspectives on the Bible*. Upper Saddle River, NJ: Pearson, 2013.

Rosen, Hannah. "Did Christianity Cause the Crash?" *The Atlantic*, December 2009. https://tinyurl.com/scu85w3.

Rowland, Christopher, and Mark Corner, *Liberating Exegesis: The Challenge of Liberation Theology to Biblical Studies*. Louisville: Westminster John Knox, 1989.

Ruden, Sarah. *Paul among the People: The Apostle Reinterpreted and Reimagined in His Own Time*. New York: Pantheon, 2010.

Runia, David T. "Philo and Origen: A Preliminary Survey." In *Philo and the Church Fathers: A Collection of Papers*. VCSup 32: 117–25 (Leiden: E. J. Brill, 1995).

Russell, D. A., and M. Winterbottom. *Ancient Literary Criticism: The Principal Texts in New Translations*. New York: Oxford University Press, 1972.

Russo, Vito. *The Celluloid Closet: Homosexuality in the Movies*. Rev. ed. New York: Harper & Row, 1987.

Said, Edward. *Orientalism: Western Conceptions of the Orient*. London: Penguin, 1978.

Saillant, John. "Origins of African American Biblical Hermeneutics in Eighteenth-Century Black Opposition to the Slave Trade and Slavery." In Wimbush, *African Americans and the Bible*, 236–50.

Sánchez, David A. *From Patmos to the Barrio: Subverting Imperial Myths*. Minneapolis: Fortress, 2008.

Sanders, E. P. *Paul and Palestinian Judaism: A Comparison of Patterns of Religion.* Minneapolis: Fortress, 1977.

Sarisky, Darren. *Reading the Bible Theologically.* Current Issues in Theology. New York: Cambridge University Press, 2019.

Satlow, Michael. *How the Bible Became Holy.* New Haven: Yale University Press, 2014.

Sawyer, John F. A. *The Fifth Gospel: Isaiah in the History of Christianity.* New York: Cambridge University Press, 1996.

Schearing, Linda S., and Valarie H. Ziegler. *Enticed by Eden: How Western Culture Uses, Confuses (and Sometimes Abuses) Adam and Eve.* Waco, TX: Baylor University Press, 2013.

Schneider, Laurel C. "Queer Theory." In Adam, *Handbook of Postmodern Biblical Interpretation*, 206–12.

Schneider, Tammi J. *An Introduction to Ancient Mesopotamian Religion.* Grand Rapids: Eerdmans, 2011.

Scholes, Robert, and Robert Kellogg. *The Nature of Narrative.* New York: Oxford University Press, 1966.

Scholz, Susanne. *The Bible as Political Artifact: On the Feminist Study of the Hebrew Bible.* Minneapolis: Fortress, 2017.

———. "Second-Wave Feminism." In O'Brien et al., *Oxford Encyclopedia*, 1:242–51.

Schüssler Fiorenza, Elisabeth. *But She Said: Feminist Practices of Biblical Interpretation.* Boston: Beacon, 1992.

———. *Democratizing Biblical Studies: Toward an Emancipatory Educational Space.* Louisville: Westminster John Knox, 2009.

———. *In Memory of Her: A Feminist Theological Reconstruction of Christian Origins.* New York: Crossroad, 1983.

———. "Interpreting Patriarchal Traditions." In *The Liberating Word: A Guide to Nonsexist Interpretation of the Bible*, edited by Letty M. Russell, 39–61. Philadelphia: Westminster, 1976.

———, ed. *Searching the Scriptures.* 2 vols. New York: Crossroad, 1993–1994.

Schweitzer, Albert. *The Quest of the Historical Jesus: A Critical Study of Its Progress from Reimarus to Wrede.* New York: Macmillan, 1968 (1906).

Scott, Bernard Brandon. *Hear Then the Parable.* Minneapolis: Augsburg Fortress, 1988.

Segovia, Fernando F. "'And They Began to Speak in Other Tongues': Competing Modes of Discourse in Contemporary Biblical Criticism." In Segovia and Tolbert, *Reading from This Place*, 1:1–32.

———. "Cultural Studies and Contemporary Biblical Criticism: Ideological

Criticism as a Mode of Discourse." In Segovia and Tolbert, *Reading from This Place,* 2:1–17.

———. "Toward a Hermeneutics of the Diaspora: A Hermeneutics of Otherness and Engagement." In Segovia and Tolbert, *Reading from This Place*, 1:57–73.

Segovia, Fernando F., and R. S. Sugirtharajah, eds. *A Postcolonial Commentary on the New Testament Writings.* The Bible and Postcolonialism. New York: T&T Clark, 2007.

Segovia, Fernando F., and Mary Ann Tolbert, eds. *Reading from This Place*. 2 vols. Minneapolis: Fortress, 1995.

Setzer, Claudia. "First-Wave Feminism." In O'Brien et al., *Oxford Encyclopedia*, 1:234–42.

Sherwood, Yvonne. "Derrida." In Adam, *Handbook of Postmodern Biblical Interpretation*, 69–75.

Shields, Mary E. "Adultery." *NIDB* 1.57.

Simkins, Ronald A. "Family in the Political Economy of Monarchic Judah." *The Bible and Critical Theory* 1 (2004): 1–17.

Slusser, Michael. "Reading Silently in Antiquity." *JBL* 111 (1992): 499.

Smith, Jonathan Z. *Drudgery Divine: On the Comparison of Early Christianities and the Religions of Late Antiquity*. Chicago: University of Chicago Press, 1990.

Smith, Mark S. *The Origins of Biblical Monotheism: Israel's Polytheistic Background and the Ugaritic Texts.* New York: Oxford University Press, 2001.

Smith, Mitzi J. *Insights from African American Interpretation.* Reading the Bible in the 21st Century. Minneapolis: Fortress, 2017.

Snell, Daniel C. *Religions of the Ancient Near East.* New York: Cambridge University Press, 2011.

Snodgrass, Klyne R. *Stories with Intent: A Comprehensive Guide to the Parables of Jesus.* Grand Rapids: Eerdmans, 2008.

Society of Biblical Literature, 2019 SBL Membership Data. https://tinyurl.com/ucfl7dk.

Spivak, Gayatri Chakravorty. "Can the Subaltern Speak? Speculations on Widow-Sacrifice." In *The Post-Colonial Studies Reader*, edited by Bill Ashcroft, Gareth Griffiths, and Helen Tiffin, 24–28. New York: Routledge, 1995 (1985).

Spöhrer, Markus. "Homophobia and Violence in Film Noir: Homosexuality as a Threat to Masculinity in John Huston's *The Maltese Falcon.*" *Journal of Literature and Culture* 6 (2016): 56–71.

Stack-Nelson, Judy. "Beyond Biblical Literacy: Developing Readerly Readers in Teaching Biblical Studies." *Dialog* 53 (2014): 293–303.

Staley, Jeffrey L. *Reading with a Passion: Rhetoric, Autobiography, and the American West in the Gospel of John.* New York: Continuum, 1995.

Stanton, Elizabeth Cady et al. *The Woman's Bible.* Parts 1 and 2. Reprint. Salem, NH: Ayer Company, 1988.

Stark, Rodney. *The Rise of Christianity.* Princeton: Princeton University Press, 1997.

Stark, Thom. *The Human Faces of God: What Scripture Reveals When It Gets God Wrong (and Why Inerrancy Tries to Hide It).* Eugene, OR: Wipf & Stock, 2011.

Stendahl, Krister. "Biblical Theology, Contemporary." *IDB* 1:418–32.

Stockhausen, Ulrike Elisabeth. "Evangelicals and Immigration: A Conflicted History." *Process: A Blog for American History.* March 18, 2019. https://tinyurl.com/uny4m42.

Streete, Gail Corrington. *The Strange Woman: Power and Sex in the Bible.* Louisville: Wesminster John Knox, 1997.

Stuckey, Sterling. "'My Burden Lightened': Frederick Douglass, the Bible, and Slave Culture." In Wimbush, *African Americans and the Bible*, 251–65.

Sugirtharajah, R. S. *The Bible and the Third World: Precolonial, Colonial and Postcolonial Encounters.* New York: Cambridge University Press, 2001.

———. "Muddling Along at the Margins." In *Still at the Margins: Biblical Scholarship Fifteen Years after Voices from the Margin*, edited by R. S. Sugirtharajah, 8–21. London: T&T Clark, 2008.

———, ed. *The Postcolonial Bible.* The Bible and Postcolonialism. Sheffield: Sheffield Academic, 1998.

———. *Postcolonial Criticism and Biblical Interpretation.* New York: Oxford University Press, 2002.

———, ed. *Voices from the Margin: Interpreting the Bible in the Third World.* Rev. ed. Maryknoll, NY: Orbis, 1995 (1991).

Sweeney, Marvin A. "Review of Greg Carey, *Ultimate Things: An Introduction to Jewish and Christian Apocalyptic Literature.*" *Religious Studies Review* 33, no. 1 (January 2007): 62.

Tamez, Elsa. *The Amnesty of Grace: Justification by Faith from a Latin American Perspective.* Nashville: Abingdon, 1993.

Thayer, Anne. "What's New in the History of Christianity?" *Religion Compass* 1 (2007): 1–15.

Thurman, Howard. *Jesus and the Disinherited.* Nashville: Abingdon, 1949.

Tolbert, Mary Ann. "Social, Sociological, and Anthropological Methods." In Schüssler Fiorenza, *Searching the Scriptures*: 1:255–71.

———. *Sowing the Gospel: Mark's World in Literary-Historical Perspective.* Minneapolis: Fortress, 1989.

———. "Writing History, Writing Culture, Writing Ourselves: Issues in Contemporary Biblical Interpretation." In Lozada and Carey, *Soundings in Cultural Criticism*, 17–30.
Tov, Emmanuel. *Textual Criticism of the Hebrew Bible*. Minneapolis: Fortress, 1992.
Tracy, David. *Plurality and Ambiguity: Hermeneutics, Religion, Hope*. San Francisco: Harper & Row, 1987.
Trible, Phyllis. *God and the Rhetoric of Sexuality*. Philadelphia: Fortress, 1978.
———. *Rhetorical Criticism: Context, Method, and the Book of Jonah*. Guides to Scholarship. Minneapolis: Fortress, 1994.
Tupamahu, Ekaputra. "'I Don't Want to Hear Your Language!': White Social Imagination and the Demography of Roman Corinth." Unpublished paper.
———. "Language Politics and the Constitution of Racialized Subjects in the Corinthian Church." *JSNT* 41 (2018): 223–45.
Ukpong, Justin S. "The Parable of the Shrewd Manager (Luke 16:1-13): An Essay in Interculturation Biblical Hermeneutics." *Semeia* 73 (1996): 189–210.
VanderKam, James C. *The Dead Sea Scrolls Today*. Grand Rapids: Eerdmans, 1998.
Vanhoozer, Kevin J. et al., eds. *Dictionary for Theological Interpretation of the Bible*. Grand Rapids: Baker Academic, 2005.
Vermes, Geza. *The Dead Sea Scrolls in English*. 3rd ed. New York: Penguin Books, 1987.
———. *Jesus the Jew: A Historian's Reading of the Gospels*. Minneapolis: Fortress, 1981 (1973).
Wahlde, Urban C. von. "Faith and Works in John VI 28–29: Exegesis or Eisegesis?" *NovT* 4 (1980): 304–15.
Wan, Sze-kar. "Betwixt and Between: Towards a Hermeneutics of Hyphenation." In Foskett and Kuan, *Ways of Being, Ways of Reading*, 137–51.
Wan, Wei Hsien. "Re-examining the Master's Tools: Considerations on Biblical Studies' Race Problem." In Hockey and Horrell, eds., *Ethnicity, Race, Religion*, 219–38.
Warnock, Raphael G. *The Divided Mind of the Black Church: Theology, Piety, and Public Witness*. Religion, Race, and Ethnicity. New York: New York University Press, 2014.
Warrior, Robert Allen. "A Native American Perspective: Canaanites, Cowboys, and Indians." In Sugirtharajah, *Voices from the Margin*, 277–85.
Webster, John. *Holy Scripture: A Dogmatic Sketch*. Current Issues in Theology. Cambridge: Cambridge University Press, 2003.

Welborn, Laurence L. "1 Corinthians" (study notes). In *The New Oxford Annotated Bible*. Edited by Michael Coogan et al. 4th ed. New York: Oxford University Press, 2010.

West, Gerald O. *The Academy of the Poor: Towards a Dialogical Reading of the Bible*. Interventions 2. Sheffield: Sheffield Academic, 1999.

———. *Biblical Hermeneutics of Liberation: Modes of Reading the Bible in the South African Context*. 2nd ed. Bible and Liberation. Maryknoll, NY: Orbis, 1995.

Wexman, Virginia Wright. "Kinesics and Film Acting: Humphrey Bogart in *The Maltese Falcon* and *The Big Sleep*." In *Star Texts: Image and Performance in Text and Television*, edited by Jeremy G. Butler, 203–12. Detroit: Wayne State University Press, 1991.

Whitters, Mark F. "Discipleship in John: Four Profiles." *Word & World* 18 (1998): 422–27.

Williams, Demetrius K. "The Bible and Models of Liberation in the African American Experience." In *Yet with a Steady Beat: Contemporary U.S. Afrocentric Biblical Interpretation*, edited by Randall C. Bailey, 33–59. SemeiaSt 42. Atlanta: Society of Biblical Literature, 2003.

Wimbush, Vincent L., ed. *African Americans and the Bible: Sacred Texts and Social Textures*. New York: Continuum, 2001.

———. *The Bible and African Americans: A Brief History*. Facets. Minneapolis: Fortress, 2003.

Wire, Antoinette Clark. *The Corinthian Women Prophets: A Reconstruction through Paul's Rhetoric*. Minneapolis: Augsburg Fortress, 1990.

Witherup, Ronald D. "The Interpretation of the Bible in Roman Catholic and Orthodox Churches." In Gorman, *Scripture: An Ecumenical Introduction*, 195–215.

Withrow, Brandon G., and Menachem Wecker. *Consider No Evil: Two Faith Traditions and the Problem of Academic Freedom in Religious Higher Education*. Eugene, OR: Cascade, 2014.

Wright, G. Ernest. "Exegesis and Eisegesis in the Interpretation of Scripture." *ExpTim* 48 (1937): 353–57.

Wright, N. T. *Paul and the Faithfulness of God*. 2 vols. Minneapolis: Fortress, 2013.

Yamada, Frank M. "Constructing Hybridity and Heterogeneity: Asian American Biblical Interpretation from a Third-Generation Perspective." In Foskett and Kuan, *Ways of Being, Ways of Reading*, 164–77.

Yee, Gale A. "Racial Melancholia and the Book of Ruth." In *The Five Scrolls*, edited by Athalya Brenner-Idan, Gale A. Yee, and Archie C. C. Lee, 61–70. Texts@Contexts 6. New York: T&T Clark, 2018.

———. "Ruth." In *Fortress Commentary on the Bible: The Old Testament and Apocrypha*, edited by Gale A. Yee, Hugh R. Page Jr., and Matthew J. M. Coomber, 351–59. Minneapolis: Fortress, 2014.

———. "'She Stood in Tears amid the Alien Corn': Ruth, the Perpetual Foreigner and Model Minority." In Bailey, Liew, and Segovia, *They Were All Together in One Place?*, 119–40.

———. "Yin/Yang Is Not Me: An Exploration into Asian American Biblical Hermeneutics." In Foskett and Kuan, *Ways of Being, Ways of Reading*, 152–63.

Yieh, John Yueh-Han. "Chinese Biblical Interpretation: History and Issues." In Foskett and Kuan, *Ways of Being, Ways of Reading*, 17–30.

Yoder, John Howard. *The Politics of Jesus*. Rev. ed. Grand Rapids: Eerdmans, 1994 (1972).

Yonge, Charles Duke. *Cicero's Orations*. Dover Thrift Editions. Mineola, NY: Dover, 2018.

Young, Frances M. "Patristic Biblical Interpretation." In Vanhoozer et al., *Dictionary for Theological Interpretation of the Bible*, 566–71.

Zainabu, Jaha. "Dear Isaac." April 6, 2013: https://www.youtube.com/watch?v=eftmI_m6sRc.

Zetterholm, Karin Heder. *Jewish Interpretation of the Bible: Ancient and Contemporary*. Minneapolis: Fortress, 2012 (2008).

INDEX OF MODERN AUTHORS

Achebe, Chinua, 132
Achtemeier, Paul, 117–18
Adam, A. K. M., 57 n. 18, 140 n. 61
Allison, Dale C., Jr., 77, 100 n. 86
Alter, Robert, 33 n. 35, 109 n. 6, 113–14, 222–24
Anderson, Cheryl B., 188
Ashcroft, Bill, 57 n. 18
Ashton, John, 100 n. 87
Ateek, Naim S., 37 n. 42
Atwood, Fiona, 10 n. 13
Auerbach, Erich, 113
Aune, David E., 136 n. 56
Aviam, Mordecai, 65–66
Avalos, Hector, 168, 171
Aymer, Margaret P., 175 n. 5
Azzoni, Annalisa, 54 n. 8

Baden, Joel, 47 n. 1, 65 n. 41, 69 n. 48, 84–85, 154
Bailey, Randall C., 36 n. 41, 102, 103 n. 94, 188 n. 51, 197 n. 78
Baker-Fletcher, Karen, 183 n. 28
Balch, David L., 2 n. 2, 54
Balmer, Randall, 214 n. 131
Barreto, Eric D., 190–91
Barrios, Richard, 10 n. 13
Barton, John, 160 n. 56, 169 n. 71
Bass, Dorothy C., 183 n. 30

Bassler, Jouette M., 21 n. 21, 185–86
Bauckham, Richard, 149 n. 26, 152 n. 37
Beal, Timothy, 174 n. 2
William H. Bellinger Jr., 79 n. 56
Berlinerblau, Jacques, 143 n. 6
Bernhard, Andrew, 65 n. 39
Bhabha, Homi, 57 n. 18
Birch, Bruce C., 167 n. 65, 170 n. 73
Blount, Brian K., 170, 187, 187 n. 46–47
Boesak, Allan A., 91, 181
Boin, Douglas, 60 n. 27
Borg, Marcus J., 72 n. 51
Borgen, Peder, 29 n. 29, 111 n. 13
Bowler, Kate, 226–27
Boxall, Ian, 91 n. 70, 174 n. 2
Boyarin, Daniel, 95 n. 76
Brasher, Brenda, 4 n. 9
Braun, Willi, 60 n. 27
Brettler, Marc Zvi, 33 n. 35, 143 n. 3, 151 n. 34
Briggs, Richard S., 146
Bright, John, 99 n. 83
Brooks, Cleanth, 115 n. 24
Brown, Michael Joseph, 102 n. 94, 187 n. 46
Brown, Raymond E., 100 n. 87

Brownson, James V., 162 n. 60
Brueggemann, Walter, 79 n. 56, 120
Buell, Denise Kimber, 211 n. 120, 212 n. 123, 215
Bultmann, Rudolf, 160–61
Burridge, Richard A., 168 n. 68
Buschart, W. David, 147 n. 20
Byron, Gay L., 102–3, 191 n. 60, 194 n. 66, 212
Byung-Mu, Ahn, 180

Callahan, Allan Dwight, 195 n. 72
Cannon, Katie Geneva, 192
Cardenal, Ernesto, 89–90
Carey, Greg, 36 n. 40, 55 n. 10, 107 n. 3, 154, 180 n. 21, 190 n. 57, 205 n. 102, 206 n. 105, 207 n. 106, 212 n. 125, 217 n. 141, 217–18, 228 n. 13
Carter, J. Kameron, 212, 215
Carter, Warren, 56
Case, Shirley Jackson, 58–59
Chatman, Seymour, 124–25
Chancey, Mark A., 67 n. 45
Cheon, Samuel, 198 n. 85
Chester, Stephen J., 144 n. 7
Chia, Philip P., 198 n. 85
Choi, Jin Young, 196–97
Clark-Soles, Jaime, 116 n. 25
Clines, David J. A., 96 n. 79
Concannon, Cavin, 155 n. 45
Cone, James H., 186, 191, 217 n. 140
Congdon, David, 160 n. 57
Coogan, Michael, 2 n. 1, 162 n. 60
Cooper, Kate, 3 n. 6
Copher, Charles B., 102
Corner, Mark, 180 n. 18
Cosgrove, Charles H., 168–70

Croatto, J. Severino, 178
Crossan, John Dominic, 56, 72 n. 51, 99–100, 106–7, 210
Crowder, Stephanie Buckhanon, 193
Culler, Jonathan, 140 n. 61
Culpepper, R. Alan, 129–30, 220–21

D'Angelo, Mary Rose, 101 n. 90
Davies, Eryl W., 171 n. 80
Davies, Philip R., 99 n. 84, 108 n. 4
Davis, Ellen F., 33 n. 35, 38 n. 45, 147 n. 15, 152 n. 37
Davis, Thomas W., 64 n. 37
DeBerg, Betty A., 4 n. 9
DeConick, April, 76
de Man, Paul, 140
Derrida, Jacques, 140
deSilva, David A., 152–54
Douglass, Frederick, 175–76, 183
Dube, Musa W., 36, 58, 90, 199–200, 207
Dunn, James D. G., 116 n. 25, 156 n. 48

Eagleton, Terry, 130–31
Ehrman, Bart D., 98 n. 81–82
Ekblad, Bob, 200–1
Kent Eilers, Kent, 147 n. 20
Elgvin, Torleif, 30 n. 31
Elliott, John H., 62 n. 31
Elliott, Neil, xi, 56, 179 n. 15
Enns, Peter, 33 n. 35, 63 n. 34, 143 n. 3
Eslinger, Lyle, 224 n. 8

Felder, Cain Hope, 102, 187 n. 46
Fewell, Dana Nolan, 232 n. 20

Fish, Stanley, 140 n. 60
Ford, Andrew, 111 n. 11
Fosarelli Patricia D., 147 n. 16
Foskett, Mary F., 197 n. 80, 198 n. 85, 199, 212 n. 121
Fowl, Stephen, 32 n. 34, 33 n. 35, 38 n. 45, 92, 146 n. 12, 147 n. 14, 147 n. 17, 150, 152 n. 36, 166 n. 63
Fowler, Robert M., 127 n. 44
Fox, Michael V., 135 n. 54
Fredriksen, Paula, 102
Frei, Hans, 114 n. 21
Friedman, Richard Elliott, 69 n. 48, 84
Frymer-Kensky, Tikva, 102 n. 92

Gafney, Wilda C., 135 n. 53, 185 n. 38, 193–95
Gallagher, Catherine, 113 n. 17
Gallagher, Sally, 4 n. 9
Gaston, Lloyd, 169–70
Gaventa, Beverly Roberts, 179 n. 15
Gilliard, Frank D., 117 n. 27
González, Justo, 189–90
Goodacre, Mark, 65 n. 39, 69 n. 49, 76 n. 53
Gorman, Michael J., 32 n. 34, 33 n. 35, 34 n. 37, 147 n. 16–17, 148, 151 n. 33
Gottwald, Norman, 55–56, 180 n. 18
Gowler, David B., 80 n. 57
Grant, Heidi, 164 n. 61
Grant, Robert M., 29 n. 28
Green, Joel B., 116 n. 25, 142, 146 n. 12, 147, 148 n. 25, 150, 151 n. 35

Greene-McCreight, Kathryn, 148 n. 24
Griffiths, Gareth, 57 n. 18
Guardiola-Sáenz, Leticia A., 194 n. 67
Gundry-Volf, Judith M., 3 n. 6
Gunn, David Miller, 232 n. 20

Habermas, Jürgen, 161
Haidt, Jonathan, 161 n. 59, 167 n. 66
Hammett, Dashiell, 8–11
Hardesty, Nancy A., 182 n. 28, 183 n. 29
Hardt, Michael, 55 n. 11
Harrill, James Albert, 40 n. 47, 52 n. 5, 58 n. 23
Harrington, Daniel J., 33 n. 35, 143 n. 3
Harris, Robert A., 31 n. 33
Hartman, Midori E., 205 n. 103
Hauerwas, Stanley, 114 n. 22
Hauser, Alan J., 29 n. 29, 31 n. 32–33, 112 n. 13–14, 144 n. 8
Hayes, John H., 99 n. 83
Haynes, Stephen R., 36 n. 39
Hays, Richard B., 33 n. 35, 38 n. 45, 147 n. 15, 152 n. 37, 169
Haywood, Chanta M., 182–83 n. 28
Heidel, Alexander, 63 n. 33
Hendicks, Obery M., Jr., 168 n. 68
Hernandez-Díaz, Rodolfo J., 194 n. 68
Herzog, William R., 81 n. 58
Hicks-Keeton, Jill, 154–56
Hidalgo, Jacqueline, 189 n. 53, 230 n. 17
Hockey, Katherine M., 211 n. 120, 214 n. 132
Hogan, Michael J., 25 n. 24

Holifield, E. Brooks, 213
Horrell, David G., 214 n. 132, 218–19
Horsley, Richard A., 55 n. 12, 56, 180 n. 18
Huber, Lynn R., 203
Hurston, Zora Neale, 187
Hutto, David, 135 n. 54
Hylen, Susan E., 109 n. 5, 110

Ilan, Tal, 102 n. 93
Isasi-Díaz, Ada-María, 194–95
Iser, Wolfgang, 126

Jacob, Sharon, 37
Jennings, Willie James, 212 n. 123
Johnson, Luke Timothy, 222 n. 5
Johnson, Thomas Cary, 39 n. 46
Jones, L. Gregory, 114 n. 22, 147
Jones, Robert P., 229 n. 14
Jordan, Clarence, 208–9, 216–17
Juel, Donald H., 158
Junior, Nyasha, 182 n. 28

Kagan, Dion, 10 n. 13
Katz, Ben Zion, 49 n. 3
Keith, Chris, 83 n. 60
Kelley, Shawn, 19 n. 18, 20 n. 19, 215–16
Kellogg, Robert, 111 n. 12
Kellstedt, Lyman A., 230 n. 16
Kennedy, George A., 110 n. 9, 113 n. 16, 135 n. 54, 138 n. 58
Kermode, Frank, 113
Kern, Kathi, 176 n. 8
Kim, Jin-Ho, 180 n. 22
Kim, Uriah Yong–Hwan, 197 n. 80
Kim, Yung Suk, 180 n. 22

Kinyua, Johnson Kiriaku, 181–82 n. 25
Kloppenborg, John S., 77
K'Meyer, Tracy Elaine, 217 n. 141
Knust, Jennifer Wright, 54 n. 8, 162–63 n. 60
Koosed, Jennifer L., 232 n. 19
Kraemer, Ross Shepard, 101 n. 90, 102
Kuan, Jeffrey Kah-Jin, 197 n. 80, 198 n. 85, 199 n. 87, 212 n. 121
Kugel, James L., 27, 122 n. 36
Kümmel, Werner Georg, 159

Laffey, Alice L., 232 n. 19
Lange, Dirk, xi
Lapsley, Jacqueline E., 167 n. 65, 170 n. 73, 184 n. 36, 186 n. 42
Le Donne, Anthony, 83 n. 60, 100 n. 86
Legaspi, Michael C., 213 n. 126
Leiter, David A., 151 n. 33
Leithart, Peter, 147
Lemche, Nils Peter, 99 n. 84
Leonard-Fleckman, Mahri, 232 n. 19
Levine, Amy-Jill, 102, 151 n. 34, 210 n. 116
Lieu, Judith M., 92 n. 75
Liew, Tat-siong Benny, 57, 188 n. 51, 196, 197 n. 78, 198–99
Linenthal, Edward T., 25 n. 23
Lipka, Michael, 16 n. 14
Lipson, Carol S., 135 n. 54
Loader, William, 3 n. 5, 95 n. 77, 117 n. 26
Lopez, Davina C., 138
Lovelace, Vanessa, 191 n. 60, 194 n. 66

Lozada, Francisco Jr., 36 n. 40, 107 n. 3, 180 n. 21, 189 n. 53, 190, 190 n. 57, 205 n. 102, 206 n. 105, 207 n. 106, 212 n. 125
Lundbom, Jack R., 133 n. 51

MacDonald, Margaret Y. 101–2 n. 90
MacDonald, Nathan 149 n. 26
MacIntyre, Alastair, 166 n. 64
Mafico, Temba L. J., 182
Malbon, Elizabeth Struthers, 123–24
Marchal, Joseph A., 203, 203 n. 98, 205 n. 101, 205 n. 103
Marsden, George M., 213–14 n. 130
Marsh, Charles, 209
Martin, Clarice J., 39 n. 46
Martin, Michael Wade, 135 n. 55
Martyn, J. Louis, 100–101
Marzouk, Safwat, 230 n. 18
Mathews, Shailer, 58–59
Matthews, Rex D., 228 n. 12
Matthews, Victor H., 59–60
Mayo, Maria, 227–28
McCormack, Bruce L., 149
McEntire, Mark, 121 n. 35
McFague, Sallie, 114 n. 22
McGuckin, John Anthony, 34 n. 36
McNair, Brian, 10 n. 13
Meeks, Wayne A., 60 n. 28
Meier, John P., 104 n. 97
Melkonian-Hoover, Ruth M., 230 n. 15–16
Mendoza, Manuel Villalobos, 203–04
Mesters, Carlos, 178 n. 13
Meyers, Carol, 66, 102 n. 92, 184 n. 36, 185 n. 37

Meyers, Eric M., 67
Míguez, Néstor, 18 n. 17
Miller, J. Maxwell, 99 n. 83
Milne, Pamela J., 184 n. 33
Mitchell, Henry H., 217 n. 138
Mitchem, Stephanie Y., 212 n. 124
Moberly, R. W. L., 148 n. 23, 150
Moe-Lobeda, Cynthia, 167 n. 65, 170 n. 73
Moore, Stephen D., 57 n. 18–21, 131 n. 48, 140–41, 143 n. 6, 168, 205
Morgan, Robert, 160 n. 56
Mosala, Itumeleng J., 181
Moss, Candida, 61 n. 29, 65 n. 41, 154
Mroczek, Eva, 62 n. 32, 152–54
Myers, Ched, 56
Myers, Jacob D., 165

Negri, Antonio, 55 n. 11
Nelavala, Surekha, 184 n. 32
Newsom, Carol A., 96 n. 78, 126 n. 43, 184 n. 36, 186 n. 42
Neyrey, Jerome H., 61
Ngan, Lai Ling Elizabeth, 197 n. 80, 198 n. 81
Nicolet, Valérie, 204–5
Noll, Mark A., 39–40
Norris, Richard A. Jr., 112 n. 14–15, 144 n. 8

O'Brien, Julia M., xii, 49 n. 2, 53 n. 7, 54 n. 8, 104–5, 184 n. 32
Odell-Scott, David W., 140 n. 61
Osborne, Grant R., 67 n. 47, 114 n. 23
Osiek, Carolyn, 2 n. 2, 54, 101–02 n. 90

Page, Hugh R., Jr., 187 n. 46, 232 n. 19
Parsenios, George A., 137–83
Parsons, Mikeal C., 135 n. 55
Paterson, Katherine, 23 n. 22
Patte, Daniel, 206 n. 104
Paul, Shalom M., 50 n. 4
Pippin, Tina, 18 n. 17
Pobee, John S., 201
Polaski, Sandra Hack, 3 n. 4
Pontifical Biblical Commission, 91, 151
Porton, Gary G., 31, n. 32
Powell, Mark Allan, 86 n. 64
Powery, Emerson B., 175 n. 3–4, 188 n. 50, 207
Premnath, Devadasan N., 198 n. 85
Pui-lan, Kwok, 206 n. 105

Rasmussen, Larry L., 167 n. 65, 170 n. 73
Reinhartz, Adele, 101 n. 88, 102
Rich, Bryce, xi
Ringe, Sharon H., 184 n. 36, 186 n. 42
Robbins, Vernon K., 138
Rock, David, 164 n. 61
Rodriguez, Rafael, 69 n. 50
Roetzel, Calvin, 156–57
Rogerson, J. W., 92 n. 75
Roncace, Mark, 206 n. 104
Rosen, Hannah, 17 n. 16
Rowland, Christopher, 180 n. 18
Ruden, Sarah, 3 n. 3, 104
Runia, David T., 29 n. 29
Russell, D. A., 111 n. 10
Russell, Letty M., 185 n. 39
Russo, Vito, 10 n. 13

Sadler Jr., Rodney S., 175 n. 3–4, 188 n. 50, 207
Said, Edward, 57 n. 18
Saillant, John, 175 n. 5
Sánchez, David A., 207–9
Sanders, E. P., 20
Sarisky, Darren, 146 n. 10, 147
Satlow, Michael, 111 n. 13
Sawyer, John F. A., 88–90, 174 n. 2, 207
Schearing, Linda S., 4 n. 7
Schneider, Laurel C., 202
Schneider, Tammi J., 63 n. 36
Scholes, Robert, 111 n. 12
Scholz, Susanne, 183 n. 30, 184 n. 32, 185
Schüssler Fiorenza, Elisabeth, 5, 19 n. 18, 62 n. 31, 101, 171 n. 78, 182–83 n. 28, 184 n. 34, 184 n. 36, 185
Schweitzer, Albert, 35–36
Scott, Bernard Brandon, 82 n. 59
Seesengood, Robert, xi
Segovia, Fernando F., 18 n. 17, 37 n. 43, 57 n. 21, 101 n. 88, 172 n. 81, 173, 180, 182 n. 26, 188 n. 51, 189 n. 53, 190 n. 57, 197 n. 78, 207 n. 106, 220
Setzer, Claudia, 184 n. 32
Sherwood, Yvonne, 140 n. 61, 143 n. 61, 168
Shields, Mary E., 117 n. 26
Simkins, Ronald A., 49 n. 2
Skinner, Matthew L., xi
Slusser, Michael, 118 n. 28
Smith, Clarissa 10 n. 13
Smith, Jonathan Z., 215 n. 133
Smith, Mark S., 63 n. 35

Smith, Mitzi J., 175 n. 6, 187 n. 46, 188–89
Snell, Daniel C., 63 n. 36
Snodgrass, Klyne R., 80 n. 57
Spivak, Gayatri Chakravorty, 57 n. 18
Spöhrer, Markus, 10 n. 13
Stack-Nelson, Judy, 107 n. 2
Staley, Jeffrey L., 210–11
Stanton, Elizabeth Cady, 176–77, 182–83, 185
Stark, Rodney, 60–61
Stark, Thom, 171 n. 79
Stendahl, Krister, 103 n. 96, 160
Stockhausen, Ulrike Elisabeth, 229 n. 14
Streete, Gail Corrington, 186 n. 43
Stuckey, Sterling, 176
Sugirtharajah, R. S., 37 n. 42, 55–56 n. 13, 57 n. 19, 57–58 n. 21, 180, 219
Sweeney, Marvin A., 154

Tamez, Elsa, 179–80
Thayer, Anne, 53 n. 6
Thurman, Howard, 168 n. 68, 186, 217
Tiffin, Helen, 57 n. 18
Tolbert, Mary Ann, 18 n. 17, 37 n. 43, 62 n. 31, 107 n. 3, 118 n. 30, 172 n. 81, 173 n. 1, 180, 182 n. 26, 207 n. 106
Tov, Emmanuel, 97 n. 80
Tracy, David, 17, 20–21, 29 n. 28
Trible, Phyllis, 133 n. 52, 184
Tullock, Janet H., 101–2 n. 90
Tupamahu, Ekaputra, 181 n. 25, 216

Ukpong, Justin S., 201

VanderKam, James C., 27 n. 26
Vanhoozer, Kevin J., 92 n. 74, 148 n. 24
Vermes, Geza, 27 n. 25, 153

Wahlde, Urban C. von, 159 n. 52
Wan, Sze-kar, 198
Wan, Wei Hsien, 214 n. 132
Warnock, Raphael G., 195 n. 73
Warrior, Robert Allen, 37 n. 42
Wasserman, Emma, xi
Watson, Duane F., 29 n. 29, 31 n. 32–33, 111–12 n. 13, 112 n. 14, 138 n. 58, 144 n. 8
Weaver, Joseph, 206 n. 104
Webster, John, 146 n. 12
Wecker, Menachem, 67 n. 46
Welborn, Laurence L., 2 n. 1
West, Gerald O., 90, 200, 207
Wexman, Virginia Wright, 9 n. 12
Whitters, Mark F., 110 n. 7
Williams, Demetrius K., 36 n. 41
Wimbush, Vincent L., 175 n. 5, 176 n. 7, 182–83 n. 28, 195 n. 72–73, 209 n. 115, 214 n. 131
Winterbottom, M., 111 n. 10
Wire, Antoinette Clark, 101 n. 90
Witherup, Ronald D., 34 n. 37
Withrow, Brandon G., 67 n. 46
Wright, G. Ernest, 159–60
Wright, N. T., 156 n. 48

Yamada, Frank M., 197 n. 80, 198
Yee, Gale A., 197, 211–12, 232 n. 19, 233
Yieh, John Yueh-Han, 198 n. 85
Yoder, Christine Roy, xi
Yoder, John Howard, 168 n. 68
Young, Frances M., 92

Zainabu, Jaha, 121
Zetterholm, Karin Heder, 143 n. 4

Ziegler, Valarie H., 4 n. 7

INDEX OF KEY TERMS

Abraham, 22, 28, 45–49, 118–21, 136, 151, 197, 230
Absalom, 108
Adam, 68, 184, 198, 226, 230
adequacy in interpretation, 161–66
African American interpretation, 36, 101–2, 170, 175–77, 182–83, 186–89, 191–95, 202, 207, 209 n. 115, 214, 217–19
Allegory, 28–31, 40, 81, 112–13, 145
Ambrose, 88–89, 118
anti-Judaism in interpretation, 19–20, 89, 92, 102, 148–55, 170, 210, 215
Antiochus IV (Epiphanes), 50
Antipas (early Christian), 52, 93
apocalypticism, apocalyptic discourse, 13–13, 18, 50, 74, 78, 90–91, 99–100, 154, 208
Apocrypha, 34, 152–54
Archaeology, 20, 63–67
Aristotle, 110–11, 166
Aqhat, 62
Asian interpretation, 196–99
Asian-American interpretation, 196–99, 211–12, 233
Augustine, 29–30, 69, 88–89, 112, 118, 144–46

Bathsheba, 108, 115, 134
Bible prophecy movement, 17, 213 n. 130, 229
biblical interpretation, history of
  Jewish, 26–27, 29–31, 68, 102, 122, 143, 150–54, 169–70, 193, 210
  Eastern Orthodox, 33–34, 91, 144
  Protestant (Reformation), 19, 28, 31–32, 40, 91–92, 113, 158–59
Brown, Antoinette, 183

Calvin, John, 28, 31–32, 91–92, 113
Cana, 65–66, 89–90
canon of the Bible, xii, 151–52
capital punishment, 166, 193, 228
climate crisis, 14, 229
circumcision, 72, 94–95, 136, 156, 204
common-sense (and common-sense realism) realism, 28, 31–32, 39–41, 212–14
complementarianism, 3–5, 11, 72, 202
creation stories, ancient Near Eastern, 62
cultural interpretation, 2, 5, 9, 13–14, 23–25, 36–38, 57–58, 88–92, 173–219

cultural or social context, 40, 44, 46–49, 53–67, 78, 104, 162, 185, 222

David, 59, 99, 108–09, 115, 125, 131, 134, 232
deconstruction, 140–41
Dead Sea Scrolls, 20, 26–27, 62, 64
devotional interpretation, 13–17, 42, 194–95
diatribe, 136–17
divorce, 12, 40, 228
Documentary Hypothesis, 46–47, 68–69, 73, 83–85, 118–19, 152
Douglass, Frederick, 175–76, 183

economy, economics, economic justice, 18, 37, 48–49, 55, 66–67, 80, 81, 89–90, 177, 181, 189, 198, 206
empire, interpretation and, 49–50, 53, 55–58, 66–67, 138, 181, 199–200, 207–10
Enlightenment, 32–35, 113, 152, 158–59, 175, 224–25
Enuma Elish, 62–63
Esau, 59–60, 68
Eschatology, 72
Esther, 176–77
Ethics, 1–5, 7, 12, 15, 29, 62, 112, 116–17, 147–48, 166–72
Eve, 68, 184, 198, 226, 230
exegesis (and eisegesis), 35, 159–61, 174
exile, Babylonian, 53, 74, 108, 231
Ezra, 188, 231–32

faith, 2, 14–17, 19, 21–22, 32–35, 37, 60–61, 71–72, 91, 98, 100, 112, 119–21, 128, 143–59, 166, 171–72, 174, 191, 192, 195, 220–21, 224, 226
faith, rule of, 29–30, 145, 148, 156, 166
family, 3–5, 14, 48–49, 53–55, 157, 193, 197, 211, 233
Farrer-Goulder Hypothesis, 69
feminist interpretation, 3–5, 18–19, 58, 90, 101–02, 110, 164, 170, 176–77, 182–86, 191–96, 199–200, 202, 210
forgiveness, 137, 179, 227–28
fundamentalism, 4, 33, 67, 92, 98

gender and sexuality, Bible and, 1–5, 8–12, 17, 37, 44, 48, 52–55, 66, 72–73, 94–95, 117, 144, 162–63, 168, 170, 177, 182–86, 188–89, 190, 191–96, 202–5, 224
Gilgamesh, Epic of, 62, 104
global interpretation, 55, 89–90, 92, 174–83, 196–201, 206, 225
Gospel of Jesus's Wife, 64–65
grace, 71, 137, 144, 147
Grimké, Sarah, 183
Grimké Weld, Angelina, 183

Hagar, 28, 46, 48, 197–98
Hammurabi, law code of, 62
Hebrew Scriptures, Christian interpretation of, xii, 19–20, 34, 119–20, 146, 148–56, 193–94
Heidegger, Martin, 161, 215–16
Hesiod, 111
higher criticism, 45–47, 67–88, 93, 98–105

Hispanic interpretation (see Latinx interpretation)
historical context (see cultural or social context)
Holy Spirit, 12–13, 121, 141
Homer, 64, 111
hybridity, 57, 189–99

immigration (and refugees), 17, 196, 201, 216, 229–33
Isaac, 28, 113, 118–21, 230
Israel, modern state, 16–17, 36–37, 229

Jacob, 54, 59–60, 68, 115–16, 121, 230
Jeroboam, 133
Jesus, 17, 19, 21, 26, 32–33, 34, 35–36, 37, 40, 41, 45, 56, 57, 58–59, 64, 65–67, 69–70, 76, 77, 79–83, 86–88, 89–90, 91, 94, 95, 97–98, 99–101, 103–4, 106, 109–10, 111, 113, 118, 119–20, 121, 122, 123–24, 128–30, 137–41, 149–55, 157–58, 168, 171, 178–83, 184, 186–87, 192–93, 196–97, 199, 200, 203–5, 208, 210, 215–17, 220–21, 224, 227, 228, 231
Jesus, historical, 32, 35–36, 41, 65–67, 81–83, 99–100, 101, 104, 139–40, 199, 210
John of Patmos, 90–91, 222
Jonathan, 125
Jordan, Clarence, 209, 216–17
Josiah, reform of, 53, 198
Judaism, ancient, 13, 14, 19–20, 56, 64, 100–102, 152–54, 170, 175, 210, 212, 215

justice, 18–19, 55, 81–82, 95, 105, 162, 177–180, 186, 198, 201, 215, 217
justification, 21–22, 144, 179–80

kingdom of God, 56, 124, 128, 187–89

Laban, 115–16
Language, 14, 21, 26, 28, 31–32, 40, 48, 88, 92–98, 138, 139, 158, 163, 181–82, 209, 216–17, 221
Latinx interpretation, 189–95
law, of Israel (see Torah), 27, 28, 31–33, 41, 50, 54, 62, 65–66, 68, 72, 106, 111–12, 118, 136–37, 152, 156, 170, 185, 187, 193, 224, 231
lawsuit motif, 134–35, 137–38
Lee, Jarena, 182
liberation theology and interpretation, 55–56, 89–90, 175–82, 186–88, 191–92, 204, 208, 214
literary interpretation, 2, 5, 11, 13, 18, 23, 33, 42, 47, 52, 57, 77–78, 106–41, 163, 202, 206, 220, 222–24, 225
logos, 62
love, rule of, 29–30, 145–47, 165, 166, 168, 169, 175
lower criticism, 44–67, 88, 92–105
Luther, Martin, 19, 28, 31–32, 91–92, 113, 144

Maccabean Revolt, 26, 50
martyrdom, 60–61, 89, 93–94
Maltese Falcon, the, 7–11
Marsh, Charles, 209

Mary, mother of Jesus, 37, 65–66, 89–90, 182, 208–9, 231
Mary Magdalene, 64–65, 122–23
Masoretic Text, 26, 96–97
medieval interpretation, 31, 112–13
messiah, 86–88, 100, 123–24, 207–08
minjung theology and interpretation, 180
Moses, 14, 32–33, 68, 111–12, 120, 122, 162, 194, 223
mujerista interpretation, 191–95
Museum of the Bible, 154–56

Nicodemus, 109–10
Nineveh, 104–05
Nag Hammadi Library, 64
names of God, 68, 83–85
Nathan, 115, 134
Nave's Topical Bible, 41
New Criticism, 114–15, 122, 124, 126
Nicene Creed, 29
noncanonical literature, 62, 71, 73, 76–77, 152–53

objectivity, 35, 149, 158–66, 171–72, 174, 224–25
Onesimus, 51–52
Origen, 29–30, 112, 145

parables, 19, 40, 41, 67, 75–76, 78, 79–82, 103–4, 106, 113, 128, 132–34, 139, 188–89, 201, 215–16, 217
Pastoral Epistles, 71
Paul, 1–5, 13–14, 19–20, 21–22, 28, 39 n. 46, 51–52, 56, 61, 62, 70–73, 74–75, 79, 94–95, 101, 104, 111, 112, 115, 116, 136–37, 138, 156–58, 162, 170, 177, 179–80, 185–86, 191, 203, 204–5, 216, 218–19, 222, 231
Peter, 13, 86–88, 113, 123, 162
Pharisees, 19, 127, 128, 165
Philemon, 51–52
Philo, 29, 62, 111–12
Plato, 14, 62, 110–11
politics, interpretation and, 5, 6, 16–17, 42, 53, 55–56, 65, 89, 178–79, 181, 188, 206, 215, 222, 228–33
postcolonial interpretation, 56–58, 181, 196–200
prayer, 13, 32, 78, 82, 86, 99, 147, 225, 226–27
prophecy, 26, 104
prophets, Hebrew, 18, 19, 30, 85, 106, 151, 168, 185
propositional interpretation, 40–42
prosperity gospel, 17, 226–27
prostitution, 104–05, 122, 184–86, 193, 204, 205
Psalms, 63, 74, 78–79, 85, 115, 133
pseudepigraphy, 71–73
Puah, 194–95
public biblical interpretation, xi, 1–25, 32, 33, 38–43, 72–73, 141, 142–44, 146, 154, 156, 161–66, 171–72, 174–78, 182, 198, 206, 214, 219, 220–33
public policy, 5, 25, 188, 228–30

Q, 70, 76–77
Qumran (see Dead Sea Scrolls)
queer interpretation, 202–5

Rachel, 54

race, racism, 6, 20 n. 19, 37, 40, 102–3, 170, 174, 177, 183–84, 186–91, 194–97, 206, 209, 210–19, 229
Rashi, 31
reader, flesh-and-blood, 37–38, 92, 126, 144, 172–219
reader, implied, 124–31
reception history, 88–92, 173–74
redaction criticism, 33, 47, 67, 81–88, 93, 103, 139
Reformation, Protestant (see under biblical interpretation, history of)
Rehoboam, 133
reproductive rights, 228
review of history, 50
rhetoric, rhetorical criticism, 112–13, 132–38, 141 n. 34, 184 n. 34, 221–22

salvation, 17, 21–22, 56, 71–72, 81, 116
Samaritan woman, 109–10, 141, 184, 223–24
Sarah, 28, 45–48, 118, 121, 151, 230
Saul, king of Israel, 96–97, 108, 125, 131
scribes, 98, 133–35
sexuality (see gender and sexuality, Bible and)
Shiphrah, 194–95
Sitz im Leben, 78–79, 82
slavery, Bible and (also, enslaved persons), 12, 14, 28, 36, 39–40, 44, 48–49, 51–52, 72–73, 79, 104, 168, 170, 175–76, 178–79, 182–83, 187–89, 193, 197, 202, 205, 207, 212–14, 231, 233

social context (see cultural or social context)
social-scientific criticism, 58–62,
Society of Biblical Literature, 143, 183
Son of God, 56, 87, 123–24
Son of Man, 87, 123–24, 205
source criticism, 47, 67–77, 81–88, 93, 118, 119, 139
spiritual care, 226–28
Stanton, Elizabeth Cady, 176–77, 183, 185
Synoptic Problem, 69–70, 76–77

textual criticism, 45, 96–98, 227 n. 10
theological interpretation, 7, 12–13, 15, 17, 20–22, 32–34, 40, 42–43, 47, 55, 59, 71, 72–73, 83, 85, 88, 89, 92, 94–98, 99, 103–5, 114, 116, 117, 119–21, 139–40, 142–58, 159–60, 164, 165, 166, 168–72, 177–81, 191–95, 202, 213, 228
Theological Interpretation of Scripture movement, 33 n. 35, 92, 146–52
Thomas, Gospel of, 73, 76, 79–80, 100
Thurman, Howard, 168 n. 68, 186, 217
Two-Source Hypothesis, 69–70, 73, 77, 85
Torah (see law, of Israel)
translation (see language)
Twelve, Book of the, 85
type scenes, 223–24

Uriah, 134

Virgin of Guadalupe, 208
Vulgate, 88

Wellhausen, Julius, 68–69
Westminster Confession of Faith, 39
whiteness in interpretation, 174–75, 210–19
wisdom, xi–xii, 13, 27, 33, 34, 62, 90, 106, 111, 157–58, 163, 167, 192, 196–97, 206, 224
wisdom traditions, biblical, 62, 106
women, ordination of, 3–4, 12, 40, 72, 101–2, 186, 202
womanist interpretation, 191–95

Yavneh, 100

Zipporah, 122

INDEX OF SCRIPTURAL AND ANCIENT TEXTS

HEBREW BIBLE/OLD TESTAMENT

Genesis
1–3…14, 46, 68, 83–85
1:1–2:4a…46, 68, 118
1:20…85
1:22…85
1:28…85
2–3…152, 184
2:4b–3:24…46, 68, 83–85, 198
4:11–16…230
6–8…83–85
6:1–4…30
6:6…84
6:22…84
8:17…85
8:21…84
9:1…85
9:7…85
12:1–3…46
12:3…119
12:10–20…230
13:14–17…46
15:1–6…46
15:6…156
15:9–21…22
16:1–16…28
16:5–6…48
17:6…119, 230
17:15–22…46
18:1–33…45–48
18:1–15…45–48
19:1…46–47
20:1–18…230
21:9–21…28
21:9–14…48
22:1–19…118–21
23:1–2…121
24:2, 9…22
24:10–61…223
25:29–34…68
26:6–11…230
27:1–35…68
27:42–45…59
29:1–20…223
30:25–43…116
32:7…59
33:9…60
33:15–17…60
47:29…22

Exodus
2:1–10…223
2:15b–21…223
4:24–26…122
14:10–31…223
15:25…223
17:1–7…223

20:1–17…68
20:20…120
23:31…36

Leviticus
19:9–10…231
19:33–34…231
20:10…193–94

Numbers
20:2–13…68

Deuteronomy
5:6–21…68
21:10–14…185

Ruth…197, 231–33
1:16…231
2:9…232
2:15…232
2:16…232
2:22…232
4:10…233
4:15…231

1 Samuel…74
13:1…96–97
16:1…131
24…131

2 Samuel…74
1:2–15…125
12:1–15…134

1 Kings…74
12:1–20…133
22:19–23…63

2 Kings…74

1 Chronicles…74
9:1…108
10:13…108
16:7–37…108
25:1–31…108
27:24…74

2 Chronicles…74
20:34…74
33:18…74

Ezra…188
9–10 231–32

Esther…125, 176–77

Job…17, 41, 85
1:6…63
2:1…63
9:32–35…134
23:3–5…134–35
38:1–42:6…134
42:6…95–96

Psalms…85
54:1…133
82…63
82:2, 7 78

Proverbs…17, 73–74
1–10…103
1:1…73
10:1…73
25:1…73
30:1…73
31:1…73–74

Song of Songs…66
3:4…66

8:2...66

Isaiah...74, 88–89
1–39...74
5:3–4...134
6:9–10...128
7:14...88
9:6...88
24–27...74
40–55...74
53...88
56–66...74

Jeremiah...53, 106
1:5...228

Ezekiel...106

Daniel...49–51
1–6...50
6:8...126–27
6:12...49
7–12...50
7:13...205
11:40...50

Nahum...104–5
3:4–5...105

Habakkuk...26–27
1:1–5...26
2:15...27

NEW TESTAMENT

Matthew
4:1...121
5:6...95
5:17–20...41
5:47...231
6:7...231
6:12...227
6:32...231
7:6...205
8:20...205
15:1–20...41
15:21–28...192–93, 199–200, 205
15:26...121
15:28...121
16:13–23...86
18:17...231
18:21–22...227
19:16–26...200
19:30...81
20:1–16...80–81
20:25...231
24:45–51...188
25:1–13...188–89
25:14–30...188–89

Mark
1:1...123
1:11...123
1:17...97
1:25...97
1:34...97
1:40–45...97–98
1:41...97–98
2:13–17...128
4:11–12...128
4:40...128
6:30–44...128
6:52...128
7:3...127
7:19...41
7:27...121
8:1–10...128
8:15–16...128

8:17–18…128
8:27–33…86–88
8:29…123
8:31–34…123
9:7…123
10:17…139
12:1–12…67
12:28–34…139
14:12–25…178–79
14:47…178
14:51–52…122–23
15:21…129
15:39…123
16:7…87
16:9–20…97

Luke
7:36–50…122
8:1–3…122
9:18–22…86
10:25–37…75, 76, 139, 217–18
12:13–21…75
12:19…76
15:11–32…75
15:18…76
16:1–13…201
16:3…76
16:19–31…75
17:7…40
18:1–8…82
18:18–30…139
23:22…118
23:34…227–28

John
1:1…62
2:1–12…89
2:11…118
3:1–21…109

3:1…109
3:19–21…36
3:19–20…109
4:1–42…109–10, 140–41, 184, 223–24
4:7…141
4:9…109
4:10–14…140
4:18…109
4:32…141
4:39…138
4:54…118
5:31–38…138
5:36…138
5:39…138
6:15…138
6:33–58…141
7:10–11…138
7:37–39…141
7:53–8:11…97
8:14…138
8:18…138
8:21…138
8:37…138
8:40…138
9:22…100
12:11…100
15:4…220–21
15:18…221
16:2…100
19:28…141
19:30…141
19:34…140–41

Acts
10:44–47…13
14:8–18…231
19:1–7…13

Romans
1:13–15...137
1:16...137
2:1...136
3:1–2...136
3:22, 26...21
4:1–25...156
4:1...136
6:1...137
6:15...136
7:7...136
8:28...17
9:19–20...136
11:1...136
13:1–7...229–30
13:14...79
14:1–15:13...157
15:22–24...137
16:1–16...3

1 Corinthians
1:10–13...158
1:18–2:5...157–58
4:16...158
6:7–8...158
6:9...95
6:12–20...185–86
7:1–4...1–5
7:3–4...186
8:1–13...157
9:12–23...158

2 Corinthians
1–7...75
1:11...75
2:3–9...75
5:1...75
5:9–11...75
6:14–7:1...75

7:1...75
7:8–12...75
8–9...75
10–13...75
10:11...75
11:2–16...3

Galatians
1:6–9...61
1:8–9...222
1:14...13
2:16, 20...21
3:1...61
3:6–14...156
3:22...21
3:27–29...79
3:28...204, 218–19
4:13...204
4:14...204
4:19...204
4:21–31...28–29, 112
5:12...61, 204, 222
6:17...204

Ephesians
2:8–10...71–72
4:24...79

Philippians
2:1–11...79, 157
3:9...21

Colossians
3:10...79
4:9...52

Philemon 51–52
2...51
16...51–52

18–19…52

Hebrews
1:1–3…149
5:5–10…149
11:37…89

1 Peter
1:1…231
2:11…231

Revelation
1:5…93–94
1:9…94
2–3…52
2:13…93
2:14…157
2:20–23…18, 222
2:20…157
3:14…93–94
12…207–9
14:1–5…18
17:15–18…18
18:11–19…18
21:24…231

JEWISH PARABIBLICAL LITERATURE

1 Enoch 30

Genesis Rabbah
1.10…31

Jubilees…30

1QpHab, *Habakkuk Pesher*…26–27

GREEK AND ROMAN AUTHORS

Cicero
Against Cataline 1.6…222

Hesiod
Theogony…111

Vergil
Aeneid 6.1.791…56

OTHER JEWISH AUTHORS

Philo
De plantatione
36…29

Life of Moses
1.1…111
2.12–13…111
2.40…111

On the Migration of Abraham
89–93…112

CHRISTIAN PARABIBLICAL LITERATURE

Apocalypse of Paul…71

Ascension of Isaiah…89

3 Corinthians…71

Letters of Paul and Seneca…71

Gospel of Thomas…73, 76, 79–80, 100

EARLY CHRISTIAN AUTHORS

Augustine
Confessions
3.5...112
6.3...118

Doctr. chr.
1.35...146
1.40...29
1.86...145
2:9–14...30
3.14...30
3.17...112
3.32...29
3.56...112
4.4...145
4.27...145

Cyril of Jerusalem
Catechetical Lectures...1.14

Origen
Against Celsus
1.18...112
4.45...112

On First Principles
4.9...112
4.12...112